THE CANADIAN FAMILY

Edited with an
Introduction by
K. Ishwaran

Canadian Cataloguing in Publication Data
Main entry under title:
The Canadian family

Bibliography: p.
ISBN 0-7715-5571-7

1. Family – Canada – Addresses, essays, lectures.
I. Ishwaran, K., 1922-

HQ559.C36 1983   306.8'5'0971   C82-094748-2

Co-ordinating Editor: Joan Kerr

Editor: Geraldine Kikuta

Designer: Jean Galt

Cover Design: Michael van Elsen Design Inc.

1 2 3 4 5 6 7 8 9   WC   87 86 85 84 83

Written, Printed, and Bound in Canada

To my father and mother

"There are two impulses which more than all others cause human beings to love and care for each other: this is my own, and this I love."

Aristotle-*POLITICS*

More Gage Books in Sociology

Contributors

Maureen Baker
University of Toronto
Toronto, ON

Eunice H. Baxter
University of Waterloo
Waterloo, ON

Merlin B. Brinkerhoff
University of Calgary
Calgary, AB

Peter M. Butler
Dalhousie University
Halifax, NS

Frederick Elkin
York University
Downsview, ON

K. Ishwaran
York University
Downsview, ON

Warren E. Kalbach
University of Toronto
Toronto, ON

Evelyn Kallen
York University
Downsview, ON

Seena B. Kohl
Webster College
St. Louis, MO

Ronald G. Landes
Saint Mary's University
Halifax, NS

Eugen Lupri
University of Calgary
Calgary, AB

Jacqueline C. Massé
University of Montreal
Montreal, PQ

Daniel Perlman
University of Manitoba
Winnipeg, MB

Karl A. Peter
Simon Fraser University
Burnaby, BC

John F. Peters
Wilfrid Laurier University
Waterloo, ON

John A. Price
York University
Downsview, ON

Henry Radecki
Laurentian University
Sudbury, ON

G. N. Ramu
University of Manitoba
Winnipeg, MB

Stephen Richer
Carleton University
Ottawa, ON

Benjamin Schlesinger
University of Toronto
Toronto, ON

Micheline St-Arnaud
University of Montreal
Montreal, PQ

N. Tavuchis
University of Manitoba
Winnipeg, MB

Marie-Marthe T.-Brault
University of Montreal
Montreal, PQ

Linda J. Trigg
General Hospital
Winnipeg, MB

Mary Van Stolk
Tree Foundation of
   Canada
Montreal, PQ

Contents

Preface

The first edition of *The Canadian Family* was published in 1971, and subsequently revised in 1976. This is not a third edition. Rather, this volume comprises a collection of new articles many of which focus on the conceptual and the policy challenges presented by Canadian families in the 1980s.

Some of the themes prominent in the earlier versions, no doubt, reappear here: the diversity of family forms, the significance of social contexts for the family, the family as a social system, and so on. They are basic to any attempt to understand the family in a social perspective. At the same time, however, articles on new themes have been added that clearly bring out some of the major predicaments and challenges faced by Canadian families in the 1980s, together with an indication of some of the coping devices that are evolving.

This volume presents some of the latest studies on the Canadian family in its diverse contexts, some more striking than others. On the one hand, there is the fascinating experience of growing up in a multiethnic society; on the other hand, the family must contend with the problems of a challenging and highly modernized society – such as the rapid increase in single-parent families, the phenomenal increase in divorce, and the increasing incidence of child abuse. Do we fully understand these problems and their implications? Are attempts being seriously made to tackle them? These articles as a whole offer insight into questions such as these.

The 1980s will certainly witness the dynamic interplay among the family, the individual, and the changing society. Will the family survive as a social form? We have reasons to believe in the vitality of the family as evident in history, but this vitality has come from the adaptive resources and responses of the family. We must explore and discuss whether this vitality still exists.

Acknowledgments

My first thanks go to our contributors who wrote new material especially for this volume.

My special acknowledgment goes to Dr. K. Raghavendra Rao, a former colleague at Dharwar, India, whose comments have been helpful in preparing my own papers.

Thanks are also due to P. G. Ganguly for his assistance in the final phase of this volume and to Jean Liebman for her secretarial help.

In addition, I wish to express my appreciation to York University's Secretarial Services Division, and to the University for its continued support of my work over the years.

K. Ishwaran

York University, Downsview

Introduction

The Canadian Family – A Profile

K. Ishwaran

A sociological understanding of any society, within the framework of the social sciences, involves a study of the social system; the social institutions and their structural-functional aspects; the social process of continuity, change, and decay; and the complex web of institutional and interpersonal relationships within the social system, conceived as roles, statuses, rights, and obligations.

Certain institutions are crucial to the existence and survival of any social system, and as such they have become objects of intensive and comprehensive scientific study, often leading to the emergence of subdisciplines within the discipline of sociology. Of these institutions, the family is one of the most important. The family has persisted in some form or another in all known social systems, and the study of its structure, functions, and processes is indispensable for an adequate understanding of the society of which it is a crucial part. It is from this broad perspective that the Canadian family attracts sociological attention.

In view of the central role of the family, it is somewhat surprising that the family theme did not enter sociological study until the mid-nineteenth century.[1] In fact, serious and systematic study of the family dates from the publication of Darwin's epoch-making work, *Origin of Species,* in 1859.

Four distinct historical phases have been identified in the development of family studies to date. The first phase (1860-1890), influenced by Darwinian theory, led to evolutionary models for the origin and growth of the family. These were cross-cultural models involving universal laws. The methods of exponents such as Lewis Henry Morgan, Fredrich Engles, J. J. Bachofen, and Edward Westermark were largely bibliographical, intuitive, and sweeping. An outstanding exception to this tradition was Frederic LePlay who used the empirical method of interview. LePlay's three-fold typology for the family comprised the nuclear or "unstable" type (husband, wife, and young offspring), the stem family (one married child living with the parents), and the patriarchal type (old parents, their male and often female children, and their spouses and children).

The second phase (1890-1920), characterized by a concern with the practical

---

[1]For an account of the history of family studies, *see* Harold T. Christensen, ed., *Handbook of Marriage and the Family,* (Chicago: Rand McNally, 1964), pp. 3-32; Wesley R. Burr and Reuben Hill, eds., *Contemporary Theories about the Family,* (New York: Free Press, 1976), pp. 1-24; Bert N. Adams, *The Family – A Sociological Interpretation,* (Chicago: Rand McNally, 1980), pp. 6-12.

aspects of social knowledge, social problems, and social reform, was particularly evident in the United States. Faced with the emergent problems of industrialization and urbanization, sociology began to show a practical orientation, as exemplified by the Chicago School of Sociology. Through its journal, *The American Journal of Sociology*, this school championed the cause of social reform. Research concern and reform concern fused in the work of this school.

The third phase (1920-1950) signalled the beginning of a period of scientific sociology, in which the family became the main focus of sociological study. Ernest Burgess (1926) shifted interest from the problems of origin and practical problem solving to the family as a system of interacting personalities. Based on the collection and interpretation of empirical data, Burgess studied virtually all the aspects of the family – marital stability, mate selection, intra-family relationships, divorce, and problems of old age.

Since 1950, the scientific study of the family has become methodologically more sophisticated and theoretically more resourceful, with an increased tendency to theorize about the family, its structure, and its dynamics. Efforts in the 1960s were spent developing conceptual frameworks to explain empirical data, while in the 1970s, family sociology took hesitatnt steps toward theory construction. The ongoing research in family sociology is comparative, aimed at structuring the variegated data and interpreting this in theoretical terms. The work of recent family sociologists, like William J. Goode (1963) and Ira Reiss (1967), has placed family sociology within a theoretical context.

Canadian Family History

The most glaring lacuna in the study of the Canadian family is the historical framework. Canadian family history has yet to be systematically investigated and its main outlines clearly identified. Some of the reasons for this laxness may be the scarcity of source data, reluctance to accord family history a priority status in research, and insensitivity to the active role of the family in a historical perspective. A survey made as recently as 1979 indicated that only 10 percent, or less, of current historical studies and research in Canada at the post-graduate level was devoted to the Canadian family history.[2] Even this work did not focus centrally on the family as a sociological phenomenon, since a considerable part of it dealt with the family in relation to other issues such as urban crime or feminism in a working-class value system. Actually, there is very little demographic data available. The Gagan survey pinpoints four crucial areas for future research. First, we need to know more about the life cycle of the Canadian family as a processional phenomenon – its formation, duration, and dissolution. Secondly, the cohort life cycle should be examined, focussing on the nature and the different stages of individual lives, and the historical changes taking place in the structure and pattern of such stages. Thirdly, the family should be considered as an institution involved

---

[2]David Gagan, "The Problem of Canadian Family History." Working paper for the workshop on the Family and the Socialization of Children, University of Western Ontario, 1979 10 26-29, p. 13.

structurally and functionally in the societal processes of production and consumption. In particular, family form and size should be related to the economic structure of the society. Lastly, a substantial research effort should be invested in the study of the kinship networks, particularly their role in preserving or changing the traditional patterns in family culture in Canada. Further, the specific aspects of the relationship between kinship network and family processes as well as wider societal processes such as geographical mobility, industrialization, and urbanization should be explored.

Conceptual Frameworks in Family Studies

Any scientific study employs a conceptual framework that designates the object of study and provides identifying criteria for the data to be assembled. While these are methodological tasks, the conceptual framework may also provide a basis for empirical theory in the sense that empirical data may be restructured into a theoretical statement by using the conceptual framework. Theoretical statements and propositions have a different status from conceptual frameworks; the latter are heuristic and exploratory, whereas the former refer to the empirical universe in a structured and meaningful way. In the papers collected here, the conceptual frameworks serve as guideposts to the relevant empirical terrain. Five conceptual frameworks are relevant to the sociological study of the family: the interactional, the structural-functional, the situational, the institutional, and the developmental.

The Interactional Framework

Originating with Burgess' focus on the family as an interacting group, this framework was subsequently established as a significant conceptual tool in American sociology and social psychology through the work of G. H. Mead (1934) and the Chicago Group of Symbolic Interactionists.

Within this framework, the family is conceptualized as a system of interacting members. The individuals act in relation to one another such that each person plays a role designated by the expectations of each of the other members within the system. The role adopted issues form the self-concept each person has as a result of his or her interaction with the other members. Consequently, the family is seen as a closed system.

The most significant contribution of the interactional framework is the notion of role-playing and its influence on the status and authority structure involved in all family processes from dating to marital dissolution. Although a useful approach that has focussed attention on the family as a micro system, this framework has overemphasized interaction within the family, while failing to consider the wider interaction between the family and society.[3]

---

[3]For further review of symbolic interactionism, *see* Ralph Turner, *Family Interaction*, (New York: John Wiley, 1970); Sheldon Stryker, "Symbolic Interaction Theory: A Review and Some Suggestions for Comparative Family Studies," *Journal of Comparative Family Studies* 3, (1972): 17-32.

The Structural-Functional Framework

Primarily an import from the neighboring discipline of anthropology, this framework has become almost the dominant theoretical orthodoxy of contemporary Western sociology, as exemplified by its major practitioners – Radcliffe-Brown (1952), Parsons (1951), Merton (1957), Homans (1961), and Levy Jr (1952). The family is conceptualized as a social system from the perspective of the individual family and the system of families, linking this framework to the institutional approach.

In actual fact, the structural-functional framework views the family as one of many subsystems constituting in their totality the overall social system, and, hence, drawn functionally into the process of maintaining the larger societal system. Within the family itself, individual members are viewed in terms of specific status-roles, coming into play under the structural pressures generated by the system.

One major criticism has been that, in its obsession with structure, it misses out the dynamics of social institutions and social systems. Moreover, it fails to acknowledge the existence and consequences of change-processes. Attempts have been made to meet such criticism. For instance, Homans has tried to accommodate change through his distinction between external and internal systems and Parsons has recently been moving toward a more dynamic and processual approach, even invoking an evolutionary paradigm.

The structural-functional framework has considerable internal variations, and its practitioners have perhaps nothing in common beyond the general commitment to the overall concept of a social system. Its strength has been that it has allowed those who adopt it considerable conceptual skill in imposing structures and patterns on apparently disorderly empirical data.

The Situational Framework

First suggested by W. I. Thomas (1931) and Lowell Carr (1948) in their theoretical writings, the basic ideas involved in this framework were later applied to family studies by James Bossard (1943) and his disciples at the University of Pennsylvania. A complementary framework, the psychological-ecological one, was advanced by Barker and Wright. As its name indicates, this framework focusses on the "situational" individuals face in their endeavor to solve the problem or the crisis caused by the "situation." The main purpose of this framework is to analyse the constituent elements and dimensions of the situation, yet not completely neglect individual behavior. Some of the major themes studied within this framework have been child development in a family context, tabletalks, and space-utilization policies. The situational tends to overlap the interactionist framework, but it differs in at least one important respect. While the interactionists do not go beyond the micro level, the situationists consider the external factors (the macro) as well as the micro level.

The Institutional Framework

The institutional framework, one of the earliest strategies used in the study of the family, has strong historical overtones and holistic implications. The key assumption is that a social system is a composite structure of institutions or "organs," developed for specific functions considered essential to the existence and continuity of the society as a whole. The family is one such functional institution.

The institutionalists maintain that many of the family's functions have been undermined by modernizing forces and hence reallocated to specialized and impersonal agencies ouside the family. However, this thesis is far from being proved. Many feel that the family has not lost status as a functional institution, but rather that it has undergone a shift in its functions.

A family study cannot dispense totally with the institutional framework. Just as the situational framework spills into the interactionist, the institutional tends to merge with the structural-functional at some points.

The Developmental Framework

In an important sense, this framework incorporates aspects from the previous four, but, in contrast to them, it stresses the dimension of time. Thus it brings back into the centre of sociological focus the historical process, reformulated as development, which the sociological tradition had discarded in its reaction against evolutionism and social Darwinism. This means that the developmental framework conceptualizes all social structures as dynamic and processional. To some extent, this has forced the other frameworks to include a developmental focus.

Like the structural-functional, the developmental framework owes its basic ideas to anthropological theory. In particular, it has drawn on the concept of the "domestic cycle" introduced by Jack Goody (1962) and subsequently refined by Frederick Barth (1960). This framework has not been employed to its maximum potential. It is our contention that it could yield substantial payoffs in terms of methodology and theory. Moreover, the family is an ideal object for a developmental focus because it is an institution characterized by progressive stages, involving changes in both structure and functions.[4]

While this framework could be advantageous in the study of any social structure, it involves long time ranges and longitudinal data collection, which are not amenable to scientific control. In general, it directs attention toward the relationship between shifting developmental functions, on the one hand, and on the other, the role expectations of the children, and the role expectations of the parents as breadwinners, as organizers and runners of the households, as spouses, and as persons. It analyses these themes within the framework of the changing developmental functions of the family.

In sum, this discussion demonstrates that the different frameworks tend to overlap, that they are not necessarily mutually exclusive, and that the devel-

---

[4]For some illustrative studies, *see* B. S. Rowntree, *Poverty: A Study of Town Life,* (London: Macmillan, 1906); Paul Glick, *American Families,* (New York: John Wiley, 1957); Evelyn M. Duvall, *Family Development,* (Philadelphia: J. B. Lippincott, 1957); K. Ishwaran, *Family, Kinship and Community* – A Study of Dutch-Canadians, (Toronto: McGraw-Hill Ryerson, 1977).

opmental framework, in spite of its high costs in time and resources, is the best able to handle the problems of understanding the family and its processes most comprehensively.

The papers in this volume are not united by a common conceptual framework, but nonetheless, without any deliberate design, the most dominant framework that emerges is developmental. However, no paper exemplifies in a pure form any single conceptual framework, though it may show a marked proclivity toward one of them.

Kalbach's demographic analysis of the Canadian family is developmental in an indirect sense, since the statistical data employed represent patterns of historical change and development in the family and its various aspects. The paper by Ramu and Tavuchis is also concerned with processes within Canadian family history that may have promoted or discouraged diversity in family forms and functions. They find that the pressures for unity are gaining an edge over the forces promoting diversity. Baxter's contribution draws attention to the role of the family in the changing occupational structure. Landes' paper on the political socialization of Canadian youth examines socialization as a developmental learning process. But what is important to note is that, no matter on what aspects of the family they may be focussing, the papers are concerned in a variety of ways and to different degrees with the processional aspects of the institutions, structures, and functions examined.

While it would be misleading to claim that the papers in this volume exemplify the developmental framework, it would, however, be quite in order to point out that most of them are sensitive to the factors of time, process, change, and history. Therefore, the eclectic conceptual framework adopted by most of the papers has not detracted from this sensitivity.

Theoretical Models in Family Studies

Although a conceptual framework should be distinguished from scientific theory in the sense that a theory is an end product and a framework is the starting point of a scientific investigation, this doesn't mean that the framework and the theory do not intersect. In fact, a conceptual framework is rooted in a theory; but it is a theory that has structured the empirical reality at the time that investigation into it began. Since such theory determines the basic operational situation of a research enterprise - its problem methods, data, strategies, and goals - it would be difficult to see how theory, implicit in a conceptual framework, could fail to affect significantly theory as an end product of a research process. Therefore, more often than not, a research process produces theoretical structures that tend to be rooted in the initial conceptual framework.

The overall tenor and direction of the papers in this volume may be characterized as integrating a variety of theoretical concerns of which the most dominant, whether implicit or explicit, is the structural-functional frame.

The structural-functional theory regards the family both as an internally structured system and as a system in patterned interaction with other systems within society. Examples of the latter are educational, religious, political, economic, and cultural systems. The key element in this theoretical stance is function. The family is, therefore, viewed as a structure performing certain specific functions in relation to the overall functions of the society. Further, family members are seen in terms of their specific role-functions in relation to the overall functions of the family.

One major advantage of this theoretical frame is that it imposes purposive patterns on empirical phenomena; thus, investing human activities with what Weber called "rationality." Virtually every paper in this volume employs a structural-functional theoretical mode. For instance, Ramu and Tavuschis examine the Canadian family in terms of two broad functions of stability and change. Ishwaran's two contributions are explicitly focussed on the urban and rural family in their diverse settings and situations. The papers on ethnicity are oriented toward a functional understanding of ethnicity in a family context. While they identify and interpret the functions of ethnic culture, community identity, and institutional patterns in relation to the functions of the family, this analysis is also related to the wider societal functions of integration. Other family-related phenomena such as courtship, marriage, and divorce are also examined generally, though not always explicitly, within a functional theoretical frame. Even the contributions on the crisis in family life are functionally formulated, in that crises arise precisely when families are unable to perform necessary functions or are called upon to perform new functions in response to wider socio-economic and cultural changes. Finally, the interactions within the families are interpreted in terms of role-functions and their interrelationships. Thus, the theoretical stamp of structural-functionalism is clearly seen in most of the individual papers and also in their cumulative impact.

The relevance of the developmental theoretical framework to articles assembled here is not as easy to delineate. This is partly because developmental theory has not yet become sufficiently crystallized and partly because most of the papers are not geared to a single methodology or theoretical frame. Yet, the developmental theoretical position frequently emerges as a systematic concern with structures as products of processes and with the formulation of processes in terms of stages, phases, sequences, continuities, and discontinuities. The developmental frame is implicitly, too, in the historical dimension articulated in some of these studies.

It would be inaccurate to consider any contribution here as an example of the developmental theoretical frame. However, Landes shows the interconnection between the learning process involving political socialization at various levels and the process of stability and change in the political system. He identifies the family as an important point of intersection between the processes. Thus, the developmental theoretical frame intrudes in most papers as a supplementary input.

Besides the structural-functional and the developmental theoretical frames, the contributors have used interactionist, situational, and exchange theories. The paper by Elkin on the role of ethnicity in socialization through the family is essentially interactionist although it also involves, to some extent, an institutional analysis. Radecki's paper on families in crisis and Butler's study of the relationship between husbands, wives, and the work factor are more clearly interactionist in their theoretical approach. The paper by Brinkerhoff and Lupri on conjugal power and family relationships, though it has an interactionist bias, uses a modified version of the exchange theory. It conceptualizes intra-family relationships as exchange relationships. And Peter's investigation into the relationship between religious ideology and social change leans toward a historically-oriented focus on processes of social change.

Perspectives in Canadian Family Studies

A fundamental question regarding the development of sociology of the Canadian family is whether the preconditions for its emergence exist. Such preconditions would include an established theoretical tradition in the specific area and the availability of relevant empirical data.

It has been argued that since, in the Canadian context, family sociology is an inter-disciplinary enterprise and since it lacks ongoing theory, there is no justification for a sociology of family in Canada. This position has been challenged,[5] but the debate raises important methodological and substantive issues relating to family studies in Canada. Methodologically, such a position is predicated on an allegedly correct scientific paradigm associated with the natural sciences. However, the model of science implicit in this paradigm is misleading even with regard to the natural sciences themselves. It is based on the fallacy of regarding scientific truth as absolute certainty. A theory need not be of this type. Thus, a sociology of the Canadian family is no less possible than is any segment of sociology. On methodological grounds, therefore, the difficulties have been exaggerated.

In substantive terms, a Canadian sociology of the family or a sociology of the Canadian family is not only possible and necessary, but already exists, however imperfectly, in the studies reported in the past, in those ongoing and scheduled for the future, on the forms, functions, and processes of the family in Canada in all its diversity and complexity. This volume reflects this faith in Canadian sociology, and it is optimistic about the possibilities of generating more and better theory in the field of the sociology of the family in Canada.

Family as a Dynamic, Changing Institution

Historically, Western sociology discarded the evolutionary framework as a theoretical tool for explaining social change at the macro and micro levels by the beginning of the twentieth century, and embraced an explanatory framework based on ideal-typical systems and models. From this latter perspective, social change was seen as a shift from one ideal type of society to another. The sociological explanation of historical shifts centred around the claim that this shift consisted in a change from an agrarian ideal type society to an industrial one. This constituted the sociological explanation of the changes brought about by the industrial revolution in European society and economy. The change entailed the rise of the factory system, the displacement of the rural home-based industries, and large-scale migration to the cities in search of a

[5]Parvez S. Wakil, "On the Question of Developing a Sociology of the Canadian Family: A Methodological Statement," *Canadian Review of Sociology and Anthropology* 7, (1970): 154-57.

better life. The industrial city became the nerve centre of the new economy and new society, representing enormous resources of capital, labor, and raw material. England was the first example of the new, urban, industrial society.

As a result of the mechanization brought into the production process by the industrial economy, the pre-industrial family-based economy died away.[6] The rural family lost its role in the production process, and hence its functions became more specialized. Within the family, role differentiation took place as members of the same family found themselves scattered as workers in different factories. Increasing urbanization undermined patriarchal authority, and the father's role as an agent of socialization into a skill or a craft became redundant. The complexity and the specializations involved in industrial technology necessitated training centres outside the family. Thus, children removed from the control of the family and thrown on the labor market were exploited to such a degree that the state was forced to legislate child labor regulations.

The institutional separation between the family and the world of work made the man the exclusive income earner for the family, while the woman and the children were concerned with domestic and school activities. Connections with the outside world were severed and the family became isolated from the surrounding urban life. The large migrations turned the city into a place of strangers, lacking in community context and meaningful relationships. Marx identified this process as the "privatization" of the family – the family turned inward. The emotional attachment earlier shown to the village community or the extended family now became narrowly confined to the immediate family and its members. This situation generated, on the one hand, anti-urban attitudes, and, on the other, nostalgic yearning for rural community life in a highly romanticized form. It culminated in the sociological tradition of dichotomy between status society and contract society,[7] and between *Gemeinschaft* or community and *Gesellschaft* or society association.[8] Max Weber (1947) and subsequent modern Western sociologists, especially Parsons (1965) and Smelser (1956), enshrined this dichotomy of the traditional and modern societies in their modernization theories implying that modern society was superior to the traditional, while the earlier community-society association dichotomy tended to be antagonistic to individualism, as, for instance, in the writings of Tonnies who felt particular concern about the effects of modern individualism on the family and the community.

As women joined the labor force, they became individualistic because they were earners. The *gemeinschaft* advocates regarded this as a destruction of the original nature of woman. The sense of family was subordinated to the self-interest of individuals. Family obligations and rights dissolved or at least significantly weakened. Both Marx and Durkheim emphasized these negative aspects of the emerging industrial capitalistic social order.

---

[6]For a changing account of the pre-industrial family, *see* Theodore K. Rabb and Robert I. Rotberg, eds., *The Family in History: Interdisiciplinary Essays,* (New York: Harper & Row, 1971).

[7]Henry Summer Main, *Ancient Law,* (London: Oxford University Press, 1931).

[8]Ferdinand Toennies, *Community and Society,* trans. Charles P. Loomis (East Lansing: The Michigan State University Press, 1957).

Against this historical background it is useful to examine briefly some of the leading sociological theories about the structure and the processes of the family. Three seminal works in the area provide a basis for such an examination – Carl Zimmerman's *Family and Civilization,* William Ogburn's "The Changing Family," and Talcott Parsons' paper, "The Forces of Change."

Carl Zimmerman

Zimmerman believed that Western civilization would face the last phase of a family crisis by the end of the twentieth century, culminating in a sickness whose symptoms had been felt as early as the 1940s. He forecast a collapse of civilization through an internal decaying process generated by the disintegration of one of its central social institutions, the family. His theory is pervaded with pessimism for the future of the family.

In a sweeping historical survey of some four thousand years, Zimmerman postulated a scheme of historical periods, each self-contained as a cycle of birth, rise, and decline of civilization. Five cyclical periods were identified: (1) the pre-Greek, (2) the Greek (1200 B.C. to 300 B.C.), (3) the Roman (600 B.C. to A.D. 700), (4) the Medieval (A.D. 700 to A.D. 1700), and the modern (A.D. 1700 and thereafter). Within each of these periods, Zimmerman identified stages such as the primitive, the trustee, and the domestic. In each of these periods, the climax of achievement is related to the domestic component or the family. Each stage generated its own specific type of family. The earliest primitive family was characterized by the ill-treatment of wives, the exploitation of children, and the suppression of individual rights. This type was followed by the trustee family which pushed the civilization toward greatness. (The trustee was the senior male in the family; he exercised authority and controlled the family property.) This system permitted neither individual rights nor divorce, and it developed into the autocratic family in which the trustees began to exercise absolute authority. It was controlled by the religious instititions and the governmental structure. As a result, the family became humanized, and transformed into the domestic type, which Zimmerman regarded as the highest development of the family, responsible for the greatness of the civilization in which it appeared.

The domestic type was based on the equitable treatment of all members by the family itself, the governmental system, and the church. While the trustee type had been potentially self-destructive, the domestic type was not immune from external influences generated by the government and the religious system. The modern period is characterized by a decline in familism and an increase in individualism. As a result, family functions are reduced and the form of the family becomes atomistic. Once reduced to a minimal function, the family becomes little more than an aggregate of individuals motivated by self-interest. Normative notions of legitimacy and illegitimacy are replaced by overriding individualism. Thus, the stage is set for the emergence of movements like feminism, for the problems of youth and other types of upset, and for interpersonal tensions, all of which render the family powerless. As a result, the whole society is engulfed in a chaotic condition.

Zimmerman believed that the United States would be the scene for the climax of this dark and destructive process. The only hope he held for the doomed North American society hinged on the power of human intellect to realize the dilemma and adopt measures to avoid the fate of the ancient Greek and Roman civilizations.

William Ogburn

Like Zimmerman, Ogburn used a wide historical canvas, but one with a comparatively narrower time frame. His development theory of the family spans the colonial period to the modern. Appropriately characterized as "passive" by Zimmerman, Ogburn did not view the family as a causal factor in the process of social change. Rather, he considered it a passive insititution, responding and adapting to the forces radiating from the wider society. Therefore, unlike Zimmerman, he located the source of social change outside the family system. Specifically, he related social change causally to changes in the technological system, especially the accelerated pace of technological innovation in modern societies. His historical analysis of the American family prompted him to conclude that there was a time lag between changes in material culture and changes in the symbolic, non-material dimensions, the former always being in the lead. The time lag, characterized by temporary social dislocation and disorganization, was designated as "cultural lag."[9]

The cultural lag was seen as an important source of change in family form and functions. The theoretical assumption was that normally the family system and the technological-economic system would arrive at a state of equilibrium. For instance, the pre-industrial family eventually became functional to the agrarian technology and economy. Then, the functions of the family were reduced by the factory system, a part of technological change that shifted material culture and produced disorganizing effects in society. Similarly, the technological invention of the automobile altered the customary courtship norms, making it difficult for parents to supervise their children's relationships.

Ogburn was very concerned with the rising divorce rates in modern society, the loss of family functions, and other "pathological" conditions in family life. His theory, while emphasizing the integrative role of the family and explaining social change in terms of changes in family functions, tended toward technological determinism. Whatever his particular emphasis, he drew attention to the interaction between technology, the economy, and family functions.

Talcott Parsons

Parsons exemplifies the structural-functional theory and his analysis and explanation of social change, including family change, are situated within that theoretical frame. Since this theory is less historically oriented, it encounters inherent difficulties when dealing with social change, especially in its more radical revolutionary forms. His theory is more conducive to explaining changes within a social system, rather than changes from one system to another.

Following in the tradition of Weber, Parsons conceptualized changes in the

---

[9]William F. Ogburn, *Social Change*, (New York: Huebach, 1923), pp. 200-37.

family in terms of ideal-type structures – from one ideal type, the traditional, to another ideal-type, the modern. However, Parsons's structural-functional framework involved a specific theory of change. Accordingly, changes in family life are changes in the structure and functions of the family as a social system or subsystem. Fusing the Weberian element with the structural-functional element, Parsons formulated his ideal type as a structure with specific functions tied to it.

In the Parsonian perspective, the historical changes due to industrialization amounted to those changes in the structure and functions of the family in the industrial society that distinguished it from its structure and functions in the pre-industrial period. Parsons held that the industrial family is isolated from its kinship structure, that it is a multilinear system, and that it is a conjugal system. Further, he maintained that the marital system associated with this family type is a prescriptive one as against the ascriptive system of the traditional family type.

Parsons saw these features as structurally and functionally interrelated. For instance, the prescriptive marital system meant that marital alliances were contracted outside the kinship network, thus weakening the kinship system and further isolating the family. Similarly, multilinearity led to a weakening of the kinship system. He related this weakening of the kinship system to the functions needed in an economy which was highly competitive and individualistic.

While the Parsonian ideal type is a useful starting point for understanding the modern family, it has sometimes proven to be a stumbling block. It has, for instance, ignored those features of the changing family that fail to conform to it. In fact, an examination of the Canadian family illustrates the deficiencies of the Parsonian model of the industrial family. Recent studies of the Canadian family on a cross-ethnic basis indicate that the modern family is better described as a modified-extended family rather than as a conjugal family. These studies, most notably those focussing on the French Canadians and the Dutch Canadians in the works of Garigue and Ishwaran, respectively, demonstrate that the kinship system continues to function as an important supportive adjunct to the family in the industrial society of Canada. Another difference is that the Canadian family is bilinear rather than multilinear. Finally, the thesis of the prescriptive marriage system also needs drastic modification since ethnicity in Canada tends to discourage intermarriage, although trends in favor of such marriages are not entirely absent.

The models of Zimmerman, Ogburn, and Parsons draw attention to the important aspects of change in the modern family; however, as can be seen in relation to the Canadian data, even allowing for the historical perspectives of Zimmerman and Ogburn, they tend to be too structural and too ideal-typical in their framework. All three overlook the complexity and the dynamism of the family as a central institution in modern society. Nonetheless, each model provides useful points of departure for further investigations into family forms and functions.

Canadian Family: Diversity and Unity

Is there such a phenomenon as *the* Canadian family, or are there different kinds of Canadian families? This question arises naturally in the context of Canada's cultural pluralism and multiethnicity. In contrast to the American melting-pot model, Canadian inter-ethnic interaction has been compared to the salad bowl, the implication being that Canadian society allows ethnic identities to flourish to a considerably larger extent. It seems, therefore, perfectly reasonable to assume that the Canadian family is characterized by considerable diversity. At the same time, however, there is a sufficient degree of uniformity running through the diverse forms to warrant the conclusion that the different forms of the Canadian family constitute variations on a common theme. Hence, for an adequate sociological analysis of the Canadian family equal attention must be paid to both aspects – diversity and unity.

The sources of diversity may be listed as (1) ecology, (2) ethnicity, (3) religious ideology, (4) culture, and (5) differential modernization. These factors either singly or in some pattern or combination account for the diversity of forms and functions in the Canadian family.

The Outpost Family

The first diversity arises because of ecological differences. From this perspective, Canadian families can be divided into three categories – the outpost family, the rural family, and the urban family. The outpost family dwells in the vast and diversified geocultural regions of Arctic and Subarctic Canada. There are some 12 000 Inuit and 170 000 Native peoples in these regions. While the outpost conditions have not shielded them from exposure to the influences of urban-industrial society, their integration into the mainstream economy has been limited because their occupational skills of hunting and fishing have little relevance to that economy.

Although information about the social structure, including the patterns of family system, is very scant, what is available points to considerable variation within the Inuit and Native family forms. While geographical isolation and ecological dependence have strengthened their traditional institutional patterns, technological advancement in the surrounding society has forced them into greater interaction with the outside world. While the effect of industrialization and urbanization has upset their traditional life style, they have been denied the benefits of occupational opportunities and economic development. A significant consequence has been a restructuring of the family into a matrifocal pattern comprised of a mother and her unmarried children, with no permanent male figure. This has not affected the functionality of the primary kin group.

In some cases, the Native peoples lived in kin-based, dispersed groups, but there was no nuclear family. The traditional bilateral cross-cousin marriage facilitated their adaptation to the ecological situation. The kinship system was organized by a separation of offspring of same-sexed and opposite-sexed siblings. The former kin were regarded as blood relatives with the status of brother and sister. The latter were viewed as non-blood kin, and hence permitted to marry one another. Thus, the categories defined as brother and sister were the same as in kinship systems elsewhere in Canada.

Demographic expansion, the outpost situation, and the distinctive kinship principles have combined to form a unique community system. The traditional, mobile, and dispersed community pattern has been replaced by a more stabilized, larger, and settled population. In the maintenance of the new community system, the role of the various urban services and the welfare amenities such as education, health care, family allowance, old age pension, and others need to be recognized. Thus, urbanization and industrialization have not favored the family.[10]

The Inuit population has suffered substantial decline primarily due to infectious diseases introduced by the Europeans. Food resources, through hunting, also declined, probably due to the introduction of the gun. The existing data, however, do not permit any systematic analysis of the relationship between such large-scale developments and the family structure among the Inuit.

For a long time, the conventional view was that the traditional Inuit family was nuclear. Recent work has shown that the nuclear family was common only among the Copper Inuit while the Netsilik and Iglulik Inuit favored a patrilineal structure, usually consisting of father-son and/or brother-brother relations. Thus their family system belongs to the extended category, not the nuclear type.

For the Inuit, too, the urban-industrial processes have created problematic situations which have indirectly affected the family. From the available data it is difficult to gauge the impact on the structure and functioning of the family in those Canadian outposts that lie on the geographical and technological periphery.

However, the impact of urban-modern forces has reinforced the traditional nuclear family adopted by the Copper Inuit, and for the Netsilik, the extended family has been strengthened in response to the innovation of wooden boats for walrus hunting. But the situation is so complex that the current array of theoretical concepts in Canadian family studies may not be adequate.

The Rural Family

The overall image of Canada as an urban-industrial modern society has tended to obscure the fact that a quarter of its population is rural. At the same time, this ruralness is under constant pressure to change from the dominant urban-industrial system. The rural social system, including its family system, is relatively more complex and diversified than the systems of the outpost communities. But it is also relatively less complex and diversified in comparison with urban society and its family system. Being agrarian, the rural society is technologically modern and therefore well integrated into the urban-industrial society and economy.

The traditional patterns of the rural family are also exposed to pull and push factors; they are reinforced by pull factors such as religious ideology or ethnic identity and weakened by push factors such as the impact of the urban-industrial processes and its values. As in the case of Canadian family studies in general, the rural family has yet to be explored more systematically to yield valid generalizations about its structure and functions. However, the few avail-

---

[10]*See* the paper by John Price on page 72. .

able studies such as those included in this volume on the French Canadians, the Dutch Canadians, the Hutterites, and the farmers and ranchers of the southwestern region of Saskatchewan may be regarded as illustrative and indicative, and yielding hypotheses for further investigation and confirmation.

The contribution by Ishwaran attempts to organize the available data to present a coherent picture of the rural family system in Canada. It quickly becomes evident that there are variations within the general form of the rural Canadian family, and rural-urban distinctions are not always easy to draw.

The Urban Family

The Jewish family displays the characteristic features of the urban family in Canada. It is highly ethnic-oriented, traditional, and committed to the group's religious-cultural system. The synagogue remains a central institution, bonding the community into a coherent group, through its distinctive religious system.

Some changes have taken place among the Jews in Canada both in the areas of intra-family relations and family-community relations. The father's increased involvement in secular-occupational activities has led to a corresponding disengagement in traditional authority and status. Since religious doctrine prevents her from substituting for the father as a figure of religious authority, the mother's role continues to be the traditional one of transmitting Jewish values from generation to generation.

Child rearing and expectations for the family and the children's future have become more liberal. The permissiveness of the wider Canadian society has penetrated to the extent that women now chafe at their traditional subordinate status and role, and they are becoming more involved in activities outside the home, despite protests from their husbands. Above all, the traditional religious commitment has weakened, transforming the role of the synagogue into a secular and cultural one calculated to strengthen ethnic identity. Hence, religiosity has become functionally subordinate to community identity. The urban Jewish family is clearly of a nuclear type, sustained less by extended kinship structures than by community-based institutions.

The general trend of urban ethnic groups has been toward a modified-extended family type, that is, one in which the nuclear type co-exists in a functional relationship with a simple aggregate model of kinship structure. The latter, a loose group of kinfolk through descent or marriage, is fairly well organized into a network of interdependence and provides the nuclear family with moral, psychological, and material support on a basis of mutual exchange.[11]

The urban family, therefore, whether in its more common modified-extended form or in its more nuclearized form has shown that it is capable of changing to meet the needs and demands of a Canadian environment dominated by technological modernization, industrialization, and urbanization. In this proc-

[11]For supportive studies of this phenomenon of mutually-supportive systems, *see also* Eugene Litwak, "Geographic Mobility and Extended Family Cohesion," *American Sociological Review* 25 (1960): 386-94; idem, "Occupational Mobility and Extended Family Cohesion," ibid. 25 (1960): 9-21; idem, "The Use of Extended Family Groups in the Achievement of Social Goals. Some Policy Implications," *Social Problems* 1 (1960): 177-87.

ess it has differentiated itself from the traditional family type in a manner unanticipated by urban sociologists like Wirth and others. Instead of discarding the kinship structure, it has merely modified it structurally and functionally to meet the challenges of modernization.

Pressures for Uniformity

The diversity found in form and function of the Canadian family does not indicate an underlying need for unity, arising from the universal functions of the family. Therefore, in analysing the trends toward uniformity in the Canadian family, it is necessary, at the outset, to conceptualize the universal functional family. Relevant theoretical literature suggests a multiplicity of such universal models, each of them designating its own set of family functions as universal. Davis (1952) refers to four functions as does Murdock (1949). However, both offer different lists that overlap. While reproduction and socialization are common to both, Davis mentions maintenance and placement, while Murdock notes the sexual and the economic. Ira Reiss (1965) suggests that the family has only one function, namely the "nurturant" socialization of the child. Other functions associated with the family are actually carried on by family-related structures such as the kin group.

In his classic survey of the literature, Goode (1959) proposes universal family functions: The reproductive function, related to age at marriage, fertility; the status placement function, determining one's life chances within society; and the socialization function relating to child rearing, enabling him or her to function as an effecive member of society. It may be expected that such universal functions tend to push family forms toward uniformity, the conjugal form, while local and specific contexts tend to produce variations of these universal functions. It is from this perspective that the specific forces and factors working toward uniformity in the Canadian family acquire meaning.

Because the literature on the Canadian family has been dominated by diversities, emerging in response to those found in ethnicity, religious ideology, ecology, historical context, and local influences, the pressures for uniformity have not been adequately noted and analysed. The paper by Ramu and Tavuchis in this volume makes an attempt in this direction. As they suggest, the main pressure for uniformity radiated from the modernization process through technology and the secularist ideology. As a result, there is some degree of convergence toward a common pattern in family structure and functions, cutting across ethnicity, class, and ecology. Such convergence is not peculiar to Canada, however; modernization is a global process, exerting pressure to create family forms functional to that process. For Canada, two major sources of uniformity may be identified – demographic changes and changes in the legal system.

Modern socio-economic factors such as mass education, commercialized mass communication, and the highly specialized occupational system impinge on the family system to reduce the diversities stemming from a variety of sources such as ethnicity or religious culture. Family and marital systems tend to become uniform. Although it would be difficult to establish precise correlations, the demographic data suggest the increasing convergence towards uniformity in family forms and functions with regard to size, residence, membership, marital system, age at marriage, and the normative assumptions and attitudes involved in family life.

The uniformities evident in family life are naturally reflected in individualistic norms and attitudes as well as in behavioral patterns in related institutional areas such as courtship and marriage. Couples exercise freedom in the choice of partners, residence, and in the desired number of children. They marry younger and move away from parental homes much earlier than did the previous generations. The increased participation of wives in the work force tends toward a more democratic family structure and intra-family functions. Thus, the demographic structure of the Canadian family pushes it toward uniformity.

Increasing standardization of legal codes involving marriage, family life, intra-family obligations and rights, family property issues, and divorce are factors that reinforce the demographic features resulting in a greater measure of uniformity in the Canadian family.

In sum, the Canadian family is currently subjected to contrary forces, some reinforcing diversity and variation, and others imposing uniformity and unity on the family system. More empirical studies are needed, not only to pinpoint in greater detail the specifics of both forces, but also to establish more precisely the patterns of interaction between these two apparently conflicting processes.

Childhood and Adolescent Socialization

From a sociological perspective, the developmental process of the child should be studied as a prelude to an understanding of childhood in its overall family setting. Although child development may be studied from several points of view, a sociological concern focusses on child development as a *social process*.

Of central importance in a study of child development is the concept of personality. From the sociological point of view, personality is defined as a socially conditioned and structured phenomenon. In the development of personality two kinds of factors are of special significance: first, the experience within an interactive group context and second, the cultural heritage as manifested in the cultural environment. The first kind of factors are socially interactive and operate in a primary group context. They also refer to the role of the group in the formation and development of the personality of the child. This is a fundamental conditioning factor in child personality development because it determines the basic pattern of growth and development itself.

The second factor is rooted in the cultural context to which the child is exposed. This context prescribes what constitutes legitimate norms and behavior. A combination of these two kinds of constraint factors controls the developmental pattern of the child's personality. In the process of personality formation, childhood is the most crucial developmental stage. Hence, the social process of personality development is virtually identical with the social development of the child. In this framework of child development, the family becomes a decisive institutional channel through which the social conditioning process takes place. This is why the sociologist can contribute substantially to a scientific understanding of child development.

The child becomes a significant object of sociological investigation because (s)he provides a link in the process of inter-generational cultural transmission. In fact, sociocultural continuity and stablility depend on the role of the family.

Hence, there is an interdependence between child development and child socialization. Further, the study of child development involves attention to the status, the factors affecting it, and the relation of the child to other people, all of which are characteristically sociological concerns.

The intellectual and ideological ethos of modern man and his world presupposes that human beings can understand, master, and alter their ecology, and, in fact, control their destiny to a significant degree. This has provided the intellectual backdrop to the increasing modern interest in the sociology of child development. Further, such a study has policy implications for industrial society whose success depends on its ability to control nature through technology and social engineering.

Socialization Process: Principles and Concept

Heredity and socialization are the two factors that determine an individual's character. Socialization, the process by which a person learns the cultural norms and patterns of behaviour sanctioned by a given society, involves the activity of the socializing agents and the socialized. It is a continuous process, moulding the individual throughout the various stages of life. As the elders mould the young, the young also mould the elders with their new sets of values and life styles. More often than not socialization is an unconscious process, and the individual becomes aware of the distinctiveness of his social identity only when (s)he encounters other types of social identities.

The parents' role in the socialization process needs to be examined against the fact that the father works away from the home and a significant number of mothers are full-time participants in the labor force. Almost 20 percent of married Canadian women with children under six years of age and 25 percent of those with children over six work full-time outside the home. The absence of working parents from the nuclear household has led, in recent years, to a demand for day care as a supportive input to strengthen the family system. Although the number of day care centres increased from 700 in 1971 to 2000 by 1977, this dramatic rise is misleading. In actual fact, only 81 000 or 22 percent of all eligible children were receiving day care in 1977. The mother's employment outside the home has tended to reduce the role distinction between the father and the mother in the socialization process. A 1970 Department of Labor survey indicated that about a third of the children of working mothers were cared for by another adult member of the household. This member was often the father. Thus, the father's role in the socialization process has become more significant, although it is substantially less than that of the other key socializing institutional agents – the school, the church, the neighborhood and playground peer groups, and the mass media, especially television. Interestingly, the cataclysmic changes initiated by industrialization-

urbanization have not dislodged the family as a primary group in the socialization of the child during his formative stages.

One of the areas in which the family plays a socializing role is in occupational choice and career commitment. Occupation itself may be studied in
terms of three aspects – perceptions of occupations, expectations about occupation, and occupational attainment and mobility. In Canada and in the United
States, occupations are similarly ranked in terms of their prestige.[12] This consensus cuts across socially significant distinctions such as age, class, sex, and
residence. Canadian children and adolescents tend to adopt the occupational
prestige hierarchy of the adults, thus pointing to the strategic role of the
family in the socialization for occupational roles. However, prestige perception emerges indirectly, through the mediating role of the family. Moreover,
the societal values related to prestige are mediated by the intra-family socialization process. Although other socializing agents may exert some influence, it
is the adult members of the family, especially parents, who provide the values
associated with occupation. There is thus a process of inheriting occupations,
occupational roles, and occupational perceptions.

Evidence suggests, however, that Canadian children are not encouraged to
follow in their fathers' occupations. This is especially true of working-class
families who have higher aspirations for their offspring. However, in certain
businesses, such as the ranches in southern Saskatchewan, sons are encouraged to enter the family enterprise. Even more influential than the family
on occupational expectations is the educational system. School plays both a
positive and negative role, depending on the relevance of scholastic qualifications to one's occupational expectations. Thus, the educational system has
differential impact, relative to the socio-economic status factor. Further, a comparative study of the aspirations of Native peoples, including Inuit and Métis,
and White high school students conducted in 1974 suggests that family and
peer groups are more important than ethnic subculture, in the formation of
occupational expectations.[13] In the final analysis, while the schools may at
times exert less influence than either the family or the peer groups, they may
also enhance the influence of the other two socializing agents if they conform
to the values of the community.

To some extent urban Canadians inherit their parents' class position, the
correlation between father and son's occupation being about 0.40. For the
working-class family influence in occupational attainment has been significant. A similar influence exists among the élite, and it is more than likely true
of the middle class. While data on occupational mobility in Canada is not
substantial or decisive, it does point to a correlation between father and son's
occupations.

Thus, while the family's influence on occupational choice is marginal, as a

---

[12]For Canadian data, *see* Peter C. Pineo and John Porter, "Occupational Prestige in
Canada," *Canadian Review of Sociology and Anthropology* 4 (1967): 24-40; for United
States' data, *see* A. J. Reiss, Jr. et al., *Occupational and Social Status,* (New York: Free
Press, 1961).

[13] Derek G. Smith, *Occupational Preferences of Northern Students,* Social Science 5,
(Ottawa: Information Canada, 1974).

mediator of occupational expectation and attainment it is quite significant.

Given the democratic nature of the Canadian political system, another important consideration is the role the family plays in political socialization. Political socialization involves the transmission of inter-generational political beliefs, attitudes, and behavior. Recent studies indicate that Canadian children start developing their political identity very early.[14] Like other areas of socialization, political learning is a continuing process. What has been learned in childhood and adolescence may later be replaced with new attitudes or beliefs, although this rarely occurs as it involves a complex interplay of inherited political identity and emergent political experience. Since politics is not a primary concern of the average Canadian, political socialization is an indirect process, mediated by a variety of social institutions, including the family, the school, the peer group, and the mass media.

The family and the school represent private and public agents, respectively. In view of the liberal democratic ideology that dominates the Canadian system, and in contrast to other more regimented or closed systems, political socialization in Canada is focussed through the private agents. In fact, virtually all political identity in childhood derives from the family since it enjoys a privileged position of control and influence over the child. Usually family influence is conservative, transmitting status quo beliefs, attitudes, and behavioral patterns. In particular, children imbibe the partisan political beliefs of their parents. But the modality of family socialization is indirect and implicit: the primary political socializing role of the family is in active competition with that of other agents such as the school, the church, and the mass media.

Native Canadians present a more complicated kind of socialization process. For instance, in the case of the Inuit of the central Canadian Arctic, the traditional conception of the children as social actors constitutes a structural element in their socialization into the cultural patterns. Yet, this traditional system is affected by a variety of change-oriented factors such as modern prefabricated residences, the Christian church, public schools, hospital facilities, and local stores. The hunting and fishing Inuit has vanished, although the image is enshrined in the fantasies of southern Canadians.[15] The lives of the native Cree who reside on the east coast of James Bay, Quebec have been disrupted by the forces of modern economy and technology as represented by the installation of the James Bay hydro-electric project. The structural frame of the socialization process has shifted from one dominated by family and bush orientations to one dominated by community and peer group orientations. Socialization into the traditional Cree culture has been undermined and the Cree children are faced with conflict and "double-bind."[16]

---

[14] *See* the paper by Ronald Landes on page 133.

[15] John S. Matthiasson, "But Teacher, Why Can't I Be a Hunter: Inuit Adolescence as a Double-Bind Situation." In *Childhood and Adolescence in Canada,* edited by K. Ishwaran. (Toronto: McGraw-Hill Ryerson, 1979), pp. 72-82.

[16] Richard J. Preston, "The Development of Self-Control in the Eastern Cree Life Style." In *Childhood and Adolescence in Canada,* edited by K. Ishwaran. (Toronto: McGraw-Hill Ryerson, 1979), pp. 83-96.

The socialization process centres on religious ideology for the Dutch Canadians and particularly for the Hutterites. The values of individual independence and autonomy are embedded in its framework, thereby reconciling individualistic and religious ideologies. In this process, the parents play a strategic role both within the family and outside of it. Of particular interest is the Hutterites' reconciliation of traditional culture and modern technology. While the children are socialized into a very strong religious ideology they are also taught to adapt to new and emerging agricultural technology. In all three cases – the Native peoples, Dutch Canadians, and the Hutterites – ethnicity constitutes a major focus and target for the socialization process. But ethnicity is a composite of sociocultural institutional patterns and religious ideology, in the case of the Hutterites and the Dutch Canadians, and of the more integrated traditional cultural patterns in the case of the Native peoples.

Prevailing socialization patterns reflect the sociocultural and demographic diversities in Canada as well as the processes of change. Therefore, it would be misleading to simplify or generalize socialization in Canada. Nevertheless, certain broad features stand out. Firstly, in Canada, as in other industrially advanced societies, the involvement of non-familial agencies in the socialization of the children and adolescents is increasing. These agencies include the educational system, peer groups, organized religion, and the mass media. Although its influence has diminished in some respects, the family continues to play a significant role. Secondly, the socialization process is no longer simply geared to transmitting traditional patterns of beliefs, attitudes, and behavior. The dynamic challenges of modernization are constantly being introduced into the socialization process, in an attempt to balance the contradictory claims of continuity and stability, on the one hand, and, of change, on the other.

Marriage in Canada

Marriage is a heterosexual relationship based on expectations of permanence and sanctioned by society. As such it forms the foundation for the family and determines patterns of interpersonal interaction within the family. From a sociological perspective, marriage may be conceptualized as a functional social institution. Its functions include the satisfaction of the marital partner's needs, provision for the organization and operation of a family system, including biological reproduction, and sociocultural transmission. Like other social institutions, marriage is subject to processes of dynamic innovation and change as well as the "pathological" condition of malfunctioning often leading to its dissolution.

Since courtship is an important premarital stage, it is the logical starting point for a discussion of marriage in Canada. Two broad courtship patterns – the assortative and the random – have been identified in sociological literature.[17] In the former, mate selection involves group intervention in the interest of the group. That interest may be religion, race, family, kinship, or ethnicity.

---

[17]William J. Goode, "The Theoretical Importance of Love," *American Sociological Review* 24 (1959): 38-47.

The individual has little to say in the matter. Random mating involves minimal interference, and the individual has maximum freedom in the choice of partners. Conventional family sociology suggests that the assortative pattern is characteristic of pre-industrial traditional societies, while random mating is a distinctive feature of urban-industrial modern societies. However, Canadian data on courtship, far from conclusive or adequate, point to a much more complicated situation. Indeed, as suggested by Ramu's paper in this volume, both types are evident. Although individual choice dominates, the Canadian courtship patterns are sometimes influenced quite significantly by social structural or situational factors, which include ethnicity, religion, race, class, and residence. The difference between the traditional assortative and the modern type is that these factors are regarded as contributory rather than decisive in the Canadian courtship pattern.

Another facet for consideration is inter-ethnic marriage. The available data suggest that inter-religious marriages occur more often than inter-ethnic marriages. This suggests that ethnic homogamy is relatively stronger than religious homogamy, although there are variations among different groups. Of the factors favoring ethnic homogamy, the most important are the recognition of ethnicity as a resource, persistent family patterns, kinship intervention in the mate-selection process, the psychological security of group identity, and the prevalent Canadian climate of sociocultural pluralism.

As suggested in Ramu's contribution, husband-wife relations are moving toward a more egalitarian pattern, in reponse to three factors – the increasing impact of feminist ideology, the rising rate of participation of married women in the labor process, and the more liberal legal framework. Education provides more opportunities for married women, and the traditional sex roles based on inequality are being undermined. In particular, the husband's role as the exclusive breadwinner has been modified. Despite these shifts, Canadian wives continue to play the traditional role of tending the household, caring for the children, and providing sexual companionship to their husbands.

Difficulties within marriage seem to be increasing. More and more, marriage is being characterized by internal malfunctioning, interpersonal conflicts, and even intra-family violence, leading to dissolution and divorce. Indeed, divorce has become a major problem, threatening the very function of marriage as a social institution. This could lead to three possible alternatives – a decline in the marriage rate, attempts to work out alternative arrangements to marriage, or a restructuring of marriage itself. Indeed, in his paper, John Peters supports one of these alternatives. He argues that the institution is in need of a radical reorientation and restructuring; this might well be the challenge of the 1980s.

The Canadian Family in the 1980s: A Panoramic Perspective

The Canadian family in the 1980s presents a situation of shifts and changes in institutional arrangements, behavioral patterns, values, and life styles. The following panoramic presentation has been assembled on the basis of available statistical data, survey reports, and sociological research findings. Its purpose is to provide a rapid, comprehensive, and fact-based chart for further exploration of emerging Canadian family styles, patterns, and problems as the current decade unfolds.

Labor Force. The nature of the labor force depends on the type of economy of which it forms a part. In 1891, 82 percent of Canada's population was rural. But, by 1971, the size of the rural population had dropped to 24 percent, only 7 percent of which was a farming population. The key to this dramatic shift lies in the technological changes, especially in production, that took place at the turn of the century. These changes stemmed from the displacement of family production by factory production, a development that had a significant effect upon sex roles and behavior.

By 1900, nearly 90 percent of the male population over fourteen years was in the labor force, and about 16 percent of the females of that age were working outside the home. Up until 1974, male participation in the labor force had declined to 77 percent, while in the same period, female participation increased steadily, climbing to about 40 percent.

In 1971, in nearly half of the Canadian families, there were two income earners, 14 percent had three or more members earning incomes, and 37 percent of all the families had only one income. This implies that married women in Canada had assumed a new role, that of co-provider. This invasion of the labor market by married women has often been incorrectly attributed to the impact of the feminist movement. In fact, it was initiated by the Second World War and, by 1951, the percentage of married women in the working force was 30; it rose to 50 percent within the next decade. This remarkable rise cannot be attributed to the feminist movement, which didn't significantly surface in Canada until the mid-1960s. From the emergence of this movement to 1971, the number of working wives rose by a mere 7 percent. In actual fact, the rise of married women workers has been the consequence of two factors – employment opportunities created by an expanding economy and the financial needs of the families. But even with this trend some 57 percent of married women stay out of the labor market.

Socialization. Prior to 1900, child and adolescent socialization was largely a matter for the family and/or the church. But with increasing industrialization and urbanization, non-family institutions became more involved in the socialization process. For instance, in 1900 about 50 percent of the children between the ages of five and nineteen attended school. By 1971, this figure had risen spectacularly, reaching almost 80 percent. Thus, society's share in the socialization of the young increased dramatically during the last seven decades.

Further evidence of the trend toward additional social responsibility for socialization is the increase in the number of day care centres. In 1971 there were about 700 of these centres. But, by 1977, this figure jumped to 2000! In 1977, some 81 000 children benefited from these centres. Thus, more children are being exposed to socializing influences outside the home and beyond parental direction.

The family, however, continues to be a significant agent of socialization. It has been especially important in the maintenance of ethnic cultural identity, particularly in the case of the French Canadians. Among French Canadians, Jews, and Ukrainians, the mother's role is emphasized during the early years of childhood. In farming and ranching families such as those in Saskatchewan, children are socialized to follow the parental way of life. This is also true of the Hutterites. Family honor and reputation are highly valued among the Greek, Chinese, and Italian immigrants, and, in fact, frequently are the motivations for higher educational achievement.

Premarital Sex. Premarital sexual behavior in Canada has been affected by the revolutionary changes in sexual norms that have taken place in North America in the last twenty years. These changes have generated a climate of sexual permissiveness and freedom, which has usually taken three patterns – premarital sex, heterosexual cohabitation outside marriage, and "swinging." Although these behavioral patterns first started in Europe and the United States, they have had significant impact on Canadian sexual behavior.

Most data on Canadian premarital sex are based on investigations into student behavior, such as those conducted by W. E. Mann, D. Perlman, and C. Hobart. These studies suggest certain broad conclusions. While in the 1960s Canadian students were less permissive and sexually experienced than their American counterparts, more recently their behavior is converging toward the American pattern. Secondly, while in earlier times Canadian men were more permissive and sexually experienced, in recent years Canadian women are approximating the behavioral patterns of men. Thirdly, while earlier Francophone students lagged behind Anglophone students in permissive behavior, since the late 1970s they have been catching up with them and in fact have now surpassed them. Finally, in the case of Anglophone and Francophone students of both sexes, there has been a behavioral convergence toward a love norm as legitimating sex, in contrast to the older ethic of sanctioning sex only between engaged or married persons.

The increasing incidence of premarital sex is a part of an overall process of ideological and moral shifts now taking place throughout the advanced industrial or post-industrial societies, including Canada.

Birth Expectations, New Life Styles, and Marriage Patterns

While it may be difficult to forecast future circumstances from the changes that are now visible in the fields of marriage, family structure, and life styles, there is no doubt that these changes are important. Coupled with ongoing diversities, such changes present a Canadian society in flux, perhaps caught up in post-industrial transitional patterns.

While the traditional structural diversities based on ethnicity, race, or religion have been responsible for differentiated patterns of marriage and family, the modernization processes of industrialization and urbanization have been generating continuous pressures toward uniformity, especially toward a modified-extended family pattern and open marriage system based on a more egalitarian husband-wife relationship. By 1971, nearly 80 percent of the population had become urbanized, and the remaining rural population had been affected by urban values and forces. However, rural patterns persist, although further differentiated by farming and non-farming groups. Geographical variations exist within demographic patterns, hence the provincial differences in marriage and family forms. For instance, British Columbia has the lowest birth rate and one of the highest divorce rates. Ethnic diversity due to the fragmentation of the population into fourteen ethnic groups is evident in different life styles, family forms, and marriage patterns. In 1971, the major ethnic groups were demographically distributed as follows: British 45 percent, French 25 percent, and the remaining groups 28 percent.

Of the three types of Canadian families classified earlier as outpost, rural, and urban, the outpost family of the Native people groups has preserved some of its traditional patterns, however, this preservation is threatened by the impact of outside industrial-urban forces. The patterns of the rural system are under similar pressure. Changes are underway toward the urban models, but it is difficult to predict the future of these developments. However, diversities continue to exist. Among the Kwakiutl peoples of British Columbia, for example, arranged marriages still take place, and, in one village studied, 60 percent of those over thirty-five years were involved in such marriages. In the rural community of the Hutterites, a system of endogamous and exogamous prescriptions has evolved to balance the community's needs for continuity and change. Marriage is within the community but not within the colony. The Jewish community also exercises some control over mate selection. Parents tend to disapprove of marriages outside the community, and indirectly discourage intermarriages through residential segregation into Jewish neighborhoods. Through the 1960s and 1970s, new life styles and arrangements have been emerging. As a result, alternative living patterns have surfaced as trends. The climate of alienation and anomie created by a variety of factors – rapid industrialization, new technologies, and new opportunities for self-expression – proved favorable to experiments in alternative life styles. Although these tend to be ignored by mainstream sociology, they are worth noting. The least radical change is the increase in extramarital sexuality. Precise data are not available, but some estimates place the proportion of urban North Americans involved in extramarital sex as high as 60 to 70 percent of the married population.[18] Very close to this pattern is the practice of living together without benefit of marriage. Cohabitation is increasing, even reaching smaller towns. More important is the developing tendency to remain single. Many people are now either avoiding marriage or, after a failed marriage have opted for the single life. As an alternative to marriage this life style has caught on and acquired some social approval.[19] The stereotypical image of a single person as an object of pity or in some sense deprived is disappearing. Today the single life is being accepted as a reasonable life style.

---

[18]Warren E. Kalbach, "The Demography of Marriage." In *Marriage, Family and Society,* edited by Parvez S. Wakil. (Toronto: Butterworth, 1975), pp. 59-84.

[19]Robert Whitehurst, "Non-Traditional Family and Marriage." In *Courtship, Marriage and the Family in Canada,* edited by G. N. Ramu. (Toronto: Macmillan, 1979), p. 170.

In terms of numbers, various forms of community and co-operative life styles are of minor significance. In Canada, the churches have attempted to evolve quasi-kin units based on the collective sharing of social and recreational facilities. These may include baby-sitting and communal sharing of household equipment. Another is the gay life style, as yet a deviation from what is regarded as the norm. Also emerging are group marriages, including triadic sex relationships. But these are essentially life styles adopted by a small segment of Canadian society.

Remarriage. A high divorce rate is usually associated with a high remarriage rate, in a society that favors remarriage. Moreover divorced persons tend to favor remarriage, unlike the widowed who tend to remain single. There is a close relationship between remarriage and marital stability, such that a union between previously married people is less durable than that between those married for the first time. Hence the divorce rate increases with successive marriage.

Children tend to pose problems in interpersonal relations between spouses, between stepchildren and stepparents, and among stepchildren themselves. But children may also be a factor that encourages remarriage. Widowed or divorced women with children are more likely to remarry than those without children. Often children have difficulty adjusting to the situation created by divorce and remarriage. While the disruption created by divorce is traumatic in itself, remarriage tends to create even more anxiety for the child.

In Canada, 18.1 percent of all marriages in 1973 were second marriages. This was an increase from the 1966 figure of 12.4 percent. In 1973, the total number of Canadians who remarried was 50 638. More men were involved in second unions than women. Of this group, 71.3 percent were divorced and 28.7 percent were widowed. The average age range of those who divorced and remarried was 35 to 39; for those who were widowed and remarried, it was 52 and 58. Over two and a half times as many divorced Canadians marry for the second time than do the widowed.[20]

In 70 percent of all remarriages, according to 1973 data, at least one of the spouses had been divorced. A divorced person preferred to marry a single person rather than one who had been divorced or widowed. Of all remarriages in 1973, 50 percent involved single persons. According to a study of Toronto remarriages conducted by Schlesinger, the average age at remarriage was 37 for males and 32 for females; for the divorced male and female, it was 36.5 and 33.5 respectively; it was 45 for widowers and 37 for widows; and for single men and women, it was 32 and 27, respectively.[21] As indicated widows were slightly older than divorced or single females at the time of remarriage. For first marriages the average age is 25 for men and 22 for women. Thus, single persons who marry widowed or divorced persons are generally older than those marrying for the first time.

There was no significant difference between widowed and divorced with

---

[20]Benjamin Schlesinger, "Remarriage." In *Courtship, Marriage and the Family in Canada,* edited by G. N. Ramu. (Toronto: Macmillan, 1979), pp. 155-57.

[21]Schlesinger, *op. cit.,* p. 158.

regard to the age at the time of first marriage being respectively 22 and 21 years. The average duration of the first marriage for divorced males was 11 years, and for divorced females it was 9 years. Marriages lasted longer for those widowed. The average time lag between the first and second marriages was 1.5 years for divorced males and 2 years for divorced females. For widowers, it was 3 years and for widows, it was 7 years. According to the study, the most frequent cause of marital dissolution was emotional incompatibility or poor interpersonal communication leading to sexual distance. Of the other reasons given, poor relations with in-laws was most frequently mentioned.

Divorce. Understanding divorce in relation to its influence on society involves three considerations – the breakdown of a key social institution, the disturbance of a culturally significant relationship concerning the conjugal situation, and the adverse effect on children. In Canada, as in modern societies in general, divorce is a legal process defining legal status in a specific manner. While there are countries without legal provision for divorce, this does not mean that marital failure or unhappiness does not exist in those societies. In these societies, absence of divorce is associated with either religious beliefs or male supremacy, as in those societies that do not allow divorce but permit polygamy. The general devaluation of divorce as a social phenomenon derives from the almost universal practice of investing marriage with a positive value.

Many theoretical frameworks have been developed within the sociological tradition to deal with divorce.[22] One focusses on the causal relationship between the proneness to divorce and background characteristics such as urban-rural setting, age at marriage, ethnicity, religious behavior, and kin attitudes. A second framework concentrates attention on three types of intramarital relationships – the aborted marriage, the moderately functioning family, and the intermittently working family. In an aborted marriage, the partners fail to work out the emotional or sexual problems in their relationship. In the second type, the necessary functional roles are performed with minimal efficacy. Marital satisfaction is questionable and, while it is a potentially divorcing situation, no divorce actually occurs. The third type represents a satisfying marital relationship, but one plagued with disturbances such as excessive drinking, extramarital activity, or extreme dedication to work at the cost of the family.

For modern society, especially as it has evolved in more recent times, a permanent availability model is predicated on a potential spouse, whether single, divorced, widowed, or married. This model is best suited to societies characterized by increasing rates of divorce and remarriage. In this model, permanent availability arises because marriage is regarded as a free association to be dissolved in response to diminished marital commitment. A more complicated framework is one which conceptualizes estrangement as a prelude to divorce. It uses three basic notions: attraction forces, barrier forces, and alternative attractions. These account for divorce in psychological and economic terms.

---

[22]For a brief review, *see* John F. Peters, "Divorce." In *Courtship, Marriage and the Family in Canada,* edited by G. N. Ramu. (Toronto: Macmillan, 1979), pp. 135-36.

With this theoretical background, it is possible to examine meaningfully the demographic features of divorce in Canada. Between 1970 and 1977, the number of divorces in Canada almost doubled, from some 29 775 in 1970 to 55 370 in 1977. The divorce rate increased from 139.8 per 100 000 population in 1970 to 277.7 in 1977. The divorce rate jumped from 166.1 in 1973 to 200.6 in 1974, registering a percentage change from 11.9 to 20.7. In 1975, the Canadian divorce rate was 222, in comparison with 480 for the United States, 308 for the USSR, and 314 for Sweden. However, a more meaningful figure would result by relating the number of divorces to the number of married women above 15 years. This would take into account only the legally married population. In 1976, there were 986 divorces per 100 000 legally married people in Canada, and from 1974 to 1979, the average annual rate of increase in divorces for legally married persons was 11.5 percent.

A comparison between the number of divorces and number of marriages for a given period of time is a demographically significant indicator of marital stability. In 1979, the Canadian ratio was around three divorces to every ten marriages annually. In the United States, it was one divorce to every two marriages. Of course, such figures do not necessarily mean that marriage is being undermined as an institution.

There are considerable inter-provincial variations in divorce rates in Canada. Such variations reflect differences in history, economic structure, political patterns, and other demographic factors. The Canadian regional and cultural diversities are fully represented in these variations. For 1977, British Columbia had the highest divorce rate of 330. Quebec's rate jumped suddenly by 50 percent in 1974, and is now moving closer to the national average. The Deckert and Langelier study of 1977 indicates that the decline of religious influence is reflected in the divorce rate in that province. In terms of absolute numbers, Ontario registered the highest number of divorces in 1977, but its divorce rate is close to the Canadian average. Prince Edward Island had an increase of 55 percent in its divorce rate in 1976. But this figure is misleading; the increase in absolute numbers was only from 75 to 116. Prince Edward Island and Newfoundland are among the provinces with the lowest divorce rates in Canada. Sociologically more challenging is the sudden 20 percent jump in the Saskatchewan divorce rate in 1977, since it involved a larger number of divorces.

In Canada, as in the United States, a low marriage age is more likely to lead to divorce. In 1976, around 24 percent of all Canadian brides and 7 percent of all bridegrooms were under 20 years of age. Of all those divorcing in that year, 42 percent of the women and 12 percent of the men had been married at this age. For the same year, 45 percent of all brides and 46 percent of all bridegrooms fell into the 20-24 year age range. The average age at marriage for the female and male in 1976 was 22.7 and 25 years, respectively. In the last few years the average age at marriage has been rising.

One of the important variables in any analysis of divorce is marital durability. In 1976, the average duration of marriage prior to divorce in Canada was eleven years compared with seven years for the United States, for the same year. But averages conceal such interesting facts as that a significant number of Canadian divorces occur at the end of three years of married life, and that in 1976 there were as many as 156 divorces within the first year of marriage. There has been a gradual increase in the percentage of divorces before the fourth year of marriage. The proportion of marriages ending in divorce after twenty-five years is comparatively small. The Canadian cities showing high divorce rates are Edmonton, Calgary, and Vancouver. While no significant study has been done on the relationship between divorce and income level, a positive correlation between higher income and higher divorce rate has been generally documented for Western societies. The Canadian data show that the divorce rate has been increasing even among lower-income groups.

Children are no longer regarded as a deterrent to divorce. In recent studies, no significant variation has been documented between the single-parent home and the two-parent home in which there is frequent tension between the spouses. There has been an increase in the number of divorced couples who have children. About 55 percent of all divorcing couples in 1976 had at least one child. However, there were some 900 divorces involving couples with children numbering five or more. In 1976, it was the wife who more frequently petitioned for the custody of children; among all divorced wives the percentage was 66. While formerly it was customary for the mother to win custody of the children, in more recent years, due to the emergence of egalitarian ideology, fathers are often gaining custody. In about 1 percent of the cases, custody is assigned to external agencies or to persons other than the parents.

In Canada, unlike the United States, divorce laws are federally controlled, and divorce is granted on two grounds, either marital offence or marital breakdown. The former includes adultery, physical cruelty, and mental cruelty; the latter comprises drug or alcohol addiction, separation for a period of three years or more, and desertion by the petitioner for a period of at least five years. During 1976, marital offence formed the basis of alleged grounds for divorce in 62.9 percent of the cases filed, and marital breakdown provided grounds for 37.1 percent. The most frequent grounds were adultery (30.5 percent) and desertion (31 percent). Between 1969 and 1972, the Canadian courts only dismissed about 0.8 percent of all divorce cases processed. This low incidence of dismissals is a reflection of the more liberal divorce laws passed in 1968. Cases petitioned on grounds of mental cruelty are more likely to be dismissed than those grounded on adultery. The law provides for voluntary withdrawal of applications which accounted for 4.3 percent of all cases during this period. Such withdrawal occurred more in the traditional regions of eastern Canada than in the central or western provinces.

Statistical data on divorce may not appear to be immediately significant or relevant for sociological analysis, but the figures provide a point of departure for more qualitative and detailed in-depth investigations into the phenomenon.

Illegitimacy. Between 1921 and 1972, the illegitimate birth rate showed an increase for all provinces in Canada except New Brunswick and Manitoba. Even in these two provinces, the rate for those in the fifteen to nineteen year age group did not decrease. In 1921, Manitoba had the highest rate followed by Nova Scotia, while British Columbia had the lowest rate. Nova Scotia had the highest in 1941 and 1951, and the second highest in 1931 and 1961. Alberta was first in 1931 and 1961, second in 1971, and third in 1941 and 1951. Saskatchewan maintained a fairly stable rank, fifth or sixth, until 1971, but it claimed the highest illegitimate birth rate in 1971 and 1972.

Abortions. In 1972, abortion rates for 100 live births was highest in British Columbia (23.7), while Newfoundland had the lowest rate. Although Ontario ranked second (16.2), it was still far behind British Columbia. Manitoba, Saskatchewan, and Alberta have very high illegitimate birth rates, but relatively low abortion rates. This challenges any assumption of positive correlation between illegitimacy and abortion rates. The decline in illegitimacy rates in the 1970s may not be exlusively attributed to the liberal abortion law. Qubec is low both on illegitimate births and abortions, which may be a reflection of the Roman Catholic influence.

Unmarried women in the fifteen to nineteen year age group had a very low abortion rate relative to that of older women. This may be due to the fact that the teen-age women were unable to take advantage of the changes in the Canadian abortion laws. The statistical data raise some significant questions. Why did the decline in the illegitimacy rate become noticeable only in 1970-1971, and why was it not reflected in the teen-age group? It is quite likely that, even though the abortion law was introduced in 1969, its consequences were not significantly reflected until 1971. The failure of teen-agers to abort might have been due to lack of awareness or their low socio-economic status. Further, they may have been influenced by family and friends. More research is needed to clarify these issues.

Evaluation

Existing knowledge about the Canadian family in all its ramifications and complexities is far from adequate to provide a basis for any substantial conclusions and generalizations. Nonetheless, the study of the Canadian family has advanced rapidly in the last two decades, revealing its multifaceted forms and its multidimensional processes.

While the forms and functions of the Canadian family have continued to reflect Canadian diversities in ethnicity, language, religion, region, socio-economic status, and ideology, there are also significant pressures driving it toward greater uniformity. These pressures stem primarily from increasing urbanization, industrialization, and technological change, and in particular, tend to converge toward the modified-extended and nuclear family. The myth of the modern family as being isolated from the kinship network has been explored by Canadian researchers, and the data conform to the general interpretation of the form and function of the family in contemporary modern societies in the West. However, caution must be exercised when making simplistic generalizations about a highly complicated and developing situation, for which the available data is anything but satisfactory. However, one fact emerges very clearly; the family is still a vital institution, both functionally and structurally adaptable to the changing needs and realities of Canadian society.

Almost all areas and aspects associated with family life in Canada, whether structural or demographic, are undergoing significant shifts. Patterns of socialization at two strategic life stages (childhood and adolescence), mate-selection patterns, the marital system and the process of its dissolution, post-dissolution patterns, and a host of other related phenomena are also showing quantitative and qualitative changes. Where these changes will lead is difficult to anticipate. Nonetheless, speculation is possible, and this profile of the Canadian family is an attempt to capture the patterns of highly dynamic, fluid, and uncertain developments that have characterized the history of the family from the turn of the century to date. What can be asserted, perhaps even emphatically, is that the family in Canada is here to stay and will continue to perform its more conventional as well as its changing functions within a changing Canadian society. It is bound to be as much a part of Canadian society in the future as it has been in the past and is in the present.

THE CANADIAN FAMILY DEMOGRAPHIC AND QUALITATIVE PERSPECTIVES

Introduction

There are several important general issues regarding the forms and functions of the family in Canada that must be clearly laid out and discussed before we can make a detailed analysis of the family forms and functions exemplified in various case studies. In other words, a general perspective on the family in Canada considered as a context for convergence of general issues must be developed. The two articles in this section are intended to provide this perspective.

Warren Kalbach guides us through the intricacies of the Canadian census data pertinent to an understanding of the changes in the family forms and functions since World War II. The census data, like all data, are dependent for their meanings and interpretations on, among other considerations, various definitions of concepts such as family, household, primary family, and so on. Kalbach clarifies the major definitions, and quantitatively documents numerous major aspects to which close attention must be paid by those interested in understanding some of the complexities of change and continuities in the family in Canada over the period considered by Kalbach.

Notable among the aspects explored are: formation, growth, and dissolution of families; family living arrangements; types of families; family structure; family size and composition; the cultural milieu of the family; inter-religious and inter-ethnic marriages; characteristics of family heads; labor force participation and family income; and women's participation in the labor force. So far as the census data permit, Kalbach documents these and other themes, drawing attention to their implications, and concluding with a discussion of the overall results obtained from his exploration.

The results of Kalbach's documentation and analysis must be grasped in their specific contexts, however, a few are noted here for illustrative purposes. For instance, we learn that even though both the total population of Canada and the number of families have increased during 1941-1976, the relationship between the two has remained relatively constant. From the discussion of the declining marital age, we learn that home ownership is still the predominant form of tenure, even though younger families are finding it increasingly more difficult to own homes to begin their married life. Another important finding is the declining size of the family due to the reduced number of children. Increasing numbers of single-parent families, in which women are preponderantly the single parent, is yet another factor disclosed. There are many general conclusions, of the type indicated here, that emerge from the data presented and the reader is encouraged to look for them.

Overall, Kalbach's discussion stresses that changes in the structure and character of family life result from interactions between the external socio-economic forces and the implications of individual efforts. The rapid decline in fertility and family size during the period is responsive both to the changing economic circumstances and the individual's evaluation of those conditions in the future in relation to larger, smaller, and no children families.

As distinguished from the variety of implications considered by Kalbach, the second article in this section, by Ramu and Tavuchis, focusses on one basic argument of general importance. They note the position of a number of social scientists, namely that various forces of pluralism operative in Canadian society make it misleading to think in terms of the concept of "the Canadian family." Ramu and Tavuchis then argue that, even though such forces are there, they are being eroded by the larger forces of urbanization, modernization, and technology. They opt to emphasize these larger forces, discussing their implications for family forms and functions, and concluding that "family patterns in Canada are indeed converging in the ways suggested by Goode and others although not uniformly or simply in response to industrialization and urbanization." Thus, they find the concept of "*the* Canadian family" useful. Their discussion will no doubt provide further opportunities for a continued debate basic to an understanding of the family in the Canadian and other national-cultural perspectives.

The Canadian Family: A Profile

Warren E. Kalbach

The family is the fundamental social unit of human societies. Yet, its form and character is exceedingly varied throughout the world. Because of this, the family has a wide range of meanings for individuals, particularly for those in Canada whose families or ancestors have emigrated from many different regions of the world. In addition to this primary source of variation between Canadian families, the forces of modernization and urbanization have wrought further changes on the traditional family forms of immigrants and non-immigrants alike. Because of continuing change, it is important to periodically assess its nature and effects. Specifically, this profile of the Canadian family reviews its major features and changes during the postwar period.[1]

The national census, Canada's major means of assessing the population, requires an enumeration of all individuals with respect to their living arrangements. The term "household" is used to identify a common dwelling unit occupied by a person or persons regardless of their relationship to one another. However, only those persons occupying a single household who are related by blood, marriage, or adoption are generally regarded as a family. More specifically, Statistics Canada defines the *census family* as a "husband and wife (with or without children who have never married, regardless of age), or a lone parent, regardless of marital status, with one or more children never married, living in the same dwelling."[2] The census definition is very similar to the concept of "nuclear" family used by social scientists to refer to a living unit comprised of parents and their immediate offspring (Nye and Berardo 1973:33).

While the definition of census family covers the most prevalent form of the Canadian family, there are many households that contain other non-family persons, multiple families, and households in which the family head is not the head of the household. In addition, there are non-family households. In 1976, there were 7 166 095 occupied private dwellings and households. Of these, 79 percent were family households consisting of a single family. Furthermore, practically all households contained only family members. Just 9

---

[1] Unless otherwise specified, the data for this paper have been taken from the published reports of the 1961, 1971, and 1976 Censuses of Canada, and from the annual reports of the vital statistics published by Statistics Canada.

[2] A family may consist also of a man or woman living with a guardianship child or ward under 21 years for whom no pay was received (Canada 1972:6). Persons living common-law were reported in the 1971 Census as married and appear as husband-wife families in the census reports. Sons and daughters who have ever married, regardless of age, are not considered as members of their parents' family, even though they may be living in the same dwelling (Canada 1978:v).

percent reported the presence of additional persons. Multiple family house-holds accounted for less than 2 percent of all family households.

The number of non-family households, while relatively small, has shown a significant gain since 1951 when they comprised only 11 percent of the total households in Canada. By 1976, their number had quadrupled and their pro-portion had increased to just over one-fifth. The importance of non-family households for understanding the nature of the family in Canadian society lies in the fact that many of them are survivors of former single family house-holds. Of non-family households, 79 percent consisted of only one person, and over half of these persons were either widowed, divorced, or married individuals living alone. While never married persons comprised just under half of the single person non-family households, a continuation of low fertility and increasing longevity will make the elderly survivors of former families an increasingly greater and important part of the social and demographic struc-ture of Canadian society. Additionally, elderly persons may be found as heads of both single and multiple family households in which none of the families are those of the household head. However, their numbers were few at the time of the 1976 census.[3]

The remaining non-family households with two or more persons number almost a third of a million. While they are not census families as formally defined, they might be construed as a type of sociological family unit. How-ever, as intriguing as these emerging family forms may be, it is not possible to examine them more closely with the available census data. Consequently, the following analysis focusses on the dominant form of the family in Canada – the census family.

Formation, Growth, and Dissolution of Families

Everyone is a member of a census family at some point and for most persons the majority of their lives is spent within the context of a family, first as chil-dren and adolescents, and then as married couples and parents. The non-family intervals in the individual's life cycle have been traditionally regarded as temporary states representing transitions from one family and marital sta-tus to another.[4]

Because of the inclusiveness of the family as the basic societal grouping of individuals, the population belonging to census families in relation to the total population has remained relatively constant, even though both the total population and the number of families has continued to increase in Canada during the postwar years. The data in Table 1 show that between 1941 and

---

[3]According to the census definition, the families in such households could be those of a son or daughter living in their parent's home where the parent would be consid-ered the head of the household.

[4]The term life cycle has been used to describe the sequence of stages and events that an individual typically passes through during his lifetime. It has been used specifically by Glick (1955) to refer to the family and the series of characteristic stages that fami-lies experience between formation and dissolution. The family life cycle begins with marriage and household formation, bearing and rearing children, marriage of the children, and the empty nest period between the departure of the last child and the death of one of the parents.

Table 1: Total Population, Census Families, Population in Census Families, and Average Number of Persons per Census Family, in Canada, 1941-1976

Year	1941[a]	1951	1961	1971	1976
Total Population	11 489 263	14 009 429	18 238 247	21 568 310	22 992 600
Number of Families	2 525 299	3 287 384	4 147 444	5 053 166	5 727 895
Persons in Families	9 937 986	12 216 103	16 095 721	18 791 904	19 783 200
Average Number of Persons per Family	3.9	3.7	3.9	3.7	3.5

[a]Excludes Newfoundland, Yukon, and Northwest Territories.

Source: CANADIAN HOUSEHOLDS AND FAMILIES: RECENT DEMOGRAPHIC TRENDS, CENSUS ANALYTICAL STUDY, Catalogue 99-753E, Table 2.1A. Data for 1971 and 1976 from 1976 Census of Canada, Catalogue 93-821, Table 1. Reproduced by permission of the Minister of Supply and Services Canada.

1966 the proportion of the population in families increased only slightly from 86 to 88 percent, then returned to 86 percent by 1976 (Wargon 1979:34). During the same period (1941 to 1976), the total population, as well as the population in families, doubled in size while the number of families increased by 127 percent. In contrast, family size has both increased and decreased over the same period, varying between 3.9 and 3.7 for thirty years before declining to 3.5 in 1976.

Changes in the number of census families and their proportion of the total population reflect earlier variations in fertility levels as well as changes in other demographic factors, such as the age at marriage, marriage and divorce rates, and the number and size of immigrant families. The prewar decline in fertility followed by the postwar baby boom and bust is visibly reflected in postwar variations in family size. Peak marriage rates from 1940 to 1942 contributed to the increase in size of the married or family population, as well as to the number of families. Favorable economic and social conditions following the war not only encouraged marriages postponed by the war, but also marriages of younger persons. Crude marriage rates peaked again in 1946, and although they steadily declined until 1962, the age of first marriage continued to decline until 1966 for brides and 1971 for bridegrooms before levelling off. One effect of the declining age at marriage was to increase the proportion married in the population which compensated to a certain extent for the opposite effects produced by a declining marriage rate (Kalbach and McVey 1979: 306-11). The postwar immigration boom and the government's increasing recognition of the importance of family immigration and reunification during the 1960s were also positive factors in the growth of the family population (Canada 1974).

Two additional contributing factors are the consequences of mortality and divorce. Both reduce the family's size by at least one, while not necessarily reducing the number of families. Mortality and divorce also contribute to an increase in the population of one-parent families and, in each case, tend to produce more one-parent families with female heads. Older one-parent families are more susceptible to dissolution with the departure of the last child or the death of the remaining parent. On the other hand, one-parent families with young female heads are more likely to be restored through remarriage.

Liberalization of divorce legislation in 1969 has contributed greatly to the rapid growth of one-parent families with divorced female heads. On the other hand, the current liberalization of attitudes toward the role of women in society seems to be responsible for an increase in both the number of female family heads who are separated and young women who have never been married. While relatively high proprotions of the younger female heads of lone parent families are not in the labor force, neither of the above trends could have developed without the increase in female participation in the labor force during the postwar period.

Family Living Arrangements

The particular living arrangement of any family tends to reflect its needs in relation to its position in the individual and family life cycle of its members.

The family's living arrangement also reflects the character and availability of housing in the community, and the earning power in relation to the cost of living, as well as the family's attitudes and values regarding the importance of kinship ties. The ideal living arrangement and type of accommodation for families has traditionally been touted as ownership of a single detached dwelling where the husband or father is both the head of the household and the major breadwinner. The wife, in her traditional role, carries the responsibility for homemaking and child care. While this may still be considered by most as the type to emulate, the effects of industrialization and urbanization, combined with fluctuating economic conditions, have made the traditional goal somewhat less than ideal and increasingly difficult to attain.

Home ownership is still the predominant form of tenure with almost two-thirds of all occupied private dwellings in Canada owner occupied at the time of the 1976 census. The proportion has fluctuated since 1941, partly in response to changes in the age composition of family heads during this period and partly due to variations in the cost of owning a home. In earlier times, persons generally did not consider marrying until they had saved enough to buy a home. The trend to marrying at a younger age has meant that few can afford to buy their own home and must seek alternative accommodations until their financial position improves. Concentration of growth and spiralling costs in the large urban centres are making the dream of owning single detached housing in these areas increasingly difficult for many people to obtain. This is reflected in the fact that in 1976 slightly less than half of the private occupied dwelling units in urban areas were single detached, and only slightly more than one half of all private occupied dwelling units in urban areas were owner occupied. The urban percentages were almost ten percent lower than the corresponding percentages for Canada as a whole, which were 56 and 62 percent respectively. In urban areas, the dream of the single detached house is being replaced by dreams of owning a semi-detached house, a town or row house, or an apartment condominium as an interim step. Until the dream of ownership can be realized, renting or sharing accommodations with family or friends appears to be the only viable alternative.

Type of Family

The census makes a clear distinction between primary and secondary families in terms of whether or not they maintain their own household. Those who do not, i.e., secondary families, are further differentiated into related, lodging, and non-related families.[5] Primary families have experienced a steady growth during the postwar years, increasing from 90 percent in 1951 to 98 percent in 1976. All of the secondary family types experienced declines during the same period with related families decreasing from 6 to 2 percent, and lodging type families declining from just under 4 percent to only 0.2 percent in 1976.

---

[5]Related families consist of a census family in which the husband, the wife or the parent in a lone-parent family is related by blood, marriage, or adoption to the household head. Non-related families are further subdivided into lodging families and other non-related families (employees' family, partner's family) (Canada 1979:26-29).

Other types of secondary families have remained relatively insignificant at less than one percent since 1971.[6]

The ability or desire to maintain one's own household varies with the age and marital status of the family head, as well as by generation and period of immigration for the foreign-born. In terms of marital status, the proportion of primary families tends to be highest for families with both married partners living at home (98 percent in 1971), and lowest for lone-parent families where the wife is the family head (61 percent). With respect to generational status, the second generation exhibited the highest proportions with primary families (98 percent), while the proportion for the most recent immigrant families was slightly lower (90 percent) (Richmond and Kalbach 1980: Table 6.2). As might be expected, all generations show higher proportions of "related" family heads in both the younger and older age groups. The differences were greatest between the oldest family heads of the first generation who came to Canada prior to the last war and those immigrating just prior to the 1971 census. In the case of the former only 3 percent were secondary families with related heads compared with almost half for the most recent immigrants (Richmond and Kalbach 1980: 207).

Family Structure

By far the most common type of family in Canada is the husband-wife family consisting of husband and wife, or persons living common-law, with or without children. In 1976, 90 percent of all families had both husband and wife at home while the remaining 10 percent were lone-parent families. Of the latter, those with female heads were the most numerous, accounting for 83 percent of all lone-parent families.

Husband-wife families increased from 90 to 92 percent between 1951 and 1966. By 1976, their proportion had declined to 90 percent, primarily as a result of an increase in lone-parent families with female heads. The proportion of lone-parent families with male heads actually declined during the same period. Between 1971 and 1976, the proportion for the latter dropped below two percent while the 465 480 female lone-parent families, reported in 1976, represented 8 percent of the total. The growth of female lone-parent families represents increases in the number of younger, separated, divorced, and never married women. While families headed by widows still comprised the single largest group of all types of one-parent families in 1976, their relative share has declined since 1951, accounting for less than half of all single-parent families.

Given the predominance of husband-wife families, little variation in the composition of the family population by type is possible. However, the slight urban/rural differences are consistent with the known effects of urbanization.

---

[6]Statistics Canada comments that the numerical increase in other secondary families from 4910 in 1971 to 7195 in 1976 may be due, in part, to an undetermined overcount in the partners component of the other category. They advise that while the extent of the overcount remains to be determined, this possibility should be kept in mind while comparing 1976 data with previous census results (Canada 1979:32).

Rural farm families, for example, have a slightly above average proportion of husband-wife families (95 percent) compared with just 89 percent in urban centers of 500 000 or more population. Conversely, the proportion of single-parent families is considerably larger for the largest urban communities with 11 percent compared with just 5 percent found in rural farm populations. It is possible that these differences might actually be greater than these data indicate, but the high degree of population mobility, which has characterized Canada's population during the postwar period, tends to blur many of the rural/urban differences.

Family Size and Composition

The postwar baby boom and bust were not caused solely by actual changes in the completed fertility of married women. Henripin and Légaré (1971) have shown that the postwar rise in fertility up to 1959 was primarily due to an increase in the proportion of the population married, and to a lesser extent to increases in marital fertility. On the other hand, they attributed the sharp drop during the 1960s to declining marital fertility heightened by changes in child spacing. The postwar boom and bust in fertility did produce similar variations in average family size even though the latter is also affected by changing marriage, divorce, separation, and mortality rates, changes in the length of schooling for children, and changes in the age at which children leave home to work or marry. Even though fluctuations in family size since 1951 appear to reflect variations in fertility, family size is less a measure of fertility per se than a measure of the average size of the functioning family unit at a particular time.

Average family size increased to a maximum of 3.9 during the 1960s from 3.7 in 1951, but then declined to 3.7 in 1971 and 3.5 in 1976. Between 1971 and 1976, the rate of family formation was greater than the growth of the population in families. Specifically, the number of families increased by 13 percent, while the persons in families increased by only 5 percent. The same pattern, although somewhat attenuated, characterized the previous decade during which families increased by 22 percent while the population in families increased by only 17 percent.

Average number of children per family. The average number of children per family tends to follow the trend in family size very closely since families are predominantly two-parent families. As is the case with family size, the average number of children in the family reflects more than variations in fertility. An increase in family formation between 1941 and 1951 was primarily responsible for the decline in average number of children from 1.9 to 1.7 in spite of rapidly increasing postwar fertility rates. Continuing high fertility during the 1950s produced an increase in the family population greater than the increase in number of families (32 percent versus 26 percent). The consequence was an increase in the average number of children from 1.7 to 1.9 between 1951 and 1961. The decline in fertility, starting around 1961, was subsequently reflected in average family size and number of children after

1966, when average family size declined from 3.9 to 3.5 in 1976 and average number of children declined from 1.9 to 1.5.[7]

Recent changes in fertility are also reflected in the distribution of families by number of children. The proportion of families with no children in 1976 (30 percent) was not much different from that reported in 1971. However, while the proportion of families with one and two children increased between 1971 and 1976, the proportions with more children showed significant declines from the peak values achieved in 1961. By 1976, just over half of all families had either no children or just one. Another 24 percent had two children with 13 percent reporting three. Less than 10 percent of all families had four or more children, a considerable reduction from the 17 percent reported in 1941, and a reflection of the dramatic decline in child bearing at the older ages since 1964 (Kalbach and McVey 1979:103).

Spacing and age groupings of children at home. The spacing and age composition of children in families is also affected by demographic factors and the social and economic conditions that influence marriage and fertility in general. The decline in age at marriage that characterized the postwar years and contributed to the rise in fertility rates, ended for females during the early 1960s and during the early 1970s for males. The interval between marriage and first births increased from about eighteen months during the 1960s to almost two years before dropping sharply to just under one year in 1975 and 1976.[8]

The intervals between children tended to increase after the postwar baby boom, continuing into the 1970s for most orders of birth. For example, the average interval between first and second births increased from 2.4 years in 1959 to 2.7 years in 1975, while the interval between fourth and fifth births increased from 1.4 to 1.9 years.[9] The evidence strongly suggests that the decline in fertility following the boom years of the 1950s was a direct consequence of the postponement of births. According to Balakrishnan, et al. (1979), the tendency to postpone births was a result of the increased participation of married women in the labor force, and an increased desire for smaller families. Moreover, the introduction of oral contraceptives during the 1960s pro-

---

[7]In 1976, all unmarried children living at home, regardless of age, were included as family members. This would, of course, produce higher averages than prior censuses that included only those children at home under 25 years of age. However, even when using the 1971 figure of 1.8, based on the new definition, the revised figure still shows a continuation of the decline that had become apparent as early as 1966.

[8]The sharp decline in the interval between marriage and the first birth is suggestive of an increase in premarital pregnancies resulting in marriage. A similar trend was reported in the United States for the period 1970-1974 during which 24 percent of all first births were estimated to have occurred during the first eight months of marriage, compared with 17 percent twenty years earlier. Estimates between 19 and 25 percent have been reported for the Detroit area circa 1961 by L.C. Coombs, et al., (1970).

[9]Calculations are based on live births by age of mother and birth order data for Canada, published by Statistics Canada in the annual vital statistics reports.

vided a more effective means of family planning than was previously available.

The overall effect of these changes appears to have been a decline in family size and a shift to relatively greater numbers of families at a more advanced stage of the family life cycle with more older children in the home. In 1976, slightly more than one-third of the families could be classified as "mature," that is with all their children either 18 years of age and over, between 15 and 18 years of age only, or just some of their children 18 and over. Families at intermediate stages of the family life cycle, that is with all their children between 6 and 15 years of age, or in both the 6-14 and 15-17 year age groups, accounted for 27 percent of the total families with children. Young families, with all of their children under six years of age, accounted for another 21 percent, and approximately 14 percent could be classified as "young transitional" families having some children between 6 and 14 years of age as well as some under 6 years. Larger families, or others with their children widely spaced across all the major age groups, accounted for only 2 percent of the total.

Several important consequences may be expected from the developing trend toward having smaller families within shorter periods of time. The exercise of more effective control over fertility, implied by this trend, means that families can be expected to change their fertility behavior more quickly in response to future social and economic conditions. This unpredictable fertility behavior will make it difficult to anticipate changes in the younger school age populations. In addition, the earlier completion of childbearing and childrearing activities has, in essence, added a new stage to the family life cycle. The combined effects of a shortening period of childbearing and increasing longevity are already evident in the longer periods of time that parents are living together without any children at home. This so called "empty nest" period will require adjustments in family living now that fathers are living well beyond the time when their children have left home.

The Cultural Milieu of the Family

Ethnic origin. Outside the major urban centres where fairly high levels of ethnic diversity are to be found, multiculturalism in Canada takes the form of relatively homogeneous regional clusterings of ethnic populations. Thus, the ethnic composition of the population as a whole does not reveal as much about the significance of ethnicity and multiculturalism as does the ethnic character of the country's regions. In 1971, just under half of all heads of family households were of British origin compared with 27 percent for French, and 28 percent for all other origins combined. Regional variations were quite significant, as may be seen in Table 2. In the Atlantic provinces, the numerical dominance of the British origins varied from 60 percent to as high as 93 percent. In Quebec, the French accounted for 76 percent of all family household heads while in the Prairie provinces, the other combined origins (mostly northern, western, and eastern Europeans) were the numerically dominant group. In Ontario and British Columbia, both the British origins and the combined other group were overrepresented in the population.

Table 2:   Ethnic Origin of Heads of Family Households for Provinces, in 1971

Province	Ethnic Origin			
	British	French	Other	Total
	(in percentages)			
Newfoundland	93.3	3.2	3.5	100.0
Prince Edward Island	82.9	13.2	3.9	100.0
Nova Scotia	75.8	10.4	13.8	100.0
New Brunswick	60.3	33.7	6.0	100.0
Quebec	11.6	76.4	12.0	100.0
Ontario	58.8	9.1	32.1	100.0
Manitoba	42.5	7.9	49.6	100.0
Saskatchewan	40.7	5.5	53.8	100.0
Alberta	45.7	5.6	48.7	100.0
British Columbia	57.8	4.2	38.0	100.0
Yukon and Northwest Territories	37.1	7.0	55.9	100.0
Canada	44.9	26.8	28.3	100.0

Source: 1971 CENSUS OF CANADA, Catalogue 93-707, Table 42.
Reproduced by permission of the Minister of Supply and Services Canada.

The ethnic composition of family heads in a region not only reflects the cultural origin and influences operating within families, it also indirectly indicates the general limits for contact and opportunities for interaction between individuals of the various cultural groups residing in the region. The relative sizes of regional ethnic populations are a crucial factor, although not the only one, in determining the probabilities of ethnic intermarriage. Differences in age distributions, the balance between the sexes in the marriageable age groups, general status differences, and prevailing attitudes between the various populations, all affect the opportunities for individuals to marry within their own ethnic group or with those of other cultural origins.

The net effects of all these factors influencing mate selection can be seen in the ethnic origin of the wives, in relation to that of their husbands. For the country as a whole in 1971, 24 percent of all family heads were married to wives of some other origin. Proportions varied widely for individual ethnic origins, from only 9 percent for Jewish husbands to 73 percent for those of Scandinavian origin. A more sensitive indicator of the propensity for ethnic intermarriage in Canada is obtained when the proportions are based on just the native born rather than on the total population of family heads (Kalbach 1974). These proportions are presented in Table 3 along with the ethnic distribution of heads of family households for Canada. Jewish males comprise only 1.6 percent of all family heads, but with 90 percent of Jewish husbands married to Jewish wives, they clearly have the lowest propensity for ethnic intermarriage. The French, one of the larger ethnic and cultural origin groups, show the next lowest propensity with 86 percent; and, somewhat suprisingly, those of British origin show the third lowest with 80 percent being married to women of British origin. Clearly, the large size of the British origin population in Canada relative to the size of the various ethnic populations can limit the range of possibilities for ethnic intermarriage. However, even the use of an

Table 3:   Ethnic Composition of Heads of Family Households, and the Percentage of Native-born Heads with Wives of the Same Origin, in 1971.

Ethnic Origin of Head	Heads of Family Households	Native-Born Family Heads with Wives of Same Origin
	(in percentages)	
British Isles	44.9	79.9
French	26.8	86.5
German	6.8	38.3
Dutch	2.0	26.9
Scandinavian	2.0	19.1
Polish	1.6	24.1
Ukrainian	3.0	45.0
Italian	3.5	30.1
Jewish	1.6	89.8
Asian	1.2	63.8
Indian and Inuit	1.0	—
Other and unknown	5.5	—
Total: Percent	100.00	75.6[a]
Number	4 933 625	3 537 120

[a]Total for all groups listed except Indian and Inuit, and other and unknown origins.

Source: UNPUBLISHED SPECIAL TABULATIONS AND 1971 CENSUS OF CANADA, Catalogue 93-707, Table 36. Reproduced by permission of the Minister of Supply and Services Canada.

index which takes into account the differences in size of the various groups does not alter the results significantly (Kalbach 1974).[10]

More interesting were the regional differences in the tendency to inter-marry. It is clear that differences in settlement patterns underlying variations in regional concentrations of ethnic populations are important for understand-ing the variations in intermarriages. Family heads of British origin show the lowest propensity for ethnic intermarriage in the Atlantic provinces and the highest in British Columbia. The French show their greatest reluctance for ethnic intermarriage in Quebec where they dominate both numerically and culturally. But, in British Columbia where they are numerically small, their propensity for ethnic intermarriage is even higher than it is for the British. Similarly, the Ukrainians exhibit their lowest propensity in the Prairie prov-inces where their cultural influence is most deeply rooted. Even those of Scandinavian origins, who have a very high propensity overall, show regional variations that reflect their pattern of early migration and settlement in the Prairie provinces.

Further analysis has shown that significantly larger proportions of north-ern and western European family heads acquire British origin wives when they marry outside their own ethnic origin group than is the case for males of other ethnic origins. The differences, however, declined somewhat between 1961 and 1971 (Kalbach 1974). Perhaps the improved socio-economic status of many of the other European origin groups has increased their social acces-sibility to the more dominant population of British origin.

Religion. Closely interrelated with ethnic origin, and sometimes inseparable from it, religion is an equally important component of the sociocultural di-mension by which Canada's population is further differentiated. In 1971, 49 percent of Canada's population was either Roman Catholic, Greek Ortho-dox, or Ukrainian Catholic. Nineteen Protestant denominations combined, accounted for another 44 percent, while the Jews comprised only slightly more than 1 percent. As with ethnic origins, the characteristics of the population getting married in any given year should reflect the general reli-gious composition of the nation as a whole, as well as that of the specific regions within which they live. The extent to which marriage and fertility patterns reinforce the regional ethnic and religious status quo would, of course, depend upon the extent to which individuals married within their own reli-gious faith and maintained current ethnic and religious differentials in both marriage and fertility rates.

Heer and Hubay (1975) have shown with respect to the major religious

---

[10]To account for the effects of differences in the size of groups, as suggested by Besanceney (1965) and Yinger (1968), propensities for intermarriage were calculated in terms of ratios of actual to expected proportions of intermarriage based on random pairing. Propensities were also calculated in terms of ratios of actual to possible proportions of intermarriage as suggested by Hewitt in Yinger (1968). While both sets measured in terms of the two types of ratios differed from the simple proportions, the rank order of the various ethnic origins in terms of their propensities for intermarriage was not significantly altered.

groupings of Protestants, Catholics, and Jews that interfaith marriages have consistently increased between 1927 and 1972. Veevers (1977) has shown that between 1963 and 1972, Catholic intermarriage increased from 13 to 22 percent, Jewish intermarriage from 8 to 12 percent, and for the five combined major Protestant denominations, interfaith marriages increased from 19 to 30 percent. More recent data for the period 1974 to 1977 have shown that the trend has continued for most of the major denominations.[11] There is some evidence that interdenominational marriages for several of the major Protestant groups that have been characterized by high levels of interdenominational marriage in the past may be on the wane. For example, the proportion for Presbyterians remained unchanged between 1974 and 1977, while the proportion for Baptists declined slightly from 62 to 60 percent.

Using the characteristics of heads of families and their wives, at the time of the national census, produces similar but not identical results. More important, the census permits a comparison of endogamous and exogamous marriages present in the population with respect to both ethnic origin and religion. In an unpublished study by Richard (1978) of ethnic and religious intermarriage in the Toronto Census Metropolitan Area (CMA), based on the 1971 census, the proportion of ethnically endogamous marriages (81 percent) slightly exceeded the proportion of families characterized by religious endogamy (78 percent). Furthermore, there appears to be a positive relationship between religious and ethnic endogamy. Of the ethnically endogamous marriages, 83 percent were endogamous with respect to religion, compared with only 59 percent in ethnically exogamous unions. Most persons still marry within their own ethnic and religious groups. However, the lower proportions of religious and ethnic endogamy among the younger heads of families and for the native born suggests a long-term trend towards greater cultural and religious heterogeneity among husbands and wives that is consistent with the results of the analyses of data for brides and bridegrooms at the time of marriage. In any event, while the long-term effects of such mixing are still unclear it would be difficult to argue that a continuation of this trend would not tend to weaken the cultural influence of these groups.

Characteristics of Family Heads

Age. Slightly more than half of all the heads of families were under 45 years of age in 1976. There has been little change since 1961. Even the proportion of older family heads, i.e., those 65 years of age and over, has remained relatively constant during this period at approximately 12 percent. This apparent stability reflected in the broad age groupings has obscured important changes that have occurred in some of the younger age groups. The effects of declining age at marriage and the increasing proportion married, that contributed

---

[11]The data for 1974 and subsequent years exclude the Province of Quebec which stopped providing this information to Statistics Canada. This is the apparent reason for the abrupt decline in the percentage of Roman Catholic brides marrying Roman Catholic grooms. In 1972, 77.7 percent of Roman Catholic brides married Roman Catholic grooms compared with 58.3 percent in 1974.

to the postwar baby boom and its subsequent reversal, plus continuing variations in the marriage rates have contributed to increasing proportions of younger family heads under 25 and between 25 and 35 years of age. However, the combined increase for these two younger age groups was almost entirely balanced by the decrease in the proportion of family heads 35-44 years of age.

The most important factor contributing to this relatively faster growth of the population of younger family heads has been the rapid increase in lone-parent families headed by young women (Wargon 1979). The proportion of young males under 35 years of age who were heads of families has changed very little for most of the period since 1951, in contrast to the proportion for women which has increased significantly, particularly between 1966 and 1976.[12]

Age differences between husbands and wives. A large increase in fertility, such as that characterized by the postwar baby boom, not only can produce a younging of the population of heads of families some twenty to twenty-five years later, but it can also affect the age differences between husbands and wives. Postwar economic conditions and changing social attitudes encouraged younger marriage, but even as the average age for first marriages decreased, the age difference between husbands and wives also decreased. Between 1941 and 1976, the average difference in median ages for brides and bridegrooms marrying for the first time declined from 3.3 to 2.1 years. Given the long established general cultural preference of men for marrying younger women, and vice versa, the trend toward parity in age at marriage has been produced, in part, by the marriage squeeze that follows significant increases in fertility. When fertility increases rapidly, as it did during the immediate postwar period, each successive birth cohort is larger than the one preceding it. Under these conditions, for any given cohort of women the pool of eligible bachelors is always smaller than the number of women. If women are to continue to marry, there is an increased likelihood that they will have to marry men much closer to the same age as themselves or younger. During periods of fertility decline, the reverse would be true and men would have greater difficulty in finding younger women. To the extent that they are unsuccessful, they would be forced to consider women closer to their own age or even older women for marriage.

Age at marriage also has an effect on the size and direction of age differences between men and women. The data in Table 4 show that the proportion of males marrying someone within their own five-year age group was greatest for those under thirty at the time of the 1976 Census. For men, the proportion marrying a woman in a younger age group increases dramatically with increasing age, from 17 percent for those 20-24 years of age to 65 percent for those 65-69. The chances of marrying a woman of an older age group

---

[12]Wargon (1979) discusses the possible overestimation of the numbers of female lone-parent families in 1971 and advises caution in their use. However, the percent of lone-parent families with female heads in 1976 was reported to be 28.1 percent. This would suggest that the rapid growth reported between 1966 and 1971, when the proportions were reported to be 16.2 and 24.3 percent, respectively, may not have been too much in error.

Table 4:   Age of Husband Showing Percent of Wives in a Younger, the Same, or Older Age Group, in 1976.

Age of Husband	Total Husband-Wife Families	Age of Wife		
		Younger Age Group	Same Age Group	Older Age Group
(in years)		(in percentages)		
Under 20	20 500	—	63.9	36.1
20-24	312 900	17.4	72.2	10.4
25-29	660 800	37.7	54.5	7.7
30-34	661 100	49.6	43.7	6.7
35-39	548 000	53.0	39.6	7.4
40-44	554 000	52.9	38.4	8.7
45-49	532 800	51.6	39.0	9.4
50-54	491 400	51.3	38.7	10.0
55-59	409 300	56.5	33.6	9.9
60-64	353 300	61.3	30.3	8.4
65-69	263 700	64.6	28.6	6.8
70 and over	331 000	49.2	50.8	—

Source: 1976 CENSUS OF CANADA, PUBLIC USE SAMPLE TAPE, FAMILY FILE.
Reproduced by permission of the Minister of Supply and Services Canada.

is highest for those under twenty years of age and generally somewhat lower for males in all other age groups. It is worth noting that the husbands who were 25-29 years of age in 1976 (i.e., born between 1947 and 1951) had a higher proportion marrying women within their own age group and in older age groups than was the case for the same age group in 1971. (Kalbach and McVey 1979: Table 12:5). Both are consistent with what would be expected when fertility rises rapidly as it did from 1947 to 1951. It should be remembered, however, that the decline in age differences between brides and grooms had been occurring prior to the postwar baby boom. This would suggest that the demographically produced marriage squeeze may have simply reinforced an existing trend reflecting changing attitudes and values in mate selection.

Educational attainment. Educational differences between husbands and wives reveals the existence of another cultural preference that appears to influence mate selection. The age graded educational system operates to facilitate interaction between persons of similar age and education so that a certain degree of homogeneity with respect to age and education can be expected among those who meet and marry. However, to be consistent with the traditional notion of male dominance, not only is the husband expected to be somewhat older and more experienced, but more intelligent and better educated as well. The exercise of culturally influenced preferences within broadly similar age and educational attainment group would be expected to produce patterns consistent with the cultural norms.

Evidence from recent censuses shows that this is, in fact, the case in Canada. Of all the husband-wife families in Table 5, 44 percent of the husbands had wives within the same general educational attainment category as themselves, while an additional 30 percent had wives with less education. A somewhat smaller proportion, 26 percent, had married women with more education. A complicating factor is the general tendency for more women to achieve higher education than men at any given level, except the highest. Thus, men who had not gone beyond grade ten were more likely to have wives with more education than themselves, while those who went beyond grade eleven were much more likely to have more education than the women they had married.

Because of the strong correlation between education and income, the education of husbands and wives is an important indicator of the family's general socio-economic status position in society, as well as having important consequences for the family's life style and expectations for their children's future. With respect to the latter, studies indicate that education of the family head is closely related to the children's chances of achieving post-secondary education. In 1976, the percentage of 18-24 year olds still attending school full time

Table 5: Educational Attainment Levels of Husbands and Wives, in 1976.

Educational Attainment of Husband	Total Husband-Wife Families	Educational Attainment of Wife		
		Less than Husband	Same as Husband	More than Husband
		(in percentages)		
Less than Grade 9	1 547 000	—	61.1	38.9
Grade 9 or 10	883 500	21.4	35.8	42.8
Grade 11	347 800	37.8	24.5	37.7
Grade 12 or 13	615 000	38.4	38.2	23.4
Post-Secondary, Non-University	775 500	53.5	36.5	9.9
Some University or Degree	970 000	60.1	39.9	—
Total	5 138 800	30.3	43.8	25.9

Source: 1976 CENSUS OF CANADA, PUBLIC USE SAMPLE TAPE, FAMILY FILE.
Reproduced by permission of the Minister of Supply and Services Canada.

in families whose father had less than a grade nine education was just 27 percent compared with 71 percent for those whose fathers had attained a university degree.

In comparison with heads of husband-wife families, the heads of lone-parent families tend to have less favorable educational attainment levels. Relatively larger numbers have less than grade eleven education whether they are male or female, the proportions being 61 and 56 percent, respectively, compared with 47 percent for husband-wife families. Given their lower educational attainment levels, it would be unlikely that they would have as high a proportion of children in the 18-24 age group attending school full time. Even when educational attainment levels are held constant, comparisons show that heads of lone-parent families have a lower proportion of their children attending school full time. For those with less than grade nine education, the proportion of their 18-24 year old children attending full time is 20 percent; and for those with a university degree it is 61 percent. The percentages fall somewhat short of those for husband-wife families which were 27 and 71 percent respectively. It would appear that lone-parent families are at a greater disadvantage when it comes to encouraging their children to continue their post-secondary education.

Labor Force Participation and Family Income

The extent and nature of participation in the labor force and family income are basic determinants of the family's social status and life style. Both participation and income vary significantly by sex, age, and education of the individual members, as well as by the marital status of the head of the family (Kalbach and McVey 1979). Males have traditionally participated more fully in the labor force than women, and they have consistently earned more money within any age group, educational attainment level, and marital status. Consequently, wives as well as children, have tended to be economically dependent on the family head; and, it has been this dependent relationship that has provided the basis and reinforcement for the dominant role of the husband and father in the family context.

The period of rapid economic expansion and population growth that followed World War II produced many social and economic changes that have had major consequences for the family. Perhaps the most important one has been the rapid increase in female labor force participation accompanied by a continuing decline in male participation. Between 1941 and 1976, female participation rates increased from 21 to 45 percent while the rate for males declined from 86 to 76 percent. The increase for women was due primarily to the rapid increase in participation by married women, even though divorced women continued to have the highest rates of any of the marital status groups.

More and more women are entering the labor force, irrespective of their marital status.[13] Women are breaking out of their traditionally defined roles, not only because of a growing desire for greater self-realization, but also for

---

[13]Female participation in the labor force has increased since 1951 for all marital statuses except for the never married which has only increased since 1971.

economic reasons. Increasing divorce and separation rates have made it necessary for many women to maintain their own households. Economically unstable and inflationary conditions during the 1970s have also made it increasingly difficult for families to maintain their living standard or to achieve their desired life style without the supplementary income of a working wife. The gradual extension of the number of years of schooling for children, combined with the postwar trend toward early marriage, have reduced the children's contribution to the family income. Consequently, wives have had to supplement the families finances (Podoluk 1968).

The proportion of husband-wife families in which both husband and wife are in the labor force has increased significantly from the 20 percent reported in 1961 to 41 percent in 1976. At the same time, the proportion of husband-wife families in which only the husband is in the labor force has decreased from 68 to 41 percent. While families with only the wife in the labor force declined to just 2 percent, those with neither husband nor wife in the labor force increased from 9 to 15 percent. Much of the latter's increase appears to reflect the effects of increased longevity and the survival of more married couples past retirement age.

Participation rates also vary significantly with age. Peak rates of over 90 percent for married men are characteristic of husbands between the ages of 25 and 50 years of age. For wives, the greatest participation, 68 percent, is achieved by the 20-24 year olds. The rate drops somewhat for the 30-34 year old group but is somewhat higher again for those just completing their childbearing years (54 percent). Beyond 45 years of age, participation rates decline without interruption. The general pattern of participation by age for all women still reflects the effects of child bearing and rearing activities on the part of married women between 20 and 45 years of age, although the effects are not nearly as great as they once were.

The importance of children at home for the wife's participation in the labor force is indicated in Table 6. For wives under 45 years of age, the presence of children at home has a considerable effect on participation rates. Note that without children, rates vary from 66 to 79 percent, but with children, the rates range from 35 to 50 percent. For women 45 and over, the effect is quite different. In their case, participation rates are higher where there are children still at home in contrast to those families where there are no children. As the average income of family heads begins to decline after age 45, families with children still at home would, perhaps, have a greater need for supplementary income.

Not only is the presence of children important, but their age distribution is also significant in determining whether or not the mother enters the labor force. Participation rates are lowest for those families in which all the children at home are under 18 and the mothers are under 45 years of age. Participation rates tend to increase as the children grow older, and when the youngest reaches 18 years of age, labor force participation increases significantly for mothers under 45, but declines in the case of older women for whom neither the need nor the desire to work seems to remain very strong.

The number of parents is also a crucial factor underlying the labor force participation of the family head. However, compared with some five million

Table 6:   Labor Force Participation of Wives by Age and Presence of Children at Home, in 1976.

Age of Wife	Total Families	All Wives With Children At Home	All Children Under 18 Years	With Children Both Over and Under 18	No Children Under 18	No Children at Home
(in years)				(in percentages)		
15-24	57.1	35.0	34.9	—ᵃ	—ᵃ	76.5
25-34	48.6	41.7	41.6	45.6	66.7	78.9
35-44	50.6	49.6	48.3	51.6	61.6	65.5
45-64	39.3	41.7	42.9	42.1	40.5	35.9
65 +	6.1	10.0	12.3	25.2	9.5	5.6
All Ages	43.8	43.0	42.9	46.0	39.2	45.5

ᵃLess than 500 cases
Source: 1976 CENSUS OF CANADA, Catalogue 93-832, Table 13.
Reproduced by permission of the Minister of Supply and Services Canada.

husband-wife families, lone-parent families are still a minority among Canadian families. Although only slightly more than a half million, their numbers have been increasing at a faster rate than those of two-parent families. Between 1971 and 1976, the increase for the former was 17 percent compared with 13 percent for the latter. What makes lone-parent families of particular interest is the fact that 83 percent of them are headed by women, making their participation in the labor force a matter of economic survival. For women in husband-wife families, in which most of the husbands work, the need is considerably less urgent.

The proportion in the labor force was, in fact, considerably greater for women heads of lone-parent families than for those in husband-wife families in 1976. However, the lower participation rates for the youngest female heads of lone-parent families indicate that those under 25 years of age are more likely to share the households and support of related families than are older women in similar circumstances. While participation levels are high for female heads of lone-parent families, the fact that they only earn about 50 to 60 percent of the income levels for male heads of husband-wife families suggests that many must rely on welfare or other sources of income. Rates for male heads of lone-parent families, while almost as high as those for males in husband-wife families, are still significantly lower, suggesting that they too must rely, to a certain degree, on social assistance programs.

Family income. Significant variations in individual income are caused by differences in age, sex, marital status, education, occupation, and hours of employment. All factors considered, average income tends to be curvilinearly related with age, peaking during the middle adult years with males continuing to earn more than females in all age groups. There is also a positive correlation between education and income, as well as between the degree of skill, experience, and income. All of these factors have significance for explaining variations in family incomes, whether the family head is the sole provider or whether other members of the family contribute to family earnings.

Interestingly, males who marry earn significantly more than those who remain single, for any given age group, with the greatest differences occurring in the age groups between 45 and 65 years of age. Marriage is selective in many ways, but whether the harder working, more ambitious males are more likely to get married, or whether they have to work harder because they get married is difficult to determine. Nevertheless, married males in 1971 were much more effective earners than those who were unmarried.

The data in Table 7, showing average income for family heads by age and schooling, illustrate the importance of age as a life-cycle variable, and education as an indicator of general skills and as a means for achieving greater financial remuneration. The pattern of changing average income, for those reporting income, reflects the value of increasing experience as one ages, up to the middle adult years, and then the effects of declining participation rates and changes in the type and amount of work as retirement age approaches. This curvilinear relationship is characteristic of progression through the individual life cycle at every level of educational attainment. However, the data in Table 7 show that the maximum average incomes are achieved at a somewhat later age for those with some university or university degree, again demonstrating the long-term rewards of post-secondary education. The importance of education for achievement and maintenance of a given standard of living or life style is also clearly demonstrated; with only one exception, additional education is translated into additional income. Only for those under 35 years of age does some university fail to produce an immediate reward, but this would appear to be only a temporary setback caused by late entry into the labor market. For older age groups, "some university" is obviously better than none.

The family appears to be a very effective economic unit. Not only do married males earn more than single males at every age level, but over half of all husband-wife families have two major wage earners. The family appears to be quite capable of mustering greater resources as its needs vary throughout the entire family life cycle. The increased participation of married women in the labor force would appear to be part of this adaptive response to the need for supplementary income to maintain the family's life style. Whether this is the major reason, or as others have suggested, the increased participation and lowered fertility have been a response to the increasing strenuousness of the mother and housewife roles (Boyd, et al. 1976), the results have been the same. The traditional family with a single male wage earner has been gradually evolving into one with two wage earners of increasing economic equality.

Table 7:   Average Incomes[1] of Heads of Husband-Wife Families by Age and Schooling, in 1970.

Age of Family Head	All Levels of Schooling	Schooling of Head[2]					
		Less than Grade 5	Grades 5-8	Grades 9-11	Grades 12-13	Some University	University Degree
(in years)		(in dollars)					
Under 35	7 248	4 963	6 055	6 901	7 725	7 468	9 829
35-54	9 163	5 667	7 094	8 640	10 457	11 534	18 754
55-64	7 724	4 734	6 064	7 887	9 867	11 080	19 716
65 +	4 566	2 926	3 810	5 144	6 211	7 794	13 676
Total	7 860	4 446	6 190	7 699	8 965	9 541	14 878

[1]Includes those reporting no income.

[2]Refers to highest level of schooling post-secondary, non-university and vocational training.

Source: 1971 CENSUS OF CANADA, Catalogue 93-725, Table 104.
Reproduced by permission of the Minister of Supply and Services Canada.

Discussion

Changes in the structure and character of family life are a consequence of external social and economic forces, as well as the results of individual efforts to develop living arrangements that are more compatible with current realities. The strength of the family lies, in part, in its ability to resist rapid change and to provide a stable and secure base for both sheltering and nurturing its members. In the long run, however, the family's success depends upon its ability to adapt to new conditions in order to continue to provide for its needs. This brief profile of the family has attempted to illuminate some of the more stable aspects of the family, as well as some important changes that have become noticeable during the postwar period.

Family formation and family size continue to be sensitive to changing social and economic conditions. Insofar as family size also partially reflects changing fertility, it is becoming more responsive to the individual's evaluation of future economic conditions and the perceived advantages or disadvantages of having larger or smaller families, or no children at all. The rapid decline in fertility and family size during the period of increasing economic uncertainty following the postwar baby boom has hastened the maturing of families and the relative decline of those with only young children. However, a significant improvement in economic conditions that might brighten the prospects for the future could quickly reverse the current trend because of the greater control presently exercised by individuals over their fertility.

Because one's preferences and tastes are shaped by the groups in which they are socialized, most Canadians marry within their own age, ethnic, religious, and cultural groups. However, there are often certain demographic imperatives that encourage or force change from customary practices. Variations in fertility, such as the postwar baby boom, interfere in the exercise of normal age preferences in mate selection, while sex differentials in educational attainment levels make it difficult at times for some males to marry less educated women. In addition, the generally high levels of physical and social mobility which characterize an urban industrial society, also tend to weaken a group's control over its individual members. The continuing increase in interfaith marriages and regional variations in ethnic intermarriages illustrate this point.

Variations in marital status, age, and educational attainment of family heads, as well as the labor force status of both husbands and wives that characterize Canadian families have significant income effects. Heads of husband-wife families exhibit higher economic achievement than male heads of lone-parent families at every age level, and both do significantly better than female heads of lone-parent families. Husband-wife families, of which almost half had both the husband and wife in the labor force in 1976, are obviously capable of mobilizing much greater resources to maintain their life style and standard of living than any other type of family. Education of family heads continues to be a crucial variable in determining post-secondary opportunities for their children. Not only does higher education reflect the presence of a more positive attitude toward the value of extended schooling, but the direct correlation of education with income of the family head at every age level indicates an increased capability to bear the financial burden of extended education.

Under the pressure of inflation and economic uncertainty, the wife's participation in the labor force has increased at such a rapid rate that it is, by far, the most significant change in the Canadian family during the postwar period. With the rise of the women's movement during the 1960s, a concomitant and significant increase in the number of lone-parent families with young female heads during the same period is hardly coincidental. How far this trend will go, or what the long-term effects of these changes will be are subject to speculation and debate. However, it is fairly certain that they will have a significant impact on the traditionally defined roles of husbands and wives and the nature of family life.

Family in Canada or the Canadian Family?

G. N. Ramu and Nicholas Tavuchis

Considerable discussion has followed Elkin's (1964:31) assertion that "There is no one Canadian family. With its distinctive history, Canada is much too heterogeneous to have one or twenty distinctive family types. As the geographical setting, social class, religions, ethnic, occupational, and other groupings vary, so too do our families." This view implies that because household and family forms reflect and are shaped by the putative pluralism of other social institutions and historical experiences, any attempt to reduce such diversity to a unitary concept, i.e., "the Canadian family," is empirically invalid and misleading. Such an approach, the argument goes, passes over the marked differences characteristic of Canadian society. Larsen (1976:53) also affirms this position with the observation, "Though scholars frequently use the term American family, Japanese family, and Canadian family..., there is little justification for these labels in complex heterogeneous societies which permit, if not encourage, multiple value systems, divergent normative proscriptions and prescriptions, and the relative autonomy of the individuals." Consequently, insofar as one accepts the principle or fact of multiple family realities, this should be linguisitically signalled by reference to the "family in Canada" or "Canadian families."

Nevertheless, the notion "family in Canada" represents a partial perspective because, as we shall argue, *all* families are subject to certain overriding changes that are driving existing forms toward a convergent and dominant paradigm that effectively undermines if not eliminates normative and structural variations. For example, Jones (1968) points to the homogenizing effects of urbanization and industrialization on the family and assumes that there is an ideal-typical "Canadian family." "As many post-1945 immigrants have been subject only to urban influences in their countries of origin as well as immediately on settlement in Canada, their families can be expected to resemble the dominant type from the outset." (Jones 1968:631) The dominant type to which Jones refers is clearly the nuclear family prevalent in urban settings, serving as the cultural point of convergence and benchmark which ethnic families emulate either voluntarily or involuntarily with respect to some standard patterns. The adaptation of the family to its surroundings tends to be gradual, selective, and contingent upon its initial structure and beliefs as well as the socio-economic stiuation it encounters – points we shall elaborate later. Ishwaran (1971:377) follows Jones when he notes that "The cumulative forces of expanding urbanization and industrialization in Canada, pressing for uniformity of familial forms, operate on a population that is ethnically diverse." Obviously, the claim here is that whatever the traditional family patterns in Canada (immigrant or indigenous) may have been, they cannot remain impervious to extra-familial sources of change attributed to the global concepts of urbanization and industrialization. Although neither Ishwaran nor Jones gives us a clue as to the emergent forms of family, we would speculate that these would generally conform to what Goode (1963:1) has delineated as the *conjugal family pattern* in his influential work, *World Revolution and Family Patterns.*

All this suggests that the concepts of "family in Canada" and "the Canadian family" are neither mutually exclusive nor antithetical but rather refer to two different aspects of family life – stability and change. This dual orientation is summed up best by Ishwaran (1971:373) when he hypothetically notes that, "While numerous factors – demographic, environmental, technological, historical, and socio-cultural – generate pressures for variation; a different but related set of factors – process of urbanization, industrialization based on modern technology – produces pressures for uniformity. Consequently what one actually finds is a whole range of variations continually under pressure for uniformity." Furthermore, legal codes governing marriage, family, and divorce act as catalysts toward convergence in marriage and family patterns among Canadians. As a result, when one uses the notion "the Canadian family," the reference is to a general pattern which transcends ethnic, racial, and social class boundaries. On the other hand, "family in Canada" alerts us to subgroup variations *on the theme of the conjugal family* with respect to courtship practices, marital and familial interaction, and socialization and as constrained by the law and economy which clearly favor and promote intentionally or not certain forms and possibilities to the detriment of others. This is not to argue that the family is essentially reactive and, hence, deny the observable tension between familial and other institutional domains. Instead, it seeks to remind us that the power to effect and legitimate changes is not equally or uniformly distributed in Canadian society or any society for that matter.

The primary purpose of this chapter, therefore, is to re-examine in detail the concepts of *family in Canada* and *the Canadian family* in the light of recent empirical research. Our thesis is two-fold. First, to the extent that families diverge from the conjugal pattern with respect to race, ethnicity, religion, class, etc., they contribute to the stability that reproduces and reinforces wider societal arrangements that are culturally authorized. Second, depending upon their position in the social structure, and hence their symbolic and material resources, families are also subject to differential modification stresses stemming from powerful standardizing forces implicit in what we loosely call urban-industrial society and explicitly expressed in law and buttressed in other spheres, e.g., work, mass media, etc. Such oppositions often defy and resist our desire for categorical clarity and methodological precision. Nevertheless, as we shall try to suggest in what follows, such an approach provides us with valid sociological insight and tools for understanding the complex realities of family life in Canada.

Family in Canada

The organization of family life centres around the ideal of stability while, at the same time, providing for and defining acceptable kinds of change and strain. In Canadian society, for example, there are widely shared beliefs about appropriate marriages (and hence family formation), division of labor within the family, ways of raising children, and a variety of rights and obligations which delineate the domain of kinship for members and groups. Such norma-tive codes not only cut across ethnic, religious, and class lines but increase in intensity and salience as one moves from the periphery to the intimate core marked initially by the husband-wife and then by the mother-child bonds. Such elemental relations are both sensitive and resistant to the myriad forces of change in contemporary society. Moreover, given the societal significance of the activities the family performs at certain key points in the life-cycle, the state tries to ensure that the family remains the first line of defense against any radical changes that are not in keeping with orthodox ideologies. In this regard, Bradway (1948:567) observes "The state . . . is interested in the development of stable and enduring families because they have definite functions to perform in connection with property, orderly adjustment of the relations between sexes and the rearing of children."

The objective of the state's protection of the family or more properly, a particular version of the family, is obvious – its own perpetuation. Of the possible social arrangements geared to the promotion of order and stability, the family is clearly strategic insofar as it provides the first endorsement of valid membership from which all subsequent statuses and life chances spring.

As the primal source of orientation and social placement, the family tends to perpetuate and reproduce its own distinctive culture as well as its position in the larger social order and, thus, serves as an essentially conservative unit with respect to the historical conditions it encounters and creates. In provid-ing us with profiles of different patterns of family life among various ethnic and class groups, the contributors to the editions preceding this volume (Ishwaran 1971, 1976) have demonstrated that the family in Canada subtly, non-ideologically, and often unintentionally reinforces the pluralistic vision of society. The family along with surrogate institutions, e.g., schools, peer groups, mass media, etc., socializes its young members according to certain enduring, but culturally distinct, variant norms and values. True, neither the family nor its members are immune to exogenous pressures of change – whether viewed as benign or subversive – but the potency of these initial epistemological moorings in such a unique unit militates against changes that come up against fundamental world views and patterns of behavior. It is not accident, as numerous analysts have shown, that the family is the prime target in any program of radical social change whatever the political or philosophical ideal pursued.

The Family and Ethnicity. By initiating the young into a group that receives, embodies, and embellishes intricately woven cultural milieux, e.g., language, religion, food, age and sex roles, authority relations, and a sense of shared historical placement from the country or origin, the family in Canada acts as a buffer against assimilative forces of the larger society. From this point of view, ethnicity is an extension of certain aspects of family culture. In discussing the linkages between the family and ethnicity, one of us has stated elsewhere that the family ". . . is ultimately and inextricably linked to the vitality and persistence of ethnicity insofar as it is able and willing to foster allegiance and conformity to traditions. In this respect, the family is the first line of defence against potentially erosive and competing assimilative pressures." (Tavuchis 1979:117) Let us consider some general patterns.

The data on family life among over thirty-five ethnic groups in Canada are sketchy and uneven. Yet, most studies document intricate affinities between the family and various dimensions of ethnic identity. For example, among French Canadians, the immediate and extended family in concert with the Church effectively combine to preserve linguistic and cultural uniqueness. Piddington's (1976) study of French Canadians in Manitoba illustrates that extensive kinship recognition and interaction over time and space, mutual aid, and frequent intermarriages of relatives weave an intricate tapestry of family and ethnic bonds. Garigue (1976:299) also suggests the manner in which the French Canadian culture complex and the family are interrelated as follows:

> The ideals about the family and kinship were not isolated but were part of a culture complex which included the French language as spoken in Quebec, a specific system of education, membership in the Catholic Church, and various political theories about the status of French-Canadians in Canada. To be a member of a French-Canadian kinship group implied attitudes and beliefs about some or all of these.

To be sure, detailed implications of such assertions have been confirmed, disputed, and revised by other observers (for a review see Ramu 1979; and Tavuchis 1979) but few, if any, have challenged the axiomatic and elemental premise that the family, in specific sociotemporal contents, is *the* effective unit in either perpetuating or turning away from ethnic identity. In a complex set of relationships that resist facile scrutiny, to say we know little, however, is not to assert total ignorance.

The Dutch, and the Germans, especially the Hutterites, form somewhat geographically or residentially insulated communities that tend to stress a distinct religio-ethnic community rather than individuality. The Hutterite colonies, for example, represent an extension of the extended family in which children are socialized into Anabaptist values that shun secular and modern influences (Hostetler and Huntington 1967; Peter 1976). The community is clearly designed to counteract any innovations or influences which threaten the Hutterite way of life. The Dutch also maintain an isolated community life consciously designed to retain their "Dutchness" in the midst of assimilative forces (Ishwaran 1977). The family remains the primary agency through which the community concept of "Dutchness" is inculcated. The close institutional ties between the family and religion are expressed in ideals and practices that accentuate male authority, maternal and domestic roles of women, rigid socialization that is sex-based, the structural importance of the eldest child as a parental surrogate, extended kin ties, and extremely conservative attitudes toward intermarriage, sex, contraception, and divorce (Ishwaran 1977). Discussions of family life among Italians (Boissevain 1976; Danziger 1971, 1975, 1976), Poles (Radecki and Heydenkoru 1976) and Natives (for example,

Cruikshank 1971; Dunning 1971; Damas 1971; Valle 1971) provide further evidence, if any is needed, for the indelible co-inherence of ethnicity and family in Canada.

If there is any profound meaning to the notion of ethnic pluralism in Canada other than the arbitrary and superficial imposition of hyphenated categories, the family is the crucial unit of analysis for distinguishing fact from ideological cant. Strong arguments have been put forth against the implications of the data presented above, i.e., ethnicity taken as culturally conditioned differences owes its vitality to the nourishment provided by the family. Kralt (1977) and Kalbach (1974), for example, seriously question the ability or desire of various ethnic groups to withstand the apparently ineluctable press toward cultural standardization and homogeneity that seem to mark contemporary urban-industrial societies. Others (Mindel and Habenstein 1976) see the family as an ethnic haven in an increasingly massified and ideologically segmented world. We would suggest that, however one interprets the available evidence or one's own experience with respect to ethnic realities, the family is the institution *par excellence* for exploring beginnings and endings.

The Family and Social Class. Any attempt to delineate the relationships between the family and social class are as problematic as our comments concerning ethnicity, given the relatively scant attention paid to this institutional intersection. This is especially puzzling when we consider that social stratification in Canada has been studied in greater detail than many other topics. The initial ascriptive status conferred by the family largely determines the life chances of an individual with regard to educational training and subsequent occupational placement which, in turn, affects his or her marriage and family position in the social structure. For example, a child born into a middle or upper class family inherits an opportunity structure and family environment vastly different from, and, superior to a child born into a lower class family. Aside from such built-in and accrued benefits and disadvantages (whatever the individual capacities), the family provides a continuous and informal atmosphere in which socially valued aspirations, skills, attitudes, etc., are either systematically cultivated or not, despite the nature of objective structures confronted.

It is true, as a general principle, that most parents expect their children to maintain if not improve their class ranks and they assist their children to the best of their abilities toward this goal. But what little data we have on this score do not allow us to infer that most parents succeed in their efforts with the important exception of those who are themselves defined as successful. The evidence suggests a close correlation between educational and occupational success of children and social class status of parents (see, for example, Porter 1965; Synge 1976; Crysdale 1976). In a review of access to education among various classes in Canada, Synge (1976:420-28) demonstrates that parents' occupational status has direct relationship to the proportion of students in grade thirteen and those who plan to complete university education. Nearly two-thirds of those in grade thirteen come from the upper class as opposed to only one-third from lower class. Obviously, one's educational attainment determines subsequent occupational status, level of income, and degree of prestige. The middle and upper classes are generally able to provide the grounds for ensuring that their children attain their superior educational, occupational, and income positions.

Such a pattern is contrary to the much heralded open-class philosophy of Canadian society. In principle, most people believe that they can attain a position of their choice with appropriate efforts and most parents strive hard to increase the opportunities for social mobility of their children. To be sure, such efforts work but only for a small, statistically insignificant, proportion of Canadians. As Pryor (1975:145) notes, "The family economic means is still the overwhelming force in determining the child's future – opportunities, abilities, and obviously economic resources." The best measure of family class, as defined by the census data, is the real income of the family. After a careful analysis of income distribution among Canadian families, Pryor (1975:154) comes to the following conclusion:

> *Certainly the hypothesis that inequalities are widening is not refuted by the data . . . The evidence would reinforce the argument that our social class system has become more rigid with our inequities relatively constant and persistent. In fact, the major and important conclusion from these data is that (the) family class system has solidified in the past two decades with remarkable stability and inequality.**

Pryor's analysis focusses on outcomes of differential initial life chances and leaves little doubt as to the family's role in reproducing and maintaining structural economic inequality and other forms of dominance in Canada which deviate from official norms and ideals. Nevertheless, such aggregate data taken alone tell us little about the complex interplay of routine and often implicit decisions, dispositions, and perceptions that crystallize within families, but exemplify accommodation to economic realities that merit further attention.

In Canada, the fundamental criteria of social class are occupation and income. Broad occupational categories (owner-manager, professional, white-collar, or blue-collar) and sources of income (dividends, profits, fees, salaries, or wages) are conveniently used, alone or combined, in assessing the social class position of individuals or families. Using these general categories we may divide the Canadian class system into three strata – upper, middle, and lower – mindful of the theoretical and empirical limitations inherent in such an arbitrary division and intra-class differences. Children from these classes would not merely have differential access to educational and occupational structures, but also tend to attribute varied social meanings and significance to education and occupation.

Upper Class. Those who inherit wealth, those who live off interest, dividends, and profits, those who have amassed wealth by their own efforts, suc-

---

*Family Income and Stratification in Canada by E. T. Pryor from *Marriage, Family, and Society: Canadian Perspectives* by P. Wakil. Reprinted by permission of Butterworths Toronto.

cessful professionals, and corporate executives who hold positions of power, prestige, and influence in key institutions (local, national, and international) constitute the core of the Canadian upper class. Although this group is numerically small, it commands enormous power to shape and influence the economic and political life of Canadian society (Porter 1965; Clement 1975; Newman 1975). The children of these élite families generally are socialized carefully in certain educational and occupational settings to succeed their elders eventually. They are, for the most part, conscious of their privileged positions and accept the obligation to maintain their class positions as well as the material and symbolic rewards they are destined to inherit. The stable financial base and the family environment insure both the income and the training that starts at birth, but not the talent (Goode 1967). Despite this latter constraint they are able to attain their family/class goals with considerably fewer difficulties than the young of other classes, even in a formally open class system. Strict endogamy or recruiting talented individuals from other classes through marriage are two modes of maintaining class interests.

Middle Class. The lower level professionals, managers, and various kinds of white-collar workers constitute the middle class, whose main source of income is salaries rather than inherited wealth, interests, profits, and dividends. Although the middle-class families maintain a comfortable standard of living, much of their time and energies is devoted to moving up and not merely retaining their position. Excellence in job performance, continuous retraining, and emulating upper-class ways of life characterize their desire to climb up the ranks. In the absence of inherited wealth and privileged entree to apical institutional positions, their children require extended and expensive training and carefully developed educational plans lest they fall from anticipated élite grace. The family environment is critical not only in assisting the development of a context of aspirations, but also in providing adequate resources. Achieved status may be taken to insure talent, but not the income and training the upper-class young enjoy. The Canadian middle-class families are in an extremely difficult position, especially in a depressed and inflationary economy and mass culture that encourages the young to deprecate their values while demanding the things and facilities that come with middle-class status.

Lower Class. The Canadian lower class is generally comprised of skilled, semi- and unskilled workers, who earn hourly wages as opposed to salaries, suffer from income instability, low prestige, and economic insecurity. In most cases, both husband and wife work hard to make ends meet, live in low-rental districts, and have given up thoughts of upward mobility. It is necessary, however, to distinguish the stable lower class from the urban and rural poor; the latter include a wide assortment of alienated social groups with socio-economic deprivations uncommon among the lower class. To be sure, stable working-class families have educational aspirations comparable to the middle class, but their efforts to escape their lot, individually or vicariously through their children, are generally abortive. Based on his study of lower-class families in south Riverdale in downtown Toronto, Crysdale (1976:325) underscores the problem of closed opportunities as follows:

> *Today, although the children of workers in the sample are staying in school about two years longer than their parents did, the economic and environmental conditions in which they are raised still do not afford them opportunities for higher education equal to those open to people in more favoured classes and areas of the city ... aspirations for education and occupation among children of manual workers were not greatly different from those of middle class children in the sample ... However, the opportunities for advancement by workers' children are restricted by low income, by overcrowded and deteriorated housing, by poor health, and by limited access to the secondary associations which in metropolitan society have an important part in facilitating mobility. Crucial among these is education.**

In sum, although there are conspicuous instances of individuals and families rising (and falling) rapidly in class position through educational or occupational achievements, such movements are likely to entail modest shifts to adjacent strata. Moreover, this observation does not negate the proposition that initial family class position exerts powerful pressure in determining the future location of its members in the system.

These fragmentary data and speculations suggest to us that Canadian society exhibits persistent class difference coupled with a steady if uneven levelling of ethnic identity over time that cannot be understood without more than casual reference to family patterns. It would be a gross oversimplification and empirically untenable to assume that the inexorable push toward standardization and uniformity has completely suppressed family diversity attributable to distinct class and ethnic experiences. One has only to peruse the sociological landscape to detect, we are told, a variety of family flora and fauna and "alternate marital and family life styles." We would argue, however, that a more careful scanning would reveal that these are confined mainly at sociocultural margins and hardly qualify as harbingers of vital challenges to the conjugal family system as it has taken root in industrial societies or appears to be emerging in underdeveloped areas. Moreover, any serious analysis must pose the question of choice versus necessity with respect to social arrangements and the ways in which family structures articulate with the larger social order. Thus, upper-class patterns are more likely to deviate from the conjugal pattern, but for reasons quite different from those of Natives, the rural and urban "disreputable" poor, isolated Hutterite colonies, recent immigrants, or middleclass single-parent households destined to return to the conjugal fold.

The Canadian Family

The main contention in the previous section was that the family in Canada continues to perpetuate certain aspects of social structure such as ethnicity and class, but that this function is being gradually eroded by the forces of modernization expressed in technology and secularism. The ramifications of such an erosion are complex, yet to be completely understood. Nevertheless, there are some clues as to the nature of change as well as its direction. As

*Reprinted by permission of the author.

Ishwaran (1976:3-45) has pointed out, the cumulative effects of industrialization and urbanization on the family bring about a convergence of its ethnic, class, and regional characteristics. Such a convergence, however, is hardly unique to Canada. In setting out a theoretical perspective to his incisive cross-cultural and historical analysis of changing family patterns, Goode (1963:1) discerns the following trends:

> *For the first time in world history a common set of influences – the social forces of industrialization and urbanization is affecting every known society. Even traditional family systems in such widely separate and diverse societies such as Papua, Manus, China, and Yugoslavia are reported to be changing as a result of these forces, although at different rates of speed. The alteration seems to be in the direction of some type of conjugal pattern – that is, fewer kinship ties with distant relatives and a greater emphasis on the "nuclear family" unit of couple and children . . . We are witnessing a remarkable phenomenon: the development of similar family behaviour and values among much of the world's population.* *

With respect to Canada, certain demographic and legal changes provide us with firm though far from conclusive evidence, taken alone, concerning the thesis of cultural standardization and structural uniformity of the Canadian family.

Demographic Characteristics. Under modern socio-economic conditions, such as mass education, specialized occupational structure, and mass media, ethnically and culturally diverse groups cultivate certain secular and standardized family and marriage patterns. Such a uniformity is evident in size and composition of the family, residential arrangements, type of marriage, age at marriage, and, more importantly, in the premise governing ideal practices and arrangements, and statistical regularities.

Without positing a rigid correlation or causal relationships, (cf. upper-class patterns noted earlier) we would note that the conjugal family system is compatible with the industrial society and that this increasingly describes Canada. In its first hundred years after Confederation, Canada has gained the status of an urban-industrial society. For example, in 1891 only 18.3 percent of the Canadian population was defined by the census as urban and, a century later, it rose to 76.1 percent. The changing occupational structure also provides evidence for this assertion (Kalbach and McVey 1971:238-42). In 1971, 55 percent of the work force was in agricultural occupations, but by 1971 this proportion had dwindled to 6.3 percent. This means that over 90 percent are in either manufacturing, service, or the professions. Such a massive transformation of the Canadian society has affected corresponding changes in the family and the demographic characteristics attest to this fact. Undoubtedly, there are a few resilient enclaves of ethnic and indigeneous social groups, but

---

*From *World Revolution and Family Patterns* by William J. Goode (Copyright © 1963 by The Free Press, a Division of Macmillan Publishing Co., Inc.). Reprinted by permission of Macmillan Publishing Co., Inc.

over 90 percent of the families tend to approximate the conjugal family pattern and domestic arrangements.

The dominant family type in Canada is nuclear, i.e., composed of a married couple and their unmarried children. Statistical trends in the average size of the family (3.9 in 1941 and 3.5 in 1976) suggest that an increasing number of couples may be having fewer than two children; this would be unprecedented and contribute to a sharper approximation to the nuclear pattern. A close examination of the provincial variations in family size suggests that the Northwest Territories have the largest (4.3 persons per family) and British Columbia the smallest (3.3 persons); most strikingly, Quebec's family size has declined from 4.5 in 1941 to 3.5 in 1976. The overall decline of the family size and provincial variations confirm the assertion that, as communities move closer to urban-industrial order, the small family norm becomes institutionalized; this is illustrated by Quebec's declining family size which is consonant with its attempt to enter the economic mainstream since the beginning of the 1950s.

Associated with the widespread nuclear family pattern is the significance attached to neolocal residence and the decline of residentially extended families. With the exception of certain farm families, religiously based communities and subgroups, and families among the northern Natives, neolocality and geographical mobility are unquestioned aspects of the Canadian family culture. By establishing separate residence after marriage, couples tend to limit the formation of residentially extended families. In fact, the small proportion of such existing families has further declined in recent years (from 6.1 in 1961 to 2.5 percent in 1976). The tendency of couples to maintain independent households has contributed to changes in the kinship structure that now exists in relation to expressed, often, ritualistic affectivity, selective interaction, and mutual exchange of goods and services (for a review on this point, see Ramu 1979). Much of the evidence upholds the view that urban kinship structures have not only adapted to changing socio-economic conditions, but also enable the nuclear family to cope with the demands of a modernizing society. Thus, small family norms, neolocal residence, and the redefinition of kinship obligations characterize the majority of families despite ethnic, class, or regional variations.

Furthermore, given the autonomy of courtship and marriage, couples make independent decisions not only on whom to marry but when, the desired number of children, where to live, forms of living, and so on. Although profoundly and systematically organized by seemingly anonymous economic, political, and technological decisions at every stage in the family cycle, this formal independence is crucial to the emergent conjugal ideology which is further accentuated by neolocal residence, decreased kinship control and influence, and the ideal images of marital and family life created and applauded by the mass media. As the present demographic evidence shows, couples, today, marry at a younger age than their parents, children leave home at younger ages, and couples now live longer than those of previous generations.

Such configurations result in an ideological and structural stress on the marital tie that colors the entire family spectrum, even in the face of high divorce rates that represent an institutional recognition of pressures and a respite before the cycle is resumed. According to various estimates, couples who married in 1976 are likely to live together for approximately sixty years, barring divorce. This demographic fact, alone, shapes interpersonal possibilities in conformity with conjugal ideals; it is buttressed by the increasing age similarities of spouses and the economic participation of wives contributing, theoretically, to a more egalitarian relationship. For example, between 1921 and 1976 the age difference between spouses fell from 4.4 to 2.3 years and the number of working wives in the population has nearly doubled in the last ten years rising to 2 303 000 by 1976, or 42.8 percent of all married women. More recent studies suggest that the gainful employment of wives brings about gradual changes in various aspects of their marital life such as in decision making, domestic roles, etc., all of which dovetail neatly with the requirements of the economic system.

In sum, even a cursory review of the demography of the Canadian family suggests that, with the exception of marginal and élite groups, standardization is occurring with respect to family size and composition, residential arrangements, kinship structure, fertility, age at marriage, and participation of wives in the labor force. Such emerging patterns conform to what Goode conceptualizes as the conjugal family.

Law as a Homogenizing Force. In Canada, as in most modern societies, rules pertaining to marriage, family formation, rights and obligations of spouses, property rights, and divorce are subject to state intervention and are uniformly applied within jurisdiction in theory, if not in practice. Although the general intent of the legal statutes is to institutionalize uniformities, there are many provincial variations because two legal traditions – the British Common Law and the Napoleonic Code – govern these statutes and also because the jurisdiction over marriage and family is shared by federal and provincial governments. Under section 91 (26) of the British North America Act of 1967, the federal parliament has exclusive jurisdiction over marriage and divorce, and provinces retain the jurisdiction over not only solemnization of marriage (Section 92 (2)), but also issues related to property rights in marriage. The provincial variations in regard to marriage contracts, especially property rights, are being reduced by recently proposed law reforms in many provinces.

Such a codification has a number of consequences: it brings about standardization of marital practices and family behavior that overrides or tempers particular religious, ethnic, or subcultural norms. For example, traditional marriage and divorce codes as stipulated in Islam are at variance with the Canadian laws. A Muslim is entitled to four wives at one time and can divorce any of them in a relatively easy and informal manner. But as long as the Muslim is a Canadian citizen or permanent resident, local rules of monogamy and divorce take precedence over Islamic norms. A second function of the uniform legal codes is to ensure that a family unit is responsible for such tasks as reproduction, primary socialization, and physical maintenance of family members, crucial for social stability and cultural continuity. Finally, the legal codes attempt to promote and preserve a particular form of marriage and family, which may or may not be responsive to changes in other institutional sectors, e.g., economy, but clearly exert an independent authority of their own.

Conclusions

Living in an urban, technological, mass production, and market-oriented milieu, dictating an extraordinary degree of predictability and centralized control, seems to almost inevitably militate against diversity in virtually every sphere of human activity, including the family. Such homogeneity is not only evident in the routine and visible aspects of family functioning, it also permeates the material and symbolic environments in which family scenarios are enacted. More often than not such interventions are far removed from their eventual point of impact. For example, the desired type of housing, furnishings and appliances, work-related recreational and mobility patterns, and segregation of work and family sites are all viewed as essential to a system predicated on mass production and consumption. These desiderata effectively preclude or subvert alternative possibilities.

Such developments have not gone unnoticed and it is instructive to contrast Elkin's earlier reflections with the following by the same author: (1975:127)

> *Despite the variations in traditional family life patterns of Canada and many isolated pockets which lie outside the mainstream, certain characteristics and trends apply to a high proportion of our population. Many of these characteristics and trends began in the United States and are a reflection of recent developments in the direction of a mass society. In some respects, for example, people everywhere in North America, no matter what their ethnic or regional backgrounds, aspire to roughly similar material benefits and standard of living goals. Throughout the continent, too, industry produces and distributes mass-produced items for mass-consuming markets.* **The result in many respects is homogeneity in a way of life unimaginable a few generations ago.** †*

Any serious analysis of the family in Canada (or anywhere for that matter) must be sensitive to larger institutional contexts in which it is embedded and cultural resonances which it registers. In numerous ways, each family reproduces itself, and, in turn, the larger system of which it is a part, according to its unique and shared properties (e.g., ethnicity, class, etc.), that converse with the past, live in the present, and mark future possibilities. In addition, there is constant pressure on marriage and families to cope privately with radical collective changes nourished by such powerful ideas as individualism, neutral and benign technology, and the reflexive conversion of "desire" to "need." Consequently, a heady array of variant sexual, marital, and family forms ranging from urban communes to homosexual marriages, offered as legitimate

---

†Emphasis added.
*Lifestyles of Canadian Families by F. Elkin from *Marriage, Family and Society: Canadian Perspectives* by P. Wakil. Reprinted by permission of Butterworths Toronto.

options to traditional arrangements, are often viewed as *prima facie* evidence of the pluralism immanent in the formulation, *family* in Canada.

We recognize that families in Canada retain trace elements of robust heterogeneous traditions and experiences but question their binding force in the face of awesome social changes that appear to dilute and neutralize diversity from birth to death. Based upon our reading of various sources and trends, we conclude that family patterns in Canada are indeed converging in the ways suggested by Goode and others although not uniformly or simply in response to industrialization and urbanization. To the question posed in the title of this paper, therefore, our tenative answer would be *The* Canadian family.

FAMILY STRUCTURES AND VARIETIES

Introduction

The three articles in this section are intended to give a glimpse of the structural variabilities of the family forms in Canada. Although such variabilities can be described and analysed in many dimensions, space limits coverage to only a few. However, these are highly significant to the overall focus of this book.

John Price's exploration of the aboriginal Indians presents a very different picture of family life. As Price puts it, "The well-adapted aboriginal mosaic of family forms is now almost destroyed." In support of this viewpoint, Price begins by offering an outline of the various traditional cultural groups and categories among the Canadian Indians in various parts of the country, focussing on the Cree, the Kwakiutl, and the Huron. Understandably, the outline stresses various aspects and dimensions of kin-based relations, including those that meshed with the political and economic contexts of social life of the Canadian Indians. Moreover, Price's account of the traditional cultures draws attention to the fact that the various Indian tribes during the pre-European contact days were at different levels of advancement and, therefore, should not be considered as an undifferentiated mass of people.

Having outlined the traditional cultures in this fashion, Price then highlights the drastic and destructive impact that the intrusion of Europeans had on those cultures which he views as well-adapted forms. His discussion of the circumstances and consequences of this European impact shows how the Indian Act of Canada, drafted by European immigrants, ran counter to a host of cherished Indian values, including those crucially related to marriage, property rights, and so on.

Apart from the impact of the Indian Act, Price also offers information, including the results of a few surveys, which more than strongly suggest great strains in male-female, husband-wife, and parent-child relations. The article indicates some of the measures that the Indians are considering to combat widespread disorganization of their social life, in general, and their family life, in particular.

The theme of family structures and varieties has also been presented in this section in two articles by Ishwaran that focus on rural-urban dimensions.

The article on the rural family is based on data from four community contexts: the Dutch Canadians of Holland Marsh; the Hutterites of the Prairie provinces; the big ranchers and small farmers of the Jasper* community; and the French Canadian St. Jean Baptiste community.

Assuming a broad ecological perspective, Ishwaran illustrates the relevance of the interplay of historical, religious, political, and economic factors in accounting for some of the important similarities and differences in the family forms and functions in all four cases.

In the Holland Marsh community, for instance, the settlers, guided by their Dutch values, were fairly successful in rebuilding many of the familiar crucial institutions of their homeland. This evolution of the Dutch Canadian community shows how the *nuclear* family became more or less significant at different times in response partly to the changing ecology and the evolving links between the community and the wider world.

In the Hutterite example, the nuclear family remains, as it has traditionally been, submerged under the wider structure of the Hutterite community. This structural submergence, justified by Biblical interpretation, positively discourages the so-called modern values of individualism and the centrality of the nuclear family.

In the Jasper case, stress is placed on differential economic interaction of the families of the big ranchers and those of the small farmers, especially in relation to the transmission of property and opportunities for the children growing up in this community. Data and analysis show that, despite the prevalence of the nuclear family in both groups, the contingencies of the life cycle tend to lead them in different directions toward different ends, at any given time.

In St. Jean Baptiste, Roman Catholicism regulates the life of the community and the family. In addition, the case illustrates the significance of kinship which goes to the extent of intensive local endogamy.

One of the major overall conclusions of Ishwaran's study of rural Canadian families is that they are more responsive than the urban family to the pressures of ecology, and, on account of the relative isolation of the rural family, the question of their identity-formation is influenced more strongly by religious considerations.

Ishwaran's article on the urban family relates to a theoretical debate concerning the relevance of extended kinship ties in Canadian urban life. Sociologists, like Parsons, emphasize the declining importance of such relations, while others, like Sussman and Litwak, notice their continuing importance, even in the modern American context, as channels for a variety of important goods and services not provided by modern institutions. Several cases – French Canadian, Italian Canadian, Greek Canadian, Polish Canadian, the urban working-class European, and the Japanese Canadian – are explored, and, in each case, the continuing significance of kinship relations in a variety of important social contexts becomes quite clear.

---

*A fictitious name

Canadian Indian Families

John A. Price

The Aboriginal Mosaic

There was much greater variety in Canadian Indian languages, customs, and types of families than there was in traditional European cultures. By contrast with the Native peoples, the immigrant ethnic cultures appear quite uniform. For example, most of the Europeans spoke languages historically related to a single European phylum, while the Canadian aborigines had fifty-two languages in nine phyla. In terms of social evolution, all the European immigrants came from state-level societies, whereas Canada's fifty societies ranged from the simple hunting *bands* of the Arctic and Subarctic; to the intermediate level of agricultural, fishing, and horseback hunting *tribes* of southern Canada; to the advanced, socially ranked, fishing *chiefdoms* of the Pacific coast. Table 1 lists the language phyla of Canada according to their general historical depth; that is, Beothuk, Kutenai, and Tsimshian are probably survivals of the most ancient migrations, while Dene and Eskimo-Aleut are the most recent, about 4000 years old.

Table 1:   The Indian Mosaic by Language Phyla

Phyla	Languages in Canada	Location in Canada	Population Registered	Predominant Level of Evolution
Beothuk	1	Newfoundland	Extinct	band
Kutenai	1	Southern B.C.	446	band
Tsimshian	3	Northern B.C.	7 730	chiefdom
Wakashan	5	Coastal B.C.	8 217	chiefdom
Salish	9	Southern B.C.	20 989	tribe
Macro-Siouan	8	Southern Canada	28 516	tribe
Algonquian	12	Prairies, East	153 594	band
Dene	12	Western Canada	24 515	band
Eskimo-Aleut	1	Arctic	20 000	band
Total	52		Total 264 007	

European immigrant families were usually bilateral with a patrilineal bias in kinship, monogamous and quite legally oriented in marriage, intolerant of premarital sexual relationships, and organized into extended families and kinship networks by simple expedient bilateral ties. In contrast, the Canadian Indian mosaic included most of the major global variations in kinship systems and forms of marriage and families.

Monogamy was the most common and the only form of marriage allowed in the Huron, Petun, Neutral, and Iroquois societies of southern Ontario and Quebec. Europeans were impressed with the freedom of courtship, romance, and trial marriages of these more female-oriented societies, in which women held a lot of power. In general, however, Indian marriages involved parental arrangements and sanctions for the young people.

Among North American Indians, the degree of potential marriageability dictates male behavior with his female relatives. There is respect and avoidance of intimacies with one's mother-in-law, a son's wife, and a sister; with cross-cousins (a father's sister's daughter and a mother's brother's daughter), there is usually a mixture of respect and intimate jesting; with a brother's wife or a wife's sister, the relationship is the most intimate, involving jocular and sexual teasing.

Puberty reckoning was universal and usually associated with some ceremony, particularly with a girl's first menstruation. However, such practices as circumcision and other modifications of the genitalia were absent among both North and South American Indians. ·

Polygny was tolerated everywhere outside of the Iroquoian agriculturalists, but occurred in more than 20 percent of the marriages only in a few of the richer tribal and chiefdom societies of the west. Sororal polygyny in which a man marries two or more sisters was the most common form. Fraternal polyandry was accepted by most societies in special cases, such as when one brother became crippled and another assumed his responsibilities as provider and mate. Table 2 contrasts the traditional marriage traits of Canadian Indians and European immigrants.

Kinship plays a more important role in primary societies than it does in modern societies. Kinship institutions are instrumental to both family and community life. In these smaller, more personal societies, marriage arrangements are an integral part of politics and economics, involving corporate enterprises such as house construction, long-distance trade, and political alliances.

Postmarital residence is a crucial factor for kinship systems because the environment determines the orientation of the children and the work arrangements of the adults. For survival, simple hunting bands must follow the erratic movements of game, hence their residence shifts from bilocal (the camp of either spouse) to neolocal (a new camp). Children raised in this environment see both sets of relatives and adults make bilateral work arrangements, often co-operating with their siblings. Thus, the simple hunting bands of the Arctic and Subarctic tended to develop bilateral kinship systems. Modern industrial society has many features in common with the simple bands, although here the social flexibility and mobility of families is related to such things as the specialization of labor and the shifting labor market. Thus, the simplest and the most complex societies have similar bilateral kinship systems, while the

Table 2:   Contrasting Traditional Marriage Traits

	Canadian Indians	European Immigrants
Puberty Ceremonies	Important	Unimportant
Premarital sex	Usually tolerated	Forbidden
Marriage	Little ceremony in bands and tribes	Elaborate ceremony
	Customary, gift exchanges	Legal and religious
	Patterned by kinship	Contractual
	Polygamy usually accepted	Monogamous
	Cross-cousin marriages in lineal societies	None
Adoption of children	Common	Less common
Divorce	Common	Less common

intermediate societies – tribes, chiefdoms, and early states – tend to have elaborate linear kinship institutions formed around lineages and clans.

Where it becomes important for a mother and daughter or for sisters to work together, the tendency is to live with the wife's family; the children are raised with a bias favoring the mother's relatives and matrilineal orientations develop in descent, social affiliation, inheritance, and succession. The matrilineal societies of Canada were in two historical clusters – the Iroquois-Huron in the east and the Tsimshian and neighboring western Dene of the Yukon and British Columbia.

Kinship terms reflect both conceptual categories of relatives and behavior appropriate for each category. Most Indian societies make age distinctions among siblings in both terminology and behavior. So we find terms equivalent to "older brother" or "younger sibling" and behavior appropriate to relative ages. In a bilateral kinship system, the term "cousin" refers to the children of both maternal and paternal aunts and uncles. Lineage is less important and cousins do not usually intermarry. The technical term for this kind of cousin terminology is *Eskimo.* (In kinship studies the word Eskimo is used for all simple bilateral systems. We use a bilateral system.) A common lineal type is called *Iroquois,* in which parallel cousins (father's brother's children and mother's sister's children) are merged with brother and sister, all in a category that is ineligible for marriage, but contrasting with cross-cousins (father's sister's children and mother's brother's children) who are always in a different lineage and eligible for marriage. Canada also had the *Crow* type, associated with strongly matrilineal societies, and the *Hawaiian* type, associated with bilateral descent in a system that groups people according to their membership in generations relative to the speaker.

The term "aunt" is classified according to whether or not the aunt is *merged* i.e., equated with one's mother or *bifurcated* i.e., distinguished from one's mother. In the former instance, a child would use the same term for his mother and his mother's sister, whereas, in the latter, a second term would be used for his father's sister. The term *collateral* refers to the siblings of lineal relatives and their descendants and in a *bifurcate collateral* system there are separate terms for the mother, mother's sister, and father's sister. The English term "aunt" is called a lineal term because the lineal relative, the mother, is distinguished from the collaterals, the aunts. The general frequency of these various "aunt" terms among North American Indians is 50 percent for bifurcate collateral, 20 percent for bifurcate merging, 23 percent for lineal, and 7 percent for a variety of specialized forms (generation, relative age, and others). (Murdock 1970) The fine distinctions between these various kinship systems might seem unimportant to us today but, aboriginally and historically, kinship and family life were central to the entire social structure of these societies.

These contrasting patterns are illustrated in three large, well-known, and very different kinds of societies: Cree, Huron, and Kwakiutl. The Cree were aboriginally a simple hunting society situated south and east of Hudson Bay. Following the fur trade system out into the Prairies and up into the Northwest Teritories, they became the largest and most widespread Indian society in modern Canada. Like band-level societies everywhere, they were egalitarian in politics, sharing in economy, and quite flexible in social structure with bilateral descent. However, they use "cousin" terms associated with lineality, "aunt" terms that are usually associated with patrilineal societies, and have a preference for patrilocal postmarital residence. Data on the James Bay Cree support the theory that the relaxation of sexual customs upon modernization leads to an initial stage of increased fertility. (Romaniuk 1974) The Indians in the rapidly modernizing region of northern Ontario also tend to have larger families. (Fels 1980:40)

In the James Bay Cree lodge, the men and their hunting, fishing, and trapping gear occupied one side, while the women and their equipment occupied the other. (Tanner 1979) When two, three, or four families camped together in winter, a large open lodge was built and space was arranged within it so that each family had its own unit. The sequence of male and female sides of each family unit was arranged so that the male space of the first family was next to the male space of the second, and the female space of the second was next to the female space of the third, and so on around the lodge to the entrance that divided the first and last families. Thus, a male and a female from different families never slept next to one another.

Several related Huron families lived in quonset-shaped, bark long houses in villages among their agricultural fields. Here the co-operative production, storage, and preparation of food, and co-operation in child tending, defence, and other activities made an easier and more secure life for the people. These conditions and the great productivity of farming led to a major population increase in southern Ontario. Because of the very ancient association of women

with plant gathering, women did most of the farming, men came to live with
their wives' kinfolk, and children were raised with a matrilineal orientation.

The Kwakiutl were an even more advanced society. They were organized
into socially ranked chiefdoms in which several related families lived together
in large plank houses in fishing villages along the Pacific coast. Marriage was

Table 3: Three Kinship Systems

	Cree (Eastern)	*Huron*	*Kwakiutl*
Evolutionary level	band	tribe	chiefdom
Culture area	Subarctic	Iroquoia	Pacific
Language phylum	Algonquian	Macro-Siouan	Wakashan
Subsistence	hunting	farming	fishing
Settlement	seminomadic	semisedentary	permanent
House	small, circular	large, rectangular	very large, rectangular
Settlement size	20-100	100-1000	400-1000
Stratification	absent	wealth distinctions	class system
Warfare	absent	raids	large battles
Slavery	absent	captives adopted	captives sold hereditary slaves
Population today in Canada	76 488	1041	2715
Sex roles			
Hunting	men	men	men
Fishing	men	men	men
Gathering	women	women	women
Farming	absent	women	absent
House building	both	men	men
Skin preparation	women	women	women
Weaving	absent	absent	women
Basketry	women	women	women
Pottery	absent	women	absent
Cooking	women	women	women

Kinship

Premarital sex	allowed	freely permitted	prohibited
Marriage mode	egalitarian gifts to bride	egalitarian gifts to bride clan exogamy	socially ranked gift exchange bride wealth village exogamy
Polygamy	rare	none	common
Postmarital residence	bilocal	matrilocal	patrilocal
Descent	bilateral	matrilineal	patrilineal
Lineal groups	none	clans	clans
Cousin terms	Iroquois	Iroquois	Hawaiian
Aunt terms	bifurcate collateral	bifurcate merging	lineal

patterned by social rank as well as by incest prohibitions and kinship rules. The higher the rank, the more property and titles were involved; thus, the more elaborate was the marriage ceremony.

In *The Ojibwa Woman,* Ruth Landes includes intimate details of family life in a band heritage society. The material, recorded in Emo, Ontario in the early 1930s, credits marital instability to the increase in community size and economic prosperity in the fur trade; marriage is characterized as brittle and divorce as "easy and often whimsical." Men were taught initiative, individuality, and fortitude in the hunt, war raids, and sexual adventures. Women were raised to be more flexible and variable in their social and economic roles, to be the recipients of male favors, but generally to be ignored by men. Both men and women were physically strong and highly skilled in the ways of survival in the country. The typical Ojibwa woman could set a broken leg, stitch a wound, and gather and administer medicinal plants for dozens of ailments. She was familiar with the use of love charms and magic, but she could also build a lodge, make clothing from skins, and hunt, fish, and trap just like the men. However, if she had a husband and children, she would normally stay close to the camp, tending the children, preparing the food, and maintaining a trapline for rabbits, squirrels, marten, and mink.

Modern Family Problems

Written by European immigrants, the Indian Act of Canada was predicated on values such as monogamy, nuclear families, male dominated households, and patrilinear inheritance. Section 10 of the Act specifies the registration of Indian males first, and then their wives and children; section 11 specifies the direct descent of the male line; and section 12 (1)(b), the most notorious, deprives an Indian woman of her legal status as an Indian and as a member of a specific Indian band, depending on her choice of husband. If she marries outside her band, she loses her rights to property and burial in her ancestral home. If she marries a person without Indian status, she *permanently* loses her own Indian status and with it a host of Indian Affairs programs. On the other hand, on marrying, the non-Indian wife of a status Indian is accorded legal Indian status and ensuing rights and privileges. Section 12 also carries a "double mother" clause by which children with a mother and a paternal grandmother who were not born with Indian status will lose their Indian status at the age of 21.

Section 12 is both sexist and racist, overemphasizing female dependency and punishing Indian women for interracial marriages. After considerable pressure from women's groups, in 1980 the government agreed to suspend section 12 (1)(b) if requested to do so by the bands themselves. In the following year, only two dozen of the 570 bands had made such a request. A variety of reasons are offered by Indian leaders for not requesting this suspension, some of which are as racist and sexist as the Act itself.

In their attempt to combat this sexist and racist section, the Indian Rights for Indian Women association have advocated that: (1) no one should lose their rights through marriage; (2) those who have lost their rights in the past through marriage should have them reassigned; and (3) status should be granted to all Metis and non-status Indians who can prove that they have at least one-quarter Indian biological heritage.

In 1980, the Native Women's Association of Canada was responsible for special services from the Employment Ministry for training programs for Native women. This group claims that: (1) about 80 percent of Canada's Native women are unemployed: (2) many face discrimination as Natives and as single parents; (3) when families break up on reserves it is the female who has to leave, because women maintain Indian status through men, therefore, the men usually own the housing units, property that cannot be divided upon divorce; and (4) Native women then tend to be forced into slum housing in urban areas. (Indian News 1981: 21:XI-1)

Breakdown of traditional marriage systems is evidenced by this article in the *Montreal Gazette* (1977 03 19). "The marriage of an Oka Indian was declared illegal yesterday because it was performed by the chief of the Lake of Two Mountains Reserve .... the man who filed suit was married by Chief Curotte according to Longhouse religion. The man sought to have his marriage declared illegal after his wife sued him for a separation allowance of $100 a week for herself and her child." This is the kind of case in which changes in traditional means of child and spouse support, including kin groups and extended families, has made traditonal marriage and divorce dysfunctional. Now the wife needs legal marriage in order to make a case for support if the marriage breaks down.

Studies in the Yukon and Northwest Territories have shown that Indian girls there (1) tend to fit in better at school than boys in their teenage years; (2) tend to get a year or two more formal education than boys; (3) are less attracted to reserve life in the remote reserves, with its male orientation toward trapping, hunting, and fishing; and (4) can readily get jobs as secretaries, waitresses, and clerks in the towns. Thus, they meet and marry Whites more than Indian men. However, Indian women have fewer legal marriages with Whites than Indian men do because, in the woman's case, she would lose her Indian status by legal marriage to a White. Common-law marriages or Indian custom marriages with non-status males allow her to retain her Indian status.

Table 4:   A Survey of Ontario Native Women

	On Reserve	*Off Reserve*
Sample size:	492	602
Employed during the year:	30%	39%
Members of O.N.W.A.:	20%	19%
Had seen a physician within the past year:	56%	61%
Had seen a dentist within the past year:	30%	33%
Use birth control methods:	26%	29%
Use traditional healing or medicines:	19%	25%

Female migration to the towns and cities contributes to a shift of the culture in the northern Indian villages to a situation of fewer marriageable women and more boredom, drinking, and fighting among the men. In the towns the tendencies toward seasonal work for males, high mobility for jobs, and common law or custom marriages lead to high levels of separation, divorce, adoption and fostering of children, and matrilocal families. These are conditions which promote the greater acculturation of Indian women than Indian men, just the opposite of what usually occurs when women stay on reserves. Spindler (1962) found that among the Menomini, the women were more conservative of traditional values than men. In an urban environment Martin (1964) found that Navajo men were less socially adjusted but more acculturated than Navajo women.

The Ontario Native Women's Association interviewed 1094 Indian women in Ontario in 1978. (Fels 1980) Some of the data they collected has been difficult to gather in the past. There was surprisingly little difference in the responses of those who lived on reserves and those who lived off reserves, mostly in towns and cities.

The following are the results of a survey of 181 Indian families, generally from the poorer segment of the downtown urban Indian community. These families were having urban adjustment problems, and were predominantly northern Ojibwa. The survey was conducted by eight women from the Native Canadian Centre of Toronto. (Bobiwash and Malloch 1980)

A Survey of Toronto Families

• Sixty percent were single-parent families.

• Ninety-four percent were nuclear families and six percent were extended families.

- The average number of children was 2.3.

- Median number of years in the city was nine.

- Eighty-six percent planned to settle permanently in Toronto proper.

- Parental orgin: northern Ontario 15 percent; central Ontario 47 percent; southern Ontario 28 percent; and outside Ontario 10 percent.

- Indian identification: status 63 percent; non-status 30 percent; Métis 6 percent; and Inuit .5 percent.

- Fifty-nine percent were receiving social assistance, unemployment insurance, and/or student allowance.

- The average annual family income was $9800.

The issues that these families were most concerned about were, by order of importance, Native cultural education, information about government services, housing, child care and services, formal education, recreation, employment, and the operations of Native agencies. Food, clothing, legal, correctional, and health issues were only of minor importance. In broader Indian surveys issues such as unemployment, treatment for alcoholism, and education needs usually rank as the most important issues.

Child Welfare Problems

In the United States, the Indian Child Welfare Act of 1978 was passed primarily to stop the abduction of Native children by zealous ethnocentric White social agencies. (Association on American Indian Affairs 1979) In states with large Native populations, one-quarter to one-third of the Indian children were being taken away from their families and placed in foster homes, adoptive homes, and youth detention centres. The Act assures the following:

(1) No foster care placements may be ordered unless there is clear evidence that the continued custody is likely to result in serious emotional or physical damage to the child.
(2) The family will be given a hearing on the placement of their child.
(3) An indigent parent or Indian guardian will have a right to a court-appointed counsel in the proceedings.
(4) The hearing will take place in the appropriate tribal court of the child, upon petition of the parents or the tribe.
(5) First preference for placement will be given to members of the child's extended family.
(6) Second preference for placement will be given to homes maintained by Indian people or tribes.
(7) Adopted children have a continuing right to their tribal membership and to the benefits associated with that membership.

In a similar way, the Supreme Court of Canada, in 1975, ruled that Native children with status rights would retain those rights, even when they were adopted. Adopting parents thus have an obligation to inform the child of his or her Indian rights. Generally, however, Indian child welfare policies in

Canada are still in the phase of widespread abduction of Indian children by White social agencies.

The Canadian Indian Act contributes to the destruction of Indian family life. By denying legal status to women who marry non-status Indians, the Act indirectly promotes common-law arrangements to which the men feel less committed and hence abandon more readily. This type of family tends to be matricentred with a connotation of illegitimacy for the children, and often results in an unnecessarily high level of government support for single-parent families. A survey in British Columbia found that 40 percent of all single Indian women in the province had one or more children, and that 57 percent of status and 38 percent of the non-status Indian births were to non-married parents. (Stanbury and Siegel 1975)

With a particular sophistication from their advanced aboriginal heritage, the Indians of British Columbia have typically led the country in the institution of modern Indian programs. One of their innovations was the British Columbia Commission on Native Families and the Law. The following are some of the recommendations of that Commission.

(1) When a child is apprehended in an urban area, the child's band should be notified and given first option in arranging for the child's care.
(2) When foster care or adoption becomes necessary Native homes should be sought whenever possible.
(3) Indian children should be informed of their band of origin.
(4) Confidentiality of parenthood should be maintained in adoptions.
(5) Non-Indians who adopt an Indian child should agree to familiarize the child with his Indian heritage.
(6) An Indian custom adoption should be recognized as a legal adoption.
(7) The qualification for social work positions should recognize the importance of Indian life experiences in lieu of academic education.

The Native Canadian Centre of Toronto (1980) considers family issues to be so crucial to its activities that it has developed its own policy guidelines. The *central problems* are seen as the breakdown of family life and other supports for good child welfare. The *symptoms* of this breakdown are (1) the surrender of responsibilities to non-Native churches, schools, and social service agencies; (2) adoptions and fostering of Native children by non-Natives; and (3) financial hardship, poor physical and mental health, alcoholism, and divorce. The *causes* of the breakdown are (1) destructive forces within the laws and institutions of the colonial system; (2) the loss by Native people of meaningful roles, responsibilities, and cultural identities; and (3) the erosion of traditional supports for families, such as the help of relatives, commmunity leaders, religious leaders, and beliefs and life styles.

The *solutions* are for Native people to resume responsibility for their own families and children by (1) insisting that federal and provincial authorities return control of child welfare matters to the Native people, communities, and associations; and (2) rebuild a network of resources to prevent family breakdown, to support families in crisis, and to support children who must live away from their parents. The *specific actions* to be taken are as follows:

(1) To encourage Native community discussion groups, research, education,

and consciousness raising in family problems, responsibilities, and the identification and development of community resources;

(2) To encourage Natives to critically monitor and to withdraw their participation from the White systems of courts and Children's Aid Societies;

(3) To seek federal and provincial funding for a separate Native child welfare system, including Native family courts, foster care by Native people, and a co-ordinating Native Family Welfare Committee; and

(4) To encourage Native operated day care centres, children's programs, Big Brothers, family counselling, and group homes.

Conclusions

The well-adapted aboriginal mosaic of family forms is now almost destroyed. Indians were forced by European-derived laws and customs to eliminate their polygyny, polyandry, matrilineality, lineal kinship practices, and customs of trial marriage, marriage, adoption, and divorce. Now in the face of a widespread breakdown of family life itself and the loss of their children through adoption and fostering by Whites, the Native people are struggling against the massive powers of the White courts and Children's Aid Societies. Indian women are protesting sexist punishment for interracial marriages and the imposition of outsider's values on the way they raise their children. The following summation shows the extent of the loss of Indian status through marriage, births outside of marriage, loss of children through adoption, and divorce rates.

Family statistics (Indian Affairs 1980; Hepworth 1980)

• The annual population rate is 1.3 percent.

• The median age is ca. nineteen.

• The average family size is slightly less than five.

• There are approximately 2200 marriages per year.

• Approximately 480 women per year lose their Indian status by marrying non-Indians.

• Approximately 560 non-Indian women per year acquire Indian status by marrying an Indian.

• The life expectancy at the age of one is sixty for males and sixty-six for females, about ten years less than the national average.

• Approximately 45 percent of Indian births occur outside of registered marriage. This is five times higher than the national rate.

• Approximately 8 percent of Indian children are adopted or put in foster homes. This is eight times higher than the national rate. There was a fivefold increase in the number of adoptions and foster parenting between 1962 and 1978, of which 75 percent are now in homes of non-Indian parents. In 1976-1977, 655 Native children were placed for adoption in the four western provinces alone.

• While the national population comprises 2.6 percent Natives, some 20 percent of all children "in care" in Canada are Natives. These "in care" figures are extremely high in the western provinces: Manitoba – 60.0 percent, Saskatchewan – 51.5 percent, Alberta – 44.4 percent, and British Columbia – 39.0 percent.

• Excluding Indian women who have lost their status through interracial marriages, the number of females living off reserves is 10 percent higher than the number of males living off reserves.

• The Indian rate of legal divorces is now about half the national rate and has been steadily rising. This is an indication of increasing Indian participation in the Canadian system, but is no indication of changes in the actual divorce rate.

The Rural Family

K. Ishwaran

In Canada, there are three broad family types – the rural family, the outpost family, and the urban family. The rural family, like the outpost family, is relatively less affected by the modernizing forces of industrialization, urbanization, and technology. But, unlike the outpost family, it has been integrated more systematically into the market economy and the socio-cultural system of the dominant urban centres, yet without losing its distinctively rural characteristics. Because of the overwhelming prevalence of the urban population, it is seldom realized that a substantial proportion of Canadians, approximately 20 percent, live in the rural hinterland.

Three broad characteristics have generated diversity within the overall rural family type. These are the multiethnic constitution of the rural population; the greater responsiveness to local ecological challenges; and the role of the rural economy as mediator between the Canadian and the international market systems. This diversity, coupled with the paucity of sociological data on the rural family in Canada, make it very difficult to generalize and theorize on the Canadian rural family. However, it is possible to construct a tentative and provisional profile of its structure and functions on the basis of the limited source material available.

Ecology and the Rural Family

Given the agrarian basis of the rural population, its closer relationship to the ecological setting is understandable. The rural society and its economy are tied to the environmental situation in a far more structured manner than is an urban community. Hence, it may be expected that the rural social system and its central institutions, like the family, will be highly sensitive to the pressures and demands of their ecological context.

The Dutch-Canadian family of the Holland Marsh area near Toronto, Ontario exemplifies vividly the close interdependence between the rural family and its ecology.[1] But it should be borne in mind that no single factor, in isolation, shapes the form and functions of the rural family, though, for purposes of sociological analysis, it is often necessary to examine one variable in detail and depth. In fact, in the Holland Marsh community, it is the environmental factor in conjunction with such other variables as religion, cultural system, and historical antecedents that determine the patterns of family life. These patterns can be examined in three different contexts: the original Dutch con-

---

[1]For details *see* K. Ishwaran, *Family, Kinship and Community: A Study of Dutch-Canadians* (Toronto: McGraw-Hill Ryerson, 1977).

text in the homeland; the developmental context of the emergence of community life in the new Canadian environment; and the present context.

The dominant family form in rural Holland is *de familie* or the extended
family, in contrast to the urban family form of *Het gezin* or the elementary
family. The former consists of two co-residential generations and is prevalent
in the eastern part of Holland. In response to variations in regional ecology, the
family form shows inter-regional diversities in its different aspects. In the north,
the ecology permits a system of large farmholdings, characterized by a high
degree of mechanization and a substantial level of integration into the urban
economy. The type of family evolved under these conditions is the patrilocal,
nuclear family, dominated by the benign and stern male head. The small-farm
economy of the sandy regions has evolved an extended domestic-based family with farming operations organized on a collective, family level. Both types
of families maintain their social status through endogamy based on property,
class, status, and religion. However, the two differ with respect to patterns of
intrafamily role relationships. The northern family type involves a high degree
of specialization in family roles, especially that of the wife. This has generated
a more egalitarian form of intra-family relationships. In the sandy regions,
there is a complete absence of such role specialization. Of course, these patterns
are constantly changing, in Holland as elsewhere, in response to forces of
industrialization and urbanization.[2]

In the historical context, the immigrant community successfully rebuilt its
community life in the new environment. Development started as a historical
process in the late 1920s, though it was preceded by antecedent processes such
as emigration from Holland and the reassembling of scattered immigrants
into the Marsh area. In the pioneering phase, the Marsh was a patch of wilderness, stubborn and inhospitable, and providing an ecological challenge. In
response, the pioneers subordinated the environment to community needs,
such as physical security, economic production, social existence, and cultural
affirmation. It meant building houses, the church, the school, and interconnecting
roads.

The pioneering family also evolved in response to the challenge of the
ecology. In an untame environment, the family had to develop co-operative
links with other families for survival. Hence, inter-family co-operation was
generated. To convert the Marsh into an economic proposition and a habita-
ble place, inter-family labor teams were created to carry out the task of re-
making the land through a process aptly described as "toiling and trusting."
The land had to be reclaimed and then transformed into farmland suitable for
a market-garden economy. Individual families found that their interests could
be served only by continuous and systematic collaborations with other families. Thus, from the struggle of scattered families to come to terms with a
hostile and forbidding ecology, a new community was born.

In the later phase of community development, the role of the ecology was
mediated through a highly-differentiated community system. In this stage, ecology was seen in terms of geophysical and climatic conditions under which the
Marsh market-garden economy had to function. As a result, the intense co-

---

[2]K. Ishwaran, *Family Life in the Netherlands* (The Hague: Van Keulen, 1959), pp. 39-87.

operation that characterized the pioneering phase had to yield to the development of an individualistic-ideological framework. Yet, at the same time, the socio-cultural needs as well as the agricultural economic needs continued to create the basis for co-operative community life.

More recently, the forces of modernization in the form of industrialization, urbanization, and technology have begun to impinge on the contemporary Marsh community. The socio-cultural ecology, which operates more powerfully than the geophysical ecology, has pushed the rural Dutch community into a transitional stage. In consequence, the family system, which as a rule was patriarchal, authoritarian, and extended in spirit, is now under pressure to move closer to the Canadian urban model of the modified extended family.

Ideological Factor in the Rural Family System

Though generalizations are often inaccurate, it may, nonetheless, be suggested that the rural family, being more stable, is likely to be more open to the impact of the ideological factor, especially the religious ideological factor. The rural Dutch community supports this assumption very well, but the best example of the impact of ideology on the rural family form is the Hutterite rural family in Canada.[3]

Members of the Hutterite sectarian fundamentalist community, originally from Europe, settled in Canadian rural communities, mostly in the provinces of Manitoba, Saskatchewan, and Alberta. Their rate of population growth is among the highest in the world, about 4.12 percent annually. Today, they number around 20 000.

The Hutterite family system is best understood in terms of its religious ideology. Essentially a historical throwback of marginal resistance to the commercialism and the political absolutism of the Reformation period, they have evolved a distinctive social structure supported by a religious ideological framework derived from the Bible. In particular, they draw on the conception of the Christian community adumbrated, though in a scattered fashion, in the Biblical text. This ideological framework defines the Hutterite community as a "community of goods." (The orginal German term used by the Hutterites was *Guetergemeinschaft.*) Hence, within this ideology, it has become a moral and spiritual community as well as a community in a material sense. However, the Hutterite interpretation of the Bible is not egalitarian. In fact, their ideology is based on a hierarchical social system, hinging on such factors as age, sex, and economic role.

The Hutterite educational system combines two curricula, one conforming to provincial legal requirements and the other aimed at socializing the children according to the Hutterite religious and moral ideology. Thus, the school is both a secular and a religious institution. The process of socialization is also influenced by the family and other group contexts, in which the Hutterite modality of perception and behavior is systematically related to primary rela-

---

[3]Karl Peter, The Hutterite Family. In *The Canadian Family*, ed. K. Ishwaran (Toronto: Holt, Rinehart and Winston, 1976), pp. 289, 309; Problems in the Family, Community and Culture of Hutterites. In *Canadian Families-Ethnic Diversity*, ed. K. Ishwaran (Toronto: McGraw-Hill Ryerson, 1980); *see also* Peter's paper in this volume.

tionships with others, rather than more characteristically modern secondary relationships. The community constitutes the main focus of each member's objectives and behavior.

Customs of courtship, marriage, and ensuing family life are all governed by the community's religious ideology. Initially, marriage was regarded in a three-level hierarchy rooted in the religious ideology that subordinated the flesh to the spirit. The highest level represented marriage between God and the soul; the next highest between the spirit and the body; and finally, between two bodies. From this it followed that courtship was an exemplification of purely carnal desires, and, therefore, did not conform to the highest level of a man-woman relationship. Hence, a system of mate selection was designed to overcome the carnal aspect. Under a matching system, marriageable males and females gathered together once or twice a year, at which time the preacher assigned to each male three females, one of whom he was to choose as his life partner. If the male was unable to choose, he had to wait until the next such occasion.

Since 1830, chiefly as a result of a young girl's refusal to marry an old man, the community has switched to a more open system in which the choice of marital partners is left to the individual. However, the religious ideology still prescribes that none can marry before being baptized, which usually occurs between the ages of nineteen and twenty-one. Today, Hutterite communities show a widely varying commitment to the religious ideology, some of them being considerably influenced by dating and courtship patterns of the wider Canadian society. The marriage itself is a religious affair, involving the church and its rituals.

The religious system exercises considerable influence on relationships within the family. The married woman is "placed" by the church in a female hierarchical labor system. The community, as guardian of the religious ideology, exerts substantial control over the behavior of married persons, forbidding public displays of affection and involving close supervision by the older people. The dominant male role is also rooted in religious ideology derived from Bibilical interpretations of male superiority. This pattern is in sharp contrast to the prevailing ideology of equality and individual freedom.

While religious ideology plays an important role in the marital and family life of the Hutterites, it is interesting to note that the same ideology does not interfere in community adaptations to modern sicentific agriculture and associated technology. Like other rural families in Canada, the Hutterite family presents a tension between a rurally rooted pattern of organization and the impact of the external ideology of urban industrial values radiating from the wider society. Part of the distinctiveness of the rural family stems from this empirical situation.

Economy and the Rural Family: The Case of the Jasper* Region

One fundamental aspect of a rural community is a rural economy; hence, its family system should be viewed in a rural economic setting. The interrelation-

---

*Jasper is a fictitious name for an actual community in southwestern Saskatchewan.

ship between the rural economy and the rural family is vividly illustrated by the rural family system in the Jasper region which is located in the Saskatchewan section of the northern Great Plains. In this rural community, there are two distinct economic groups – the ranchers and the farmers – each with its own family form and functions.[4] In the ranching community, a crucial aspect of family life lies in the process of succession to the ranch.

A thinly-populated territory, the Jasper region is characterized by a variegated landscape. The ranchers, who were the first to arrive, settled along the creeks, while the farmers established their homesteads on the level plains, spreading to the south and north of the lushly vegetated hills. The town itself had a modest population of 2500 (in 1962), and is an important trading centre and railhead of the area. It is a relatively undeveloped area to which modern facilities have been gradually introduced, in the last decade or so.

Because of the different spatial distribution of the two communities, the kinship network of the ranchers is dispersed, while the kinship circle of the farmers is highly localized and spatially concentrated. The kin relations have evolved either through marriage or consanguinity. In the early stage, marriages tended to be spatially restricted. But later, marital alliances established connections with relatively dispersed centres. Although by the 1970s, marital alliances were increasingly contracted outside the region, this still did not account for more than a quarter of them.

The nuclear family is the dominant form for both groups, however, their different patterns of transferring resources is reflected in their differing household compositions and residential arrangements. Newly-wedded couples live in the same or separate domestic units, but within the same enterprise, the assumption being that eventually the young man will take over the family enterprise. This pattern is comparatively more prevalent among the ranchers than among the farmers because of their different economic base. The financial implications of starting a ranch are far more demanding than they are for starting a farm. Since ranchers need a greater amount of both land and capital, their sons are more dependent on parental resources than are farmers' sons who can fission into separate households more easily. Although patrilocality is the norm, it is not unusual for newly-married couples to stay with the wife's parental establishment for economic reasons.

One of the conventional conceptions of the rural society is that, in the context of industrialization and urbanization, it tends to be characterized by substantial rates and quantity of out-migration. In this context, it is significant that out-migration among the ranchers has been relatively insignificant and most of the ranches remain under the ownership of their founding families. In fact, by 1972, the sons who came of age in the preceding decade and succeeded to parental ranches accounted for 67.8 percent of all the sons of ranchers in a similar situation for the same period. This pattern can be explained in terms of the dominance of the ranching tradition and the consequent devaluation of formal educational qualifications. Hence, it is not so much tradition as it is the desire to take over the parental enterprise that tends to

---

[4]For details *see* Seena B. Kohl, *Working Together: Women and Family in Southwestern Saskatchewan* (Toronto: Holt, Rinehart and Winston, 1976).

lower educational accomplishments for the rural youth in Jasper, irrespective of whether they are ranchers or farmers. This is further complicated by those farmers' sons who are attracted to ranching, causing inter-generational conflict.

While ranching continues to evoke sentimental and romantic attachments, recent economic pressures have pushed ranchers' sons out of parental enterprises. This has not been a big problem for farmers' sons since they have always been socialized into a diversified ideal of occupational goals. Hence, they have tended to pursue formal education as a matter of course, and this is true of both boys and girls.

For the sons of both the ranchers and farmers, there is a regular period of apprenticeship. This is in some sense a throw back to the pre-modern traditional family paradigm in which the family was actively involved in occupational training. Beginning as young as four or five years of age, the child accompanies the father as he carries out the chores. Since ranching is more closely dependent on terrain and topography, such apprenticeship is crucial to familiarize the heir with the ecological conditions. In a comparative perspective, the ranching son finds it more difficult to sever the ties to his father, than does the farming son. However, this difference should not be overemphasized since even the farming son is substantially dependent on his parents. In the process of transferring property and status through succession, the father plays a crucial part. While the kin group does extend support, this is a very unusual development.

The surplus sons leave the region and seek semi-skilled or skilled urban occupations, but they tend to return to work with their fathers or to buy new business units. This pattern of out-migration followed by in-migration provides ample opportunity for the resolution of inter-generational and familial conflicts and tensions. For women, out-migration is a common practice among both ranchers and farmers. The woman stays in the region only if she marries locally. It is understood, as matter of course, that a woman does not become a rancher or a farmer. However, she may be forced to participate in these occupations if there are no sons in the family. The ideal for a woman is married life. This norm makes it easy for a woman to emigrate from the region. She may emigrate either because she marries outside the region, or because she is in search of career opportunities. The girls are expected to attain higher educational levels and generally do better in school than the boys. While sons tend to be socialized into the rural way of life, daughters are socialized into urban, middle-class values and norms by their mothers.

The rural families of Jasper preserve regular contacts, through correspondence and visits, with members of the kin group outside the region. This relationship is interdependent and mutually supportive. During the summer, younger relatives visit their country uncles, and there are frequent stopovers by relatives en route to other places. Thus, there is a systematic contact between the rural and urban components of the kinship group, but there is little support extended by the urban component of the extended family to the rural families in Jasper. However, this urban kin network has particular relevance for rural girls who can derive reference models and worldly sophistication from their urban kin.

Thus, the rural family of Jasper is indicative of the close interrelationship between the rural economy and the patterns of family processes. While the economic factor is not the only factor shaping the form and functions of the rural family, it is certainly one of the most crucial.

The Cultural System and the Rural Family Among French Canadians

St. Jean Baptiste, a farming community of some 1500, is a typical French-Canadian rural community in Quebec. The people are predominantly French Canadian, with the exception of a single English-Canadian family and a sprinkling of descendants from original Métis settlers. The basis of community life is the Roman Catholic Church, which controls a variety of socially useful organizations such as the school.[5]

While the data on this rural community are not comparable in quality and quantity to the data for urban French-Canadian families extant (see, for instance, the data compiled by Garigue[6]), it is clear that the range of kinship awareness is far wider for rural French Canadians than for the English population. The mean of kin who could be identified and named in St. Jean Baptiste was as high as 256, according to a study by Piddington, whereas Firth's study of a London area yielded a mean of only 102.[7] As with the urban French Canadians, interest in kin who were contemporary or closely contemporary was very high. For the informants' generation and that of their parents, the named kin constituted 62 percent while the unnamed accounted for 25 percent. The kinship bondage is further reinforced in this rural community by kin endogamy. Almost everybody in this community is related to everybody else, in however a distant sense, and this tends to promote community coherence, which is reinforced by the Church.

The conventional assumption that rural communities tend to be locally oriented and geographically rooted is challenged by data about this community. As already noted, the kinship network is one manifestation of what one may call a process of establishing external linkages. The other manifestation is the considerable scale of emigration from St. Jean Baptiste. This out-migration to nearby urban centres which are also predominantly French Canadian, for example, Winnipeg and St. Boniface, has not upset the structure of the rural society and culture.

Though the kinship network plays an important role in the rural community, this role should be distinguished from that played by the kin group in pre-modern societies. If kin members can be classified as priority, chosen, and non-effective kin, the pre-modern societies tend to have a wider range of priority kin with a more structured system of social relationships between

---

[5]Ralph Piddington, A Study on French-Canadian Kinship. In *The Canadian Family*, ed. K. Ishwaran (Toronto: Holt, Rinehart and Winston, 1976), pp. 555-79.

[6]Philippe Garigue, French-Canadian Kinship and Urban Life. In *The Canadian Family*, ed K. Ishwaran (Toronto: Holt, Rinehart and Winston, 1976), pp. 518-30.

[7]Raymond Firth, ed., *Two Studies of Kinship in London* (London: University of London, Athlone Press, 1956).

them. The priority kin consist of those belonging to the individual family and those closely related to the spouses. In the pre-modern systems there is a closer integration of economic roles into kinship roles outside the family. In St. Jean Baptiste, this exists to some extent. But the existence of the kin group network does not, as in pre-Western systems, obliterate the reality and functioning of the nuclear, individual family.

The kinship system of the rural French-Canadian community of St. Jean Baptiste is not essentially dissimilar to the kinship structure of its urban counterpart. This implies that, despite rural-urban distinctions, French-Canadian ethnicity and culture dominate the French-Canadian population. The nuclear family, which is the normal family form among this group, serves to strengthen the ethnic-cultural identity. But its kinship network, which is an aggregate of nuclear family units into a system of extended kinship, also plays a significant role in the perpetuation of French-Canadian cultural identity. Thus, there exists a close interrelationship between the rural French-Canadian family (and also the urban family), the extended kinship system, and the cultural system.

The extant views tend to hypothesize that French-Canadian culture predates the modernization process and, as such, is necessarily hostile to the modern processes of migration, industrialization, and urbanization. But evidence does not support this view. In fact, the French-Canadian culture harmoniously co-exists both with the rural and urban community systems. The situation can be theoretically explained by conceptualizing culture as a dynamic process responsive to changes in economy and ecology. The French-Canadian rural community tends, paradoxically, to demonstrate the vitality of French-Canadian cultural identity. Whatever the context, rural or urban, the family and the extended kinship network play a crucial role in the persistence and perpetuation of French-Canadian culture as a historical phenomenon.

Socialization in the Rural Family

Given the total context of the rural community – its isolation, its relatively greater cultural homogeneity, and its high degree of social cohesiveness – its socialization processes are likely to be more personalized and largely family centred, than those of the urban family.

If we consider the four rural communities focussed on here, it is possible to arrive at some general patterns of rural socialization in Canada. Although some of these generalizations may also apply with modifications to other immigrants – the Greeks, the Italians, the Japanese or the Polish – who have come from rural backgrounds and preserved some elements of their rural origin even in an urban environment in their new country.

A Hutterite child spends only the first two years of his life with the family, then he is entrusted to the community-controlled kindergarten, for eight hours a day, until he is six years old. Thereafter he attends a school supervised by a German teacher, who inculcates ethnic values and religious principles, and a teacher appointed by the regional School Board, who introduces the secular curriculum. At fifteen the children are enlisted into sexually segregated labor forces. From the ages six to fifteen, the child is part of a formally structured peer group, supervised by the German school teacher and his wife. Thus, the socializing task is shared by the family and a whole complex of community-controlled institutions. The objective of this process is to suppress individuality and personal angularities and shape the child in the image of the community – a distinctive religious ideology. Though the Hutterite socialization process may appear close to the urban pattern of non-family socialization, it differs in one important respect; while the urban pattern involves highly impersonal agencies, the rural Hutterite pattern involves personalized non-familial agencies. This is inevitable because the Hutterite community is a closed system, based on intensive interpersonal interactions.

Among the rural Dutch Canadians of the Holland Marsh, the socialization process is geared to generating normative and behavioral properties associated not only with the ethnic-religious system, but also with the class system. Further, the style of socialization itself is differentiated along class lines. The upper class adopts a more flexible and open pattern of socialization, and the family permits the child considerable individuality. In lower-class families, the process is more rigid and corrective. This is also true of middle-class families, where children are socialized into a value system based on aggressive and competitive behavior. This value system, however, is located within a Christian matrix. Besides socially necessary behavior, socialization also aims at producing good Christians, persons who accept and follow the commands of God as embodied in the Bible. Besides the family, agents of socialization include the Church, the Sunday school and Church-sponsored clubs.

In the Jasper region, the family is the principal socializing force and the extended kin group is secondary. In this somewhat closed, agrarian community, the non-familial institutions play a relatively less important role in the socialization process. For the ranchers, it is assumed that the son will succeed to the family enterprise and, therefore, he is socialized into the ranching way of life. For instance, he is taught to accept a dependent role for a considerable waiting period at the end of which he takes over the parental enterprise. For the farming sons, dependence on the family is necessary before they can start on their own. For the daughters, socialization has a different objective. They are socialized to look outward either for a career or marriage outside the region. But socialization is not the only significant factor in determining the behavior of the young. Situational pressures, especially of the economic or personal kind, may modify or even nullify the values, behavioral norms, and expectations a person has acquired. The kin group located outside the rural community also influences the young toward an alternate way of life. But the family performs the main role in socializing the young, especially the sons, into the traditional pattern of values and behavior.

In the rural French-Canadian community of St. Jean Baptiste, the family and the Church play an important role in the socialization process. The values and institutional patterns of French-Canadian culture are well defined and crystallized. The family and the Church, together with the Church-sponsored school, play a crucial role in the process of socializing the young into the French-Canadian cultural context. Further, the kinship network contributes to the reinforcement of the socio-cultural self-identity of the community. The extended kin group also plays an indirect role. Thus, as in the other rural communities, we find that the socializing task is carried on by personalized and relatively primary groups. But this situation is not a stable one, and already the impact of external forces such as industrialization and urbanization, through the media and through migration, are changing the situation.

Ethnicity and the Rural Family

While ethnicity is an important feature of Canadian contemporary society in general, the intensity of its impact on rural communities is relatively greater than on the urban society. The most important distinction is that the urban context is predominantly multiethnic, while the rural is predominantly uniethnic. In the case of the Dutch-Canadian community of Holland Marsh, the Hutterite community, the rural community of Jasper, and the St. Jean Baptiste community, there is an overwhelming uniethnic dominance of Dutch Canadians, German Canadians, British Canadians, and French Canadians, respectively.

Geographical isolation coupled with ethnic insularity and relative economic autonomy tend to reinforce the community patterns of values and behavior. This, of course, means a continuous and institutionalized strengthening of the ethnic factor. In this process of ethnic reinforcement, religious ideology and religious institutions play an important role, excepting in the case of Jasper region.

The family, as the guardian of ethnic values and patterns, together with the extended kinship network are the main institutional mediators in this process. In fact, ethnicity is a highly family oriented factor, though it has inter-family dimensions. Thus, the ethnic aspect of the rural Canadian population is systematically preserved and sustained within the framework of intra-family and inter-family processes. In turn, ethnic identity has enabled the rural community to enjoy a considerable measure of psychological security. It has also tended to provide institutional support, not only psychological but also material, to the families. The source of this mutual support is ethnically sanctioned interdependence in a variety of contexts.

Family Roles and Relationships: Husbands and Wives

Within the rural family system, the intra-family relationships, especially that of husband and wife, present a contrast to the patterns discernible in the urban family. Initially, there is an impression of male dominance, however, closer scrutiny reveals a more complicated situation.

In the case of the Hutterite family, it is clear that the religious ideology which forms the foundation of the community upholds the Biblical doctrine of male dominance and subordination of the woman to the man. This, however, does not mean any direct dominance of the husband over the wife. In this totalitarian community, there is a systematic control of individuality in the interest of the community goals, which are set by the religious ideology. This situation is now changing toward a pattern prevalent in the mainstream of

Canadian society. For instance, the courtship pattern is now more inclined toward one in which individual choice is permitted. The married couple is regarded by the community as a basic element in its life structure. Their material resources for marital and family life are distributed by the community. There is a clear-cut sex-based role differentiation between the husband and wife. The wife, for instance, is involved in domestic chores. Not only sex, but age and family status also define the role of the wife. Similarly, the husband is involved in the community structure of division of labor and social hierarchy. Married life is, in fact, private to a very restricted extent. Yet, within this framework male dominance, which is willingly accepted by the wife, is a significant factor of Hutterite marital life.

In the Dutch-Canadian family of the Holland Marsh, the husband is the "boss." However, this does not necessarily imply inequality between husband and wife. He is the boss only in the ultimate sense, but in terms of routine situations husband and wife share responsibilities and powers without any rigid sense of inequality. There are a substantial number of cases in which the father and mother exercise authority jointly, however, a relatively larger number of children tend to ascribe superiority to the father. But the wife's authority and status derive from her function within the family system. Since the Holland Marsh rural community is a literate modern farming community, it operates as a modern business involving maintenance of regular accounts of income and expenditure. The responsibility for this task varies. In only a small number of families is it the wife's task. However, in a substantial number of families it is a joint responsibility. Thus, though the trend toward joint responsibility is egalitarian, the dominant pattern of husband-wife relationship in this rural community is characterized by husband dominance and role specialization on the basis of sex difference. The latter implies that the wife tends to specialize in housekeeping, while the husband attends to farming operations.

In the rural community of the Jasper region, one finds a similar pattern of male dominance and sex-based role differentiation. In both ranching and farming families, only the boys are expected to take over the enterprise from the father. Among the farmers, girls are provided an alternative to married life in terms of urban careers outside the Jasper region, whereas among the ranchers, women are more specifically socialized into domestic roles. Hence, there is clearly a male dominance supported by a sex-based role specialization that confines the wife to domestic chores while the husband concentrates on the agricultural occupation.

Thus, from the three rural communities for which some data are available about husband-wife relationships, it is clear that there is convergence toward certain broad similarities of pattern. Given the nature of the rural economy and system of production, wives tend to be exclusively concerned with the process of production and income-earning. This inequality is reinforced by the religious and cultural ideology of male dominance. Thus, we find that the intra-family relationships between the spouses in the rural Canadian family are characterized by the ultimate dominance of the husband, and unequal role related to sex differentiation.

Parents and Children

Our examination of rural communities suggests that the rural Canadian family functions on an authoritarian basis. Complementing male dominance, there exists a systematic dominance of the parents over the children.

In the case of the Hutterites, while children are placed under parental control, the parents themselves are under the overall control of the community-sponsored, regulatory institutions. Nonetheless, within the framework of the family life, the Hutterite pattern implies parental authoritarian control. However, in practice, this may be negligible since children spend most of their time outside the family context.

Although children in the Holland Marsh community are subject to the control of both parents, there is a noticeable difference between the roles of the father and the mother. The father is regarded as the more authoritarian figure, associated with fear and punishment, while the mother is seen as a more benign and benevolent figure, associated with love, tenderness, and affection. As a result, she is more accessible and supportive during times of crisis and trouble. Her constant presence enables her to establish better rapport with the children. Even when the father's support is necessary, it is through the mother's intervention that it is actually obtained.

In the Jasper communities and the French-Canadian community of St. Jean Baptiste, parental authority over the children appears to be very strong. This may be partially attributed to the fact that the family performs the function of training the children for the rural occupations. This necessarily requires imposition of discipline on the young. Thus, the authoritarian pattern flows logically out of the rural economy and social structure. Further, among the ranchers, especially for the sons, dependence on the fathers is crucial as a supportive economic input. This gives the father a certain leverage in exercising his parental authority.

Evaluation

In contrast to the urban family, the rural family in Canada has certain distinctive features. First, it is more responsive to the pressures of ecology. This arises from the fact that the rural community is far more dependent on the ecological setting than is the urban family.

Second, the isolation and cultural insulation of the rural family creates the conditions for a stronger religious cultural identity. The rural communities, and hence their families, tend to emphasise the importance of sociocultural identity as a necessary foundation for a strong community identity and integration.

Third, ideological factors exert greater impact on the rural family than on the urban. This may be due to the fact that the rural family is less exposed to the external environment, and finds it necessary to root itself in a religious ideology.

Fourth, the rural family reflects the economic context of rural life. The nature of the agricultural operations tend to be reflected in male dominance, sex-based role differentiation within the family, and the authoritarian parental control over the children.

Fifth, ethnicity tends to have a stronger influence on the rural family than on the urban, though it should be noted that this is a relative matter. The most important reason for this is the fact that the rural community is predominantly uniethnic in contrast to the generally multiethnic urban demographic aggregates.

Sixth, the extended kin groups play as important a role in the rural family as among the urban family. The extended kinship network has an external impact on isolated rural communities, providing non-agrarian role models for the rural young, and thus contributing toward the process of out-migration from the rural areas.

Seventh, the rural socialization process is relatively more personalized and hence more intense. In this process the family plays an important role, both directly and indirectly; directly, the family consciously imparts its values and behavioral norms to the young, while indirectly, the children tend to assimilate unconsciously the values and norms of the family. The very closed nature of the rural society makes intensive interpersonal socialization both necessary and possible.

Finally, any generalization and characterization of the rural family must come to terms with the dynamics of rural social processes. In response to the increasing and insistent pressures emanating from the external, urban sociocultural environment and the external economic systems, the rural community and family have been undergoing changes in form and function. But this process has not reached the point where the distinctiveness of the rural family has dissolved. From one point of view, the rural family may be conceptualized as converging toward the urban family. But from another, and perhaps a more important perspective, the rural family must be seen, not as an urban family in the making, but as a distinctive family form rooted in the realities of rural society, economy, and culture. In this sense, it may be changing but it is changing within the framework of its own history and specificity.

Family Structures and Functions in Urban Canada

K. Ishwaran

The family, like the other institutions that constitute a social system, must be viewed in terms of the functions performed for it. Since the family emmeshes systematically with the other components of a social system, its structure as well as its functioning should be examined as articulating with those other components. Some of these, such as the marital and the kinship structures, are closely related to the family.

In a historical and global perspective, family structures and functions have been characterized by variations and divergences. At one end of the typological range is the nuclear and conjugal family, while at the other end is the extended family. In between lie transitional structures of the modified-nuclear and the modified-extended types. The nuclear and conjugal family is characterized by self-sufficiency, including in its economic aspect a significant degree of intra-familial socialization, a near total autonomy from kin influence, and kin network communication through letters or telephone but with limited personal contact. The extended type, in contrast, is characterized by economic inter-dependence on the kin network, a considerable degree of dependence on the kin group for emotional security, socialization, and protection, and an authority system based on a linear inter-generational pattern, and frequent and physical interaction with the kin network. Of the traditional forms, the modified-nuclear is closer to the nuclear while the modified-extended is closer to the extended type.

Historically, the nuclear-conjugal family has been causally linked to the process of industrialization, urbanization, and modernization. But empirical evidence points to a very complex interrelationship between these factors. It shows this type of family as being more a norm than a reality in modern, industrial societies. In fact, the transitional types have evolved to meet the conceptual situation created by this discovery. The earlier tradition of emphasizing the urban-rural distinction in family form was primarily a sociological response to the historical shifts in European society, created by the industrial revolution. The typology produced in this tradition remained too broad to accommodate the complexities of the empirical situation. In the 1920s and 1930s, this tradition was represented by the Chicago School, as exemplified in the work of Louis Wirth[1] and Robert Redfield.[2]

One of Wirth's major concerns was urban family life, and his study in this

---

[1]Louis Wirth, "Urbanism as a Way of Life," *American Journal of Sociology* 44.1 (1938): 1-24.

[2]Robert Redfield, "The Folk Society," *American Journal of Sociology* 52.4 (1947): 293-308.

field has left a permanent mark on the sociology of the city, a model that would transcend its particular historical and local variations. He emphasized size, density, and heterogeneity as the three key variables determining the distinctive nature and structure of the city and its life. These three factors dissolved personal relationships, depersonalized and fragmented human interactions, turning them into generalized, transitory, and casual transactions. They ruptured social structures and stimulated social mobility, disorder and rootlessness. Among the important consequences of city life Wirth notes was "the declining social significance of the family."[3] This was because in the urban system responsibility for the traditional family tasks of training in skills, education, and recreation shifted from the family to impersonal institutions.

Taking the position of the Chicago School as a whole, Redfield depicted city life in negative terms while presenting a somewhat romanticized and rosy picture of the rural community. This was particularly true of the School's treatment of the urban family. Preoccupation with the negative and disorganizing aspects of city life obscured the positive and integrative role of the city in relation to the family and the community. The Chicago School's approach to such issues as urban poverty and disadvantaged ethnic groups within the general framework of city life led to the culture of poverty theme. This, too, prevented the School from dealing with these problems in a dynamic manner, as they viewed them in terms of structural determinism.

This urban-rural dichotomy was further reinforced in positive portraits of city life. While the Chicago School emphasized this dichotomy to extol the rural family, the Parsonian paradigm sharpened it to emphasize the virtues and the progressive superiority of the modern, industrial, urban family over the traditional family. Parsons suggested that the urban, modern nuclear family, was an adequate institution in terms of its functionality in modern society, as it enabled its members to cope with the psychological and affective as well as the material and economic needs of its members.[4]

The Parsonian emphasis on the isolation and autonomy of the urban family has had to be modified in the light of the more recent sociological discovery of the existence and operation of extended kin network relationships in contemporary North American family life.[5] In their classic summary of the re-

---

[3]Wirth, op. cit., 21-22.

[4]Talcott Parsons, "The Social Structure of the Family," in *The Family: Its Function and Destiny,* ed. Ruth N. Anshen (New York: Harper and Brothers, 1959), pp. 241-74. *See also* Talcott Parsons, "The Kinship System of Contemporary United States," *American Anthropologist* 45 (1943): 22-38.

[5]For illustrative studies, *see* Marvin B. Sussman, "The Isolated Nuclear Family: Fact or Fiction?," *Social Problems* 6 (1959): 333-40; Marvin Sussman and Lee Burchinal, "Kin Family Network Unheralded Structure in Current Conceptualizations of Family Functioning," *Marriage and Family Living* 24 (1962): 231-40; Eugene Litwak, "Occupational Mobility & Extended Family Cohesion," *American Sociological Review* 25 (1960): 9-21; Eugene Litwak, "Geographic Mobility & Extended Family Cohesion," ibid., pp. 385-94; Wendell Bell and Marion D. Boat, "Urban Neighbourhoods and Informal Social Relations," *American Journal of Sociology* 62 (1957): 395; Morris Axelrod, "Urban Structure and Social Participation," *American Sociological Review* 21 (1956): 17; Paul J. Reiss, "The Extended Kinship System: Correlates & Attitudes on Frequency of Interaction," *Marriage and Family Living* 24 (1962): 334

search in this field, Sussman and Burchinal[6] called serious attention to the need to locate the urban American families within a kinship network system based on exchange of goods and services. They found that the extended kin structure played a significant and supportive role during illness, in times of financial need, in the care of children, in solving personal and business problems, and in the exchange of gifts. Litwak showed that extended family kinship structure was actively present and functionally significant in the modern urban life of Buffalo, New York. However, the new urban extended kinship structure differed from the traditional extended family form in certain important respects; it lacked an authoritarian figure, used modes other than geographical mobility for contact, and was not characterized by occupational similarity. The modified-extended family involved an aggregation of independent nuclear families on the basis of equality and mutual support. It also differed from the nuclear family in that it showed considerable dependence on a kin network.

In the light of these developments, a central emergent issue has become the theoretical reconciliation between the earlier thesis of the nuclear urban family and the later findings about the existence of the modified-extended family in contemporary North American cities. In reconciling these apparently opposed accounts of the urban family, historical specificity is a crucial variable. What went wrong was not the empirical account of the earlier sociologists, but rather their attempt to hypothesize historically specific experience into a transhistorical ideal typical model. Their empirical version of the urban family was valid for the period when, in the context of the immigration process, differential socialization patterns were imposed on inter-generational families. Such differential socialization experiences led to a transformation of identity of family members, in the context of the high social mobility during the early phases of industrialization and urbanization, with the younger generation experiencing a weakening of kinship ties. In the early stage of industrialization and urbanization, geographical, social, and cultural mobility disrupted relations between inter-generational families. Today, in the context of the expanding middle-class urban segment in American life, inter-generational differentials are unlikely to result in class differentiation. The extended family members, therefore, are able to establish cross-class kin network relationships. Upward mobility in the American middle class does not lead, as in the past, to differences in socialization between generations. This facilitates better kin network communication. The recent thesis of the extended kinship structure should be related to the historically specific situation emerging after the Second World War. While its existence in any earlier period is uncertain, recent research has identified this type as existing during the later nineteenth and early twentieth centuries. Such historically specific evidence tends to undermine the utility and relevance of overly narrow conceptual typology. Part of the explanation for this situation is epistemological and must lie in the inability of the ideal typical methodology in the post-Weber period to come to terms with the dynamic and procedural aspects of social phenomena. This does not apply to Weber himself whose efforts were sustained by high-level historical scholarship.

---

[6]Sussman and Burchinal, op. cit.

The structure and functions of the urban family in Canada should be examined against the background of this theoretical and empirical debate. The key issues are whether the Canadian urban family today exemplifies the Parsonian paradigm or whether it confirms the thesis of the existence and operation of an extended kin structure in modern urban family life.

The Kinship Network and the Family in Urban Canada

Kinship is a system of structured relationships that links individuals through complex, interdependent, and ramifying bonds.[7] Therefore, it involves a system of socially-defined interrelationships, based on rights and duties attached to specific kinship statuses. It also presupposes a normative order governing its relationships. As an extensive and multifocal system, it covers a wide range of consanguine categories – parents, children, siblings, grandparents, uncles, and aunts. The family functions within such a kinship system in the pre-modern or traditional societies. However, the assumption that industrialization and urbanization would drastically weaken, if not destroy, the extended kinship network, has been found untenable for contemporary industrial societies. This fact became increasingly established in sociological literature in the 1950s.[8] More recently, Garigue has shown the prevalence of the extended kinship network as a resource to family life among the French Canadians, and similar evidence from other industrial societies has established it as a significant institutional context for the family in the United States, England, Canada, and Holland.

The French Canadians

Garigue's pioneering study[9] of the French-Canadian community of Montreal in the 1950s disclosed a clear functional interdependence between kinship and urban society. Every family and each of their individual members were found to be structurally involved in a system of obligations based on kinship ties.

Basically, this kinship system is a modified version of the one dominant in modern, industrial Western societies. Technically, it is a patronymic bilateral system, characterized by two dimensions, namely lateral range and generational depth. Though a general sense of pride in the geneology is wide spread, the

[7]G. P. Murdock, *Social Structure* (New York: The Macmillan Co., 1949) p. 9.

[8]Raymond Firth, ed., *Two Studies of Kinship in London* (London: University of London, 1956); Raymond Firth, Jane Herbert, and Anthony Forge, eds., *Families and Their Relatives* (London: Routledge & Kegan Paul, 1969); Michael Young and Peter Willmott, *Family, Kinship in East London* (London: Routledge & Kegan Paul, 1957); K. Ishwaran, *Family Life in the Netherlands* (The Hague: Van Keulers, 1959).

[9]See the following by Phillippe Garigue, "French-Canadian Kinship and Urban Life," *American Anthropologist* 58 (1956): 1090-101; *La Vie Familiale des Canadians Français* (Montreal: Presses de l'Université de Montreal, 1962); "The French-Canadian Family," in *Canadian Society,* ed. Bernard R. Blishen, et al. (Toronto: Macmillan, 1968).

strongest interaction is between the members of the same generation, transcending consanguineal and affinal bonds. Different behavioral patterns have developed in relation to the lateral and generational dimensions. Between generations, there is a formal pattern of expected obligations, while between members of the same generation it is an informal pattern based on personal preferences. The parent, child, and siblings constitute the nucleus of the kinship structure. While the domestic family is a more active unit, the overall kinship group remains in the background excepting on a few formal occasions such as a funeral. While a high level of compliance with kinship obligations prevail, there are also segmenting factors, the most crucial of which are social mobility and cultural differentiation. The latter lead to declining kinship contacts or even a total breakdown of contact.

The French Canadians show a high level of knowledge and awareness about their relatives. The mean number of those about whom knowledge is shown is estimated to be 215. The smallest range is 75; the highest is 484. The most knowledge about kin pertained to one's own generation and that of one's parents. This accounted for from 50 to 67 percent of the persons known. The knowledge of the second generation upward involved from one to eight ancestors, and the knowledge about the next ascending third and fourth generations tends to be limited to one ancestor.

The French-Canadian kin group is spatially widely scattered. Though everybody had a relative in Montreal, the proportion of those located outside in Quebec, Canada, and even the United States was very high, around 75 percent. Outside Montreal, the largest number of contacts existed with the parents and siblings, and the factors of space became important only in the case of more distantly-related kin. There were cases of persons meeting in a month as many as forty to forty-five relatives, on the average, belonging to generations older and younger than themselves. In one case, a person claimed to have visited practically every one of his ninety-three relatives residing in Montreal.

The pattern of exchange of services within the kinship structure among the French Canadians shows a distinct preference for kin of one's own group to those of the married partner. Additionally, there is a marked preference for members of one's own sex. The services involved reveal a variety of inputs of mutual aid, including the borrowing of goods required, baby-sitting, shopping assistance, household chores during a mother's illness, exchange of gifts, making loans on a significant scale, and other kinds of financial commitment. For a family reunion, all the adult females work together as a team in the purchase, preparation, and serving of food, as well as in the subsequent clearing up operations. If there are relatives in the medical profession, their services are easily called on, and if an affinal and consanguinal kinsman is a lawyer, his services are available at rates based on the economic status of the kinsman client. There are other extensive transactions involving mutual assistance such as patronizing shopkeepers who are kin or seeking moral and spiritual advice from kin who belong to religious orders. Even more remote kin, who have power and status, are approached for recommendations or introductions. Thus, the French-Canadian kinship network is utilized to promote the self-interest of its members. To an outsider this may seem like nepotism, however, the French Canadians refer to it as a show of family solidarity. Thus, the kinship ties sustain a regular system of mutual obligations and duties.

However, the kinship system is not structurally overdetermined, and allows for considerable flexibility in operation. This is because the kinship recognition process is selective. The priority kin, in fact, constitutes a very small group. The formal exchange relations between the generations are also highly restricted in number. The lateral dimension of the kin network, based on personal preferences, implies a wide range of choice and multiple kinship obligations. A French Canadian's normal background of socialization within a large household facilitates his adjustment to multiple kinship obligations.

The kinship structure in which a French Canadian is socialized is characterized by a narrowly-defined male authority and a pattern of emotional need satisfaction oriented toward sibling, cousin, mother-child, grandmother and aunt relationships. The same pattern continues during adult life, though with the greater freedom stemming from a wider range of personal choice. Since personal preference arises from approximately similar status and background, it ensures a high degree of cohesion in the subgroup. Such peer groups provide the context for leisure activities, but they also become the kinship groups in which the new offspring of couples undergo socialization. Such socialization tends to strengthen one's sense of kinship obligation. This is because a larger family socializes the young into the cultural and moral ethos of the kin community, especially into its system of multiple obligations.

The French Canadians are among the most populous groups in the West, and it is natural that they have developed as one of their familistic ideals, the desirability of a large sibling group. This remains as true of the urban French Canadians as of the rural, although the former have a relatively lower birth rate. Thus, the extended kinship network is as strong among urban French Canadians as among their rural counterparts. Increasing industrialization and urbanization have not affected in any significant manner the extended kinship structure among the French Canadians. This fact has a direct bearing on the ongoing debate over the relationship between industrialization and urbanization, on the one hand, and the kinship system, on the other.

Against this background of a strong and functional kinship network among the French Canadians, the Parsonian thesis that the nuclear and conjugal family is a distinctive product of the industrial and urban North American society is no longer tenable. Theoretically, Litwak's concept of the modified-extended family is, therefore, more relevant to an understanding of the French-Canadian family structure. Litwak's concept postulates a union of nuclear families, on a basis of equality, and not "involving geographical propinquity and occupational similarity."[10] Geographical mobility does not fragment the kin network because the extended family accommodates and approves such mobility. Moreover, modern communication facilities also help overcome the disruptive effects of mobility. The extended family, in this context, implies a structure consisting of bilaterally linked nuclear families. This family system provides simultaneously for individual achievement and for group security. It tends to

---

[10]Eugene Litwak, "Geographical Mobility and Extended Family Cohension," op. cit.

minimize nepotism and authority conflict. The French-Canadian family is an extended type in which spatial scattering does not weaken the relations with kin members outside the family of procreation.[11]

The nuclear families, in the French-Canadian context, function as the units of exchange and interaction within the extended kinship structure. There is substantial interaction with parents and grandparents, as well as with siblings. The contact ratio for them is as high as 96.8 percent. That is, the proportion of those with whom contacts were established. The contact ratio was highest for the kin residing in one's own city and within a distance of two hundred miles.

The mobile family, however, had fewer effective consanguines than the non-mobile family. Further, the actual kind of contact is not the same. Naturally, those with relatives residing in one's own city or town have an overwhelmingly greater contact, ten times more visits and twenty-five times more telephone conversations, than do the relatives of mobile families. But written communication is significantly higher for the mobile than for the non-mobile family. While the frequency rate differs, the number of "effective" remains the same for both types of family.

For both mobile and non-mobile families, there is a regular exchange of services and goods between relatives, although the exact nature of such aid is considerably different. In terms of quantity, the non-mobile families are involved in a larger number of exchange transactions than the mobile families. Such short notice aids as child care, assistance during illness, and personal advice are contingent on physical propinquity and non-mobile families are in a better position to accommodate such requests. Other kinds of help such as financial support are not affected by distance and in these cases the difference is not significant. Thus, geographical proximity determines to a considerable degree the extent and kind of mutual aid between kin, especially in relation to the differentiation of mobility and non-mobility.

The kindred behavior among the French Canadians is associated with a set of specific attitudes. In the first place, the relatives regard each other as a special group, bound by mutual obligations and duties, rooted in a particular culture system.[12] A large majority of the group, around 75 percent, believe in the principle that "blood is thicker than water." As many as 93.4 percent feel they have an obligation to assist needy relatives. Many French Canadians, from both mobile and non-mobile families, cited the following as kindred benefits: sense of identity and belonging, a sense of security, and a variety of supports including advice, affection, and companionship. The mobile families emphasized particularly the benefits of affection and companionship. Geographical nearness tended to enhance the possibilities of tension and disagreement for non-mobile families, whereas, for mobile families, it had the opposite effect of strengthening the ties. The mobile families usually made short and infre-

---

[11]Helgi Osterreich, "Geographical Mobility and Kinship: A Canadian Example," in *The Canadian Family,* ed. K. Ishwaran (Toronto: Holt, Rinehart and Winston, 1976) pp. 531-44.

[12]J. D. Freedman, "On the Concept of the Kindred," *Journal of the Royal Anthropological Institute* 91 (1961): 192-220.

quent visits, while the non-mobile families generally got involved in more intense and more frequent interaction.

The French-Canadian kinship structure is reinforced by its marital system which encourages a large number of intermarriages.[13] Sister exchange, brothers marrying sisters, cross-cousin marriages, and marriages between distant cousins are some of the forms of this intermarriage. The result is that virtually everyone, barring a handful of new arrivals, is related to everyone else in a close and complicated criss-cross of kinship. The remote relatives, despite absence of personal contact, contribute considerably to sense of community cohesion.

While the nuclear family continues to be crucial to the survival of the community, extended family combinations exist to provide a variety of mutually supportive inputs. In the French-Canadian regions, the increasing dominance of Anglo-American business units may well pose a threat to the continuation of the French-Canadian kinship system. However, urbanization and migration have not significantly deflected the French Canadians from their distinctive kinship pattern. Economic development has not resulted in any appreciable change in the value system or in the patterns of interpersonal behavior.

The French-Canadian community preserves its traditional cultural patterns through its social structure, of which its family and kinship system are the most important components. The members of the community are socialized to consider it a pious duty and a patriotic gesture to uphold the traditional way of life.[14] This pattern has been preserved in the face of industrialization through a process of sociocultural adaptation. The case of the contemporary French-Canadian community exemplifies what Piddington has called "emergent development,"[15] a process of greater differentiation, but not necessarily on the model of Anglo-American society. In particular, the French Canadians have resisted materialistic values and have continued to show a strong commitment to the Church, participating significantly in a variety of Church-sponsored institutions. In this development, the French kinship system has played an important role.

Primarily, the kinship structure provides a network of interlocking relationships which enable French-Canadian families to cope with their problems and situations within a French-Canadian culture and society. This network has equipped them with an institutional infrastructure and value system that have helped them maintain their community identity and solidarity, while at the same time absorbing selectively the influences from the external environment.

---

[13]Horace Miner, *St. Denis* (Chicago: Chicago University, 1939).

[14]L. Gérin, "The French-Canadian Family: Its Strength and Weaknesses," in *French Canadian Society* Vol. 1, ed., Marcel Rioux and Yves Martin (Toronto: McClelland and Stewart, 1964): 32-76; Philippe Garigue, "Change and Continuity in Rural French Canada," ibid., pp. 123-36; Everett H. Hughes, "Industry and the Rural System in Quebec," ibid., pp. 76-85.

[15]Ralph Piddington, "A Study of French-Canadian Kinship," in *The Canadian Family*, op. cit., p. 573.

Family and Kinship Among the Italian Canadians

In Italy, the family is a pivotal institution from which emanate moral authority and community values.[16] An individual's status and honor are dependent on his capacity to perform two basic functions – to successfully promote the economic prosperity of the family and to preserve the chastity of the women in the family. In other words, a person's value is rated in terms of his ability to uphold the moral and material prestige of the family. Any attempt to thwart his efforts invites intrigue, force, and, if need be, direct violence.

Each individual is located at the centre of a web of relatives, stemming from both maternal and paternal sides. It is the norm of this vast kinship network that members aid one another unhesitatingly whenever called upon to do so. But the quantum of such aid, formulated in terms of mutual obligations and duties, is proportionate to geneological closeness among individual members. It is common for obligations to go beyond consanguine relatives, including cousins up to the fourth degree. This is, in fact, the range within which the Church permits marital relations.

For Italians, kinship generates a powerful sense of identity that sharply differentiates the non-kin from the kin world. While those of the kin world are friends with whom one shares mutual obligations, duties, rights, and support, those of the non-kin world are regarded as either enemies or, at the least, as potential enemies. The families and their kinship networks are involved in a competitive process in which families are anxious to achieve success even at the expense of other families. The Italian-Canadian families are tightly-knit structures, involving intense interaction among their members. The kinship structure, however, is the focal point for interaction and exchange between families spatially scattered and socio-economically differentiated.

One of the primary functions of the Italian-Canadian kinship network is the promotion of emigration of kin from Italy. Compared with other immigrant groups, Italians have the highest number of immigrants actively assisted by kin already established in Canada. Such assistance comprises lending money, providing shelter, and offering legal guarantees when necessary. For instance, it has been estimated that most of the immigrants live in the same buildings as their relatives or in buildings within five minute's reach. Thus, the Italian Canadians of Montreal tend to segregate residentially.[17] The kinship structure helps immigrants overcome the shock and isolation of a new environment, facilitating better and faster acculturation. Even the Canadian-born Italians are involved in strong kinship ties. Kin privileges and bonuses include hospitality,

---

[16]For Italian-Canadian family studies *see* Jeremy Boissevain, *The Italians of Montreal Social Adjustment in a Plural Society* (Ottawa: Queen's Printer, 1970); Kurt Danziger, "Attitudes to Parental Control and Adolescents' Aspirations – A Comparison of Immigrants and Non-Immigrants," in *Childhood and Adolescence in Canada,* ed., K. Ishwaran (Toronto: McGraw-Hill Ryerson, 1979) pp. 179-94; Frank Sturino, "Family and Kin Cohesion Among Southern Italian Immigrants in Toronto," in *Canadian Families – Ethnic Variations,* ed., K. Ishwaran (Toronto: McGraw-Hill Ryerson, 1980) pp. 84-104.

[17]Jeremy Boissevan, op. cit.

discounts in business, assistance during illness, and help to the poor and needy.

With residential proximity goes frequency of visits between members of the kinship group. It has been estimated that, during a specified week, 2.59 percent of immigrants had contact with near relatives, and in one day 36 percent has been recorded. Contacts are greater among those born in Canada, of whom 76 percent had contacts with close relatives in one week, and 71 percent in one day. Important visits among the Italian Canadians involve parents, cousins, aunts, uncles, and, to a lesser extent, brothers. Besides formal visits on Saturday or Sunday afternoons, there are informal visits to one's parents. Births and weddings are celebrated occasions. According to Boissevain, there are 2400 births, 550 weddings and 3000 other occasions annually. These occasions reinforce ethnic identity.

The small Italian-Canadian communities are modelled after those in the homeland within a framework where face-to-face relationships are possible. The role of the neighborhoods is very crucial. It functions as a self-perpetuating community of friends and relatives with property stakes. It is significant that the second generation elects to reside in an neighborhood earlier chosen by the parents. Thus, the kinship network has become the primary means of ethnic reinforcement among the Italian Canadians.

Among the Italian immigrants, a distinction is made between the nuclear family – the "famiglia," and the extended family – the "familiari." Personal choice has some role in the interrelationships, rights, and obligations extended to the kin. The kinship group takes a co-operative form, binding its members through rights and obligations. Even the nuclear family is viewed as a co-operative unit, held together by rights and obligations, but the latter are pervasive and implicit rather than explicitly formulated.[18] It is understood that every member has a moral claim in the family with regard to a variety of supports.

The extended kin group works as a co-operative team for common purposes and interests. For instance, the group purchases material in bulk for distribution, such as grapes for wine-making. In such activities, both men and women participate, although the men usually perform the physically hard tasks. Such work teams are part of a wider and more comprehensive kinship network. Apart from gathering together on occasions such as baptisms, confirmations, and marriages, the members are also bound together by exchanges of gifts.

Kinship Among the Greeks

The Greeks, like the Italians, are from a society with an original background, economy, and culture dominated by kinship networks.[19] It has long been the

[18]J. K. Campbell, *Honour, Family and Patronage* (Oxford: Clarendon Press, 1964).

[19]For further studies on the Greek-Canadians *see* Peter D. Chimbos, "The Greek-Canadian Family: Tradition and Change," in *Canadian Families – Ethnic Variations* op. cit., pp. 27-40; Judith A. Nagata, "Adaptation and Integration of Greek Working Class Immigrants in the City of Toronto, Canada: A Situational Approach," *International Migration Review* IV (1969): 44-67; C. A. Price, "Report on the Greek Community in Toronto" (Master's thesis, York University, Toronto, 1958).

custom for relatives to come to one another's aid during family crises such as illness, crop failure, or death. In times of general distress such as the German occupation and the Civil War (1946-1949), kinship ties come into full play. In Canada, the Greek immigrants help each other through the kinship system by providing the moral and material assistance needed to adjust to the socio-cultural environment. For example, those already established aided the new immigrants in the 1950s and 1960s, finding them homes and jobs and thus minimizing their culture shock.

Substantial assistance in business matters is offered by established relatives. When an immigrant needs financial help or a partner to open a restaurant, a relative is the obvious choice. Through successful enterprise, the immigrant is able to improve his economic situation and gain upward social mobility in his new environment.

A significant aspect of the Greek-Canadian kinship system is the support extended to kinfolk in Greece. In addition to clothing, food, and other gifts, they are also given financial assistance to renovate their homes, buy farms, and educate their children. Such assistance was especially important and appreciated in the 1950s, because it helped the Greeks recover from the effects of war and return to their normal economic standard.

Kinship is a cultural value among the Greek Canadians and is socially expressed by relative participation at such events as baptisms or naming ceremonies. On such occasions, feelings of kinship solidarity are exchanged and reinforced. The Greek attachment to the family as a value – to familism – places great emphasis on solidarity, interdependence, and obligations. This has a tendency to invite conflict between kinfolk over family issues and business relationships and often leads to total hostility. The Greeks also believe that consanguine relationships are mutually binding and must be maintained at least symbolically. Kinship obligations survive fierce conflicts to the extent best articulated in a popular Greek saying "the blood never becomes water, and even when it becomes water, it is never muddied."

Religious and spiritual activities play an important role in the Greek family's social network. Baptisms and marriages provide occasion for the spiritual affirmation of family solidarity. Marriage is regarded as an event binding previously unrelated persons into a spiritual relationship.[20] Such a relationship entails moral rights and duties. This spiritual kinship system provides socio-economic support and assistance during times of need. In the early phases of Greek immigration into Canada, spiritual kinsmen already settled here provided extensive sponsoring. Subsequent to their arrival, new immigrants were assisted in finding employment and housing.

In Greece, the culture and social system emphasizes the importance of children. From the time of birth, the child is the centre of solicitude in the family, and his or her needs take precedence over the needs of others.[21] This is no less true of the Greek immigrants in Canada. The earliest interaction of the child is with his parents, grandparents, and other relatives. From the age of six, the child receives considerable physical warmth – hugging, kissing, touching, and playing – from his parents, siblings, and relatives. Such

---

[20]J. K. Campbell, op. cit., p. 222.

[21]J. K. Campbell, op. cit., p. 154.

gestures of physical closeness continue even into adult life. It is common for relatives of the same sex to greet each other by hugging, kissing, and shedding tears of affection.

The Polish Family and the Kinship System

As many as 80 percent of Polish Canadians live in urban areas. Once settled, the immigrant families began to replicate their original home and kinship networks, in the new country.[22] Prior to 1956, kinship ties were preserved through correspondence. In the years following the two world wars, kinship ties were maintained through substantial gifts of food, clothing, and money to relatives in Poland. Trading companies were established to handle the shipment of goods to Poland. Such help still continues, though on a reduced scale. Since 1956, kinship ties with the homeland have been strengthened by frequent visits to Poland by economically successful Polish Canadians.

In Canada, the Polish kinship structure is three generations deep. This means that as long as the patriarch or matriarch is alive, family reunions are normally attended by the children and grandchildren. In particular, two traditional and religious events are regarded as most important – the Christmas eve supper, *Wigilia*, and the Easter Sunday celebration. In the Polish-Canadian community in Toronto, in a particular year, as many as 93.2 percent of the members celebrated these days, and in the company of some extended kin. Such occasions strengthen kinship bonds and obligations through the exchange of gifts and joint observance of traditional Polish rituals and customs. In addition, the extended kinship network encourages displays of affection, counselling, and provides companionship and material assistance.

The situation, however, has been changing in recent years. For example, the traditional obligation of caring for the elderly is being accepted less and less. By 1972, a number of Polish senior citizens' homes had opened in Vancouver, Edmonton, Winnipeg, and Toronto. This development may be attributed to several causes. The first is the rise in the number of working wives, which limits the amount of time and attention available for the elderly. The second is the shrinking of living space in urban homes. The third is the inevitable appearance of inter-generation friction and tension. The fourth is the fact that the institutions offer them better living conditions.

During the early phases of Polish immigration to Canada, a normal household comprised two generations of members, modelled after the households in Poland where parents lived with their married children. When new babies came, these became three-generation units. The recent changes may either restore the two-generation household pattern or may popularize the nuclear family norm. In conformity with the prevalent urban Canadian pattern, the

---

[22]For further studies on the Polish-Canadian family *see* Henry Radecki, *Ethnic Organizational Dynamics* (Waterloo: Wilfrid Laurier University Press, 1976); Henry Radecki, "Polish-Canadian, Canadian-Polish or Canadian?," mimeographed (Toronto: York University, 1970); Henry Radecki and Benedykt Heyden Korn, *A Member of a Distinguished Family* The Polish Group in Canada (Toronto: McClelland and Stewart, 1976).

new Polish-Canadian generations are oriented to neo-local residence, with the old folk often preferring either a new household or an institution.

Thus, among the Polish Canadians, there are signs that, while the kinship network continues to operate, the structure of the family itself is undergoing some change in the direction of a nuclear, conjugal family.

Extended Family in an Inter-Ethnic Urban European Working-Class Population

While the existence of the extended family for the French Canadians has been extensively documented, and for the several other ethnic groups also noted, its prevalence in other demographic contexts has not been adequately studied. Therefore, the study of a particular urban working-class area with a mixture of ethnic groups – Italians, British, Hungarian, and Polish – gains significance. Hamilton, Ontario, provides this example.[23]

In terms of geographical propinquity, about a third of the respondents had relatives in the immediate neighborhood, while 85 percent had relatives living outside the immediate vicinity but in the Hamilton area. The contacts between relatives was fairly high. Some 68 percent had weekly contact with at least one relative. The immigrant groups in the area helped and encouraged their kin back home to join them. Frequent visits were reported between relatives living in the immediate neighborhood and elsewhere in the Hamilton area. This conforms with the extended family pattern found elsewhere in Canada, the United States, and Great Britain.

The extended family identified is patrifocal in structure; this means that visits will be more frequent with the husband's parents than with the wife's. The extended family has to be seen in the context of social mobility arising from the individuals' search for better economic and occupational prospects. The cities where such opportunities arise are centres of industrial and bureaucratic systems, based on the recruitment of qualified, technically competent, and achievement-oriented persons. Although these cities provide a setting for changes in the family and kinship structure, such changes have not significantly weakened the kinship network and its function for the urban nuclear family. In fact, the family system has taken the form of the modified-extended type in order to accommodate structurally and functionally a balance between the traditional and the more modern, nuclear-conjugal family form. In the process of the evolution of the latter, the kinship network has played a crucial role.

The Japanese Kinship Structure and the Family

The traditional Japanese family was patrilineal and patrilocal, and organized essentially as a collectivistic institution in which the overall goals and interests of the family took precedence over the needs and aspirations of its individual members. The lineal family comprised relatives belonging to the descent line

---

[23]Peter C. Pineo, "The Extended Family in a Working-Class Area of Hamilton," in *The Canadian Family* op. cit., pp. 545-54.

and, in principle, no limit was set to their number. The family functioned on the basis of well-defined patterns of residence and succession. The membership consisted of the members of a nuclear family – grandparents and/or the parents of the husband or the wife. Usually the eldest son stayed on after marriage. The authority system within the family was patriarchal, with the women assigned a subordinate status. A woman's subordination, to the father prior to her marriage, to the husband after the marriage, and later to her sons, was emphasized as a central value and norm of the family system. A pronounced role-differentiation based on sex existed within the family – the man making all the crucial decisions of an economic or managerial nature, and the woman performing the domestic tasks. The cultural system placed the highest premium on male offspring and, in fact, the goal of the family and marriage was defined in terms of male procreation. The patriarchal authority extended not only over the women but also over the children. Parents generally did not allow initiative and independence for the children. The family was a system of hierarchically arranged rights and duties. Roles and statuses within the family were very clearly defined and closely followed. This family type formed part of the sociocultural baggage of the Japanese immigrant in Canada.

While the conditions of industrial and urban Canada, especially social and occupational mobility, have encouraged the substitution for the traditional patriarchal and patrilineal family of the nuclear type, the former process is not attributable entirely to the Canadian environment. Part of the reason stems from the very process of immigration itself which disrupts the traditional family structure. In fact, historically the extended kinship system had already weakened in Japan itself at the time of immigration; hence, the immigrants did not bring with them any tradition of an extended kinship structure.

There are no systematic studies of the Japanese-Canadian kinship structure and network. In the absence of relevant data, it is only possible to surmise and speculate in terms of the implications, impressionistically perceived rather than systematically investigated, of the working of the Japanese-Canadian family. It is likely that the Japanese kinship structure in Canada has moved in the direction of the model prevalent among the other ethnic groups, especially those coming from homelands dominated by traditional family and kinship forms. This would mean that the Japanese kinship would extend a variety of supportive inputs such as psychological security and material success into the urban Japanese-Canadian family.[24]

The Kinship Network and the Canadian Family: An Overview

Some broad generalizations can now be made regarding the interdependence of the kinship structure and the family in Canada. The first significant point is

[24]For further details on the Japanese-Canadian family see the following by Minako Kurokawa Maykovich, "The Japanese Family in Tradition and Change," in *The Canadian Family* op. cit., pp. 162-81; "Japanese and Mennonite Childhood and Socialization," in *Childhood and Adolescence in Canada*, op. cit., pp. 195-207; "Acculturation versus Familism in Three Generations of Japanese-Canadians," in *Canadian Families: Ethnic Variations*, op. cit., pp. 65-83.

that the extended kinship family has not become dysfunctional to the emerging nuclear and conjugal family in the context of industrialization, urbanizations, and modernization. Contrary to the assumptions of the Chicago School and more in tune with the findings of Sussman and Litwak, the Canadian family, for all the ethnic groups examined, has not disintegrated but simply undergone structural modification. Secondly, it has taken the form of a loose congeries of nuclear families held together by frequent contact and communication, despite spatial diffusion. Thirdly, it performs crucial functions for the survival and progress of the families. Such functions include emotional security through reinforced kinship solidarity and identity, assistance during crisis situations, and material and economic support needed for the social mobility of the member families. Lastly, while these generalizations hold broadly, there abound differences of detail and emphasis only with regard to these aspects as between the different ethnic groups.

Ethnicity, Urbanization, and Family

The ethnic diversity of the Canadian population is evident in the census figures for any period. For instance, the census data for 1951 illustrate the extent and nature of this diversity. While, on the one hand, these figures show that there are as many as sixteen ethnic categories in Canada, on the other hand they underscore the fact that of these, two occupy a dominant position. About 43.8 percent of the population is of British origin (i.e., English, Irish, Scottish, and other) and some 30.4 percent are French. The other groups together represent the remaining percentage. Though questions have been raised about the accuracy of these figures, they are, nonetheless, characteristic of Canadian ethnic demography. Numerical size should not be confused with sociological significance in terms of social structures and identities involved.

On the basis that a population of 1000 or more in an unincorporated territory and 5000 or more incorporated settlements is qualified as urban, the demographic trend in Canada since 1871 has been one of decline in the rural population, with large-scale migration to the urban centres, presumably in search of greater opportunities. The census data also reveal that the overwhelmingly dominant family form in urban Canada is the nuclear, conjugal family, accounting for over 90 percent of households, though sociologically this figure may conceal the micro-changes taking place within the urban family system.

Thus, demographically, there is a correlation between urbanization/industrialization, ethnic diversity, and the nuclear family. But the statistical picture misses the sociological nuances of ethnic differentiation and interfamily linkage structures. Moreover, even the very processes of industrialization and urbanization are differentially distributed within Canada. Therefore, in assessing the role of ethnicity in the family structure, it is important to remember that this role may be significant to different degrees in different ethnic groups. Ethnicity depends not only on the specificity of the ethnic group involved, but also on location and rural-urban distinction. The cumulative impact of ethnicity and industrialization on the family structure and functions in Canada is to produce two forces acting in different directions – one toward uniformity and the other toward diversity.

Ethnicity has a dual and contradictory role in the process of industrialization, but this role is mediated through the family. The Canadian ethnic family tends to strengthen its ethnic identity through its socialization process. The ethnic family has become generally the guardian and the chief promoter of ethnic values, behavioral patterns, institutional arrangements, and identity. On the other hand, ethnicity has also served as a major resource in enabling ethnic families to make psychocultural adjustments to the Canadian environment and to enjoy social mobility in the new competitive society. Therefore, ethnicity performs the paradoxical role of being simultaneously a promoter of change and a preserver of tradition. This duality and ambiguity make it difficult to generalize about the interaction between ethnicity and the family system in Canada.

In addition, the specific nature of its role varies among ethnic groups, from a more conservative role to a relatively dynamic one. At one end is the Jewish case where ethnicity reinforces family solidarity and is reinforced by the family processes. At the other end is the Scandinavian case in which ethnicity plays a relatively change-oriented role, pushing the family structure and functions in the direction of the Canadian mainstream model of the modified-extended family type. But these are not exclusive positions, and most ethnic groups are able to balance the push and pull forces of progress and conservatism, although in different proportions.

The conservative role of ethnicity lies in its emphasis on the traditional life style, value system, and institutional pattern, but this role cannot be performed without the mediation of the family, which socializes the individuals into the ethnic way of life. The family's dynamic role consists in its being converted into a psychosocial and material resource, which enables its members to face with assurance the demands and challenges of a modern, industrial society. For instance, ethnicity enables the individual to absorb the cultural shock through ethnic identity and to gain material support from the ethnic community in the struggle for upward mobility. As in the case of its conservative role, it is the family in its dynamic aspect that mediates institutionally to convert ethnicity into a resource for modernization. Conceptually, it is through a process of "ethnicizing" the family that ethnicity becomes an operative social force.

But ethnicity is reinforced not only at the level of the individual family. It becomes strengthened at the inter-family level through the kinship structure. Ethnicity, thus, becomes an overarching structure uniting the family and kinship networks into a higher ethnic identity. The Canadian modified-extended family and the new kinship structure based on a loose unity of nuclear families combine to perform the dual function of preserving the ethnic tradition and of generating adaptability to the industrial society.

The Nuclear Family and the Kinship Network

A systematic examination of the available data about the structure and functioning of the Canadian family shows that, in general, the nuclear family is the dominant type in the urban areas. But the urban Canadian nuclear family does not conform to the model celebrated in the Chicago School tradition as an isolated unit, bereft of any kinship support, arising in response to the demands of the emerging modern, urban, industrial society. Evidence indicates that the Canadian nuclear family is not so isolated and that it depends functionally on a kinship network. Conceptually, this means that the term, nuclear family, may be slightly misleading, insofar as the urban Canadian family is enmeshed with a kinship structure. Therefore, it has been suggested that this new type of family may be designated as the modified-extended family or the modified-nuclear family. It is more appropriate to use the former term since the kinship network is involved functionally in family activities. The kinship network, in this new context and as distinct from the traditional kinship structure, requires a redefinition. It is a looser structure comprised of an aggregate number of nuclear families united on the basis of consanguine and affinal relationship.

The kinship structure and the nuclear family are functionally interdependent. While the kinship structure itself is sustained by the nuclear families, the nuclear families depend on it for a variety of services and benefits, based on system of mutual rights and obligations and an exchange of material inputs. The services rendered by the kinship network are various, differing from one ethnic group to another. In general, they comprise assistance in the very process of emigration and post-immigration settlement including help during times of crisis, financial and other material support, and perhaps most important, the emotional empathy of kinship identity. Given the geographical scattering of families and the degree of social mobility, the Canadian kinship network has evolved its own pattern of inter-family communication. It ranges from close and immediate interpersonal communication to remote connections through correspondence. Just as the specific services rendered by the kinship group differ among ethnic communities, so the specific nature of the communication channels employed for maintaining the kinship network differs from one group to another, and from one family to another. Such differentiation in the communication mode is determined by geographical propinquity.

If one cuts across the variations in the kinship functions and communications channels, what emerges is a functional interdependence between the nuclear family and the extended kinship structure.

Summing Up

The forms and functions of the urban Canadian family are related, on the one hand, to wider historical forces such as industrialization and urbanization and, on the other, to more specific factors such as ethnicity.

The process of industrialization and urbanization in Canada since the mid-nineteenth century has brought about a highly industrialized and urbanized social system committed to materialistic and individualistic values. These forces have guided the Canadian family toward a nuclear form – a model characterized by relatively greater equality between the roles of husband and wife, a more liberal child-rearing culture, and serious involvement in the process of social mobility. Paradoxically, the complexity and the pressures of an industrial society have also produced opposite consequences, requiring some modification in the nuclear and conjugal family. In fact, it would be no exaggeration to suggest that industrialization, urbanization, and modernization have caused the emergence of the nuclear family and, at the same time, have evolved a family form inadequately equipped to cope with the demands and tensions of modern society. As a result, the Canadian urban family has found it necessary to develop its own distinctive kinship structure to support the nuclear family. Therefore, while the Chicago School rightly saw that the modernizing processes of industrialization and urbanization would weaken the traditional extended family with its supportive kinship network, they failed to see that the nuclear family itself would become modified in response to the very conditions which called it into existence. The result has been the emergence of the modified-extended family and the supportive kinship structure, with variations due to such factors as ethnicity.

Being multiethnic, the Canadian social system has naturally responded to the factor of ethnicity. In particular, one of the basic institutional components of that system, the family, has been influenced by ethnicity in a significant manner. But the nature of that influence has been complex and ambivalent. While ethnicity has reinforced family solidarity and the kinship network thus generating an institutional ethos in opposition to the prevailing mainstream Canadian value system, it has also served and continues to serve the family in the process of sociocultural adaptation and economic competition. Thus, the Canadian family has successfully harnessed ethnicity as a resource in its efforts to survive and prosper. However, as ethnic groups become more firmly rooted and historically better consolidated in the new environment, ethnicity may weaken, with the result that the variations within the urban family forms and functions may become gradually reduced, if not eliminated. On the other hand, ethnicity might prove to be more resilient and adaptable to the changing situation.

The Canadian family has demonstrated its capacity for dynamic adjustment and functional adaptability. It has responded adequately to the challenges of modern urban, industrial society. Besides performing the transhistorical and primary functions of the family such as procreation, socialization, and social control, it has attended to the special needs and demands of a modern society. It has provided its members with such resources as psychological security, material satisfaction and moral-cultural identity. Above all, it has balanced the contradictory processes of conservation and change, and enabled Canadian society and its members to absorb the dynamic impact of modernization without disruption or destabilization. The urban family, more than the rural, has played the crucial role of harmonizing the pull and push goals of stability and continuity. In this task, it has been well strengthened and supported by ethnicity and the kinship network.

SOCIALIZATION: FAMILY AND SOCIETY

Introduction

The articles in this section examine three specific contexts of socialization, and the role of the family in those contexts, that have become particularly crucial in Western societies, including the Canadian society: sex-role socialization, occupational socialization and political socialization. The three authors use somewhat different approaches, but collectively they document their argument in a fashion that draws attention to the intricacies of the processes of socialization which, among other social groupings and processes, involve the family.

Stephen Richer focusses specifically on a set of issues related to sex role socialization – that is, the processes of training through which biological males and females become males and females in a cultural sense. Utilizing the results of his own studies and those of other scholars in Canada and the United States, Richer conceptualizes and uses a model comprising the concepts of agent, content, relationship, and outcome. Among the agents, he discusses the roles of the family, the school, the peer group, and the media. His general conclusion is that "despite the activities of feminists, as well as the increasing numbers of women in the labor force, ... children continue to receive quite traditional conceptions of sex role attitudes and behaviors." Richer also indicates several aspects of the processes of sex role socialization that require serious investigation.

Eunice Baxter's article discusses the question of influence of the family on occupation in the Canadian context. Three aspects of occupation are considered – perceptions of occupation, occupational expectations, and occupational attainments or mobility. Baxter's contention is that the family influences these three aspects of the occupational context in different ways, and perceptions of occupations seem to be the least influenced by the family.

By perceptions of occupation Baxter means perception of prestige attached to various occupations. She argues that the prestige hierarchy of occupations is "largely a product of the economic system of a particular society (or, perhaps, a system of societies)," and the family by itself is a weak but persistently relevant factor.

When, according to Baxter, we focus on the context of occupational expectations, the family has an important role up to the high school level. Up to this level, however, the role of educational institutions, perhaps, is more important than the role of the family. Baxter argues that beyond the high school level, the role of the family becomes increasingly important.

So far as the influence of the family on occupational achievement for the society as a whole is concerned, it is impossible at the present stage of knowledge to reach any firm conclusions, but she believes that further studies would show that the family does play an important role in this context not only among the lower classes but also among the middle classes.

In general, Baxter's article argues for the idea that education and various aspects of the economy, independently and in conjunction with the family, must be explored to deepen our understanding of continuity and change of occupational status in Canada.

Ronald Landes' article in this section deals with the interesting and important theme of political socialization of the Canadian youth. Political attitudes and behavior, like all human attitudes and behavior, are learned, that is, they are acquired through socialization. Attempts to understand adult political attitudes and behaviors have led thus to the sources of early socialization processes in which the family, in general, plays an important part. Landes summarizes the results of the relevant studies, indicating major gaps in our knowledge and the rudimentary state of available research.

Systematic study, argues Landes, will require that we address ourselves to the questions: When does political learning develop? How does political learning take place? Where do children obtain their political beliefs? What is the focus in the content of political learning among children? Landes attempts to answer these questions tentatively by discussing the differing, and reinforcing roles of the family, the school, the mass media, and so on.

One of the major substantive conclusions of Landes' study is that the processes of political socialization in Canada are far from systematic and their contents tend to promote indifferent understanding of the Canadian political system in action. Another major conclusion is that political socialization in Canada, such as it is, tends to generate regional loyalties. We also learn that, on the whole, political socialization in Canada is basically a conservative process with political values, attitudes and behaviors being transmitted from parent to child.

Thus, the three articles clarify some of the significant aspects of the processes of socialization in the Canadian society, while exploring the varying degrees of relevance of the family to those aspects.

Sex Role Socialization: Agents, Content, Relationships, and Outcomes[1]

Stephen Richer

This discussion of sex role socialization will focus on those concepts that capture the salient elements in the socialization dynamic – agents, content, relationships, and outcomes. The behavior and attitudes that are expected of the individual by virtue of his or her gender constitute a *sex role*. Sex role socialization, then, is the process whereby these behaviors and attitudes are acquired and/or reinforced.[2]

The socialization process involves the presentation by various *agents* of a set of expected behaviors and attitudes, the *content,* to an individual or individuals.[3] The link between agent and child constitutes the socialization *relationship,* the results of which are referred to as the *outcome.* This notion of outcome, however, is not to imply that there is a discernible point when the socialization process is complete. To varying degrees, daily interaction with others, as well as exposure to the mass media and other potential agents provide a continuity of socialization relationships. Although perhaps not as explicit as the childhood process, socialization occurs throughout our lives as attitudes and behaviors are reinforced or even changed as the structural features of our society undergo change.

Socialization Outcomes: Attitudes and Behavior

Socialization outcomes can be classified into three categories – attitudes regarding appropriate behavior for the sexes in general, attitudes regarding one's self, and actual behavioral outcomes. Firstly, there is a fair amount of research in both the United States and Canada supporting the notion that children have different social expectations for males and females. Lambert's

---

[1]This article, which includes both Canadian and American data, is primarily based on observational and projective research conducted by the author on young Canadian children in a school setting.

[2]As noted in Richer (1979) the term, reinforced, has been added to accommodate those arguments that maintain that various aspects of gender roles are genetically based (see Mazur and Robertson 1972; Bardwick 1971; Money and Ehrhardt 1972).

[3]This paper is concerned exclusively with children as learners.

1969 survey of 7500 Canadian children, for example, found that children were clearly cognizant of traditonal societal expectations for the sexes. They readily assigned "appropriate" behavior, tasks, and authority relations to males and females. Similarly, Schlossbert and Goodman (1972) indicate that five-year-old boys and girls show a strong tendency to choose occupations reflecting traditional male and female work.

Not only do children hold different attitudes regarding appropriate behavior, they have also learned that male activities are more highly valued than female activities. Indeed, studies by Brown (1957), Goldberg (1968), and Markle (1974) substantiate the lower rank attributed to female activity by both children and adults. The Richer (1979) study of Ottawa kindergarten children lends additional support to this conclusion. A recurring negation of girls by boys was manifested in the phenomenon of "girl germs." Among the children observed, a boy coming into physical contact with a girl was the occasion for the enactment of an activity which can be described, with some apology to ethnographers, as a purification ritual. The only way to ward off girl germs was for the victim to cross his fingers as soon as possible, preferably while still in contact with the girl. The fact that the expression "boy germs" was never used and that, in general, the girls made no effort to challenge the girl germs label is indicative of the very early acceptance by both sexes of a hierarchical division between males and females.

Given these findings, it would not be surprising to learn that boys had more positive self-conceptions than girls. In fact, studies show that this area is somewhat more complex. Maccoby and Jacklin (1974, 1977), in their exhaustive review of the research on sex differences, conclude that boys and girls are similar in overall self-satisfaction and self-confidence throughout childhood and adolescence. There are two qualifications to this statement, however. They suggest that, while overall self-image is similar, boys and girls do differ in *areas* of perceived confidence. Boys see themselves as stronger and more dominant than girls do, while girls see themselves as more socially competent than boys do. A second qualification concerns the rather tenuous base for their childhood conclusions. They indicate that American research on self-image in childhood is meager; generalizations with regard to childhood self-image are thus to be made tentatively, if at all.

Richer's (1980) study on self-image and behavioral images among school children was conducted in one Ottawa school and included children from kindergarten to grade six. Children in regular classroom art periods were asked to draw a picture of themselves engaged in their favorite sport or game, and to circle themselves once the picture was completed. Various measures were extracted from these drawings, including: size and prominence of the circled figure (which was argued are indicators of self-image)*; type of activity depicted (whether competitive team, co-operative team, competitive inter-individual, co-operative inter-individual, or single person activity); sex composition of picture; and whether the setting show was indoors or outdoors. The major findings of the research were: (1) boys were just as likely as girls to

---

*For a discussion of the validity issue, see Richer 1980.

draw themselves as the largest figure and were slightly more likely to draw themselves as the most prominent; (2) boys were more likely to depict competitive team activities, whereas girls drew inter-individual or solitary activities; (3) boys were more likely to draw outdoor settings, while girls depicted indoor ones; and (4) both boys and girls, with virtually no exceptions, depicted same-sex activities, i.e., boys drew only boys and girls drew only girls.

The first finding is consistent with Maccoby's and Jacklin's conclusion that boys and girls are generally similar in self-image, while our large behavioral image differences are very consistent with work done previously in the United States on behavior differences between the sexes. (See Maccoby and Jacklin 1974; Schwartzman 1978)

It should be noted that there are three commonly believed omissions in the above consideration of sex differences, namely, that girls are more compliant than boys, that girls are more dependent than boys, and that girls are more passive than boys. Maccoby and Jacklin argue convincingly that the sexes are equally dependent on others during childhood, while the data on compliance and passivity are inconsistent; for the moment these issues must be classified as unresolved. In Canada, more research is needed on outcomes of socialization, particularly behavioral outcomes. This necessitates detailed observational studies of children in natural settings with a view toward establishing the extent of consistent differences.

Research is also needed on the extent of variation in both behavioral and attitudinal outcomes of socialization in Canada by such variables as social class, ethnicity, and family structure. For example, some scattered support exists in the United States for the notion that working-class children have more traditional conceptions of sex roles than middle-class children (Gaskell 1975; Mussen 1969), yet there is virtually no Canadian research on this phenomenon. Further, while there is some support for the idea that French-Canadian children manifest more traditional sex role attitudes than English-Canadian children (Hobart 1973), we have yet to examine in any depth variation in sex role socialization by linguistic/ethnic origin.

Family structure variables are variations in internal family organization and composition which could affect socialization outcomes. Factors such as the presence of only one parent, the sex and age composition of siblings, the presence of extended family members in the same household, and parental employment patterns are undoubtedly relevant to the development of sex role related attitudes and behaviors. We are beginning to understand the role of some of these, but again much work has yet to be done.

Perhaps the most work on family structure has been carried out on the consequences of maternal employment. In general, it appears that the children of mothers in the labor force have more flexible definitions of appropriate male and female behaviors than do children of non-working mothers. For example, Propper (1972) found that sons of employed mothers were more likely to be involved in traditionally female activities such as dancing, art, and music. Similar results were obtained by Gold (1976). Because of the very small number of studies in this area, however, these must be regarded as rather tentative conclusions.

Agents of Socialization – Family, School, Peers, and Media

Concern with the issues addressed in the previous section lead to an explicit concern with agents of socialization. The attitudinal and behavioral outcomes discussed raise the question of their source. How do children come to view their world and to act in the ways described?

As authors of introductory textbooks in sociology are fond of pointing out, the family remains the major agent of socialization. Regarding socialization into sex roles, it is clear that parents are in the most strategic position to transmit their views of appropriate sex role behavior to their children. The content of this socialization in Canada appears typically to reflect traditional definitions of sex roles. A study by Mackie (1971) in Alberta asked adults to describe women in general. The most common description reflected the perceived importance of the expressive role of women; they were categorized as warm, nurturant, emotional, and concerned with family responsibilities. These definitions of sex-related attributes are perhaps most clearly manifested in the kinds of toys parents purchase for their children. Several researchers (Chafetz 1974; Cook 1976; Ambert 1976) have documented the prevalence for girls of toys that reflect their potential positions as mothers and wives, while boys are given toys that reflect their anticipated entry into the outside work force.

Not only does there appear to be widespread agreement among parents as to appropriate sex role differences, but there also seems to be a consensus about the greater value attached to males and male activities. This supports the attitude of the children indicated earlier. Among parents, the most forcible indicator derives from the set of studies on sex preference of children. Markle's (1974) study, for example, showed that couples were significantly more likely prefer a boy over a girl as their first child. Further, when more than two children were anticipated, the desire was for a majority of boys rather than girls.

This discussion implies that most children in North America will be exposed to parents who espouse different and relatively traditional expectations for boys and girls. However, as indicated earlier, these conclusions must be regarded somewhat cautiously. Females with working mothers would appear to provide a more egalitarian conception of sex roles. Further, scattered studies indicate that as parents' educational and occupational status increases, so does their tendency to deviate from traditional sex role definitions. (Lambert 1969; Gaskell 1975)

There is little doubt, however, that the family is the prime inculcator of sex role attitudes and behaviors. This was quite evident in a study examining the school's role in sex role socialization. (Richer 1979) In this work, four-year-old children were observed from the first days of school in an effort to gage the extent to which they were exposed to sex role related curricula and teaching. Although there was evidence of sex role influence, the far more striking findings concerned the strength of their preschool sex role exposure. By the age of four, children are already displaying well-entrenched sex role behaviors and attitudes. Observations as early as the first week of school showed that boys and girls had developed very strong sexually segregated play patterns; boys were significantly more aggressive than girls, and a clear distinction between the sexes was evident in type of play. Boys tended to play with trucks, cars, and building blocks, while the girls favored the doll's house, playing at "mommy cooking," "mommy shopping," or "mommy taking care of baby." Similar findings appear in the works of Selcer (1972), Fagot and Patterson (1969), and Ward (1969).

A major conclusion of this study was that the school's role in sex role socialization is best seen as a reinforcer of *existing* sex role related differ-ences,[4] rather than contributing to *fundamental* sex role development. This reinforcement occurs through school personnel and textbooks. Although there is very little research explicitly aimed at examining sex role related attitudes of teachers and school counsellors, there is some research on their *behavior* from which one might infer attitude sets. For example, both Lambert (1969) and Pietrofesa and Schlossberg (1972) present evident that counsellors tend to treat boys and girls differently in offering educational and occupational guidance. Advice for boys tends to direct them toward long-term careers of a generally high status level; girls, on the other hand, tend to be presented with a much narrower range of occupations, or directed to the homemaker role. There is an accumulation of research indicating that in the classroom, teach-ers interact with boys and girls in ways that reinforce traditonal sex differ-ences, stressing traditional masculine and feminine behaviors.[5] (Serbin et al. 1973; Pellegreno and Williams 1973; Serbin and O'Learly 1975)

School textbooks have been charged with transmitting sex role images. The depiction, in readers, math, and other texts, of boys engaged in outdoor activities involving exploration and adventure, while girls are presented in more passive, supportive, and domestic roles has been well documented. (Lipman-Blumen and Tickamyer 1975; Royal Commission on the Status of Women 1970) An extensive study by Pyke (1975) shows that such stereotyping extends as well to preschool books. (see also Weitzman et al. 1972) In a survey of Canadian books for very young children, Pyke found that (1) males were much more likely than females to be portrayed as central characters; (2) male figures were depicted in a greater variety of occupations; (3) more males than females were shown in occupational contexts; and (4) certain occupa-tions were restricted by sex (e.g., male doctors and deliverers, female nurses and dental assistants).

One of the lacunae in this literature, however, is the lack of data on how, if at all, these books actually teach sex roles. The assumption underlying re-search such as Pyke's is that through these books, children receive the mes-sage that girls are one thing and boys another and that the texts therefore play important roles in developing sex role attitudes and behaviors. Unfortunately,

---

[4]These existing differences may be partially due to the influence of people other than family members. For example, given the increasing time they spend with children, baby-sitters are likely to prove very important. The nature and extent of their influence, however, is so far undetermined.

[5]This tendency will be discussed further under Behavioral Theory.

this assumption has not been directly tested. The questions of what the child actually absorbs from these books, and whether the sex typing which appears so obvious to content analysers is also clear to children remain unanswered.[6]

The same unwarranted assumption is frequently made in the literature on the mass media's role in socialization. One can find evidence of sex stereotyping on television, such as Sternglanz and Serbin's (1974) study of children's programs in the United States. Their research indicates not only greater aggressiveness depicted by male characters and greater passivity by female characters, but a much higher number of male characters. Similar results obtained from content analyses of newspapers, a salient example being Brabant's (1976) examination of the Sunday comic page. Again, however, it is not known how much, if any, of this material is actually absorbed by children. Further research focussing on the relationship between child and the media agent, whether television or textbook, is necessary.

Another agent of socialization is the child's peer group; unfortunately, very little research has been conducted in this area. Yet, the importance of peers, in general, on one's self-image, attitudes, and behaviors is undeniable, as witnessed by Coleman's classic study (1961) of adolescent peer groups and the countless studies in the social psychology literature on peer pressure and conformity (e.g., Asch 1952; Sherif 1935). More attention needs to be paid to such groups. The fact that boys and girls play largely in groups isolating one sex from another may perpetuate stereotypical thinking regarding the other sex. As Mackie (1979) has said, such segregation "permits continued fictions about the opposite sex to survive untested."

One example is the belief in male superiority. A recurring theme in the relationship between the sexes among kindergarten children was the "girl germ" phenomenon mentioned earlier (Richer 1979), in which physical contact with girls was akin to contamination. The purification finger-crossing ritual, together with the absence of "boy germs," evoke a caste hierarchy with the little girls as untouchables.

The strength of this feeling and the power of the peer group to influence behavior was evident in the game "Farmer in the Dell," played by the kindergarten children. Despite the fact that the farmer had to choose a "wife" and the child a "nurse," the vast majority of choices were same-sexed. On several occasions, however, there were insufficient boys in the class to allow the last boy chosen to select yet another male. In these instances, the boys squirmed in embarrassment, one refusing to continue the game, as they were forced to welcome a girl into the circle amid the taunts and hoots of their fellows. On the other hand, girls were not nearly as upset over having to select a boy.

Apart from their role in maintaining same-sex identities and reinforcing the hierarchical aspect of male-female relationships, peers undoubtedly learn other sex role related information from one another. Mackie (1979) speculates, for example, that boys' greater involvement in organized sports teaches them to accept criticism of their performance, thereby better preparing them

---

[6]There is also, of course, the prior issue of the distribution of such texts. Which children in our society are more or less likely to have access to various texts is a question which remains largely unexplored.

to benefit from criticism as adults. Further, because of the nature of girls' versus boys' games, attitudes toward competition, group versus individual play, the value of aggression, and general definitions of appropriate play for boys and girls might be inculcated largely through peers. Much work remains, however, before conclusions can be grounded.

In addition to more research on agents other than the family, research which systematically explores the connection between type of agent and type of outcome is also required. As intimated earlier, certain agents may be more responsible than others for producing particular outcomes. Indeed, some agents may be "specialists" in inculcating various aspects of sex role awareness. It has already been suggested that peers may reinforce the hierarchical dimension of male-female relationships more than other agents. It is also possible that the mass media, mainly through depictions of males and females in advertisements, reinforce the image of women as passive and domestic, and of males as relatively independent and engaged outside the home. More research in such areas would provide a more complete theory of sex role socialization, as well as suggestions for particular policy changes regarding stereotypical practices of various agents.

Finally, it may be quite possible, as suggested, that the type of agent important in sex role socialization varies with the structural features of the child's family. For example, are peers and media more important agents for children in some families and not in others? The general question of the conditions under which particular agents are primary or secondary sources of sex role attitudes and behaviors is an important one and demands research attention.

The Socialization Relationship

The dynamic of the agent-child relationship seems to be the most nebulous aspect of the socialization process. The assumption made by various researchers that documented sex stereotyping in the media is sufficient to conclude a socialization effect is unwarranted without additional research to establish both the existence and nature of a learning connection. Similarly, showing that parents and children hold similar sex role attitudes and/or behaviors does not in itself establish a socialization connection, nor does it throw any light on the nature of the learning process which may be involved.

A systematic explication of this process might explore the relevance of three major learning theories for the study of sex role learning. The three theories – behavioral, cognitive developmental, and modelling – are complementary rather than competing models.[7] All three point to salient learning processes which may occur virtually simultaneously in any given agent-child interaction.

Behavioral Theory

The basic premise of behaviorism is that learning occurs largely through the systematic encouragement and discouragement of particular behaviors via

---

[7]The summaries of each theory are drawn from Richer (1979).

the manipulation of rewards and punishments. Regarding sex role learning, the argument is that various people in the child's life positively reinforce boys for "masculine" behavior and girls for "feminine" behavior, while cross-sex behavior is either punished or discouraged.

Evidence of such a dynamic in a parent-child interaction was found in a home observational study by Margolin and Patterson (1975). In examining parents' reactions to their children's conforming and deviant behaviors, the authors found that boys, in general, received significantly more positive responses from their fathers than did girls, while there was no difference in the positive reactions given by mothers to each sex.

The Kindergarten study (Richer 1979) focussed directly on teacher-child and peer-child interaction. In the former case, there were two recurring instances which supported the notion of reward and punishment of sex role related behavior. Firstly, teachers were more tolerant of aggressive behavior from males than from females; they were significantly more likely to punish girls for kicking, hitting, and pushing than they were to punish boys for the same behavior. Secondly, teachers called on boys rather than girls for help in physical-type tasks, such as moving chairs and athletic equipment. The teacher's expectation was the traditional one – that certain kinds of behavior were more appropriate for one sex than the other – and this expectation was directly transmitted into classroom activity.

Sex segregation appears to be the area of the sex role learning influenced most by peer interaction. As noted earlier, individual departures from this pattern were quickly sanctioned by the boys who were clearly more concerned about cross-sex mixing than were the girls. Such behavior undoubtedly reinforces same-sex identity and discourages cross-sex behavior.

Cognitive Developmental Theory

A major premise underlying this perspective is that learning is essentially a process of conceptual growth, consisting of the ordering of external reality into a classification scheme developed as the individual learns to attribute constancy of characteristics to various environmental elements. With regard to gender, the child learns that boys and girls belong in different categories and that this is an invariant phenomenon, an instance of what Piaget (1947) terms "the conservation of the identity of physical objects." Here, the question is to what extent do parents, teachers, peers, and the media provide clues to the child which would enable him or her to "properly" classify the two sexes. It is suggested that any regularly occurring situation in which boys and girls are (i) treated differently in interaction, (ii) spatially separated from one another, or (iii) verbally or physically reacted to as different social units, would support the notion that boys and girls should be relegated to different conceptual categories.

Lewis (1972) indicates that from a very young age boys and girls are treated very differently from one another – girls are hugged and caressed and related to verbally more than their male counterparts; boys are generally handled in a rougher, less cautious manner. These phenomena, along with different dress codes, masculine and feminine Christian names, and assigning toys by gender, are all parental activities which reinforce the child's bipolar conception of gender. The maintenance of sex-segregated play patterns by peer groups and reinforcement of this segregation, such as separate lines to move children from classroom to classroom, to retrieve snacks and clothing from the lockers, and for dismissal at the end of the day, have the same consequence. Further, daily utilization of sex to motivate participation – who can do it faster, the boys or the girls? – helps crystallize the child's cognitive map regarding proper gender classification of self and others.

Finally, it is reasonable to suspect that the media also contributes to this role. Magazines, books, television, and newspapers depict sexes as constituting different consumer groups, different activity groups, and different interest groups, providing further clues for gender identity to the child.

Modelling

Although many studies have been done using the concepts modelling, imitation, and identification, very little data on the actual dynamics of these processes is available. Characters in books and on television, as well as parents and teachers, are often referred to as "models" for children in sex role development (Nett 1979), but direct evidence linking these models and the child is scanty. Under what conditions and with what outcomes are some agents and not others utilized as models?

Regarding the media, for example, there is evidence that children will imitate, in given situations, violent acts of film characters. (Bandura, Ross and Ross 1963) However, to what extent this phenomenon is also characteristic of sex role activity remains unknown. What is required is research aimed directly at capturing the agent-child encounter, such as detailed observations of sex role related modelling resulting from television exposure.

Conclusion

Despite the activities of feminists, as well as the increasing number of women in the labor force, the major research findings with respect to sex role socialization indicate that children continue to receive quite traditional conceptions of sex role attitudes and behaviors. To reverse this trend a good deal more research is required in three major directions: (1) More information is required on outcomes of sex role socialization in Canada, particularly behavioral outcomes, and including data on outcome variation by family structure and location in the wider society. (2) The role of agents other than the family in inculcating sex role related behaviors and attitudes should be studied. Moreover, research is required on the relationship between types of agents and types of outcomes, and on the relative importance of various agents for different types of children. (3) Finally, there is very little information available regarding the dynamic of the agent-child relationship in sex role socialization. This should be explored for different types of agents, utilizing observational research in the child's natural settings of home, school, and playground. Development of these areas would contribute to a richer theoretical understanding of sex role socialization and a more solid base from which to launch social policy changes.

The Mediating Role of the Family in Occupational Perception, Expectation, and Achievement

Eunice H. Baxter

Introduction

The family is regarded, in functionalist theory, as one of those important institutions having profound influences on the individual. A tenet of functionalist theory is that the family has interrelationships with other institutions, both directly and in a mediating role. The purpose of this paper is to examine the influence of the family *vis à vis* economic institutions – specifically, the influence of the family on occupation in Canadian society.

Few studies have addressed this question directly. Family studies have tended to concentrate on the internal dynamics of the family, whereas occupational studies have tended to be highly statistical, employing structural characteristics such as social class, sex, and ethnicity. This article will rely heavily on those few occupational studies which relate directly to the family and its relationship to the occupational world. These studies suggest that statistical correlations showing relationships between social class and occupation in part reflect the role of the family of origin. Where data for Canada are scarce, they shall be supplemented with data from studies of other countries.

Three traditional approaches to the study of occupations will be considered here – perceptions of occupations, occupational expectations, and occupational attainment or mobility. The influence of the family differs considerably with regard to each. Of the three, perceptions of occupations seems to be the least influenced by the family, and this will be examined first.

The Occupational Hierarchy

In 1925, George Counts, who was interested in occupational aspirations, made the startling discovery that there is a great deal of consensus among Americans about the relative prestige of occupations – differences in age, class, sex, residence, and so on make little difference in how prestige is perceived. Since then, many studies, some with representative national samples, have confirmed his finding. (See especially Reiss, et al. 1961, for the United States, and Pineo and Porter 1967, for Canada.)

Even cross-cultural comparisons yield high correlations. That between Canada and the United States is among the highest – .98 (Pineo and Porter 1967) –

but correlations among industrialized nations are usually in excess of .80. (See Hodge, et al. 1964, for discussion and bibliography.) Data gathered from less industrialized populations, such as Brazilian (Hansen and Converse 1976) and rural Japanese (Haller et al. 1972) populations, have other hierarchies based on other traditions. Industrialization is a Western European product; when a country industrializes, it adopts prestige evaluations as well as organizational techniques.

What determines the prestige ratings of occupations? A common answer is that the ratings reflect values; every person has values, many of which they share with others of the same society, subculture, and so on. They evaluate a particular occupation in terms of the degree to which it offers the rewards that they have come to value. Hatt (1950) states this position particularly clearly, from a functionalist point of view. However, generally speaking, this argument is not convincing. Agreement among different subpopulations on what the rewards are is lower than agreement on prestige itself. (Compare Garbin and Bates 1966, with Reiss et al. 1961:31-34; 192-193, and see Davies' review 1952:135-138.) Asch et al. (1938) argue that correlations between rewards and prestige are the result of "halo effect"; people are less sure about the rewards an occupation offers than they are of its prestige. It appears that prestige determines rewards perception, not the reverse.

From the literature, one gets the impression that over time there is considerable change within a country, and much variation from country to country in the perceived rewards or "reasons why" a given occupation has high or low prestige; it looks as though fashions in verbal explanations may play an important role. Longitudinal studies of particular countries would allow one to test this idea, but at the moment, such studies do not exist. However, this explanation is consistent with the findings from cross-cultural research, even when one ignores studies where the number of common occupations is low and the correlations thus artificially raised. (See Haller and Lewis 1966, for a cogent discussion of such correlations.)

This impression from the literature, that researchers are tapping different verbal behavior patterns, does not mean that attitudes and behavior are uncorrelated, but that the relationship between them or the conditions under which they are related is not well understood. People from different cultures and subcultures learn different rationalizations for their behavior, and these change over time.

Another research strategy for examining the relationship between values and prestige perception is to look at class or ethnic differences in prestige perception. If family values influence occupational perceptions, we would expect this to be reflected in class and ethnic values, since social interaction is patterned by such factors. (See studies of élite groups such as Kelner 1970; and of suburban middle-class groups such as Seeley et al. 1956.) This approach, the "culturalist" approach, does not seem fruitful either. Hunter (1977), for instance, found some differences among French and English Canadians in prestige perceptions, particularly among blue-collar respondents. His results do not support the culturalist explanations, however, since consensus on prestige is high and no clear pattern attributable to class values emerges.

A somewhat more direct approach is to study the development of views on occupational prestige among children and adolescents. Among children (the youngest studied by Lehman and Witty 1931, were eight and a half) there seems to be a tendency to give high prestige to "romantic" occupations, such as cowboy, movie actor, and sailor, and to conspicuous occupations, like homemaker, doctor, policeman and teacher. There is less consensus on prestige among children than among adults, and lower correlations between the perceptions of boys and girls than between men and women. Although most studies of children were so designed that direct comparison with studies of adults, or even with other studies of children, are difficult, there is a marked tendency, with increasing age, for children to come to see prestige as adults do. (See also Weinstein 1956; Gunn 1964.)

An earlier study (Baxter 1976) explored the relationship between prestige and rewards among children and adolescents of different ages (eight to eighteen) and social class (lower and middle). Perceptions of prestige gradually became more like those of adults; perceptions of rewards, however, showed no clear pattern. Correlations between prestige and rewards were similar to those found in earlier studies, but remained relatively the same for different age groups.

The most plausible explanation of such findings is that prestige is a product of the economic system; there is a high correlation between perceived prestige and both income and education. (Blishen 1967, for Canada; Reiss et al. 1961, for the United States; Teckenberg 1977, for Russia) Exceptions, for example the high prestige of religious leaders, suggest that historical factors are of some importance as well.

We cannot, then, expect a study of family values to clarify the perception of prestige. There are, however, two common findings that may reflect family influence. The first is that the conventional view of prestige develops somewhere between late childhood and early adolescence. Baldus and Tribe (1978) found that the recognition of social class differences begins to develop around the age of eight, and is well established by the age of eleven.

The second finding of interest, the "aggrandizement effect," (Pineo and Porter 1967) is the tendency for adults to "over rank" their own and related occupations, and for children and adolescents to "over rank" their fathers' and related occupations. Besides the change in prestige perception with age, this is the only other bias consistently found in perception of the occupational prestige hierarchy. Although usually discussed as a social class difference, it is more likely to be a family influence; first, because social class seems to influence only this part of the hierarchy, and second, because a number of studies have shown that there is considerable similarity between the views of occupation by children and their parents. (Dyer 1958; Morgan et al. 1979) Other factors are doubtless at work – peers, school, and so on – but work experience is probably not important, since few adolescents have more than limited work experience. Among adults, the association between rewards and prestige probably persists because of the adoption of what has been called "work ideologies." (Samuel and Lewin-Epstein 1979; Pavalko 1972; Knight 1979) Only a few descriptions of such ideologies have been published, but from primary and reference group theory we would expect such ideologies to exist. Such occupational values would interact with family values, and, to the degree that people in common job situations interact, directly or indirectly, contribute to the small ethnic and class subcultural correlations with prestige and rewards. Such a phenomena may contribute to the "inheritance" of occupations or occupational type, and in the next generation again reinforce the bias toward the father's occupation.

Various studies show that occupation receives considerable discussion in the family, especially in the lower class. (Aberle and Naegele 1955; Knight 1979) However, studies such as *Crestwood Heights* (Seeley et al. 1956) suggest that in the middle class, in spite of a conscious effort to separate work and home life, occupation is of considerable concern.

In summary, existing evidence suggests that family influence is reflected in perception of occupations in a restricted way. The occupational hierarchy is largely a product of the economic system of a particular society or, perhaps, a system of societies, but the family creates a weak but persistent bias in the perception of the occupational hierarchy.

Occupational Expectations

Although bias toward the father's occupation might be expected to increase expectations of following one's father's occupation, existing direct evidence shows that this is not generally so. On the contrary, families encourage their children to follow other occupations, particularly in the working class where pressure seems to be directed toward "bettering" oneself, and where job satisfaction is lower. (Dyer 1958; Harvey and Harvey 1970) There are, however, exceptions. A study interesting in this respect is Kohl and Bennett's (1976) study of ranchers and farmers in southern Saskatchewan. In this community the common expectation is that on the father's retirement, one son will assume his responsibilities while the other sons will leave to take up other but similar occupations. Daughters are expected to marry local farmers or ranchers, or to take up a profession, such as teaching or nursing. For this reason, girls are likely to have more education than boys.

This study illustrates one aspect of the strong relationship between education and occupational expectation. Available evidence suggests that the school is the single most important factor in shaping the expectations of adolescents. Clearly, the educational system has a close relationship to occupational prestige; there is a consistently high correlation between educational attainment and occupational prestige (Blishen 1967), at least in highly industrialized societies. For many occupations, certain levels of education are required. Increasingly, such learning takes place in high schools, trade schools, universities, and community colleges.

The relationship between expectations and education is two-way. On the one hand, as the Kohl and Bennett study shows, drop-out is more likely if one expects to enter an occupation that does not require formal education; on the other hand, occupational expectation is influenced by success in school. Breton (1970) argues that the internal structure of the high school is the most important factor in determining expectations. Of particular importance is the program the student is enrolled in and next, the student's performance and the failure rate of the school. (These findings are based on a national although not representative study of 360 Canadian high schools.) Of less importance are IQ scores and socio-economic status.

Breton's conclusions have been challenged by other writers. Gilbert and McRoberts (1977), using a random sample of Ontario high school students from Grades 8, 10, and 12, carried out path analysis to show that family factors strongly influenced what program students enrol in. They found, as did Breton, that the program in which the student was enrolled was highly related to expectations, but as an intervening variable. They concluded that families encourage students who are highly confident of their own abilities, especially if this is associated with high academic achievement and higher socio-economic status. Such encouragement is a much better predictor of expectations than either academic performance or mental ability. Unlike Breton, they conclude the family is the primary mechanism in determining expectations.

The relative effect of schools and family might be expected to differ from student to student. For instance, the group least influenced by their father's expectations for them were lower-class boys who were very successful in school. (Harvey and Harvey 1970) Being assigned to the less prestigious programs increased drop-out rates and lowered student expectations. Since low socio-economic status is related to being in non-university programs, students enrolled in those programs are, in effect, locked into the lower class.

Some light is thrown on this issue by Smith's (1974) interesting study of Inuit, Indian, Métis, and White high school students' aspirations and prestige perceptions, carried out in four settlements in the Canadian Arctic. Subculture had some influence on students' aspirations, particularly among Whites and Métis, but much more important was what school the students attended and what community they lived in. This suggests that family and peer influences, rather than ethnic background, are the important factors. The teachers seem to have had little influence on students' aspirations; they were quite unsuccessful in predicting these. The students aspired to the higher prestige occupations available in the community, such as doctor and airplane pilot, while teachers had stereotyped, but perhaps more realistic expectations. For instance, they overestimated the degree to which Indian and Inuit students would expect to choose trapping as an occupation.

Schools probably do not have as much influence on expectations as do families or peer groups. Their influence seems to be enhanced when they are well-integrated into the community, and diminished when they are not. (Morgan et al. 1979) In other words, schools augment the effect of family and peer groups when they are in agreement with them, but have little influence when in conflict with them.

At higher levels, at least in universities, the importance of the family is greater. Pavalko (1967), in a study of Grade 13 students in Thunder Bay, Ontario, found that socio-economic status was more important than IQ. Thus, with IQ controlled, 75 percent of Grade 12s from the higher class enrolled compared with only 52 percent from the lower class.

Robert Pike, in a study of the effect of government financial aid on university enrolment, suggests that the "boom" in high school and university attendance during the 1960s was more beneficial to students from higher than from lower socio-economic backgrounds. The percentage of the school-age population attending educational institutions rose for all classes, but increase in enrolment for children of unskilled and semi-skilled parents was considerably less than for children of skilled and higher occupational backgrounds. (Pike 1970:55-62) He draws attention to Porter's (1965) data, showing the strong relationship between social class and university attendance. For instance, Porter found that children from professional backgrounds were ten times more likely to attend university than would be expected on the basis of population, while children from unskilled backgrounds were only half as likely to attend. Increases in enrolment during the 1960s suggest to Pike that increase in university places will widen the "accessibility gap" for lower-class students. The study does not take into account such factors as academic and intellectual ability, but the figures are, nevertheless, quite disturbing; first, because such abilities are not independent of family background, and second, because losses of able students due to high school drop-out are considerable and are higher for lower-class students. Cuneo and Curtis (1975) argue that the net result is that achievement factors have been overemphasized, masking the importance of ascriptive factors in determining expectations and achievement.

In summary, the family can be seen as having an important role in shaping expectations up to the high school level, although perhaps not as important as educational institutions. Beyond high school, the importance of the family increases; higher education gives access to the higher prestige jobs.

Occupational Attainment

Clearly, there is some tendency for people to inherit their parent's social class position – for Canadian urban populations, the correlation between father and son's occupations is around .40, about the same as in the United States. (Goyder and Curtis 1977) However, the study of mobility is difficult, partly because of the methodological difficulties of getting adequate data, and partly because of problems in separating the influences of different factors.

Which institutions, besides educational ones, increase inheritance of occupation or social class is problematic. Other factors would include economic ones, such as technological change and urbanization. Other evidence, too extensive to detail here, shows that regional factors such as jobs and training available (Ossenberg 1971) and ethnic considerations (Beattie et al. 1972) have to be considered. Some of these are mediated through the family, but further research is needed to sort out specific effects.

The direct consequences for occupational attainment arising from the family has, for Canada, been most clearly shown by studies of élites. (Porter 1965; Clement 1975; Presthus 1973; Kelner 1970) These suggest that mobility into élite groups is much more limited than a .40 correlation for the population as a whole might suggest.

In his study of interlocking directorships in business and industry, Porter concluded that there has been a great deal of family continuity, maintaining the historic dominance of the business sector by Protestant English Canadians. Private schools and universities were clearly instrumental in the control of access to élite positions, and inter-marriage among the economic élite was high. Generally speaking, the picture Porter and others present is that such élites are caste-like in their exclusion of outsiders. Clement's more recent data suggest that this concentration of power is growing, making social mobility into such élites less likely.

Kelner's study of the Toronto élite is particularly interesting because it suggests that achievement is an important factor only into what she calls the "strategic élite" and not the "core élite," i.e., ability may allow someone of lower socio-economic status to enter into the lower echelons, but it is almost impossible to penetrate the higher levels.

Goyder and Curtis (1977), in their study of occupational mobility over four generations in Canada, conclude that members of the working class are most likely to perpetuate their status over several generations, a conclusion that suggests that the lower class also has certain caste-like characteristics. One is reminded of Pike's suggestion that the growing relationship between education and occupational achievement may be contributing to a division of Canada into two societies – unskilled and semi-skilled on the one hand, and the skilled, entrepreneurial, and professional on the other. For their sample as a whole, Goyder and Curtis found that the relationship between the occupations of different generations weakens, as more generations are considered, such that considering the great-grandfather's occupation does not have any explanatory power, i.e., this relationship is random. They note that this seems contrary to studies of the élite.

Clearly, it is not possible, given present information, to come to firm conclusions about the influence of the family on occupational achievement for the society as a whole. Much more research is required of how the family interacts with other social institutions to affect occupational attainment, particularly for the middle class. This group is subculturally very heterogeneous. Studies such as those of Seeley et al. could be quite enlightening when combined with the more social-anthropological approach of Kohl and Bennett, and the studies of élites. Studies of this type might show that the family is an important influence on attainment for the middle class group, as well.

Conclusion

The data available suggest that the family has a minor role with regard to occupational prestige, but an important mediating role vis-à-vis occupational expectation and attainment. Education and various aspects of the economy, independently and in conjunction with the family, are important factors that have to be studied in order to understand continuity and change of occupational status in developed industrial economies such as Canada's. In light of studies of élites, it seems likely that the family is of greater importance at higher occupational levels – professional and managerial – than at lower levels.

The Political Socialization of Canadian Youth

Ronald G. Landes

In the Canadian federal elections of May 22, 1979 and February 18, 1980 about eleven and a half million voters dutifully trudged to the polls to cast their ballots for their favorite candidates and parties (a cynic might suggest that they had voted for their least objectionable preferences). Unless one makes the probably unwarranted assumption that such behavior is a reflection of inherited lemming-like traits on the part of the Canadian voter, we are left with the basic question of all social scientific endeavor: why did this pattern of behavior take place? At first glance the answer appears to be deceptively simple: since human behavior is learned behavior, political behavior is likewise the result of the learning process. Man is not born a political animal, but may become so as a result of his socialization experiences. The political behavior of adults, such as voting in elections, is in part a reflection of the general socialization and learning processes which begin with birth. As Alexis de Tocqueville (1945:27-28) observed a century and a half ago, "the entire man is, so to speak, to be seen in the cradle of the child."

The attempt to understand adult political beliefs and behavior has thus led back to an investigation of their origins and development, that is, to a concern with the political socialization process. The basic assumption of political socialization research is that the initial learning of political values and ideas in childhood and adolescence influences, to a greater or lesser extent, the later political values and behavior of adults: "political ideas – like the consumption of cigarettes and hard liquor – do not suddenly begin with one's eighteenth birthday." (Niemi 1973:117) Thus, the study of political socialization is concerned with the "personal and social origins of political outlooks." (Dawson et al. 1977:1)

Investigation of the origins of political outlooks focusses our attention on *when* political learning occurs. An initial assessment of civic education in Canada concluded that political orientations were not learned at an early age. (Hodgetts 1968:9) The past decade of empirical research in Canada indicates quite clearly that this initial assessment by Hodgetts was wrong: political learning develops early among Canadian children on a variety of topics, including political information, political affect, and partisan identifications (see, for example, Pammett 1971; Landes 1973). Although political learning may begin in childhood, it is also important to remember that it is continuous throughout a person's life. (Zurick 1971:186) While many orientations and attitudes may be formed in childhood and adolescence, actual experience with and participation in politics as an adult may modify and change previously held ideas. In addition to being continuous and beginning early, the political socialization process, for most people, is also cumulative in nature: that is, the orientations acquired later in life are grafted onto and mixed with those previously acquired in childhood and adolescence. It is difficult to discard years of learning, political or otherwise, and to start over with a fresh set of beliefs. The infrequency in Canada of political conversions suggests the importance of the cumulative nature of the political socialization process.

Concern with the origins of political outlooks also leads to an analysis of *how* political learning occurs. For most Canadians politics is not a salient or important focus of concern. Canada is not atypical of other liberal democracies in which "politics is a sideshow in the great circus of life." (Dahl 1961: 305) The fact that politics is not a "central concern to most people" (Pammett and Whittington 1976:5) has important consequences for the nature of the political socialization process. For most Canadian youth the learning of political orientations is indirect and implicit. Few parents consciously seek to teach their offspring a particular set of political beliefs. Instead, children usually acquire values similar to those of their parents as a result of observing the values their parents exhibit. Even when children are exposed to political content in the educational process, there is usually an attempt made to avoid partisan debate. (Ogmundson, 1976; 179-182) As a result, the learning of political orientations by Canadian youth is indirect and implicit and, perhaps, based on the assumption that "politics, like sex, should be learned in the streets rather than the classroom." (White et al. 1972:193) Political learning among youth also takes place through "intermediaries, usually referred to as agents of socialization." (Pammett and Whittington, 1976:22) A brief consideration of the major agents of political socialization will provide additional insight into the nature of the political learning process in Canada.

The Agents of Political Socialization

Since political beliefs are acquired, not inherited, they must be obtained from somewhere in the learning process. A concern with *where* children obtain their political knowledge and beliefs focusses our analysis on the agents or intermediaries of the political socialization process. Few children have direct contact or experience with the political régime (i.e., one cannot vote in Canadian federal elections until the age of eighteen). However, perceptions, knowledge, and feelings about politics begin much earlier than the age of formal political participation would indicate. As a result much of the child's initial awareness of politics must be mediated by the major agencies of the political socialization process (i.e., family, schools, peer groups, and the mass media). For example, few ten-year-old youngsters would decide on their own initiative to attend a constituency nomination meeting. However, those children who do attend such political functions do so because their parents wish to participate. In the process of attending the meeting, the parents will probably explain to the child the mechanics and the significance of the nomination meeting. In other words, in this example, the parents are mediating the child's contact with the political régime. It is reasonable to assume that the younger the child, the greater will be the mediating role of the various socialization agents. As the child matures he or she will increasingly come into direct contact with the political system. Such contact may be voluntary (distributing party literature in an election campaign) or involuntary (exposure to political advertisements). The increasingly direct contact between the individual and the political system in adolescence and the early adult years indicates that the impact of personal experiences with the polity may be an important socialization mechanism. For most individuals, political beliefs reflect a mixture of the influence of socialization intermediaries and direct experiences with the political régime.

The agents of political socialization can be classified as either public or private in nature. (Pammett and Whittington 1976:22) The family, peer groups, and personal contacts with the political régime are private agencies, while the schools and the mass media are public intermediaries. In liberal democratic countries such as Canada, the extent of state or government control and manipulation of the political socialization agencies is minimal by comparison to authoritarian and totalitarian political systems. The schools and the mass media in Canada are expected to be "objective" in their discussion of politics and current events. If the schools deal with politics at all in their curriculum (usually in civics or history courses), the content is expected to be nonpartisan. Thus, the Canadian child is exposed to a mixture of public and private socialization agents, with the family, a private intermediary, providing much of what the child initially learns about the political system.

The role of the family as a primary agent of political socialization results from the near monopoly of access the family has over the child in his formative years and from the strength of the emotional bonds created within the family unit. (Dawson et al. 1977:114-15) As a result the family is usually seen as a conservative force transmitting, at least in part, the political beliefs of one generation to the next. (Jaros 1973:78) For example, Zurick's (1971:188) data on children in British Columbia revealed that the home environment acted as "a reinforcing element in fostering a favorable image of politics among the offspring." Several studies have stressed the role of the family in the transmission of partisan orientations from parents to children. (Rush 1972:317) For example, an investigation of Nova Scotian adolescents discovered "a high level of correspondence between parents' and children's partisan identification" which indicated that "for a majority of students, there appears to have been a positive transmission of party identification from parent to child." (Jabbra and Landes 1979:66)

Although specific political orientations such as partisan attachments may be passed from parent to child, as a general pattern, "most Canadian families, however, are not consciously involved in politically socializing their members." (Kornberg et al. 1979:228) The family's impact is usually indirect and implicit by providing the child with certain "circumstances of birth" (i.e., a social class position and a place of residence in a particular region of the country) which initially may look nonpolitical, but which have important consequences for what the child eventually is taught and learns about his political environment. (Jaros 1973:80, 88) In addition the influence of the family as an agent of political socialization depends in part on the homogeneity of the family unit. If the mother and father have the same political outlooks, then their effect on the child will be greater than if their political beliefs are contradictory. (Landes and Jabbra 1979:67-68) Finally, while the Canadian family in the 1980s remains an important agent in the political socialization process, it is increasingly in competition with the other intermediaries in the political learning process.

The significance of schools as agents of socialization is suggested by the frequent battles over attempts to censor school textbooks and reading materials. Censorship disputes are concerned with which community forces will control the content presented by the school as an agent of socialization: "some people fear that insidious professors or evil books may politically subvert the young." (Jaros 1973:113) Although schools are important agents of political socialization, the specific effects of schooling on political orientations appear to be highly variable, depending on the social and political composition of the school, the influence of particular teachers, the content of the required textbooks, and the influence of peer groups on the attitudes of individual students. (Niemi 1973:131)

The role of Canadian schools as agents of political socialization can be summarized with respect to the following major points. First, since under the British North America Act (section 93) education is made an exclusive provincial jurisdiction, "political socialization via the schools is fragmented because of the ten different provincial systems." (Ogmundson 1976:181) Second, as a public agent, the schools provide for most Canadians the only "exposure to formal political socialization by an instrument of the state. . . ." (Kornberg et al. 1979:228) Third, the extent of explicit political exposure through the schools is minimal, confined mainly to history and civics courses. (Hodgetts 1968:18) Fourth, what little political content is presented is done so in nonpartisan terms, stressing a censensus version of Canada's political experience. (Pratt 1975:120) Fifth, the result of the schools' efforts is an uninformed citizenry: "most high school graduates lack basic knowledge of Canadian political studies." (Symons 1978:50; see also Hurtig 1975)

The social and technological developments of recent decades have eroded the role of the family and schools as agents in the political socialization process: "the socialization potential of such groups has been reduced by increasing competition." (Jaros 1973:124) The increasing competition, especially evident in the adolescent years, has come from two main sources: peer groups and the mass media, particularly television. Peer groups, defined as "a form of primary group composed of members sharing relatively equal status as well as close ties," (Dawson et al. 1977:183-84) have been described as the "ultimate modern agent of socialization." (Jaros 1973:133) One study of Canadian adolescents in Toronto found that the peer group served as a "primary agent of socialization," providing "emotional support and important role models" in the individual's transition from childhood to adult status. (Kallen and Kelner 1976:220; see also Rush 1972:318) While peer groups first become important as agents of political socialization during the adolescent years, their impact continues throughout the adult years in "shaping, sustaining, and altering political outlooks." (Dawson et al. 1977:185)

The potential impact of the mass media as a socializing agent rests on two considerations: first, the nearly universal access most people have to newspapers, magazines, and television and second, the ability of the mass media to bypass other intermediaries of socialization and to provide information directly to children and adolescents. For example, one study of Canadian children (ages three to five) discovered that they spent 64 percent of their time watching television (Ogmundson 1976:180) Thus, it is not surprising to find that children and adolescents depend on television and the mass media for political news and for help in understanding political events. For example, among English-Canadian students in Ontario, by the eighth grade level, 27 percent would rely on the mass media for help in making their electoral decision, while only 16 percent would consult with their parents. (Landes 1973:274) Similar results were found among Nova Scotian adolescents: by the grade twelve level, 32 percent would look to the mass media, while only 4 percent would consult with their parents. (Jabbra and Landes 1974:52) Depending on television for political information may also have some important consequences for the child's view of the political process. A study of children in Kingston, Ontario suggested that "children who have much of their contact with the political world through television may be in danger of coming to regard political officials much as they do other 'actors' seen on television, as players in a drama played out for their entertainment," a view of reality which might reduce their interest and participation in the political process in later years. (Proudfoot and Pammett 1976:147)

An often overlooked agent of political socialization is the individual's direct contact with the political system: "political experiences provide an important learning tool for political socialization." (Dawson et al. 1977:111) Personal experiences in the political process may reinforce, modify, or drastically alter the political orientations which have been previously acquired and formed with the help of the family, school, peer group, and mass media. For example, a study of Canadian adolescents who participated in the "Action-Trudeau Campaign" of 1968 found that participation in the political process had produced both political (i.e., a better understanding and appreciation of the workings of the political process) and nonpolitical consequences (i.e., personality and ego development) among the group's members. (Pammett 1976:190-93) Early direct contact with the Canadian polity also appears to have a profound impact on the political recruitment of individuals to party careers later in life. (Kornberg et al. 1979) However, much additional empirical research is needed before we fully understand the significance of personal experiences on the formation of political orientations in childhood and adolescence.

To this point in our analysis of the political learning process we have dealt with three basic questions: (1) *When* does political learning develop? (2) *How* does political learning take place? and (3) *Where* do children obtain their political beliefs? A fourth important consideration concerns *what* is learned, that is, a focus on the content of political learning.

The Content of the Political Socialization Process

Much of the existing research on the nature of political learning in Canada has centred on the content of the political socialization process. A brief summary of these findings will focus on the following major areas: political knowledge, political affect, partisan attachment, and various group identifications (i.e., regional, ethnic, and continental attachments). Finally, we will consider the relationship between the agents of socialization and the content of the political learning process in Canada.

Political Knowledge: The acquisition of political information begins early in the elementary school years and is focussed primarily on political leaders rather than on political institutions. (Landes 1976) A majority of students can correctly name the prime minister by the time they reach the fifth grade, with over 50 percent able to make a correct identification by grade eight. (Landes 1977a:72) However, other political leaders rank considerably lower in the child's developing perception of the political system: provincial premiers and mayors are less well recognized. (Pammett 1971; Landes 1977a; Zurick 1971) The ability to name the occupants of the formal executive positions falls well below the recognition of the political executives. For example, among Nova Scotian adolescents in grade twelve only 22 percent and 14 percent could correctly name the Governor General of Canada and the Lieutenant Governor of Nova Scotia, respectively, while 99 percent and 89 percent correctly identified the Prime Minister of Canada and the Premier of Nova Scotia. (Jabbra and Landes 1976a:87)

If we consider more complicated aspects of political understanding, such as the child's perception of roles rather than simply the ability to name political leaders, we find that the level of knowledge is minimal. For example Pammett (1971:135) found that while 74 percent of the Kingston, Ontario students could correctly name the prime minister by grade eight, only 13 percent had a reasonably accurate understanding of his role in the Canadian political system. A similar pattern was discovered among Nova Scotian adolescents in their ability to name and to describe the role or functions of various political leaders. (Jabbra and Landes 1974:22-32) Such data are consistent with the results of the Canadian Student Awareness Survey (Hurtig 1975) which found that 68 percent of high school seniors were unable to name the governor general, 61 percent were unable to identify the BNA Act as Canada's constitution, and 70 percent had little or no idea what percentage of Canada's population was French Canadian. Thus, the average Canadian adolescent would appear to have a rather low level of political knowledge by the time he becomes an eligible participant in the formal political process on his eighteenth birthday. As one researcher phrased these findings, "I feel as though someone out there waged a war on knowledge, and I've been shell-shocked by the 'Ignorants'. Knowledge of Canadian geography is almost nonexistent, political awareness unbelievable, cultural knowledge abysmal." (Hurtig 1975:10)

Political Affect: Even though levels of political information or political cognition are low, children and adolescents still develop an emotional tie (usually positive) to political leaders and the political system. The typical pattern is for the child to "personalize" the political system (i.e., to perceive politics in terms of leaders) and to develop supportive attitudes and positive feelings toward the polity and its leaders and institutions. (Landes 1976:66-68) For example, a comparative study of English-Canadian and American school children (grades four through eight) found that the Canadian child's affective response to government in terms of benevolence, dependability, and leadership was greater than for his American counterparts. (Landes 1977a:68) Similarly, Zurick (1971:191) discovered a "benign outlook" toward politics among children in British Columbia, while Nova Scotia students have shown a marked prediliction to favorably evaluate political leaders. (Jabbra and Landes 1974:32-36) Although the initial pattern of political affect is usually positive or supportive of the political régime, typically the level of political affect declines during the adolescent years and may even turn into feelings of alienation and cynicism among a segment of Canadian young people. (Rush 1972; Hodgetts 1968; Cohen 1975; Skogstad 1975)

Partisan Attachment: One of the earliest emotional ties that a child develops with the political system is an attachment to a specific political party. Identifications with political parties begin surprisingly early among many Canadian children. Several studies of Ontario children discovered that approximately 50 percent claimed a party attachment by the eighth grade. (Landes 1977a:75; Pammett 1971:139) However, the development of party orientations among young people shows significant regional variations, with the West having the lowest and the Maritimes displaying the highest rate of partisan attachments. (Gregg and Whittington 1976:78) One study of Nova Scotia adolescents found that by the grade seven level, 85 percent were willing to express a partisan choice. (Landes and Jabbra 1979:62)

The potential significance of this early attachment to political parties results from the fact that these emotive ties precede knowledge and understanding of political issues and the political structure. (Pammett 1971:137-39; Landes and Jabbra 1979:69-73) Such initial attachments to parties provide the basis for later acquired orientations and evaluations of the political system. Moreover, the early acquisition of partisan loyalties has a rather direct impact on the individual's later participation as an adult, helping to determine, at least in part, which party to support in specific election campaigns.

Regional Political Cultures: Numerous studies of Canadian adults have found strong regional patterns of voting behavior, political attitudes, and political loyalties. So consistent have these regional patterns been that Canada's overall political culture (i.e., the total pattern of political beliefs) is usually described as a composite of a number of regional political cultures or subcultures. These regional political cultures exhibit varying patterns of political participation, party support, and political attitudes, perhaps humorously summarized in the saying that in the Atlantic area politics is patronage, in Quebec a religion, in Ontario a business, in the Prairies a protest, and entertainment in British Columbia.

Political socialization studies have discovered that these regional patterns begin early in the learning process and help to produce strong patterns of regional loyalties by the adolescent years. Differences in patterns of partisanship and political cognition led Gregg and Whittington (1976:80) to conclude that "there are significant regional differences in the basic orientations to politics even among very young children." In a similar vein, a study of Nova Scotian adolescents found that they "perceived greater similarities among Maritimers than between Nova Scotians and other Canadians living in other regions of the country." (Jabbra and Landes 1976a:86) This early acquisition of regional loyalties indicates that attempts to reform the structure of the Canadian political system which involve a readjustment of provincial or regional boundaries are likely to meet considerable resistance. (Jabbra and Landes 1976b) One particularly interesting consequence of these regional attachments is the identification by young people in some regions with the provincial, rather than the national or local units of government. (Johnstone 1969:16-22; Gregg and Whittington 1976:80-83; Landes 1977b) These strong and early attachments to regions and provinces are a possible explanation for the weak level of national identifications in the Canadian polity. (Richert 1974a) As Johnstone (1969:22) has concluded, "during the adolescent years Canadian young people become aware of the important sectional, regional, and provincial interests in Canadian life," so that the "adolescent years . . . could be characterized as the period of emergent sectionalism."

English-French Differences: Given the fact that historically English-French differences have been the most significant internal political cleavage in Canada, it is not surprising to find that English-Canadian and French-Canadian children and adolescents not only hold different political values, but also view each other with less affection than might be hoped for in a country still trying to develop a common national identity. Numerous studies have shown that English-Canadian and French-Canadian youth are taught different political values in the political socialization process. (Johnstone 1969; Lamy 1975; Forbes 1976) For example, a study of English and French Canadian history textbooks found that almost totally contradictory pictures of Canadian historical figures and events were presented. (Trudel and Jain 1970) As a result "children overwhelmingly identified with historical figures of their own culture" and "Francophone and Anglophone children identified with different eras of Canadian history." (Richert 1974b:156) One interesting finding is that Francophone students identify with the provincial level of government to a much greater degree than their Anglophone counterparts. (Richert 1973; Gregg and Whittington 1976; Johnstone 1969) Differing views of political authority and levels of political affect have also been discovered between English-Canadian and French-Canadian youth, with Francophone students more likely to display a personalized view of the polity. (Richert 1973:313) In terms of national identity and the images held of the Canadian polity, "Canada is two nations not just sociologically, but also psychologically." (Forbes 1976:302) More important, perhaps, is the finding that differences between Francophone and Anglophone perceptions increase during the adolescent years (Johnstone 1969; Lamy 1975), making unlikely the later emergence of any common national identity. Such findings as the above lead to the conclusion that "political socialization in Canada, then, seems to be for young French and English Canadians a process of socialization into discord. . . ." (Lamy 1975:278)

Continental Political Socialization: In both historical and contemporary terms the impact of the United States on Canada has been profound. From sports to culture, education to the economy, American influence has been pervasive. (Lumsden 1970) The American impact on the learning of political values is what is meant by the concept of continental political socialization. (Redekop 1978:44) Two agents of the political socialization process have been particularly affected: the mass media and the required textbooks utilized in the school system.

American domination of the mass media has meant that children are socialized to many American rather than Canadian political values. For example, among grade twelve Nova Scotian adolescents it was found that 70 percent read *Time* magazine, while only 33 percent read *Maclean's* and 5 percent read the *Globe and Mail*. (Jabbra and Landes 1974:11) Not surprising then is the finding that Canadian children often know more about the American political system than their own polity. (Jabbra and Landes 1974:19; Hurtig 1975) A similar situation is evident in school textbooks of which an overwhelming number are produced by American publishers. (Redekop 1978; Robinson 1979) For example, a "standard Grade 6 history text used in Winnipeg in 1975, *Canada-The New Nation*, has not one word on the Winnipeg General Strike but has two full chapters on Abraham Lincoln." (Redekop 1978:49) As a result students learn little of the Canadian political tradition but much more about American history and politics. As one student in the Canadian Student Awareness Survey concluded, when asked to identify a series of cultural and political leaders, "never heard of them, so they must be Canadian." (Hurtig 1975:13)

An important consequence of the American influence on the political socialization of Canadian youth is a low level of national identity among Canadians and the perception of similarities across, rather than within, national boundaries. Several studies have found a greater perception of similarities between English Canadians and Americans than between English Canadians and French Canadians. (Forbes 1976:302-03; see also Johnstone 1969:22-36; Landes 1977a:77-78) Combined with the early development of regional loyalties and English-French differences in political outlooks, the American penetration of the political learning process certainly exacerbates the development of a Canadian national identity.

Agents and Content of Political Learning: In briefly examining the existing research findings concerning the content of the political learning process in Canada, we have indirectly suggested an important relationship: the content of the political socialization process is heavily influenced by the nature of the socializing agents. For example, the Canadian family is usually described as a conservative agent of socialization because, in most circumstances, it tends to transmit political orientations from one generation to the next. The promotion and perpetuation of regional loyalties and French-English differences has been constitutionally facilitated by providing that education (i.e., the schools as agents of political socialization) is an exclusive jurisdiction of the provincial governments. Likewise, the promotion of a common national identity has been hindered not only by provincial control of education, but also by the dominance of American textbooks in the schools and American domination of the mass media. Such relationships as these between the agents and content of political learning has meant that the "socialization process has thereby contributed to regional loyalties within Canada, and to extra-national loyalties." (Forcese and Richer 1975:28) Finally, the indirect nature of political socialization through such agencies as the family and peer groups, and the minimal levels of political content presented to the child through the formal political socialization agent of the schools, has meant the production of an uninformed citizenry. Any reform of this situation must contemplete major changes in both the content and agents of political learning. Such changes would greatly alter the impact of the political socialization process in the Canadian context.

The Consequences of the Political Socialization Process

The effects of political learning are evident in relation to both the individual and to the political system of which he is a member. For the individual the political socialization process determines the initial content of his acquired political beliefs and influences his political participation as an adult member of the polity. The political learning process creates for the individual a "political self," which can be defined as the "individual's entire complex of orientations regarding the world of politics, including his views toward his own political role." (Dawson et al. 1977:39)

From the perspective of the political system, the political learning process has several important consequences. First, in most circumstances, political learning is conservative in nature, transmitting, at least in part, the political values from one generation to the next. However, this conservative impact need not always be paramount – political learning can also be used as a tool of political change, perhaps best exemplified currently by the attempts to increase the amount of Canadian content presented to the young in the schools and by the mass media. Second, at the élite level, political socialization experiences are a crucial component in the recruitment of individuals to positions of leadership in the political system. Third, at the mass level, the political learning process influences the loyalty, participation, and political beliefs of the average citizen. Finally, political socialization processes help to determine the stability or instability of the polity. In Canada the political learning process, through the perpetuation of regional identities, French-English differences, and extra-national loyalties, has helped to maintain the basic conflicts and sociopolitical cleavages which continue to challenge the Canadian political system.

FAMILY, ETHNICITY, AND IDENTITY

Introduction

In the multiethnic Canadian society, ethnicity must be carefully considered in the process of describing and explaining the major social forms that collectively make up this society. This consideration also applies to family studies. The four articles in this section explore, both substantively and conceptually, some of the aspects of interconnections among the family, ethnicity, and the strategies of identity-formation, identity-use, and identity-modification that operate as part of the mechanism of all contexts of group and personal interactions.

Using available data on Canadian ethnic families of European origin, Frederick Elkin's article discusses some of the issues involved in the use of the concept of ethnic identity in the Canadian context. Such issues arise from evidence suggesting the loss of ethnic identity in some cases and persistent display of it in others. Consequently, Elkin investigates both the circumstances in which the child's ethnic identity takes root and others that alienate the child from this particular kind of identity.

The overall approach considers ethnic identity as one of several identity options available in Canadian society, and that various configurations of factors, emerging at different times, tend to encourage, suppress, or revive ethnic identity to varying extents.

Elkin also recognizes that the family is not all-important in establishing ethnic identity. Other kin, peer groups, clergy, teachers, ethnic media, and institutions play a significant role in a child's development of feelings toward or against his or her ethnicity.

In the case of the Jews in Toronto, however, Evelyn Kallen finds that the family has remained the ethnic socializer *par excellence*, providing the basic (primordial) institutional focus for the symbolic-expressive goals of Jewish ethnicity of its members. This is particularly true at the macro-community level. Kallen presents her case in terms of three generations of immigrant Jewish families and in categories of Jews – the committed Orthodox, the Conservative, and the Reformed – and their varying degrees of commitment to Jewish ethnicity.

Based on a framework established by Fredrik Barth, Kallen's article shows how various aspects of Jewish ethnicity may be emphasized or de-emphasized, in response to national and international circumstances. In this approach ethnicity is conceptualized as a cultural resource base, and the family is seen as the most significant provider of practical models for the use of this resource.

In response to the question – why have the Hutterites, while showing amazing resilience in accepting modern farming and related technologies, successfully insisted on maintaining the encapsulation of their ethnic identity? – Karl Peter considers both the historical aspect and the overriding values of the Hutterite community, particularly those that relate to salvation. One of the predominant values is the submergence of the individual and the family in the community, accomplished through a highly ritualized social mechanism in which the concept of "community of goods" is pervasive. Although directly opposed to this, the acceptance of modern technologies is related, according to Peter, to the problems of survival in the changing, wider society that has hosted the Hutterites. Use of such technologies enables the Hutterite community to enter into rational economic transactions with these societies, and utilize the benefits to finance their continued ethnic identity.

The final article, by Ishwaran, explores some of the issues of interconnections among the processes of socialization, religion, and ethnic identity in two Dutch-Canadian rural communities – Ansnorveldt and Springdale – in the Holland Marsh region near Toronto, Ontario. Intentionally, the author adopted a historical approach as his overall guide to explore the changing nature of the Dutch-Canadian ethnic identity.

In this community, religion, in the form of a certain version of Calvinism, is very much a pervasive force, mediated through the church and the church-sponsored school. To complete the loops of interrelations, the family supports the church in a variety of ways, just as the church supports the family.

The Dutch-Canadian child's encounter with religion and other norms and values takes place within the family, where the father is instrumental in bringing God's message to the child. Clustered around this fact are many sociocultural processes and patterns that relate to the generation of specific ethnic identity. Ishwaran documents and explores such processes and patterns, showing how, over the past forty years or so, the Dutch Canadians in the Holland Marsh region have been able to maintain and continuously generate various forms of ethnic identities.

Family, Socialization, and Ethnic Identity*

Frederick Elkin

The Concept of Identity

In reports on Canadian ethnic groups, few concepts are as widely used as identity. Members of ethnic groups designate themselves as members and feel an affiliation with those of common ancestry. Without such an identification, we would not, in any meaningful sense, have ethnic groups or ethnic group activity.

Yet, in its application to particular situations, the concept of ethnic identity is far from clear. In modern society, ethnic identity is but one of several identities - we also identify with our sex, age group, nation, race, occupation, social class, labor union, neighborhood, fellow club members, those in similar family roles, those who concur with our political stands or participate in the same sports, and innumerable other groupings - and these identities may be attached to one another in innumerable ways which both link and set us apart from others. (Breton, 1978)

In Canada, of these many identities, which vary in significance depending on the context and issues at hand, ethnic identity is surely one of the most basic, often becoming a "terminal identity, one that embraces and integrates a whole series of statuses, roles, and lesser identities." (Epstein 1978:101) Yet, it is but one identity which, for purposes of analysis, we abstract from reality to help us understand ethnically associated phenomena.

Even as an abstraction, however, ethnic identity is far from a simple and clear designation. Within larger ethnic groupings, divisions are common - on religious grounds as, for example, between Old Order and Progressive Mennonites, or Christian and Muslim Arabs, or Orthodox, Conservative, and Reform Jews; on political grounds as between Ukrainians or Poles who accept and oppose policies of Soviet Russia; or social class and economic grounds as between Italian or Greek employers and employees. Even when divisions are not pronounced, apparent identities may shift, for example, from Azorean to Portuguese or vice versa. (Fernandez 1979) The members of ethnic groups may, depending on the circumstances, identify sometimes with a larger ethnic label and sometimes with subunits, or sometimes with one ethnic group and sometimes with a variation thereof. (Nagata 1979)

A further complication stems from the very subjective nature of identity. Ethnic identity, in general, is likely to be consciously self-designated, but it

---

*The author wishes to thank Maria Chow for bibliographical assistance.

may also be deeply embedded and unconscious with its significance overtly denied as in the case of certain second-generation rebels. British anthropologist Epstein speaks of negative identity "where the image of self rests chiefly on the internalized evaluations of others, and where accordingly much of one's behaviour is prompted by the desire to avoid their anticipated slights or censure." (1978:102) Likewise, of course, the intensity of the identification may vary, from a complete absorption with the ethnic group, or particular segment thereof, to a mild affinity which comes into view in crisis or other extraordinary situations. For research purposes, we often find it difficult to use such an ambiguous concept as identity and look for some manifest index of it, which raises other methodological questions.[1]

Ethnic Identity in Canadian Studies

Yet, the concept, despite any conceptual difficulties, is crucial. Activities associated with the ethnic group, by members or by non-members, implies an ethnic identity and such identity, in one form or another, is a taken-for-granted variable in studies and analyses of Canadian ethnic groups. The concept is perhaps most obvious in reports dealing with ethnic retention, acculturation, and assimilation. As high proportions of the descendants of immigrant Ukrainians, Hungarians, Dutch, Greeks, Italians, Lithuanians, Portuguese, Germans, and others come to lose their language, traditional customs, and symbols of their groups; as they intermarry with men and women from other ethnic groups; as they come to feel "Canadian" and participate in non-ethnically identified activities – we ask, what happens to their ethnic identity? The question is constantly raised. Writers, in the past, in speaking of North American immigrants and their descendants, often approached ethnic identity as a zero-sum concept – the more, for example, one gained an American or Canadian identity, the more one lost a previous ethnic identity. Kosa, for example, writing in the 1950s of the larger kin groups, or sib, of second generation Hungarians, said:

> *As they become independent in life, they lose their interest in their "relatives," and after the death of their parents they tend to withdraw from the remaining sib, a decisive step in their assimilation. When saying farewell to the sib, they say farewell to the Hungarian ethnic group as well. From this time on they can be regarded as Canadians only. (1957:21)**

More recent analyses are likely to view this perspective as unduly simple and to stress the many forms and types of identity which vary by generation

---

[1]One technique is to ask respondents to which ethnic or cultural group they belong and then perhaps how they usually think of themselves. Such questions have the advantage of simplicity and directness; they do not of course seek to get at the subjective meaning of identity to the respondents. (O'Bryan, Reitz and Kuplowska 1976; Richmond 1976)

*From *Land of Choice: The Hungarians in Canada* by John Kosa. Copyright © 1957.

and context. Thus, the adoption of a Canadian identity for an immigrant or his child may or may not accompany a loss of a former ethnic identity; the two may go hand in hand, with each varying in saliency and intensity, to some degree independently of one another. (Isajiw 1975; Breton et al 1976; Goldlust and Richmond 1976).

The importance of ethnic identity is also assumed and almost always included as a relevant variable in studies of language retention. Reporting on a survey of Italian, German, Ukrainian, and Polish urban Canadians, Reitz writes, "Whatever the intentions of parents, children raised in an environment conducive to language retention are far more likely to remain within the ethnic fold than those who are not." (1974:118) Driedger, writing of Ukrainians, links ethnic identity and language retention with urbanization:

a majority of the Canadian-born Ukrainians no longer know their language and very few use it at home. If Ukrainian identity depends on ethnic language use, then the future for metropolitan Ukrainian identity is not encouraging. (1980:131)

In institutional studies, too, ethnic identity is taken for granted. Breton, for example, speaks of institutional completeness in which members of ethnic groups are more likely to maintain interpersonal and informal relationships with members of their own ethnic groups (1964); and Jansen, writing of Italians in Toronto, describes the various institutions and organizations that have grown up in the community (1978). Ethnic identity in such reports presumably is both a factor underlying, and a consequence of, the establishment of such ethnic institutions.

Also in the political sphere, ethnic identity is assumed in the policy of multiculturalism. Cultural diversity is held up as a value and not considered to be antithetical to a Canadian identity. It is the official policy of the federal government (as well as provincial and municipal governments) to support ethnic language classes for schoolchildren, performing groups, associations, and other group initiatives. (Ziegler 1979) Presumably such activities also both reflect and reinforce ethnic identities.

Other areas of study likewise assume an ethnic identity. Reports of intermarriage (Chimbos 1971), inter-ethnic attitudes and behavior (Ziegler 1979), and ethnic residential patterns all look for measures of ethnic identification. Without an assumption of ethnic identity, such studies would often have little basic rationale.

We must not assume that ethnic identity is only an ascribed characteristic; it may also have a strong situational component and be "used" as a resource by ethnic members in order to gain other ends, perhaps from fellow ethnic group members, perhaps from others. Brettel, for example, speaking of the Portuguese in Toronto (1977), and Harney of the Italians (1979), describe the travel agent and others who use their ethnicity to establish themselves as intermediaries and make profitable links with their respective ethnic communities. And on a broader level, Goldenberg argues that ethnic groups may stress their collective ethnic identity when they believe this will help achieve economic or other gains in the larger community (1977).

The Importance of the Family

Thus, ethnic identity, in one form or another, is a key concept in a wide range of Canadian ethnic studies and analyses. One important and crucial question follows: Wherein and how does this sense of ethnic identity arise? Surprisingly little attention has been given to this question. An ethnic sense of identity is not innate; presumably it develops early in a child's life when he is still ordinarily very much a part of his family.[2] It is difficult, however, to determine the exact age at which a child becomes aware of his ethnic group status. Aboud writes that the "spontaneous use of an ethnic attribute when describing oneself may occur as early as five years of age." (1981:43) Ziegler, referring to studies in the United States and elsewhere, suggests that a child becomes aware of his ethnicity at the age of three or four, following awareness of his sex. An ethnic orientation and attitudes associated with ethnic groups do not emerge until later. According to one researcher, awareness and understanding of ethnic differences with others comes at the age of six and probably becomes increasingly salient with age.[3] (Ziegler 1977:375) When thinking of ethnicity, a young child is more likely to think in terms of external attributes such as language, place of residence, and holiday celebrations rather than such internal attributes as values and belief systems. (Aboud 1981:52) Reitz has found that the ethnic child in Canada, assuming the ethnic tongue is spoken in his milieu, acquires the basic knowledge of the language before the age of five. (1974:115)

In this paper, we shall explore ethnic materials in Canada which deal with the process by which a child in the family both learns and reacts against his ethnic identity. Our focus is primarily on those families of European origin who tend not to live segregated lives. Thus, although the processes and problems of ethnic socialization are undoubtedly similar, we do not include such visible minorities as the Blacks, Native peoples, or East Asians or such relatively isolated groups as the Hutterites, rural Mennonites, and Lubovitcher Jews. How, we ask, in our European-origin families, does ethnic identity take root? And how too is the foundation laid for possible reactions against the ethnic status? The data on such issues, we shall see, are sparse. Our concern in this paper is with the sociopsychological aspects of individual rather than collective identity. The latter perspective is relevant for those questions that concern the ethnic group as a whole such as government multicultural policy, the ethnic institutional apparatus, political movements in support of the home country, and voting patterns. The two perspectives of course are intimately related; any action in the name of the ethnic group implies that at least some

---

[2]For the sake of convenience, we shall use the masculine "he" to represent the child, male or female.

[3]Artist William Kurelek writes that he first became conscious of being "ethnic" at the age of seven when he called a fly by its Ukrainian word and the "teacher stared icily and the classroom roared with laughter." But by this time his basic ethnic identity was deeply engrained. (1977:46)

members, both among those who lead and those who follow, experience this identity.[4]

The family of course is not all-important in the establishment of an ethnic identity. Other kin, peer groups, clergy, teachers, ethnic media, and institutions play a significant part in a child's development of feelings toward or against his ethnicity. Yet, the immediate family, as the child's first group, and that in which he experiences close and intense emotional relationships, is ordinarily foremost. (Elkin and Handel, 1978) Ethnic identity, since it does involve one's self-image and self-esteem, generally includes an extension of one's self so that a member experiences the group's glories and threats, including a strong affect or emotion. Unless a child learns and experiences his basic ethnic identity within his family and other early primary groups, it seems unlikely that he will ever strongly feel it thereafter. Ethnic identities can of course be modified. (Horowitz 1975) Conversions among adults to other ethnicities, although not common, do occur. (Boissevain 1970:70; Kallen 1977:88) Certainly, too, an ethnic identity may change over time as it has for some "French Canadians" to "Franco-Ontarians" (Lee and Lapointe 1979) and among the many who have become "hyphenated" Canadians. But these are modifications within limits that are learned in a new context over a period of time and they do not necessarily imply a complete surrender of a previously learned and experienced identity.

Identity and Family Processes

The Cultural Heritage. Ethnic families do not often deliberately set out to teach their children an ethnic identity. Rather, in the same way that the parents take their own ethnicity for granted, so too do they take their child's, and the child learns his ethnic identity in the course of day-to-day activities of family living. This is most readily seen in descriptions of immigrant families who adhere closely to their ethnic group and follow without question the patterns of their culture. These families, in their activities, live their speech, religious practices, holiday celebrations, handicrafts, food customs, distinctive expressions and gestures and topics of everyday conversations. Their ethnic identity is never questioned. Writing of the Greek family, Antoniou says:

> *Work and play, eating, conversation, celebration are in terms of the family and the way through which belongingness is taken on. Contacts with the outside world are made through the family and its extensions. A child's friends are the family friends and their children. He goes visiting and to social gatherings with the family, by day or by night, no matter how late. He goes to church with his parents, to social gather-*

---

[4]For a discussion of links between individual identity, as evidenced in inter-generational assimilation studies, and collective identity, as evidenced in ethnic residential communities and organizational life, see Darroch (1981).

ings or wherever his parents are invited...The expectation is that the child will adjust the rhythms and pace of its life to that of the family's. (1974:1)*

Writing of the Arab family, Sharon Abu-Laban says:

It is within the family, also, that second and third generation Arab Canadians learn of ancestral origins. Stories and customs which differentiate kin from non-kin lay the groundwork for ethnic awareness. Even if physical differences begin to merge with the larger society, even if distinctive language is lost, there are the idiomatic expressions, the unique foods, the holiday celebrations or the family reminiscences which are reminders of ethnic heritage. Second and third generation Arab Canadians can find representations of their ancestral origins in the manners, values and customs of parents or grandparents. (1980:158)**

A very young child, in such circumstances in which he is a taken-for-granted member of a practicing ethnic unit, learns his identity along with his cultural heritage. He knows no other culture and other ethnic identity and it would not ordinarily occur to him that it could be otherwise.

Interaction Boundaries. Closely associated with the experience of the cultural heritage is the distinction between those who are and those who are not members of the ethnic group. The way of life of participating ethnic group members tends to set apart those who belong from those who do not. Lambert considers this distinction basic.

It seems that young children's ethnic identities take their start in the contrasts *that children are induced to draw between their "own" ethnic group and various comparison groups. It also seems the "contrast training" is relied upon by adults because it has proven to be a very effective means by fixing group boundaries and thus satisfying children's inquisitiveness about who or what they are.****

The boundaries and the differences in interaction patterns may or may not be explicit; they may be evidenced in the topics of conversation, use of the eth-

---

*C. Antoniou, "Greek Family Life." In *Outreach for Understanding,* a report on intercultural seminars, edited by George W. Bancroft, Ph.D., 1980, pp. 62-63. Reprinted by permission of the Minister of Citizenship and Culture.

**From *An Olive Branch on The Family Tree: The Arabs in Canada* by Baha Abu-Laban. Reprinted by permission of The Canadian Publishers, McClelland and Stewart Limited, Toronto.

***From R. C. Gardner and R. Kalin, eds. *A Canadian Social Psychology of Ethnic Relations* (Toronto: Methuen Publications, 1981) p. 57 © Copyright 1981. Reprinted by permission of Methuen Publications.

nic language or ethnic phrases, different degrees of self-awareness, facility of expression, and general feeling of ease and rapport. Speaking of Orthodox Jewish socialization, Kallen writes:

> *Traditional Judaic prescriptions and proscriptions provided strong*
> *boundary maintaining mechanisms ensuring that social relationships*
> *with outsiders were confined to the public sphere of business, school,*
> *and market-place. On the other hand, continuing and comprehensive*
> *interaction with ethnic insiders was encouraged. Primary relation-*
> *ships were confined to fellow Jews, and private Jewish institutions re-*
> *mained largely insulated from the cultural influences of Anglo-Canadian*
> *society. (1977:66)**

Speaking of the rejection that accompanies intermarriage among the Dutch of Holland Marsh, Ontario, Ishwaran writes: "In such a situation, Dutchness quite understandably forces cultural inbreeding; it becomes part of the socialization of children and an element of community pressure." (1977:175) And quoting a local resident: "There are about twenty nationalities here in this little Marsh. We all live by ourselves and know little about other groups. There is no visiting, friendly relationship. Well, we live in a common territory, and, sure enough, we are not enemies anyway." (1977:173)

In learning boundaries and in experiencing different interaction patterns between his own group and others, a child cannot help but become aware of his ethnic identity. Cognitively, whether he views himself from the position of his own group or from the position of others, he is designating his ethnicity and emotionally, in experiencing different self feelings with his own group and others, he reinforces a sense of difference.

Control of the Environment. Besides practising the cultural heritage and de-fining interaction patterns, parents also indirectly help "teach" a child his ethnic identity by controlling his external environment. Parents, for example, may place the child in an environment in which ethnic culture and contacts are likely to be reinforced. This is most readily done through a choice of a neighborhood in which to live. Demographic studies indicate the persistence of ethnic communities in urban areas. (Darroch and Marston 1971; Richmond 1972) Boissevain, writing of the Italians in Montreal (1970), and Driedger and Church, reporting on a study of six ethnic groups in Winnipeg (1974), show the importance of residential segregation for the maintenance of institutional completeness. Kallen cites the specific example of reform Jewish parents who report that they "moved back into the ghetto" when their teen-aged children began dating non-Jews. (1977:91) Ziegler in a report on Italian and Chinese adolescents goes further and finds a correlation between ethnic density and an index of high ethnic self identity. (1979:20)

Closely associated with ethnic segregation is the establishment of ethnic institutions and organizations. On coming to Canada, immigrant groups al-

---

*From *Spanning the Generations: A Study in Jewish Identity* by Evelyn Kallen. Re-printed by permission of Academic Press Canada.

most invariably established their own churches and associations in which they could find a greater sense of security and maintain some community life. Over the years, with adaptation to Canada and with new waves of immigrants arriving under different circumstances, these institutions underwent ups and downs along with considerable modifications. In recent years, however, it seems, there has been an "unmistakable increase in formally organized ethnic social and political activities." (Darroch 1981:94) One major concern throughout the years among all the groups has been the ethnic socialization of the young. Recognizing and fearing the strong influences pulling children away from a traditional ethnic culture and toward an Anglo-Canadian way of life, leaders of the ethnic groups have sought, partly through religious and other institutions, to exert a counteracting influence by fostering a knowledge of the ethnic language and an appreciation of the traditional ethnic heritage. Also as parents, many certainly wished a greater apppreciation from their children and the establishment of closer ties through sharing common interests and a common culture. To some degree, too, parents were passing on to other institutions socialization tasks for which they were no longer effective.

One major institutional effort has focussed on language classes. A major study of urban ethnic groups in the early 1970s reports that over half of the respondents considered more ethnic schools as a means of language retention to be important, with the Greeks and Italians ranking highest. (O'Bryan, Reitz and Kuplowska 1976:136) Reports on specific ethnic groups cite many programs designed to encourage the children to learn the ethnic language and heritage and to associate with fellow ethnic members, with one hope, among others, that romantic attachments develop within rather than without the group. To illustrate: Anderson and Higgs write that Portuguese are "sent to Portuguese schools, held on Saturdays or after regular school hours. There they relearn the language and study the history and geography of their parents' homeland." (1976:138) Chimbos writes: "There is no doubt that the Greek parents (immigrants and even second-generation Greeks) are determined to provide their children with adequate knowledge of the Greek language and culture. In 1976 more than 12 000 children attended Greek afternoon schools." (1980:84) Radecki and Heydenkorn cite various Polish, parish and secular, youth groups, including the Polish Boy Scouts and Girl Guides Association in Canada with a membership of about 2250. (1976:74) Kallen speaks of the Jewish Conservative and Reform congregations which are "decidedly child-oriented" and provide a variety of "youth-oriented activities – educational, religious, social, and recreational – designed to draw members' children to the congregation and create lasting ties that will ensure the children's participation and commitment as adults." (1977:103)

Such efforts to control and guide the environment, to the degree that they are successful, undoubtedly help reinforce an ethnic awareness and identity although it is a different type of identity than that of the parents. The child participating in such programs views himself as an ethnic group member. Insofar, too, as others in the group become "ethnic reference" points, whose roles he takes and from which he views his own behavior, his ethnic identity is further reinforced. In the light of other influences, however, we cannot generalize on the general success of such efforts. Researches on the Dutch

(Ishwaran 1977) and the Jews (Kallen 1977), for example, generally report successful institutional efforts; researches on the Poles (Radecki and Heydenkorn 1976) and the Ukrainians (Petryshyn 1980) are more qualified.

Ambivalance in Family Influence. It is widely recognized that the ethnic child in Canada experiences many aspects of the larger society which differ from and tend to pull away from his ethnic identity, including teachers and the public school, television and movies, non-ethnic and sometimes ethnic peers, secular holidays, and many other facts of our popular culture and contemporary way of life. In some respects, the immigrant family, knowingly or unknowingly, also contributes to this process by "pushing" the child away from his ethnic and into an Anglo-Saxon world. First, just by virtue of being foreign and not knowing Canadian society, an immigrant parent may "push" the child to non-ethnic sources. Speaking of Hungarian parents, Kosa writes:

> *They are 'ignorant' in many respects when compared to Canadian parents. They do not read comic books or know the rules of baseball, they are rather poorly informed about the banking system or the geography of the new country. In such fields the children are superior. (1957:57)*

Another ambivalent aspect of immigrant ethnic socialization stems from the one-time common use of the child as family translator. The ethnicity of the child is not questioned here, but compared with the parent, the more anglicized child is placed in a position of superiority and power to the detriment of the ethnic background. (Gavaki 1979:12; Kosa 1957:57)

In other ways, too, the immigrant ethnic family contributes to this general process. In its eagerness to adapt and succeed in the new world, it may play down its ethnicity by replacing an ethnic-sounding name with an Anglo-Saxon one (Radecki and Heydenkorn 1976:180; Chimbos 1980:68) or by encouraging an identity which extends beyond the specific ethnic group itself such as the Roman Catholic church (Boissevain 1970) or the wider ethnicity of Slav or Arab. Parents, too, for the sake of household peace or other immediate reasons, might approve any television program or peer group participation that keeps a child's interest, regardless of the non-ethnic influences. Further the immigrant family may uphold values which push the child into a non-ethnic world such as achievement in public school or participation in local athletic teams or working in a fast-food outlet.

Encouraging non-ethnic "Canadian" ways of course does not in itself mean a loss or decrease of ethnic consciousness, but it does introduce other values and reference groups which differ from and may run counter to an ethnic culture and identification. Some ethnic families of course are very much aware of this dilemma. Speaking of Polish immigrants, for example, Radecki and Heydenkorn say: "The parents were happy that at least their children, exposed to Canadian education, had chances to enter and participate fully in the new society." Yet they also note that most parents "were alarmed that in the process of acquiring a new language and cultural identity their children quickly forgot the Polish language, values and customs." (1976:97)

Ethnic immigrant parents, adhering to ethnic traditions may also behave in such a way that their children who internalize more modern Canadian norms react against them and the ethnic patterns and values they represent. For example, that the parents use old world gestures, that widows and sometimes other older women always wear black, that men believe they have the right to use physical force against their wives and children – these and other patterns may be seen by the children as relics of an archaic world. Such reactions have a long history. In earlier days, some Ukrainian daughters viewed the ways of dress and speech of their parents as uncouth and even "foreign." (Lysenko 1947:239)

Commonly cited in the literature are those areas of disagreement and conflict which stem directly from parental demands on the children themselves; demands which the children find unduly restrictive. One is the general claim that children should respect and obey their parents. More striking are those demands for closer adherence to stricter old world norms in dating and courtship which are sharply at variance with the freer Canadian norms. Abu-Laban, writing of Arab parents, refers to problems arising from sleeveless dresses, bathing suits, dancing, and co-education "with parental fears of waywardness on the part of daughters and their definitions of female propriety." (1980:169) Anderson and Higgs, writing of the Portuguese, cite the bitterness among many Portuguese young women. The authors note that men who are allowed more freedom "prefer to go to non-ethnic dances, so that they will not come under the watchful eye of parents" and that they "are more likely to marry outside their ethnic group than are second-generation women." (1976:133) Chimbos, speaking of the Greeks, writes that parents "often do not approve the Canadian courtship patterns" and that when children reach the dating age "the parents become disturbed lest their children date or marry non-Greeks." (1980:112)

Such dissension and conflict are not ostensibly about ethnic identity. The child in such families, by the time he can dispute with his parents about particular issues, already knows and feels his ethnic identity. Rather, the disagreements deal with parental authority, rights of decision making, reference groups, values and norms. In themselves, such disagreements do not lead to a loss of ethnic identity but, to the degree that the parents represent the ethnic group, the disagreements may lead a child to react against his ethnicity and dispose him to look elsewhere for satisfactions and more sympathetic relationships which, in turn, might help draw him closer to other identities. The result may then be a weakening of his ethnic identity compared with others. In one classical characterization, those individuals torn between a traditional and more modern peer oriented culture, and not completely at ease in either, are spoken of as "marginal men." (Stonequist 1937; Radecki 1976:132)

Our interpretation of ethnic family differences which may influence identity stems primarily from reports on immigrant families and their children. We have little systematic, or even anecdotal, information on such problems for third- and fourth-generation ethnic families in Canada. It seems likely, however, that in these later generations, parent-child issues reflecting ethnic considerations are less acute. The children are generally less concerned about familism and maintaining close relationships with relatives. (Hobart 1976) Ethnically concerned parents may be unhappy with their children's lack of interest in or defection from the ethnic group, but often they are less certain of the rightness of their own ideas and hesitate, on the basis of ethnicity, to demand that children follow their own beliefs. Disagreements, again leaving aside the closely knit segregated ethnic religious groups, are more likely to be seen as personal rather than ethnic problems. To reinforce an ethnic identity and to keep children within an ethnic fold, these parents, if they are concerned, are more likely to resort to persuasion and indirect pressures rather than authority. They sponsor and send their young children to ethnic language classes, and establish and encourage their children to join ethnic church clubs and youth organizations which include modern social activities as well as aspects of the ethnic culture. They argue rationally the advantages of ethnic affiliation and identity and the disadvantages of inter-ethnic courtship and marriage. They develop new customs which combine aspects of the traditional and contemporary Canadian such as, distinctive engagement showers for the prospective bride among Italians in Toronto. (Sturino 1981; see also Greenglass 1972; Kallen 1977) And in some instances, it seems, the younger groups themselves take the initiative to reinforce their identities. Speaking of third- and fourth-generation Romanians in Saskatchewan, Patterson writes:

Much of the culture is imported rather than being continuously handed down; dances, songs and some ceremonies are often learned from records, books, materials from the Romanian Embassy in Ottawa and visits to the homeland rather than by parent-to-child cultural continuity. (1977:46)

Sociopsychological Processes

The specific psychological process by which a child learns his ethnic identity and the associated ethnic attitudes and behavior is basically no different from that by which he learns other basic status identities. The process is complex and we know too little to go beyond a general formulation. Parents and "significant others" act and respond to a child in terms of their own needs, feelings, and values. In so doing, they define a world for the child; they suggest, explicitly or implicitly, what they consider to be good and bad, right and wrong, appropriate and inappropriate. (Elkin and Handel 1978) They also act toward a child in terms of their image of him, which includes his ascribed ethnic membership. Thus parents, in the course of their everyday activities, knowingly or unknowingly, approve and reward a child for behavior associated with his ethnicity such as knowing his ethnic status, understanding the ethnic language, knowing the ethnic symbols and participating in ethnic ceremonies and institutions. They may give him presents, compliment him, smile, or merely give him more attention. They also, as we have observed, may, knowingly or unknowingly, reward the child for activities which may lead him away from, and even possibly to reject, aspects of his ethnic world such as friendship with a non-ethnic teacher or coach, knowing the English language well, achievement in public school, quietly watching television, and participation in Canadian holiday activities. Punishment or negative sanctions, which may range from a direct slap to a reprimand to mild disapproval to lack of response, follows the same principle for both unacceptable ethnic and non-ethnic activities. The child also learns by observing the rewards and punishments that others receive for ethnically-defined behavior. Chimbos notes that Greek adults may gossip about deviant children. (1980:114) In reality, of course, in individual cases, it is difficult to identify positive and negative sanctions and to distinguish – both in the minds of the parents and the children – those associated with ethnic status from those associated with sex roles, family ordinal position, social class level, broad moral standards or other positions and values.

Parents and significant others also serve as models of identification and insofar as they express their own ethnic identity and manifest attitudes and behavior associated with an ethnic status, they may encourage or discourage an ethnic identity in the child. The type of relationship between the child and the adult of course is crucial. In theory, if the identification is basically positive – in the sense that the child places himself in the position of the parent and, to the degree that he can, thinks, feels, and behaves as he does – he would adopt the parent's ethnic attitudes and beliefs and perhaps feel more comfort, as does the parent, with members of his ethnic group. If the identification with the parent is basically ambivalent, the child may feel discomfort or react against ethnically associated attitudes and behavior and then be more open to other identities and influences. In real life situations, such modelling and identification is a complex developmental process in which the child must attempt to integrate many many models.

Members of the family, in their ethnic activities as definers and identification models, themselves change considerably over the years. The parents, as immigrants or descendants of immigrants, become socialized into the ways of the social worlds in which they live. They are influenced by workmates, spouses, children, community leaders, and others with whom they come into contact. Even in the short run, as Anderson and Higgs note among the Portuguese, immigrant parents may be considerably less demanding of younger than of older children. (1976:133)

Also of crucial importance in the socialization process is the child's conception of himself. A child first learns his ethnic identity, as he does his sex, before he can judge its significance or its problems. He defines himself as ethnic and over a period of time comes to know the associated behavior expected of him. He also comes to have feelings toward his ethnicity, as he has feelings toward his other status and personality characteristics. As he grows and develops, coming to know other people and undergoing a wider range of experience, these self definitions and feelings change. And to the degree that he can view himself and his feelings and can direct his own behavior, his direction of development is not predetermined. Various questions follow including: Which behavior and sentiments does the child come to associate with his ethnic status and which does he not? To what degree might an ethnic identity lie latent, perhaps to be revived when a crisis, momentous event, or new personal relationship develops? The difficulties of obtaining systematic and meaningful information on such topics is undoubtedly one reason why we have such little pertinent research data.

Conclusion

To a great degree, our analysis of the limited academic Canadian materials dealing with the family, socialization and ethnic identity is speculative and does not take us far beyond our common knowledge. We recognize the importance of the early experience of the child in the development of an ethnic identity and can point to various reports which illustrate the family's role. But basic questions remain: theoretical, substantive, and methodological. One question concerns the very concept of ethnic identity which assumes a commitment to the ethnic group and presumably some sharing of common values, behavior patterns or symbols different from those of the larger society. (Isajiw 1975) It includes both cognitive and affective aspects. Cognitively, a young ethnic child, viewing himself from the position of those close to him, comes to define himself as ethnic and asks what is expected of him as a member of the ethnic group. As he gets older and views his own behavior, he may, depending on the context, choose to carry on, give special emphasis to, or play down various aspects of his ethnicity or of the ethnically associated culture, patterns, and symbols.

Affectively, a child develops feeling toward his ethnic self. He may feel comfortable or uncomfortable in this status. Epstein distinguishes theoretically between a "positive identity" which is built on self-esteem and a feeling of the worthiness of the ways and values of the ethnic group and a "negative identity" in which the self-image rests chiefly on the presumed negative evaluations by others. (1978:102) Such affective aspects of ethnic identity have their roots in the early experience of the child and the development of his basic personality. The ethnic group becomes, to some extent, an extension of the child's self, and his feelings toward the group, depending on the situation, may bring forth pride, exhilaration, shame, or anxiety. We need only note the intense interest of Canadian Jews in the fate of Israel and the holocaust, the interest of Canadian Poles in the election of a Polish Pope and the political turmoil in Poland (Matejko 1979), and the response in 1980 of Italian Canadians to the earthquakes in Italy. We should know more about the nature of ethnic identity experiences and the functions they serve the individual.

A closely-related question concerns the place of ethnic identity in a child's life. There is no one type of ethnic identity: that of the non-English speaking immigrant is different from that of the second-, third-, or fourth-generation ethnic child reared in Canada; that of the visible minority child is different from that of the child who can "pass"; that of the established segregated rural religious ethnic group child differs from that of the recent immigrant urban child from Europe; that of the child whose family is "purebred" differs from that of the child of an ethnic intermarriage. We ask, also: What, in a changing world, is the place of an ethnic identity among other identities? We have noted the close link between sex role identity and ethnicity among the Greeks, Italians, Portuguese, and Arabs, but, in the context of the women's movement, this is surely changing. The ethnic literature especially stresses the structural and cultural assimilation of ethnic group members and the development of a Canadian or hyphenated Canadian identity. (Reitz 1980) Other identities, depending on the context, may also change in significance over time such as social class level, occupation, marital status of parents, or community. We ask: How are these identities related? Under what circumstances does the ethnic or a particular subethnic identity assume a greater or less significance? To what degree can one return to an ethnic identity, or variation thereof that, in the course of development, has been shunted aside?

A further question suggested by our review concerns the complexity of the role played by the ethnic family in Canada. We have suggested that parents and other primary group figures, knowingly or not, teach a child his ethnic identity; at the same time, they may, in various ways, be encouraging a "Canadian" identity and pushing the child away from certain ethnically associated patterns of behavior and values. Also, as the child develops and changes, so too do the parents and other influential figures – in part influenced by the children themselves – so that the teaching of ethnic culture and ethnic identification is not the same from year to year and not the same for each child. Once we consider too that each person is unique and the mother and father, let alone other family figures, may not agree, the question of analysis becomes complicated indeed.[5] Ethnic intermarriages which have become more and more common add still further complexities. The task for the researcher is, while crystallizing the topic, clarifying concepts, and gathering data, to keep the important questions in mind.

---

[5]In his studies of Italian families in Toronto, Kurt Danziger demonstrates that definitions of family behavior patterns may differ considerably among members of the same family (1971).

FAMILY, ETHNICITY, AND JEWISH IDENTITY

Evelyn Kallen

Introduction

The primary role of the family as ethnic socializer par exellence has long
been demonstrated by scholars of inter-group relations. Yet, paradoxically, in
their attempt to account for the apparent resurgence of ethnicity in contemporary North America, social scientists have paid little attention to the critical
part played by the family in this process. This seeming lack of scholarly concern with family ethnic socialization is particularly surprising, in the case of
the Jews, where the mythology surrounding the Jewish family has spread beyond the confines of academe and has permeated popular North American
culture to a marked degree.[1]

The present paucity of empirical research on the familial component of
ethnicity renders the present attempt to directly address this theoretical
question as suggestive only.

Theoretical Perspective: From the Old to the New Ethnicity

The current social scientific usage of the concept of ethnicity reflects a shift in
theoretical perspective among scholars of ethnic studies from a biocultural-
territorial isolate frame of reference to one of expressive-symbolic and
behavioral strategy.[2] The former perspective, that of the old ethnicity, focussed
on the distinctive characteristics of racial and/or ethnic groups; these groups
were conceived as corporate entities uniquely capable of maintaining their
membership and cultural continuity through time. Ethnic group distinctiveness
rested on three fundamental assumptions: common ancestry (the biological-

---

[1]An article in the *Globe and Mail* (Toronto 1979 09 20) draws attention to the
entrenched tradition of the American Jewish mother, in its report on a recent study by
Nell Hughes, a historian at the University of California, entitled: "The Myth of the
Stereotype of the Jewish Mother."

[2]See, for example: N. Glazer, and D. Moynihan, eds., *Ethnicity: Theory and Experience*;
and J. Bennett, ed., *The New Ethnicity: Perspectives from Ethnology.*

peoplehood referent); common ancestral territory (the geographical-homeland referent); and common ancestral heritage (the cultural-tradition referent). From this perspective ethnic identity was seen as a corollary of ethnic group distinctiveness which, itself, was moulded and maintained through geographical and/or social isolation.

The shift from the old to the new ethnicity owes much to the seminal work of Fredrik Barth who argued that the old "ethnic group as culture bearing unit" perspective could not (indeed, was never designed to) account for the persistence of viable ethnic units despite continuing contact across ethnic group boundaries.[3] Barth argued that, if we are to explain ethnic group persistence in the face of migration, culture contact, intermarriage, and miscegenation, we must shift our focus of investigation from the "internal constitution and history of separate groups to ethnic boundaries and boundary maintenance."[4] In Barth's definition the critical feature of ethnicity is not geographical and/or social isolation, but "the characteristic of self-ascription and ascription by others."[5] Barth argued that, as a status, ethnic identity is superordinate to most other statuses because an ethnic ascription categorizes a person in terms of his "most basic, most general identity, presumptively determined by his orgin and background."[6] This aspect of Barth's conceptualization has some important implications for the role of the family in ethnic socialization. For the family would seem to offer the most likely, indeed natural, focus for ethnic identification ascriptively defined in terms of one's presumptive origin and background. From this, it can be argued that the family provides the most appropriate symbolic-expressive focus for ethnic identity expressed in terms of the idiom of kinship at the micro-community level, a thesis which will be developed later.

However, it was not this aspect of Barth's thinking that most profoundly influenced his followers. Rather, it was Barth's contention that ethnic group identity needed to be defined *with reference to some outside group* which influenced others to view ethnicity as a dependent variable, whose centrality and salience is contingent upon the social environment.

The new ethnicity is viewed as a symbolic system which can be manipulated situationally to satisfy members' expressive and/or instrumental goals. From this perspective, ethnic group persistence is seen as a function of the ability of ethnic leaders to mobilize resources from within and without in pursuit of corporate interests and common goals. Ethnic identity is no longer viewed as a function of ethnic distinctiveness; rather it is seen as a function of individual and/or group priorities governing intra- and inter-ethnic relations. The centrality and salience of ethnicity is contingent, on the one hand, upon the continuing effectiveness of various ethnic socializers, and, on the other hand, upon the limiting nature of prevailing ethnic policies, priorities, and practices within the greater social environment.

---

[3] F. Barth, *Ethnic Groups and Boundaries*.

[4] Ibid., p. 10

[5] Ibid., p. 13

[6] Ibid., p. 17

The Thesis

The foregoing conceptual schema provides the theoretical framework for the analysis of changing expressions of Jewish identity, over three generations, at the micro level of the Toronto Jewish community.

The thesis of this paper is that the family, at the micro community level, has remained the ethnic socializer par excellence providing the basic institutional focus for the symbolic-expressive goals of Jewish ethnicity; and further, that changing expressions of Jewish identity are strongly associated with the nature and effectiveness of parents as ethnic behavioral role models.

This thesis will be supported with specific reference to studies of Canadian Jews residing in the city of Toronto.[7]

The Old Ethnicity and Jewish Identity

From a biocultural-territorial isolate perspective Jewish ethnicity can be traced back through biblical sources to the patriarch Abraham. Pre-Jewish ethnicity was fragmented along tribal lines. With his adoption of the Judaic religion Abraham *and his descendants* became heir to a Divinely ordained ancestral homeland, *Eretz Yisrael.*[8] Hence, the three core components of Jewish ethnicity – common ancestry (descent from Abraham), common ancestral religion (Judaism), and common ancestral homeland *(Eretz Yisrael)* became inextricably intertwined.

The Diaspora.[9] From the time of their dispersion from Palestine in A.D. 70 to the formation of the state of Israel in A.D. 1948, the Jews were an ethno-religious minority in the European host nations in which they lived. During this period, Jewish ethnic group persistence was highly contingent upon the social environment of host nations whose hostile attitudes and discriminatory practices against Jews varied only in degree. Whenever and wherever the policies and acts of their national hosts gave rise to anti-Jewish violence in *pogroms,* the

---

[7]In order to create comparative, cross-generational profiles, quantitative data are presented here in descriptive form only. Readers are referred to the original studies for numerical data.
See: E. Latowsky (Kallen), "Three Toronto Synagogues: A Comparative Study of Religious Systems in Transition." Ph.D. dissertation, University of Toronto, 1969.
E. Kallen, *Spanning the Generations: A Study in Jewish Identity.*
Y. Glickman, "Organizational Indicators and Social Correlates of Collective Jewish Identity." Ph.D. dissertation, University of Toronto, 1976.

[8]The notion of a promised homeland, *Eretz Yisrael*, was an integral component of the Divine Covenant between the Jewish people and their Deity. According to this Covenant, the Jews agreed to observe 613 Divine commandments regulating everyday life, in order to be cherished as the "Chosen People" and rewarded in the "End of Days" by the coming of the Messiah and the return of all the Jews to the "promised land." See: R.J.Z. Werblowsky and G. Wigoder, ed., *The Encyclopedia of the Jewish Religion*, pp. 205-06.

[9]For an excellent account of this period in Jewish history, see: M. Wurmbrand, and C. Roth, *The Jewish People: 4000 Years of Dispersion*.

Jewish minority responded with a strategy of migration, initially within Western Europe, and later from Western to Eastern Europe. From the sixteenth to the eighteenth century, increasingly restrictive national policies in Eastern Europe created a social environment in which the Jewish minority was accorded little more than pariah status. Denied the franchise and citizenship, prohibited from land ownership and from residence in large cities or rural areas, Jews were confined to segregated quarters – *ghettoes* of small cities, or small Jewish towns *shtetls* – where they were economically restricted to marginal, intermediary pursuits, such as peddling.[10] Closely watched by government officials and police, Jews were granted communal autonomy and religious freedom in their segregated quarters. In this social environment Jews were unable to mobilize resources from without; hence, the persistence of the Jewish ethnic group was contingent upon their ability to maintain community-wide consensus on core values – family, religious education, and ritual observance – and to mobilize collective resources from within.

Daily observance of the myriad details of Judaic law by the various ethnic socializers within the segregated Jewish community, ensured the continuing centrality of the old ethnicity; while mutual attitudes of mistrust and suspicion between Jews and their national hosts reinforced the salience of the religiously-defined ethnic boundary between them. Particular Judaic practices, such as observance of Sabbath and dietary laws and the use of a distinctive language, served simultaneously to reinforce intra-ethnic bonds, and to sharpen the edge of the inter-ethnic boundary.[11] Thus, the religious self-definition of Jewish ethnicity, reinforced from within and without, gained in centrality and salience.

The New Ethnicity: Jewish Identity in the Canadian Context

The majority of contemporary Canadian Jews are second and third generation descendants of Eastern European immigrants who came to Canada as refugees feeling the pogroms during the mass migration (circa 1880-1920).

These Jewish immigrants saw Canada as a land of boundless freedom and opportunity. Unlike previous Jewish migration, overseas migration to Canada

---

[10]A somewhat idealized but fascinating reconstruction of Jewish culture in the Eastern European Diaspora period is given in M. Zborowski, and E. Herzog. *Life is With People: The Culture of the Shtetl.*
See also, Wurmbrand and Roth, op. cit.

[11]Sabbath observance, from sundown Friday evening until sundown Saturday evening, clearly distinguished the Jewish day of rest from that of their Christian hosts. Similarly, dietary regulations which prohibited various categories of foods, required strict separation of milk and meat diets and imposed many other restrictives on Jewish consumption patterns, effectively prevented commensality between Jew and non-Jew. In addition, the everyday use of ethnically distinctive languages (Yiddish, for ordinary discourse, and Hebrew for ritual purposes) provided clear and strong boundary maintaining mechanisms, separating Jews from the world of outsiders – the *goyim* (strangers).

represented the acquisition of the long dreamed of goal of ethnic equality. In other words, it was regarded as an opportunity to shed their Jewish minority status.

In Canada, Jewish immigrants were accorded opportunities for public participation in the political, economic, and educational spheres; opportunities denied them in Eastern Europe. Yet, to their disappointment they found that they were not accepted as social equals by their Canadian hosts.

The First Generation: Jewish Immigrants and the Toronto Social Environment.[12] The ethnic visibility of these Jewish newcomers, particularly within the predominantly Anglo-Christian and British-oriented social environment of Toronto, provided a clear boundary marker and a continuing symbol of their minority status. Within this environment, their social acceptance hinged on their willingness to shed their foreign ways in favor of Anglo-Christian norms.[13] But Eastern European Jewish immigrants, unwittingly or willingly, clung to their ethnic institutions; within a short time, the Toronto Jewish community was marked by a proliferation of synagogues, ethnic newspapers, Jewish schools, mutual aid and sick benefit societies – frequently named and patterned after the East European ethnic enclaves from which their members stemmed. The fragmentary nature of this pattern of institutional development was offset by the fact that Eastern European Jewish immigrants had a strong sense of Jewish peoplehood – *Klal Isroel* – which provided an expressive symbol of Jewish unity over and above the local community level.[14]

Ethnic Socialization Among Immigrant Jewish Families.[15] Research data support the thesis that, in Toronto, the Jewish family over three generations

---

[12]The remainder of this paper will focus on empirical studies of family and ethnicity among descendants of these Jewish immigrants (and others) at the local level of the city of Toronto. The reader is cautioned that the patterns of family socialization and ethnic identity elaborated in this paper are based on a narrow range of field studies and thus cannot be taken as representative of Canadian Jewish identity. Nevertheless, they do reflect some of the main expressions of contemporary Jewish ethnicity, particularly within the context of the social environment of Toronto.

[13]Upon arrival in Toronto, Jewish newcomers found an embryonic Jewish community composed predominantly of well-to-do and highly acculturated English (and Western European) Jews. These earlier Jewish immigrants had gained religious equivalence in the eyes of their Anglo-Christian hosts, because, like their hosts, they defined the ethnic boundary solely in terms of religious differences. Alternatively, the newcomers defined themselves ethnically in terms of Jewish *peoplehood* as well as religion, and, unlike the older residents, they were unwilling to shed their foreign ways in order to gain social acceptance.

For a historical account of this early period, see: B. Kayfetz, "The Evolution of the Jewish Community in Toronto," in *A People and Its Faith*, ed. A. Rose, pp. 14-29.

[14]Ibid.

[15]The following profiles of three generations of Torontonian Jews are abstracted from data based on two research studies carried out by Latowsky (Kallen) 1969, op. cit. and Kallen 1977, op. cit., chs 4 and 5.

has been the primary source and symbol of ethnic group continuity. Differences within and between second and third generation Jews in expressions of Jewish identity, such as the centrality of the various components of ethnicity and in the salience of ethnic group boundaries, are related, in large part, to differences between Jewish families in their effectiveness as ethnic socializers and behavioral role models. In general, the greater the dedication of parents and relevant others to distinctively Jewish life ways, the stronger and more positive the ethnic identity and commitment among the younger generation.

Traditional Socialization. Second generation Orthodox Jews tend to stem from traditional immigrant families where strict observance of Judaic law, especially Sabbath and dietary rules, provided clear and strong ethnic boundary markers distinguishing the "good Jew" from the outsider and limiting behavioral access to the stranger. The latter was of considerable importance in the Canadian social environment where children of Jewish immigrants attended public school alongside their Anglo-Christian peers. To counter the perceived threat to ethnicity posed by these outside influences, children within traditional Jewish families were given an extensive religious education after public school hours, and were expected to accompany their parents to the synagogue for services of worship on the Sabbath and other religious occasions.

Traditional socialization was characterized by a high degree of consistency among primary ethnic socializers in their commitment to a traditional Jewish life way. Parents provided effective behavioral role models, and networks of kin and friends within the Jewish residential enclave reinforced parental values. Not surprisingly then, the children of these traditional immigrant families tended to develop and retain a strong and positive commitment to a traditional, religiously-defined Jewish life way. As adults, they came to define themselves as committed Orthodox Jews.

Transitional Middle-of-the-Road Socialization. Second generation Conservative Jews tend to stem from immigrant Jewish families where value priorities of parents, kin, and friends appear to have been considerably more influenced by the prevailing social environment. Within the home a relaxation in observance of Sabbath and dietary laws followed from the priority given to opportunities for economic achievement. Not infrequently, both parents worked long hours on Saturdays, the Jewish Sabbath, as well as week days, rationalizing their commitment in terms of secular educational goals for the younger generation. In these immigrant families, secular education was accorded priority over religious studies and the responsibility for the children's religious education was delegated from working parents to *cheder* – the supplementary Jewish school. But poorly-trained immigrant teachers provided weak substitutes for parents as religious socializers. Nevertheless, like their more traditional neighbors within the Jewish residential enclave, these parents continued to provide strong ethnic role models in their commitment to Jewish peoplehood: they continued to confine their close personal relationships to networks of Jewish kin and friends. Thus, while the children of these families did not develop a strong, positive sense of religious commitment, they did tend to develop and retain a strong sense of Jewish peoplehood. Later, as adults, they expressed their identification with the Jewish people through synagogue affiliation, defining themselves as Conservative Jews.

Anglo-Dominant Socialization. Second generation Reform Jews tend to stem from immigrant Jewish homes where value priorities of parents were decidedly weighted in favor of Anglo-Christian over distinctively Jewish life ways. For these parents, work and secular education were conceived as the twin means not only to economic achievement, but also to broader social mobility within the larger Anglo-Christian social environment of Toronto. Accordingly, these upwardly mobile Jewish parents abandoned distinctively Jewish life ways that marked them as foreigners and impeded their pursuit of economic and status interests. Although some retained a nominal synagogue membership, they rarely attended services; although some sent their children to *cheder,* religious education was de-emphasized and many children were given none. In some families, parents opted out of the Jewish community altogether, taking up residence in predominantly Anglo-Christian areas of the city.

The process of ethnic socialization for children of these Anglo-dominant Jewish families was characterized by a vacuum in distinctive ethnic content and a lack of clarity in the definition of ethnic group boundaries. Consequently, the second generation tended to be somewhat marginal in ethnic identity. As adults, they lacked both the commitment to religious observance and the broader sense of Jewish peoplehood basic to Jewish ethnicity. Nevertheless, their family ties remained strong and they retained a narrow sense of peoplehood expressed within a small circle of Jewish friends and kin. Oriented largely to Anglo-Christians as a reference group, they adopted a religious self-definition which was highly convergent with that of their surrounding social environment: they defined themselves as Reform Jews.

Comparative Ethnic Socialization Within Immigrant Families. For the immigrant generation of Eastern European Jews, the social environment in Toronto offered compelling new opportunities for participation in occupational and educational spheres. However, ethnic discrimination while not as virulent in its expression as it had been in Eastern Europe, nevertheless, remained a salient feature of the social environment. For Jewish immigrants to improve their social status beyond the world of work required a high degree of Anglo conformity. Where Jewish and Anglo-Christian values conflicted, families were constrained to choose between them, and their choices reflected the priority accorded Jewish ethnic distinctiveness vis à vis upward mobility within the status hierarchy of greater Toronto. Where value priorities favored the former, as among traditional families, ethnicity among the second generation was strongest and most deeply rooted. Where value priorities favored the latter, Jewish ethnicity was thereby weakened and ethnic identity was more shallowly rooted.

The Second Generation: Orthodox, Conservative, and Reform Families and Jewish Identity

The Post World War II Social Environmental Context. The social environment for second generation Jewish families raising their children in the post World War II period was markedly different from that of their immigrant forebears. Second generation Jews had achieved middle-class status,[16] and this economic success had resulted in a shift of focus from ethnic and economic survival to ethnic status enhancement. The postwar environment reinforced the peoplehood component of Jewish ethnicity in two important ways. First, the Holocaust – the death of six million Jews in Nazi gas chambers – provided an indelible reminder of their vulnerability as an ethnic minority. Second, and more positively, the postwar environment was characterized by a new humanism and a spirit of religious tolerance. This new postwar spirit and the inter-faith activities through which it was expressed provided strong legitimation for religious diversity in Canada. Given this social environment, Canadian Jews, in the two decades following World War II, began to turn back to the religious institution, that many had long abandoned, as the primary vehicle through which to express their ethnicity.

The postwar return to religion among second generation, middle-class Jews gave rise to a proliferation of grander and more modern synagogues throughout the Jewish community.[17] For many non-Orthodox, second generation, Jewish parents, a major reason behind their affiliation was to provide for the religious education of their children, through the auspices of the congregational religious school. Ideological differences among the three de nominations, as well as differences in practice among congregations within each movement reflected growing disparities among Torontonian Jews in postwar priorities governing intra-ethnic and inter-ethnic relations. Differential religious affiliation thus had serious potential for generating factionalism within the Toronto community.

However, this pattern of institutional fragmentation was offset by the

---

[16]Richmond's (1972) comparative analysis of the socio-economic status of ethnic groups in Toronto revealed that Jews ranked highest of all the categories (including the British) as measured both by the Blishen Index and in terms of years of education, annual income, and proportionate representation in high level occupations. See: A.H. Richmond, *Ethnic Residential Segregation in Metropolitan Toronto*.

[17]This phenomenon led one Toronto rabbi to comment upon the postwar, Jewish "edifice-complex!"

The modern synagogue is expressed in three denominational forms – Modern Orthodox, Conservative, and Reform – roughly representing a continuum differing in degree of traditionalism and in degree of acculturation to Anglo-Christian norms. In the postwar era the newer and grander synagogue structures served simultaneously to provide religious legitimation for Jewish ethnicity and to symbolize the achievement of middle-class status of their membership. In its Conservative and Reform (Temple) expressions, the modern synagogue, through its supplementary congregational school offered an important added attraction: an appropriate vehicle for the religious socialization of the young.

overwhelmingly unifying effect of the formation of the State of Israel in 1948.[18] The centrality of the ancestral-territorial component of Jewish ethnicity, newly defined in terms of Israel's statehood and nationhood, increased markedly; and since this time support for Israel has provided an instrumental goal with a remarkable degree of value consensus at the community-wide level. This latter development has had considerable import in overcoming potential factionalism of religious denominational divisions within the Jewish community.

Within synagogue congregations, commitment to Israel provides strong expressive/symbolic underpinnings for Jewish ethnicity. Contemporary congregations are marked by a proliferation of Israel-oriented social, philanthropic, and education programs and activities involving the participation of members from all age categories.

Within Conservative and Reform congregational schools the curriculum has increasingly incorporated Israel-oriented studies: Hebrew as a living language, the history and culture of Israel, summer study programs in Israel, and so forth. In many congregations, these Israel-oriented studies take precedence over more traditional, religious studies. Yet, despite the revitalization of the synagogue and the ethnicization of the congregational school curriculum, neither the religious institution nor its educational adjunct have served to provide effective substitutes for the family in the ethnic socialization process.

At the micro level of the Jewish community, the family continues to provide the primary source of ethnic roots and the most effective ethnic socializer for the young. Accordingly, differences among Orthodox, Conservative, and Reform Jewish families in ethnic versus wider priorities and commitments have generated differences in the centrality and salience of ethnicity among third generation Jewish youth.

Family, Religious Diversity, and Ethnic Identity: Ethnic Socialization in Second Generation Jewish Families

Orthodox Socialization. For committed Orthodox adults, the traditional tenets of Judaic law continue to provide their primary ethnic referents and behavioral imperatives. Within and outside of the home they continue to observe the Sabbath and dietary laws; they attend synagogue services regularly, and they accept the traditional interpretation of *Eretz Yisrael*. Committed Orthodox Jews thus experience some ambivalence with regard to their strong loyalties to the secular State of Israel.

These Jews tend to live in a predominantly Orthodox neighborhood centred around the Orthodox congregation with which they are affiliated. Their

---

[18]For many non-Orthodox Jews, the achievement of Israeli statehood and the later miraculous victory of Israel in the Six Day War (1967 06) symbolized the coming of the Messiah and the return of the Jews to the promised land. For the Orthodox, however, the secular state of Israel does not represent *Eretz Yisrael*, and the Messiah has yet to come.

day-to-day life continues, like that of their parents, to be dichotomized be-tween the two ethnically distinct worlds of Jews and outsiders. The strength of the old ethnicity among committed Orthodox Jews is expressed in their cus-tomary disapproval of interfaith marriages even when the non-Jewish partner converts to Orthodox Judaism.[19] Because of their strong stance against inter-faith marriages committed Orthodox Jews consider participation in any inter-faith activities as dangerous.

The parents in committed Orthodox families tend to be highly effective ethnic socializers, and their effectiveness as religious behavioral role models is constantly reinforced by relevant others within Orthodox Jewish neighbor-hoods, networks of kinship and friendship, and ethnic organizations.

An important aspect of Orthodox socialization is the overwhelming parental support for separate (two-track) religious day schools where their children receive both Jewish and secular education and are effectively isolated from daily contact with non-Jewish peers. For children of the committed Or-thodox, the process of ethnic socialization is characterized by a high degree of consistency among ethnic socializers and a high degree of value consensus within the Orthodox subcommunity. Thus, the role of the family in generating the old ethnicity is constantly reinforced by relevant others.

Conservative Socialization. Second generation Conservative Jews stem largely from less traditional immigrant families in which religious observance had declined and ethnicity was expressed largely through ties of family and kinship. Accordingly, as adults, they express their sense of Jewish peoplehood through the revitalization of selected ethnic rituals and customs centred around Jewish home and family life. The expressive-symbolic role of the family is most clearly demonstrated in the dichotomy in life ways maintained between the Jewish home, wherein some attempt is made to adhere to distinctive ethnic ritual and custom, and the broader social environment, wherein life ways reflect the priority given to economic, educational, and professional interests.

Conservative families tend to draw their own line of ritual observance, even within the home. Although some attempt is made to maintain a kosher-style dietary pattern, many of the rules of *Kashruth* are rationalized away. Similarly, while some attempt is made to usher in the Sabbath with a lavish Friday evening dinner and the customary candlelighting, little attempt is made to observe the Sabbath as a day of rest and prayer. Nevertheless, for Conserva-tive Jews, maintaining even the appearance of *Kashruth* and Sabbath observance is significant, in an expressive-symbolic sense, for it provides family members with a focus for their ethnicity and with a feeling of cultural continuity. Conservative Jewish parents, like their immigrant forebears, tend to be

---

[19]According to Judaic law, a convert to Judaism should be accorded full status as a Jew. A Jew is religiously-defined as the offspring of a Jewish mother *or* a convert to Judaism.

See: Werblowsky and Wigoder, op. cit., p. 211.

effective ethnic socializers in terms of community-wide values of Jewish peoplehood and Israeli statehood. They continue to provide a home and family atmosphere which stresses loyalty and obligation to family and, by extension through kinship, a feeling of collective responsibility for *Klal Isroel.* Like the committed Orthodox, Conservative Jewish families tend to reside in predominantly Jewish neighborhoods and to participate in a variety of ethnic organizations where personal networks of kinship and friendship reinforce the sense of peoplehood promulgated within the family. They also tend to disapprove strongly of intermarriage, but their disapproval is neither as un-qualified or as religiously-grounded as that of the Orthodox. The realization that such marriages will not gain social approval from either Jewish or non-Jewish families acts as a strong deterrent. Endogamy, on the other hand, is embraced not only because it reinforces the bonds of kinship within the Jewish community, but also because it maintains good will between Jews and Anglo-Christians by *respecting the ethnic boundary of intimacy between them.*

The desire of Conservative Jewish adults to maintain good will in inter-ethnic relations is further reflected in their support for interfaith programs. They regard these interfaith activities as strategies designed to reduce anti-Semitism, thereby enhancing Jewish opportunities for upward social mobility. However, these activities are not viewed as strategies for ethnic assimilation. The bound-ary of intimacy is subtly reinforced by the covert understanding of Conserva-tive Jews *and* Anglo-Christians that neither will violate the other's norms of endogamy.

Although Conservative Jewish parents are neither able nor willing to as-sume the role of Jewish religious educator, they tend to place a high value on Jewish education as a vehicle for ethnic group persistence. Responsibility for religious socialization of the young has been shifted from parents to religious teachers under the auspices of the congregational school. However, the dis-parity between behavioral norms espoused by the Conservative synagogue and religious teachers and the everyday life styles of Conservative parents has reduced the effectiveness of both Jewish parents and religious teachers as religious behavioral role models. Further, within the broader context of the Jewish community, Conservative Jewish children are exposed to a plethora of life styles and a high degree of inconsistency among the various ethnic socializers. Nevertheless, the centripetal pressures of networks of Jewish friends and kin, strongly reinforced by commitment to Israel, keep Conservative youth clearly within the ethnic fold.

Reform Socialization. Second generation Reform Jewish adults stem largely from immigrant Jewish families wherein value priorities favored upward social mobility within the Anglo-Christian community over maintenance of ethnic distinctiveness. As adults, the Reform-oriented children of these fami-lies tend to identify strongly with both Jewish and Anglo-Christian reference groups with the consequence that they are somewhat marginal in ethnic iden-tity. In part, their marginality stems from the fact that, as Reform Jews, they have de-ethnicized the boundary between Jews and non-Jews and have redefined their ethnicity in universalistic, *ideological* rather than particularistic, *behavioral* religious terms.[20] Because their primary ethnic referents are ideological, they are uniquely able to manipulate their ethnicity to their situational advantage in both intra- and inter-ethnic contexts.

Reform Jewish families have rejected most of the particularistic behavioral requirements of Judaism such as dietary and Sabbath laws which are viewed as incompatible with their commitment to the concept of the brotherhood of man. Because this concept dovetails well with Anglo-Christian norms, Reform Jews tend to view themselves as mediators across the ethnic divide, as the appropriate ambassadors of the Jews to the Anglo-Christian community. This Reform definition of their ethnic role is most clearly expressed in their dedication to interfaith programs.

Reform Jewish families tend to reside in predominantly Anglo-Christian neighborhoods and open their homes to their Anglo-Christian neighbors in the hope that the Jewish spirit of brotherhood will be reciprocated. However, their attempts to gain social acceptance *beyond the ritual limits of interfaith activities* have been rebuffed. Reported personal experiences of anti-Semitism relate largely to their unsuccessful attempts to penetrate the private networks, clubs, and cliques of Anglo-Christian acquaintances. In response to this ethnic impasse, some Reform Jewish families have begun to revitalize ethnic symbols and to redefine the ethnic boundary in more particularistic terms. Accordingly, they have begun to reintroduce at least a modicum of distinctively Jewish content into their homes, Reform temples, and congregational schools.

The revitalization of ethnic symbols within the Reform Jewish home is expressed in patterns strikingly similar to that found among Conservative Jews: reintroduction of the Friday night Sabbath dinner and even the reintroduction of a limited kosher-style dietary pattern. Also, as among Conservative Jews, the observance within the home of child-centred Jewish holidays, such as *Chanukah* and *Passover,* serves to revitalize the importance of the Jewish family as a source of ethnic roots.

As ethnic socializers, Reform Jewish parents provide decidedly ambivalent behavioral role models, for their revitalized ethnic behavior is inconsistent with their universalistic Reform ideological commitment. This ethnic ambivalence comes to the fore in their attitudes toward Israel. The carry-over of long-term anti-nationalistic (anti-Zionistic) Reform sentiments conflict with currently-held strong feelings of loyalty and attachment to Israel.

This ethnic ambivalence is extended to the Reform temple and congregational school wherein attempts to reintroduce ethnic custom mitigate against the salience of Reform ideology. Reform Jewish parents, like Conservatives,

---

[20]Traditional Judaism stresses a behavioral rather than an ideological commitment: a good Jew is an observant Jew. Reform Judaism, on the other hand, deviates from both Orthodoxy and Conservatism in this respect in stressing an ideological commitment based on the ethical teachings of the biblical prophets. Because Reform Judaism has rejected the notion of Divine revelation, Reform Jews and congregations may discard their rules and may effect changes in ritual which bring their practices into line with those of the prevailing social environment. Orthodoxy and Conservatism, on the other hand, are bound by the notion of Divine revelation of Judaic law in Torah and Talmud and may only make changes in *interpretation* of the rules governing Jewish behavior. For a fuller discussion of denominational differences, see: S. Rosenberg, *Judaism.*

depend on Jewish education to compensate for the lack of Jewish content in the home. Responsibility for the religious socialization of the children is therefore delegated to the congregational school. But again, the gap between religious teachings and familial behavior reduces the effectiveness of both home and religious school as primary ethnic socializers. Hence, ethnic socialization is characterized by a marked degree of incongruence in ideological values espoused by the various ethnic socializers and by considerable inconsistency among ethnic behavioral role models. Further centrifugal pressures emanating from daily contact with Anglo-Christians influences the child's perception of the ethnic boundary as being highly permeable. Thus, their ethnicity is highly contingent upon the limiting nature of the greater social environment.

Comparative Ethnic Socialization Within Second Generation Orthodox, Conservative, and Reform Jewish Families

By the post World War II period, Torontonian Jews had achieved a high level of economic and educational attainment. Comfortable in their suburban, middle-class homes and neighborhoods, second generation Jewish parents shifted the focus of their ethnic interests from economic survival to status enhancement. The return to religion among second generation families represented a postwar Jewish strategy designed to fulfill both instrumental and symbolic-expressive ethnic goals. The modern synagogue provided religious legitimation for Jewish ethnicity, as well as a visible symbol of middle-class status. Thus, the modern congregation was viewed by its members as conferring both ethnic legitimacy and prestige upon them in the eyes of both the Jewish and Anglo-Christian élite.

Denominational differences between Orthodox, Conservative, and Reform congregations were reflected within Jewish families in differential priorities governing intra- and inter-ethnic relations and in different parental life ways and patterns of ethnic socialization. As among immigrant Jewish families, the more traditional the second generation family and the more consistent the values and behaviors of its various ethnic socializers, the more effective have been the parents as ethnic behavioral role models. Thus, from Orthodox through Conservative to Reform, the effectiveness of Jewish families as ethnic socializers decreases. Among Conservative and Reform Jews (who far outnumber the Orthodox within the Toronto community),[21] parental expectations

---

[21]Glickman's figures, here recalculated to represent synagogue membership among Jews in Toronto at large, diverge somewhat from Richmond's, based on a smaller Jewish sub-sample; but both find that the alternatives to Orthodoxy in synagogue affiliation predominate in Toronto.

| | Percentage of Sample | |
Synagogue Affiliation	Richmond (1972)	Glickman (1976)
Orthodox	19	17
Conservative	45	32
Reform	20	15
None	16	36

that the congregational school would provide a meaningful substitute have not been fulfilled, and the Jewish family remains the ethnic socializer par excellence.

The Third Generation: Forces Shaping Ethnic Identity Among Orthodox, Conservative, and Reform Jewish Youth

For the third Jewish generation, raised within middle-class affluence in the decades following World War II, the most salient features of their social environment – the Holocaust and the State of Israel – lay outside the local Toronto context. These young Jews have interacted with Anglo-Christians far more than their parents, and have, in this process, experienced far less overt ethnic discrimination. Hence, their ethnicity is far less contingent upon the local (Toronto) Anglo-Christian social environment. However, the spectre of the Holocaust provides an indelible reminder for the *first* postwar generation of the degree to which their own and indeed the destiny of the Jewish people remain contingent upon the social environment – the policies and practices of the dominant powers. In contrast with this past negative symbol of Jewish passivity and death, the State of Israel provides a highly positive Jewish symbol for the present and the future – a symbol of a young and vigorous nation dedicated to the goal of Jewish self-determination. For third generation Jewish youth, Israel symbolizes both Jewish expressive goals and jewish corporate interests. At the macro level of the Toronto Jewish community, a high level of value consensus regarding the common goal of support for Israel crosscuts differential interests among third generation Jewish youth and provides a unifying basis for their Jewish ethnicity.

Family, Religious Diversity, and Ethnic Identity: The Third Generation

At the micro level of the Toronto Jewish community, differential socialization with Orthodox, Conservative, and Reform Jewish families has generated differences in expressions and depth of Jewish identity between Orthodox, Conservative, and Reform Jewish youth.

Third generation Orthodox youth were raised within a mutually reinforcing institutional environment of Orthodox home, family, synagogue, and day school within a largely Orthodox subcommunity sector. Thus, their socialization was characterized by a high degree of consensus concerning traditional Orthodox Jewish values and a high degree of behavioral consistency among primary ethnic socializers; both of which emphasized their Jewish ethnic distinctiveness in terms of the old ethnicity. Not surprisingly, then, the majority continue to identify strongly and positively as Jews in terms of the Orthodox referent of religious observance. However, their religious self-definition of Jewish ethnicity is strongly reinforced through their attachment to Israel and the two components are linked with Jewish peoplehood through the idiom of kinship.

Conservative Jewish youth were raised within a far more fragmented Jewish institutional environment where the values and behavioral role models were far more inconsistent. The process of ethnic socialization was thus characterized by a higher degree of value incongruence and behavioral inconsistency. Ethnic socialization emphasized Jewish peoplehood, symbolized primarily by family ties and obligations and reinforced by close networks of Jewish kin and friends. The decline in religious observance and the consequent ineffectiveness of both parents and religious teachers as behavioral role models markedly weakened the religious component of Jewish ethnicity. As a result, many third generation Conservative youth tend to reject their parents' religious self-definition of ethnicity and define themselves as non-religious. On the other hand, they tend to identify strongly and positively as Jews in terms of Jewish peoplehood and Israel, two components of Jewish ethnicity closely linked through the idiom of kinship.

In contrast, third generation Reform Jewish youth were typically socialized within an ethnically mixed social environment where the primary ethnic socializers in the home, neighborhood, Reform temple, and school minimized ethnic distinctiveness and encouraged intimate social intercourse with non-Jews. As primary ethnic socializers Reform Jewish parents provided weak and ambivalent behavioral role models; their life ways were patterned on those of the Anglo-Christian élite, yet they attempted to provide a modicum of particularistic Jewish content in their homes, temples, and religious schools to ensure the continuing commitment of the younger generation. The ineffectiveness of these ethnic socializers has similar results for Reform as for Conservative Jewish youth. Like their Conservative peers, Reform Jewish youth tend to reject their parents' religious self-definition of ethnicity and define themselves as non-religious. Morover, in contrast to both Orthodox and Conservative youth, third generation Reform youth do not confine their friendships to fellow Jews. They have as many non-Jewish as Jewish friends, and their relationship with non-Jewish friends is reportedly as close as it is with their Jewish friends. This observation has significant implications for the question of intermarriage among Reform youth. Except for the committed Orthodox, the majority of third generation Jewish youth, in contrast to their parents, profess approval of intermarriage *without qualifications.* Yet, the social behavior of Conservative youth, like that of the Orthodox, is expressed in predominantly Jewish friendships. Thus, their behavior lags behind their reported attitudes toward intermarriage. However, in the case of Reform youth, behavior is consistent with expressed attitudes; hence, the likelihood of intermarriage is greater. For Reform Jewish youth, the centrality of Jewish ethnicity appears to be far weaker than for Orthodox or Conservative. Lacking a strong sense of Jewish peoplehood their primary ethnic referents, family and Israel, are not closely connected. Thus, the salience of their Jewish ethnicity is far more contingent upon their perception of actual or potential threats to Jewish survival emanating from the surrounding social environment.

Continuity-in-Change: Jewish Identity Over Three Generations

The foregoing profiles clearly support the thesis that the Jewish family remains the most important ethnic socializer as well as the most important focus for expressive-symbolic goals at the micro level of the Jewish community. The Jewish family continues to provide an unambiguous source of roots and a primary symbol of ethnic commitment in terms of the Jewish idiom of kinship. Despite the decreasing effectiveness of non-Orthodox parents as religious behavioral role models, they remain the most effective ethnic socializers in terms of the expressive-symbolic goals of Jewish ethnicity. In contrast, the non-Orthodox congregational school has failed to substitute for Jewish parents as the primary agent of religious socialization; and its covert role to draw Jews back into the religious orbit of the synagogue has not been fulfilled.

At the micro level of the Jewish community, different expressions of Jewish ethnicity are related to differences in family ethnic socialization and generations. Among the immigrant generation, some families continued to adhere insofar as possible to traditional, Judaic life ways; while others gave priority to economic and/or status interests over religious observance. In the more traditional families Jewish ethnicity continued to be rooted in the ancient triumvirates – religion, peoplehood, and promised land; while in the less traditional families religious observance declined and Jewish ethnicity was expressed largely in terms of the peoplehood component.

Among the second generation, committed Orthodox families continued to adhere to traditional Jewish life ways, hence the ancient triumvirate remained central to their Jewish ethnicity and they defined themselves as Jews primarily in terms of religious orthodoxy. Among Conservatives, and more so among Reform Jewish families, life ways became far more acculturated to Anglo-Christian Canadian norms, and economic and status interests gained priority over religious observance. Although Conservative and Reform Jewish parents continued to define themselves as Jews in religious terms, their Jewish ethnicity was more firmly rooted in family ties and in growing identification with the State of Israel.

Among third generation Jewish youth, only the committed Orthodox remain highly and positively identified as Jews in religious terms. For Conservative youth, Jewish ethnicity rests on a strong sense of peoplehood symbolized by family and Israel, and reinforced through primary networks of kin and friends. For Reform Jewish youth, kinship has lost salience; yet, Jewish peoplehood, symbolized by the family and strongly reinforced by the reality of the State of Israel, continues to provide a limited, if not central, ethnic referent.

Jewish Identity at the Macro Level of the Jewish Community: The Toronto Jewish Community in the Present Decade

Recent research on correlates of Jewish ethnicity at the community-wide level in Toronto reveals that support for Israel and Jewish education currently provide the overarching bases for value consensus.[22] The primacy of these ethnic interests at the macro level is clearly expressed in the high priority they are given in community wide philanthropic endeavors.

Between Jewish family and community in Toronto, a wide range of Jewish

---

[22]Glickman, op. cit., ch. 10.

voluntary organizations, religious and secular, provide institutional bases for different expressions of Jewish ethnicity. The Toronto Jewish community is not only highly institutionally complete, but is also characterized by a high rate of active participation by adult members in various ethnic organizations. Despite a general decline in institutional participation over the generations, the majority of Jewish youth remain affiliated with at least one ethnic organization.[23] At this intermediate level of Jewish community organization the religious institution remains the single largest sphere of voluntary organizations. Here, the incorporation of Israel-oriented social, educational and philanthropic programs and activities within the synagogue structure (especially among Conservative and Reform congregations) provides strong reinforcement for the community-wide value of support for Israel.

Probably most significant, however, for the question of Jewish identity among the younger generation and for future generations of Jewish youth, is the high priority given religious education at the macro-community level. The strong value consensus within the adult Jewish community on the vital importance of religious education for ethnic group persistence is most clearly expressed in the rise to prominence within the last decade of the two-track (Hebrew and secular studies) Jewish day school.

By the mid 1970s, the North American Jewish day school movement had gained considerable support within the Toronto Jewish community, not only among Orthodox Jews (long-time supporters of Jewish parochial schools) but also, and perhaps more importantly, among Conservative and even, most recently in 1975-1976, among Reform Jews (long-term opponents of Jewish parochialism).[24] This increasing "return to particularism," which crosscuts denominational differences among contemporary Jews, reflects a widespread North American response of Jewish parents to the failure of supplementary Jewish schools to produce highly identified and positively committed Jewish youth. Postwar supplementary programs of Jewish education have been "blamed" for the (alleged) current "identity crisis" among Jewish youth, which is increasingly expressed in the alienation of Jewish youth from the synagogue and from Jewish organizational life in general, in the increasing representation of Jewish youth in integrated or Christian sectarian movements (Hebrew-Christians, Jesus Freaks, and so forth), and in the currently expressed approval of and dramatic increase in rates of intermarriage reported in the United States.[25]

The deep-seated fear of Canadian Jewish parents that future generations

---

[23]Ibid., p. 142.

[24]Ibid., pp. 320-24.

[25]Figures from the National Jewish Population Study (1973) suggest a national average of 31.7 percent for Jewish intermarriages in the United States from 1966 to 1972. Canadian Census data for 1971 reveal a much lower national rate (under 10 percent) for reported Jewish intermarriages in Canada.

For a fuller discussion of the Canadian data see: W.E. Kalbach, "Propensities for Intermarriage in Canada...," paper presented at the annual meeting of the Canadian Sociology and Anthropology Association, University of Toronto, 1974. Despite the difference between American and Canadian statistics, Torontonian Jewish adults fear that influences south of the border will inevitably spread to the north.

will increasingly skip over the ethnic boundary is based on two salient features of contemporary inter-ethnic relations in Canada: the decline in Jewish ethnic distinctiveness and therefore the increasing congruence and compatibility between Jews and Anglo-Christians, and the current nature of legitimation for ethnic diversity under the federal government policy of multiculturalism.[26]

While the multicultural policy supports ethnic group persistence in terms of its symbolic-expressive goals – providing the individual with a personal sense of roots – it emphasizes the *voluntary* nature of ethnic commitments. It also allows for movement across ethnic boundaries by defining the various ethnic units as equivalent options for personal identification and commitment. Further, in the decade following the implementation of multicultural policies at both federal and provincial levels, the pluralist Canadian social environment has spawned a variety of *options* to ethnicity, such as born-again Christians and various liberation movements, which draw strongly from other primary identities and compete with ethnic loyalties for primary group affiliation. Given this social environment, Jewish parents have begun to positively re-evaluate the effectiveness of traditional, particularistic, and segregationalist Jewish practices in the light of their effectiveness as Jewish boundary maintaining mechanisms. This process of re-evaluation, particularly among Conservative and Reform Jews, has led to a dramatic increase in support for separate Jewish education in the contemporary two-track Jewish day school. Separate schools are perceived as uniquely designed to revitalize Jewish ethnic distinctiveness and to reinforce the boundary of ethnic intimacy between Jews and non-Jews in the interests of Jewish ethnic continuity.[27] However, available evidence suggests that there is no statistically significant relationship (at least in the Toronto context) between the degree and type of Jewish education and the degree of Jewish identification.[28] Clearly, the *substitution* of the religious school (whether supplementary or day school) for the parent as ethnic socializer (what contemporary Jewish educators refer to as Jewish education in a vacuum) has failed as an effective strategy of ethnic socialization. At the macro-community level, the evidence strongly supports the micro level thesis that the Jewish family rather than the religious school remains the primary ethnic socializer.[29] Moreover, given the general decline in religious self-definition, religious observance, voluntary organizational participation, and approval of endogamy among third generation Jewish youth, the symbolic-expressive role of the Jewish family may indeed be the critical variable, at the micro level, for the future of ethnic group persistence.

---

[26]House of Commons Debates, 1971. Statement of Prime Minister Trudeau, 1971 10 08.

[27]Glickman, op. cit., p. 322.

[28]Ibid., p. 355. It should be pointed out that Glickman's sample was not stratified by parental synagogue affiliations, therefore potential differences between Orthodox, Conservative, and Reform Jewish families were not revealed. The author's findings, on the other hand, suggest that only in the case of the Orthodox youth, where influences emanating from family, day school, and other ethnic institutions were mutually reinforcing, did the educational institution appear to play a positive role in reinforcing Jewish ethnicity.

[29]Ibid.

Religion, Community Relations, and Self-Identity Among Hutterites

Karl A. Peter

Hutterite society is characterized on one hand by a traditional social order and on the other by the pursuit of rationally structured economic activities. How is it possible to combine these seemingly contradictory characteristics in the daily life of communities that hardly exceed 140 members?

Would it not be more reasonable for Hutterites to uphold their traditional social order and to follow economic pursuits as some of the Old Order Amish do? How is it possible for the Hutterite individual to give at one moment detailed technological instructions for the repair of a complicated machine over short-wave radio, and an hour later expose himself to a religious sermon, the text of which has not changed for 350 years?

If we follow Max Weber's line of reasoning, the Protestant ethic facilitated the rationalization of the everyday life of the Puritans, Calvinists, and Baptists. Is it possible that the Protestant ethic under certain conditions might facilitate traditionalization of the life of certain sects and rationalization of the conduct of others? Moreover, is it possible that the Protestant ethic might facilitate the traditionalization of some societal institutions and the rationalization of others?

The following suggests that the routinization of the certainty of salvation among Hutterites is correlated with the ritualization of religion and the traditionalization of the social order. The rationalization of economic activities among members of this sect, on the other hand, seems to have originated as an adaptive response to secure its survival within a given host society.

The theoretical framework through which this analysis is conducted borrows from Max Weber's attempt to correlate certain religious doctrines of Calvinism with the economic conduct of the Calvinist. The classic study of the relationship between religious ideologies, community structure, and personal identity began with Weber's essay "Die Protestantische Ethik und der Geist des Kapitalismus" first published in the *Archiv fuer Sozialwissenschaften and Sozialpolitik*, Vol. XX and XXI, 1904-1905. This essay was intended as the first step toward a comparative study to determine the influence of certain religious sanctions on the development of an economic spirit. In 1920, the incomplete results of this study were presented in his book *Gesammelte Aufsaetze zur Religionssoziologie*.

Although Weber's primary concern was with the correlations that seemed to exist between religious affiliation and a particular type of economic conduct, he nevertheless saw this correlation in a much wider framework. He says:

> *We are interested in the influence of those psychological sanctions which, originating in religious belief and the practice of religion, gave a direction to practical conduct and held the individual to it. (1958:97)*

This relationship between religious beliefs and practical conduct in the case of the Calvinists and the Puritan sects was traced by Weber to the workings of protestant asceticism. He found that:

> *Protestant asceticism . . . created the force which was alone decisive for its effectiveness: the psychological sanction of it (faithful labours) through the conception of labour as a calling, as the best, often in the last analysis the only means of attaining certainty of grace. (1958:178)*

The active self-control which the individual derived from protestant asceticism and applied to his economic activities, however, could be generated in different ways.

Weber recognized that all Baptist communities desired to be pure churches, in the sense of the blameless conduct of their members. A sincere repudiation of the world and its interests, and an unconditional submission to God as speaking through the conscience were the only unchallengeable signs of true rebirth. Thus, a corresponding type of conduct was indispensable to salvation.

Inasmuch as each Baptist sect spelled out in some detail its understanding of the unconditional submission to God, the repudiation of the world, and the blameless conduct of its members, one can see the specific psychological sanctions at work in those sects that gave direction to the practical conduct of its members.

But as a group moves away from the religious preoccupation and fervor of its founders, and struggles for survival within a larger society, it must adjust itself to the conditions of that society. The nature of these societal conditions interacting with religious doctrines ultimately determines the final relationship between the psychological sanctions that are felt by the individual and the practical conduct which is directed by them. Weber summarized this process in his concept of "elective affinity."

Here an attempt will be made to show that the attainment of salvation among Hutterites changed from a spiritual phenomenon speaking through the individual conscience to a gift bestowed on the individual for faithful participation in the group life. The *Guetergemeinschaft* (community of goods) became the means by which salvation was achieved, and the Hutterite secured his salvation through participation in this community of goods.

The ritualization of the religious institution and the traditionalization of the social relations of the community of goods can be seen as attempts to preserve this precious storehouse which bestowed such valued gifts on its participants.

Economic activities, in contrast, had no eternal value whatsoever, and were regarded as temporary necessities. Certain religious restrictions were imposed mainly in the areas of consumption, financing, and distribution. However, Hutterites were free to develop a rational approach toward production. This structural freedom made it possible for them to use economics as the principal means of establishing mutually beneficial relations with their respective host societies, and thereby enhance their probability of survival as a group.

Methodologically speaking, a baseline will be established to show how the founding generation of Hutterites understood the repudiation of the world, submission to God's will, and the blameless conduct of its members. Then, the transformation of this basic interrelationship will be traced to its contemporary manifestations.

Roots of the Hutterite Doctrine

The Hutterite repudiation of the world shortly after the Reformation took a very radical form not shared by many other Baptist sects. The rejection of infant baptism by the Anabaptists amounted to a challenge of post-medieval civil society based on the unity of religious and societal membership.

The interrelationship of social classes, occupational stratification, and religious adherence formed a perceptual unity that allowed no alternatives. As the unfortunate example of the Jews demonstrates, there simply was no place in society for the religious nonconformist.

The reaction against adult baptism among the established churches was so violent that Felix Mantz, one of the very first Swiss Anabaptists, became the first individual put to death by a *Protestant* power – the city state of Zuerich – which had just completed a Protestant Reformation. (Farner 1954:IV, 112 ff.)

The Anabaptist movement might well have been arrested at this juncture had it not been for a number of strong-willed individuals who formulated the idea of "total separation from the world" and combined it with the immediate practical means of migrating to those parts of the German Empire where a degree of religious toleration traditionally existed. It was here that the concept of "separation from the world" developed its logical implications. These included the strictest pacifism, non-payment of taxes for wars and non-payment of tithes for churches, rejection of worldly office, and refusal to swear the oath. For all practical purposes, these early Hutterites had stripped themselves of the major prevailing civic responsibilities. (Zieglschmid 1947:1-40)

The physical and behavioral separation from the world was quickly followed by a mental and emotional separation. The governments of the day were perceived as the "Rod of God to punish evil doers." There was no intrinsic value assigned to the political authorities; they were regarded as the tool by which God punished the world. (Rideman 102-108) Such a perception effectively neutralized any traditional loyalties, or national or tribal affinities. In the end, the Hutterite not only rejected civic responsibilities and all established churches, he was also stripped of any emotional or rational attachment to existing sociocultural interests or institutions including forms of art, music, and non-biblical literature.

The doctrines of submission to the will of God and the blameless conduct of the individual were realized in a number of behavioral forms, the most important of which was the renunciation of all private property. As God gave the sun, the air, day and night, intending them to be shared by all men, and as he offered sharing his spirit with all men who truly desired to be with him, private possessions in spirit and in property were seen as sinful acts. The *Guetergemeinschaft* incorporated the material aspects of this sharing.

But more important was the spiritual community. To achieve a society where everyone truly shared in the spirit of God, it was deemed necessary to re-move all private spiritual possessions, such as the private love between hus-band and wife and between parent and child. A husband and wife could love one another through sharing in the spirit of God; only through this sharing was bodily union justified. The same applied to parent-child relationships. (Rideman 97,130) As a result, the institution of the family became practically restricted to the bedroom relations between husband and wife, while all other functions such as child rearing, socialization and inter-personal attachments, the expression of love, etc., became community affairs. The transfer of emo-tional attachments from husband, wife and children to the community, and the spiritualization of those emotions in religious doctrines that prescribed specific expressions, subjected the Hutterite to enormous psychological stresses and strains. The blameless conduct of the individual in the community there-fore depended on effective forms of self-control, that made it possible to engage in the prescribed forms of behavior. This was not a problem for first generation Hutterites since membership was self-selective, and self-control, self-denial, and self-sacrifice were voluntarily adopted. Self-control increases the probability of the emergence of rational conduct. As Weber noted:

> *This active self-control, which formed the end of the exercitia of St. Ignatius and of the rational monastic virtues everywhere, was the most important practical ideal of puritanism ... (1958:118)*

If, however, one adds self sacrifice to self control, it is possible to see the emergence of an entirely different type of behavior – the behavior of the martyr.

Hutterites were preoccupied with demonstrations of truthfulness in faith and righteousness in group conduct. Self-control in the daily conduct of the ordinary member and the sacrifice of their martyrs, many of whom reported themselves to the authorities thereby inviting a cruel death, demonstrated their truthfulness and righteousness to an unbelieving public. In this sense, sacrifice displays power on the part of the powerless. And indeed the calm acceptance of the martyr's death by so many Hutterites left a deep impression on even the most hostile enemy of their faith. It was the Hutterites' readiness to die for their faith which often forced a re-examination by their persecutors of their own faith. Hutterites, however, were not lonely martyrs; they were intensely group-oriented individuals even when they died the seemingly lonely death of the heretic. The proliferation of Epistles written in prison, and the multitude of "Confessions of Faith" written by the condemned and addressed to their brothers and sisters in faith, testify to their group orientation.

In the fullest meaning of the word, Hutterites who shared the goods of this and the rewards of the next world also had to assume responsibility for each other's conduct in daily life. This collective responsibility made it legitimate and mandatory to be concerned with every other person's most intimate thoughts and activities. Watching over and assisting one another were seen as expressions of the most valued form of love. (Rideman 132) When this type of love took hold of an individual, it led to a state of mind called *Gelassenheit*. This state was characterized by a fearless and carefree attitude. It was the child-like freedom which flowed from the complete assurance of God's grace and, for the individual who possessed it, all worldly concerns were completely insignificant. (Friedmann 1961:83-85)

The "calling," which Weber perceived as a pattern of conduct incorporating the psychological sanctions activated by submission to God's will, and therefore the rejection of the world, was given a peculiar twist by Hutterites. They insisted that the calling could only be achieved in the context of the *Guetergemeinschaft*, that is in the spiritual and material community where the spirit of God, the material resources of men, and the attainment of eternal grace were shared equally and simultaneously by all members. The individual, his work, and his eternal future were unalterably welded to the state of the total community to the extent that he could be saved only if the total community were saved, he in turn had to do his share to make such communal saving possible. In his own calling, the individual carried the burden of saving his neighbors and his kin.

Thus, *Gelassenheit* was a state of mind that accompanied one's conduct in the calling. It was the result of a constant and rightful participation in the community and at the same time it was a precondition of it. It was marked by the absence of conflict between the individual's wants, wishes, and desires, and the demands and standards of the group. *Gelassenheit* for Hutterites constituted the highest form of self-discipline and self-denial. It signified the stage where the individual became completely submerged in the group. As time passed and the composition of the sect changed from voluntary group affiliation to natural reproduction, the fervor and the intense spiritual demands of *Gelassenheit* and the calling could not be maintained.

A change occurred which shifted the emphasis from the state of mind of *Gelassenheit* to the performance of required behavior in the *Guetergemeinschaft*. It meant a shift from self-control through the individual's conscience to the social control of the group in the form of traditions and customs. This change was greatly facilitated by the increasing ritualization of the religious institution.

The spiritual religious creativity, which so characterized the first generation Hutterites, steadily declined in successive generations, and disappeared altogether around 1660, some 130 years after the founding of the sect. (Peter 1967:127-254) The *Lehren*, the explanation of Bible chapters sentence by sentence, were originally nothing more than verbal interpretations by learned individuals for the illiterate. Under these circumstances it was unavoidable that individuals would give different explanations for the same Bible passages. To avoid theological strife, it became necessary to standardize and record these interpretations. A series of written lectures from elected "servants of the word" gave rise to a liturgical calendar, since some of their explanations suited certain occasions better than others. The sacraments retained by Hutterites – adult baptism, marriage, and the Lord's supper – likewise needed a standardized ritualistic format, and they progressed from relatively freely conducted ceremonies to highly structured ones.

The spiritual sharing explained earlier excercised an enormous pressure toward spiritual singlemindedness and conformity. The faith and the ceremonies associated with it had to be uniform among the scattered Hutterite communities. Such conformity was assured by the ritualization of the entire religious institution. With ritualization came traditionalization in the sense that authority and value were assigned to these elements. However, traditionalization had an inhibiting effect on the religious creativity of Hutterites. They were reluctant to replace the Biblical interpretations of their forefathers who had been willing to die for their faith.

A visitor to a Hutterite church today would be surprised to learn that the *Lehr* (the lecture), which constitutes the main element of the sermon, was written at least 300 years ago; as were the songs intoned by the congregation. Hutterite preachers do not write their own sermons, but faithfully copy the old ones. Almost all of the religious literature was created by first- and second-generation Hutterites.

Under these circumstances, the psychological sanctions of *Gelassenheit* could not be maintained. *Gelassenheit* could not be taught; it had to be experienced, and the societal conditions which gave rise to such experiences no longer existed for Hutterites born into the communities. Without *Gelassenheit*, the psychological sanctions that had originated in the individual's conscience and had governed the individual's conduct faded away. It was replaced by the value of participation in the community of goods. It was no longer conscience that assured the Hutterite's salvation, but rather actions. Salvation was guaranteed for all who participated in the *Guetergemeinschaft*. Self-control, which had earlier been directed toward innermost thoughts, motives, and desires followed by behavioral restrictions, now concentrated on the acting individual. But individual behavior did not require critical rational examination; it could rely on the forces of social control in the community. Hence, social control mechanisms, such as authority positions, customs, etc., assured appropriate participation in the group, while this participation in turn bestowed salvation as a matter of routine. By the time these social controls had been traditionalized, the Hutterite mental focus had shifted from an active, value-oriented conscience to passive, traditionally-defined group conformity that secured eternal fate. Basically that is the situation as it exists today.

The Roots of Economic Rationality

The economic ethic of Hutterites had a traditional orientation which has not appreciably changed during the ensuing centuries. The work of traders and merchants was regarded as sinful and Hutterites do not engage in it today. The market regulation through supply and demand was rejected and the exacting of interest forbidden. As Peter Rideman formulated it:

*Therefore do we allow no one to buy to sell again, as merchants and
traders do. But to buy what is necessary for the needs of one's house
or craft, to use it and then to sell what one by means of his craft hath
made therefrom, we consider to be right and not wrong. (126)*

Wages were set to allow a decent living for those who applied their work to a
product and prices reflected costs plus wages. No market speculation in regard
to wages and prices was allowed. These ideas reflect the sentiments of those
individuals of the social strata from which Hutterite membership was largely
recruited – peasants and journeymen. The work ethic of these individuals was
derived from the village crafts and guilds before the capitalistic transformation. The identification of the individual with his product was expressed in
good workmanship with little distinction between work and life style.

The changes that led to traditionalization do not account for the economic
rationality of the Hutterites. It is not traceable to the economic ethic of the
sect nor is it directly traceable to the psychological sanctions of religious
doctrines as asserted by Weber. Hutterites never developed a spirit of capitalism. As indicated in the previous section, it was participation in the *Guetergemeinschaft* that ensured salvation. However, this participation was not necessarily in the form of faithful work. Any other form of participation would
suffice and indeed there were historical periods when the lack of an active
work ethic proved to be a major problem. What then was the nature of the
Hutterite economic rationality and where can the roots of such rationality be
found?

The economic rationality of Hutterites was and still is, first and foremost, a
rationality of production. (Klassen 1964:93) When the sect was founded it
attracted individuals from a cross section of crafts and was faced with the task
of organizing them in such a way as to maximize their contribution to the
community. There was an immediate advantage to be realized. Most guilds
outside the Hutterite community had adopted restrictive regulations in regard
to the technology of the craft, the securing of raw materials, the hiring of
labor, and the marketing of goods. Hutterites, however, were not hampered
by these regulations and therefore could organize the various crafts in such a
way that a succession of craftsmen would transform the raw material into a
finished product all in one place. The tanner, for example, would prepare the
hides which later would be used as raw material by the harness maker, glove
maker, and others who used leather as a basic material. This semi-industrial
mode of production needed a rudimentary bureaucracy, a planning staff, and
supervisory personnel, all of which were supplied by the emerging authority
of the *Guetergemeinschaft*. Detailed regulations for the various crafts appeared
thirty years after the founding of the sect and increased in frequency and
complexity over the next 100 years. (Peter and Peter 1980) Hutterites were
the first community in central Europe to create a viable planned mode of
production contained under one roof. However, they also were the first to
experience the breakdown of same as demonstrated by the disappearance of
the *Guetergemeinschaft* after 150 years.

The Hutterites were in competition with the guilds, but unlike the guilds, they had no political power to secure markets and supplies of raw materials. By organizing the crafts in an efficient way they were able to produce better products cheaper. There was another important factor at work, however. Hutterites needed a place to live where they would be physically tolerated and protected. The cities with their elaborate religious and sociopolitical structures were quite hostile to Hutterites and offered no such protection. If ever a territorial authority was to afford refuge to Hutterites, it had to be one which might realize enough benefits from their presence to outweigh the dangers which protection of Hutterites created, even for the protector. (Klassen 1964:106-113)

Such territorial authority was found among the members of the lower nobility in Moravia. Within the confines of their estates, Moravian aristocrats were able to grant a degree of protection to these religious dissidents. But what status were they to be given on these estates, and what benefits would they bestow on their protectors? How would their positions relate to the Hutterite doctrine of separation from the world? Whether as serfs, tenured peasants, or employees of noble households, there was little chance of remaining separated from the world since the world of the aristocrat lived off the fruit of their labor.

After some initial experimentation, Hutterites made it a practice to enter into contractual relations with those who offered refuge. In a *Hausbrief* (house contract) very similar to present-day union contracts, the aristocrat and the Hutterites detailed each other's obligations, privileges, and benefits. (Hruby 1935:1-20) The idea was not entirely new; Jewish groups had attempted to do the same for centuries. There was, however, an important difference. The only economic benefits Jews had to offer were financial, since no other occupations were open to them. However, Hutterites had professional skills, organizational talents, and honest, efficient management to offer. As many insightful Jewish leaders recognized, throughout the medieval period financial services were of marginal value in exchange for toleration when the benefits from expropriating the financial sources became greater than the benefits that originated with their toleration. The benefits derived from the professional skills and organizational talents of Hutterites likewise attained marginal utility when either these talents became redundant in the larger society or when the positions of political power were held by those who could afford to be unconcerned about these benefits.

Hutterites, therefore, came under pressure to maximize the benefits of their presence for their protectors. This was achieved by various means. The Hutterites offered a detached, skilled, objective, and honest personnel, who remained reliable and loyal to the aristocrat as long as the socioreligious demands of the sect were respected. Further, they offered products which in quality, design, and workmanship could not easily be duplicated, an outstanding example of which is majolica or faience pottery which was a preferred luxury item of the nobility before the introduction of porcelain. But there were other products such as coaches, an assortment of glassware, kitchenware, iron and steel products etc., which were also of excellent quality. (Klassen 1964:83-97)

During their 450 years of travel through Eastern Europe and North America, the survival of the group was always dependent on the value of those benefits which they could offer through contractual economic relations. The sect, therefore, was forced to develop its economic potential in such a way as to maximize the probability and endurance of such exchange relations. This maximization was obtained through an extraordinary degree of economic rationality applied to the productive aims of the economic enterprise, while consumption continued to be regulated by the principal of sharing in the *Guetergemeinschaft.*

Another factor that contributed greatly to the development of the Hutterite economic rationality was the realization of their own material needs. A sect that adopted a doctrine of separation from the world could not allow inter- ference from the outside world even in a helping capacity. Hutterites in past centuries refused even to be enumerated for census purposes. During the sixteenth and seventeenth centuries, the Hutterite leadership deposited sur- plus funds from each community into a common treasury as insurance against war, plunder, and other casualties. In the nineteenth and twentieth centuries there has been no common treasury, but each Hutterite colony has set aside funds to accommodate the enormous natural increase in the population. (Peter 1967:294-323)

While the rational organization of production had to be geared to maxi- mum profitability to meet the contractual agreement and the requirements of the sect, the accumulated surplus capital posed a threat to the community. For if this surplus was consumed, the material sacrifice demanded of the individ- ual was reduced; this, in turn, devalued the spiritual benefits the individual acquired through participation in the community, thereby endangering the sect's reason for existence. The most effective and legitimate means of maintaining the mode of production at a most rational level, therefore, was to expropriate any surplus for emergencies and to increase the population of the sect to such an extent that there was no surplus available for consump- tion. Their failure to employ either of these mechanisms resulted in the total collapse of the *Guetergemeinschaft.*

In summary, the economic rationality of Hutterites was only indirectly re- lated to the sect's doctrine of separation from the world. Its particular form cannot be traced to the workings of individual psychological sanctions, as Weber asserts, but to the societal situation in which Hutterites found them- selves. As a dissident religious minority, their survival as a group apart from the host society could only be secured by entering into contractual economic relations with that host society. Once established, the rationalization of pro- duction was perpetuated by its own successes.

Contemporary Manifestations of Economic Rationality and Hutterite Doctrine

Separation from the world except for contractual economics precludes Hutterite participation in the emotional, moral, esthetic, and political frame- works of the host society. Although the individual might very well be acquainted with some or all of these aspects, his situation can best be compared with the detachment with which a eunuch views the behavior of those motivated by sexual desires.

This emotional detachment contributed to the development of a personality structure which, through self-control, was capable of dealing with these conditions. The rationality and constant maintenance of contractual relations were only possible if objective criteria were brought to bear by the Hutterite individual on his own behavior. The anticipated actions of the world had to be incorporated into the planning of future Hutterite actions. This required an accurate anticipatory knowledge of the world which was only possible by objective assessment. The effectiveness of the individual's action, on the other hand, depended on the ability to dissect one's own behavior and to rationally judge the consequences of each behavioral element. Such rationality has, of course, gone through a certain evolution over the centuries. The form that it takes today can perhaps be characterized in a few statements.

Hutterites are masters of practical thinking and reasoning. It is almost impossible to convince them of anything by verbal means alone. They judge individuals by their behavior, not by their words; and they prefer experiment over theory. The result is a certain neglect of abstract thinking. But postponement of judgment until experience or demonstration can be supplied is very useful in all practical situations. Confusion about abstract cause and effect relations is widespread but not very consequential for Hutterites, since their practical life produces very few encounters of this kind. They perceive the world in primary terms, emphasizing primary means of communication rather than secondary ones, and relying on personal relations rather than impersonal forms of interaction.

Another pronounced aspect of Hutterite rationality is the ability to discern the source of any event. In human relations it takes the form of searching for the power of an individual or an office. "What can he do and what can't he do?" is the crucial question. In mechanical terms the question is "How does it work?" Since in the religious realm the questions about power are sufficiently answered, there is a certain compatibility between this mode of religious thinking, the thinking applied to economic relations with the outside world, and the mode of thought concerning economic production.

On the other hand, there is an abundance of traditionalized thinking and acting. Why is it important for Hutterite men to wear suspenders instead of belts? Why must garments be made in dark colors rather than lighter ones? Why must a younger person show deference when talking to an older one and why is it the privilege of certain people and not of others to say grace in the community dining room?

Although a degree of habitualness is evident in Hutterite colonies, tradition is more than just habit. The maintenance of traditional forms of thinking and acting must have a more immediate and compelling force in order to be as persisting and effective as they are in Hutterite society.

Hutterite traditions have crystalized around the religiously important concept of the *Guetergemeinschaft* and have become the manifestations by which this institution has become reified. As the original means by which a mental state of *Gelassenheit* could be obtained, in turn assuring salvation, participation in the community of goods in and by itself now produces this effect. The early Hutterites who worked themselves painfully slowly into the mental state of *Gelassenheit* in order to obtain salvation must be seen in contrast to modern-day Hutterites whose participation in the *Guetergemeinschaft* routinely secures their salvation.

The customs and social relations practised in the *Guetergemeinschaft*, no matter how odd or dysfunctional they appear from a practical point of view, nevertheless visibly demonstrate the existence and effectiveness of this institution. The participating member feels secure in complying with these traditions handed down by successive generations. The fact that these traditions impose restraints that he must struggle to obey, increases the value of the *Guetergemeinschaft* for him.

That the Hutterite *Guetergemeinschaft* of today is vastly different from that of past centuries matters little. The interaction between economic rationality and traditional elements has produced constant but subtle changes in the Hutterite culture. The nature of these changes is insignificant as long as noticeable discontinuities and obvious incompatibilities are avoided. Traditions depend on living memories; since there are three generations in each Hutterite colony, change that is compatible with the generational memory structure of Hutterite society is permissible. What Eaton called "controlled acculturation" (1952:331-40) is in reality a balancing act between economic rationality (which aims at change), and social and religious traditionalism (which aims at constancy), all in relation to the scrutiny of the three-generational traditional memory in Hutterite communities.

The extraordinary holding power of the *Guetergemeinschaft* now becomes clearer. It is understandable why the communal system that disappeared around 1680 was recreated around 1760 and why, when it disappeared a second time in 1818, strenuous efforts were made to reinstitute it forty years later. The analysis also sheds some light on why few Hutterites permanently defect from the colonies and why those that do suffer from lifelong yearning to return.

Weber's analysis of the Protestant ethic assumed that the effective action of psychological sanctions, mainly in the form of asceticism, held the individual to his economic conduct. The rationality of economic action was shaped and sharpened by the rationality of searching for the signs of salvation in the individual that gave him certainty of that salvation. This analysis has sought to show that Hutterites were, and still are, traditional in their economic ethic, and that they never developed any spirit of capitalism despite the fact that the state of *Gelassenheit* demanded as much self-control as that of the Puritans. Moreover, in spite of the traditionalization of salvation in the *Guetergemeinschaft,* Hutterites nevertheless developed an economic rationality of production. This development cannot be credited to the religious sanctions of *Gelassenheit* which disappeared quickly, but rather to the development of rational economic relations necessary for the survival of the group. This does not, however, invalidate Weber's thesis.

On the contrary, it is suggested that when religious doctrines and practices assume collectivistic and separatistic aspects the type of conduct that follows might differ from what Weber observed among the Calvinist and Puritan sects. Weber's concept of "elective affinity" implies the spontaneous and gradual convergence of a religious ethic and the material interest of its articulators. The data presented here seem to indicate that the Hutterite sect's ideal interests were realized in the traditionalization of its socioreligious institutions while its material interests were served by the rationalization of production. The routinization of salvation and the traditionalization of its religious practices served the ideal interests of the Hutterite individual by making salvation a certainty. Through participation in the *Guetergemeinschaft* salvation was assured; yet through faithful labor in rationally structured productive activities demanding the denial of private possessions, the very existence of the community was perpetuated. The religious interests and the material interests of Hutterites therefore converged in the traditionalization of the first and the rationalization of the second.

Religious Socialization and Ethnic Identity Among the Dutch Canadians

K. Ishwaran

The Holland Marsh area about forty miles north of Toronto, Ontario was settled by Dutch immigrants. This rural community is characteristic of a Dutch village in the northern provinces of Holland, and the residents have typical Dutch names – Boneschanker, Horling, Jansme, Van Dyke, Hyma, and Miedema.

The Holland Marsh community is divided into two rural communities, Ansnorveldt and Springdale. The economy of the community is based on commercial gardening which is integrated into the adjacent urban market. The sociocultural system is predominantly Dutch, adapted to suit the local ecology. This paper is an exploration of the interrelationship of the socialization process which is aimed at generating a strong self-identity, and the religious system and ethnicity that contribute to it.

The data for this analysis are drawn from fieldwork between 1965 and 1975, and October 1977 and March 1978.[1] The advantage of such a long period is the opportunity to perceive and reflect on the changing nature of the community life.

Of the total population, the Dutch account for 60 percent. Other ethnic groups in the community are Poles, Hungarians, Ukrainians, Germans, Chinese, and Japanese. However, the population is highly segregated and the Dutch display very little meaningful interaction with the other ethnic groups. Classified by age, about 41 percent of the respondents were between 14 and 16, 42.5 percent were between 16 and 18, and the balance were between 18 and 20. Females accounted for 65.9 percent and males 34.1 percent of the sample. Although there are slight variations, the Ansnorveldt and Springdale communities can be viewed as a single community in terms of their value system, institutional patterns, and behavioral norms.

The community is committed to the religion of the pioneers, i.e., the Dutch Reformed Church, which plays a dominant and crucial role in the life of the community. The two churches and the two denominational schools have been largely instrumental in consolidating and strengthening the Calvinistic and familial cultural values and institutional patterns of the community.

Most of the pioneering families came from an agricultural background and

---

[1]Survey data were derived from closed questionnaires supplemented by prolonged interviews with 155 heads of households and their 72 adolescent children, from both rural communities.

it was natural for them to transform the Marsh wilderness into an agricultural setting. In the 1930s, this developing agrarian system generated the simple two-class system familiar in the homeland. However, the need for intense community interaction during the community building phase conflicted with the hierarchical system and it had to be abandoned. As the community prospered through expanded and intensified vegetable cultivation, especially after 1950, a new class system emerged. Prosperity implied differential resources giving rise to a three-tiered class system identified by the size of landholdings, modes of cultivation, and marketing techniques and life styles. Today these classes are identified as small farmers owning an average of 5 to 14 acres, middle farmers having between 15 and 39 acres, and upper farmers with 40 acres or more. By 1970, according to their own assessment, 73.6 percent of the population were middle-class, 12.9 percent were lower-class, and 2.6 percent were upper-class farmers.

The contemporary family in this community is undergoing a change toward a nuclear model. The family of the pioneers had been a nuclear type, but building a farming community required the subordination of the family to interfamily community life. The present development is, therefore, a resurgence of the earlier model. The rise of the nuclear family has not resulted in a decline in the community identity, however. The dominant position of the church has meant that the nuclear family functions within the framework of a church-defined culture and value system supported by church-controlled institutions such as the school. In fact, the contemporary Marsh community resembles the pioneer system in all essential respects, although, more recently, it has been under pressure to assimilate some elements of the surrounding mainstream society. The defining features of the culture, religion and value systems are friendship, mutual support, family sense, kinship support, and male dominance, especially that of the father in the family system.

The Religious Imperative

Religion is a basic sociological imperative in the Holland Marsh Dutch community with the church playing an important role in its development from the pioneer days. The social structure of the early settlers was organized, as it was in Holland, on a distinctly religious basis. The church and the church-sponsored schools were the foundation of this religious dominance over the community.

The family as an institutional system and an ideological structure can hardly be separated from the activities of the Dutch Reformed Church. Religious dominance has become such a part of the family system that they accept it automatically and implicitly. Consequently, the function of the church is merely to provide an institutionalized symbol for an active religious life.

The denominational school, an instrument of the church, disseminates the Calvinistic faith and way of life, forging the integration and cohesion of the community on the basis of its religious ideology. Although this is a central role, the school is only one component in a complex institutional system; the other two are the family and the church.

The religious basis of the family is reflected in its functioning. The family acts as a sifting mechanism permitting only external literature that is consistent with the religious value system. For instance, the family system orders things in such a way that a heavy input of religious newspapers and journals, such as the *Young Calvinist*, the *Christian Vanguard*, and *De Watcher*, is systematically injected. Virtually every family keeps two Bibles, one in English and the other in Dutch. There are cases of extreme religiosity as, for example, one family that had thirteen Bibles, five of which were printed in Dutch. Even secular reading material is indirectly related to religious themes and concerns. Above all, the family is involved in a series of rituals that strengthen the religious bond – baptisms, weddings, funerals, and Christmas celebrations. The informal grace before meals relates even the most commonplace domestic acts to religion. Biblical quotations abundantly adorn the walls of the home. The ethical and value systems that govern the family life are rooted in religious doctrines and scriptures, supporting a strong belief in God and the Bible.

Marriage is conceived as a religious relationship, sacred and indissoluble, sanctioned by God. Opposition to divorce is consequently quite substantial, as many as 51 percent of family heads opposed it, and some 15 percent were vehemently against it. Only 28 percent felt that divorce may be justified in special cases involving adultery, alcoholism, and deliberate physical violence or mental cruelty. Religious endogamy tends to reinforce the religious influence. Because marriage is regarded as a religious act, interfaith marriage is neither encouraged nor accepted. Seventy-eight percent of the parents surveyed were opposed to their children marrying outside their religion, claiming that it would interfere with the life style sanctioned by their religion.

Religious Socialization

In general, the socialization process is designed to reinforce certain basic sociocognitive categories. Of these, the three most important are age, sex, and class differentiation (lower, middle, and upper). On one level, children are socialized into roles related to these categories. However, these three aspects are subordinate to religion – the central element in the socialization process. In fact, they function within an explicitly religious-ideological framework.

Thus, religious socialization remains a crucial community process through which the young are made aware of their roles and the behavioral norms associated with them. The values and behavioral patterns involved in the socialization process are products of historical interaction between the traditional homeland equipment and the overall environment of the adopted country. This historical aspect is very important because it suggests a complex socialization process involving the continuous dynamics of interaction. In other words, the socialization process produces certain static categories but, at the same time, must leave room for changes within these categories. Otherwise, socialization would not help explain the central community process of maintaining a dynamic equilibrium between the goals of continuity and of change. In this instance, the balance of forces is tilted significantly toward the traditional ethnic-religious community model.

Religious socialization takes place in the context of the family, the church, and the school on an interrelated basis. The Dutch child's first encounter with the faith, norms, values, and life goals that (s)he is likely to embrace for a lifetime takes place within the family. (S)He is socialized into the religiously-based community life and its institutional patterns through the mediation of a series of well-marked ritual situations. The first experience is infant baptism, signifying induction into the culture of the community. Then the child becomes involved in the family ritual of Bible reading before meals. From this early routine induction, the child becomes familiar with the teachings of the Bible, the foundation for the Dutch Calvinistic religious life. The recitation of grace before meals affirms the goodness of God and the status of the father as the representative of the Holy Ghost. The authority and the pervasive presence of the Lord are evident in every aspect of the home – the theme of discussions at mealtimes, the family books, toys, and wall plaques.

The Calvinistic religious ideology and system of values into which the child is socialized is a structure of balanced and contained contradiction between an individualistic emphasis on self-effort and private conscience on the one hand, and the notion of God's absolute authority on the other. At bottom, the system has evolved a balance on the basis of a fundamental identity between the two values – the individual's self-identity derived from God's authority without any mediation. But for the child it must be mediated, and the father performs the mediating role. In contrast, the mother's role in the socialization process has no explicitly religious connotations. However, she assists the father in his role, and she also contributes to the socialization of behavior patterns which are not overtly religious, but are designed to be consistent with, and supportive of, the religiously approved way of life. Further, given the sex dimension of the socialization process, the mother provides a role model for the daughter.

Because the church is a specialized religious institution in the community, its socialization is unmediated and directly religious. The youth are socialized into the religious ethos by a variety of church-sponsored voluntary organizations. But in theory, the church is itself a voluntary institution in the sense that one is not born into it. In practice, this means little since community ethos is such that very few find it necessary or possible to opt out. In fact, the church plays a crucial role, next to that of the father, as a mediator between God and the individual. In terms of socialization into a religiously-legitimated pattern of behavior, the church emphasizes the non-individualistic aspect of the religious belief system. This means that the thrust of the church socialization is toward an authoritarian model of behavior in which the individual is subordinated to the complex of community structures of which (s)he is a member. Above all, the church today, employs a sophisticated and modern instrument in performing its role, i.e., a church-controlled bureaucratic organization. This structure, with the pastor at the top, comprises a consistory, normally a body of nine members, the council of five elders, and a group of four deacons. The structure is centralized in the office of the pastor who is the president of these three structures as well as the formal head of all committees associated with the church.

Highly formalized in terms of procedures and regulations, the church bureaucracy exercises a quasi-judicial function in relation to complaints pertaining to unacceptable behavior. It has punitive powers ranging from expulsion of the delinquent from the Lord's Supper to expulsion from the church membership itself. In a closed and isolated community, these are formidable fates which individuals have to reckon with seriously.

The church is in a strategic position since it co-ordinates the religious activities of the community as a whole, especially those under the auspices of the family and the school. It is, therefore, not surprising that the Dutch pastor in the Holland Marsh community is a person commanding respect and influence. Most children regard him as a figure of authority and a correct reference model. Under his comprehensive care and control, the church functions as the guardian of the right behavior in the religious, ethical, and social life of the community. It is in this role, as much by its mere presence as by its overt activities, that the church plays its part in the religious socialization of the young. In sociological terms, the consequence of such a process is to perpetuate a community identity rooted in the Calvinistic values of asceticism, industry, parsimony, and thrift.

In the early days, religious instruction was a family reponsibility; now it has been taken over by outside agencies which include Sunday school, the catechism, clubs, summer camps, church-controlled conferences and recreational activities, in addition to the Christian Reformed denominational primary and secondary schools. The objective of this religious exposure is to orient the young toward the Calvinistic beliefs, norms, and values. Regular religious training for all children is an essential part of the Calvinistic doctrine. The authoritarian context of this early socialization makes them dogmatic and authoritarian in their values, beliefs, and attitudes; consequently, they become quite intolerant of a non-Calvinistic viewpoint.

Religious socialization also takes place in the school. The church-controlled parochial schools provide religious and moral training which contributes to the personality structure of the Dutch-Canadian youth. These educational institutions extend beyond the Marsh area. Besides the Christian junior school in the Marsh, they include the secondary school in Woodbridge, Ontario and Calvin College in the United States. The educational system functions as an effective barrier against the secular impact of the public schools. Normally, the children are sent to denominational schools, and only rarely do they attend secular institutions. The parochial schools are preferred because they produce the "right kind" of youth, those who conform to the community tradition.

Thus, the Dutch-Canadian children in the Marsh experience a prolonged and pervasive socialization process in the triple context of the family, the church, and the school. These agencies generally succeed in producing persons who are disposed to subordinate their individual inclinations to the traditional community system, a system founded on a clearly Calvinistic basis.

The Ethnic Dimension of Socialization

The socialization process, while clearly religious in content and form, cannot be explained merely in terms of the religious system of the community. Its other basic dimension is ethnicity – identity based on belonging to a specific ethnic group – which, in this case, is Dutch ethnicity. Dutch ethnicity derives from the nationality, history, culture, and social geography, as well as the physical ecology of Holland. The Dutch immigrants brought this heritage, which included the Calvinistic religio-ethical system. Thus, we find that ethnicity and Dutch religion are inseparable components of a single historical structure.

From this it follows that religious socialization as well as what little non-religious socialization there is are both aimed at producing individuals who identify systematically with Dutch culture and social organization, and who have a sense of Dutch community identity. Hence, to understand the content of the socialization process, it is necessary to comprehend the nature and pattern of Dutch ethnic identity.

Like any national community sense, the Dutch identity contains regional variations; it is not totally homogeneous. But these inter-regional distinctions in sociocultural patterns or value systems are contained within a common national community framework. The deviations from a predominantly national pattern are too marginal to threaten the national community identity. The Canadian Dutch identity, as it has evolved historically in the Holland Marsh over the last half century, may be conceptualized as a structure characterized by five basic and distinctive aspects: religiosity, familism, extended kinship, paternal authoritarianism, and Dutchness. Each of these will be examined briefly.

Since religious socialization and the dominant role of religion have been discussed in detail, only a brief recapitulation is necessary. The Dutch-Canadian community has a distinctive religious system, characterized by the Dutch Reformed Church and the Calvinistic religio-ethical ideology. Contrary to theories that view modernization as virtually identical with secularization, the "modern" rural Dutch-Canadian community of Holland Marsh draws systematic sustenance from its religious value system, behavioral norms, and institutional complex. From both their own assessment and that of outsiders, this religiously rooted community is defined as a distinctive group of people who subscribe to puritanical norms, abstain from alcoholic beverages, live a simple economic existence, and equate labor with service to God. The pattern of daily living demonstrates the religiosity of the community which stands in dramatic contrast to the prevailing mainstream Canadian pattern of dominant secularism.

Familism – attachment to the institution and ideals of family life – is a basic constituent in the self-identity of those in the Dutch-Canadian community. The family holds a central place in the Dutch social life and scale of values; and the religious system reinforces, and is reinforced by, this element of familism. The role of the father symbolizes and upholds the ideal of familism, which is reinforced by his ever present consideration of "the interest of the family." The mother, though subordinate to the father, has her functional distinctiveness as a loving person and her autonomy within the framework of family and community life. The daughters reinforce familism through the mediation of the mother as their role model. The Dutch-Canadian family in the Marsh is crucially involved in the primary processes of socialization; this enables the community to preserve its ethnic identity. The modernization of this rural community has resulted in a strengthening rather than a weakening of the family system and its ideal of familism.

The third important feature of Dutch ethnicity is its emphasis on kinship as an institutional resource and as a value. As the community has developed, kinship has undergone some changes, but it remains functional to the community system. Historically, the evidence suggests that the role and significance of kinship relations have declined over the years, especially in comparison with the situation during the earlier phases of pioneering and consolidation. The frequency of their mobilization has shown a perceptible downswing. This, however, does not imply that they are not potentially present to be activated should the occasion arise. Even today, the kinship relations can be invoked for psychological and material support.

In the Marsh, farming operations often necessitate kin support during certain seasons. The duty of the kinguard, collecting and preserving information about kin groups, has not declined in significance. This information enables Marsh inhabitants to draw on their kinship relations, when necessary. Behavior toward non-kin is significantly different from that accorded kin. The kinship network, however, is not closed or confined to the Marsh area. It extends well beyond in spatial terms as well as in terms of closeness of relationship. The kinship system presupposes a moral exchange of values and a material exchange of goods and services. No doubt the effective kinship network is much narrower than the formal structure, but it exists, and continues to be one of the resources individuals and families may call on for support.

The fourth aspect, authoritarianism, is a widely accepted and shared value that dates back to the traditional social system in Holland. The most significant interpersonal interactions and relationships of the community are characterized by authoritarian behavior, involving dominance, subordination, and negation of individuality. Like most aspects, the authoritarianism of the Dutch-Canadian community is traceable to its religious system. But whatever its probable source, it has become a feature governing most relationships and transactions in the community. In the family, the father represents this principle as a surrogate of the Divine Father. Although there are functionally-based role distinctions within the family, the final authority belongs to the father. The role of the mother is to minimize the authoritarian role; she symbolizes God's other aspect, love and affection. All crucial family decisions ultimately rest with the father, although other members do participate in varying degrees. The father's authority descends directly to the eldest male child, who represents the surrogate of the earthly father. While children may experience the authoritarian power through physical punishment, adults realize it through more subtle moral and psychological pressures. The same pattern extends to the school where the teacher represents authority and to the church and church-based structures under the authoritarian control of the pastor. Authoritarianism is functional in this community and, contrary to conventional modernization theories, has not been a serious obstacle to modernization.

The last feature of ethnicity is its Dutchness. This is the most comprehensive and distinctive aspect of the community. Dutchness lies in the pattern of sociocultural, institutional, and interpersonal relationships that have evolved into a complex structure through a long historical process. It involves a certain emotional commitment to the history and tradition of Dutch society. It underscores each of the other aspects of ethnicity – religiosity, familism, kinship, and authoritarianism. This Dutch-Canadian community has organized its social, economic, and cultural systems to ensure the continuity and continued reproduction of the essential community system, allowing for minimal changes consistent with the ideal community. This ethnic identity is further reinforced in a multiethnic context. The rivalries between religious denominations – the Protestant and the Catholic – and diverse ethnic groups – the Poles, Hungarians, Germans, etc. – have also tended to strengthen the Dutch identity. The religious and ethnic aspects have been intensified and structurally fused by these conflicting interactions. The perception and the associated behavior of being Dutch and not being Dutch have contributed to this process of identity consolidation by the community. The sociocultural life in Holland Marsh is dominated by community stereotypes that reflect community prejudices, if not hostilities. Just as the Dutch emphasize their Dutchness, so do the other groups stress their ethnicity. In consequence, interethnic interactions have remained largely negative. Self-affirmation has been achieved, to some extent, through a process of other-negation.

The Dutch ethnic identity is most vividly exemplified in the community's distinctive dimensions of time and space. In this rural community, social time is bound to the repetitive nature of farming operations, but it is also church-oriented and church-defined. Socially, it is a closed community with a crystallized identity, and the outside community has no structural relationship to it. Space is also socially-defined in relation to the home, signifying the central role of the family in the community. The spatial arrangements of the architecture and the landscape reiterate the social themes and motifs of a distinctive ethnic community.

Religion and Ethnic Identity

In this community, religion and ethnicity cannot be separated. The social structure, the cultural system, the cognitive dimensions of time and space, and the family system emphasize the intermeshing of religion and ethnic identity among the Dutch Canadians.

In the first place, the social system, the value system, and the behavioral patterns that characterize the community are overtly religious in that they reflect the teachings of the Bible elucidated by the Dutch Reformed Church. Secondly, the community structures and processes that reinforce the religious system have become institutionalized in the Marsh. Moreover, the contrasting backdrop of multiethnicity and the non-Marsh environment contribute to the persistence of Dutch identity encased in a religious framework.

As indicated earlier, the socialization processes, whether overtly religious or outwardly non-religious in terms of the agents involved and the content socialized, constitute the basis of a historical persistence and reproduction of the religious-ethnic identity of the Dutch community. The degree of integration is such that the community's identity is both Calvinistic and Dutch. The

Dutch Canadian's answer to the question – Who are you? – involves three components – religion, ethnicity, and Canadianism. The complexities, ambiguities, and self-contradictions of being a Dutch Canadian in Holland Marsh stem from this diverse source of community identity.

The Changing Situation

While the Dutch-Canadian community structure and identity are predominantly Dutch and Calvinistic, there are now new social trends and patterns that suggest a departure from the traditional system. However, it is difficult to foresee the cumulative impact of these changes. It is very unlikely that the traditional community identity will remain constant. At the same time, it is unlikely that the traditional identity will be destroyed. Conceptually, this is a situation in which contradictory elements appear to be structurally balanced; community tradition and identity seem strong enough to meet the challenge of outside pressures. However, it is too early to predict whether the increasing challenges from the mainstream Canadian system will undermine and destroy the self-identity of the Dutch Canadians in Holland Marsh. Clearly, the community is beginning to experience contradictions.

In addition, there are internal contradictions. The first is rooted in the history of the community, especially in its pattern of immigration. Historically, the immigrants came from different regions in Holland. This diversity of origin is reflected in the diversity within the Dutch community pattern. Cognition and behavior tend to be related to inter-regional distinctions. In the early years of community building and consolidation, these diversities were submerged; more recently, they have been consciously articulated and focussed. One minister interviewed made sharp reference to intra-Dutch parochialism, declaring that immigrants from the northern provinces were highly conservative and hence resistant to new ideas such as family planning. Some respondents believed that the community would never overcome the fragmentation resulting from these diversities. However, in the face of the Canadian environment, internal differences will no doubt be forgotten in the interest of community unity.

A second source of internal contradiction is inter-generational conflict. The older generation zealously guards the traditional ways through institutionalized and socialized behavior, but the younger generation, who are more exposed to the external environment through non-denominational schools, the mass media, and the opportunities afforded by mobility, find it more difficult to accept traditional patterns without some questioning and doubt. This situation has brought about slight but symptomatic shifts in family life style. For instance, the pioneers gave their offspring only Dutch names, but their children and their grandchildren followed the practice of giving two names – one traditional Dutch and another representing the culture of the dominant Anglo-Saxon group. This is an instance of pragmatic compromise. Today, Dutch names have been virtually abandoned, signifying the results of a Canadianization process.

Inter-generational behavior within the family has also undergone change.

While it is still the practice for parents and children to dine together, the children now leave the house after dinner to avoid parental pressures. This behavior runs counter to the traditional norm.

Inter-generational differences are also evident in attitudes toward the church. In contrast to the commitment of the old, the younger generation see the church as a constricting and undesirable obstacle, and attendance is irregular. Their departure from expected behavior has caused genuine concern to the ministers and elders.

Even more alarming for the older generation is the fact that the young have even begun to court outside the local Dutch community. Often in these instances, the minister will attempt to dissuade the couple, warning them of the unhappy consequences of their behavior. Thus, interfaith marriage is severely denounced by both church and parents.

While the tradtional pattern was strongly and exclusively Dutch, changes are evident. Originally, the church was totally Dutch, with all services conducted in the Dutch language. However, since 1955, this pattern has changed. English is now used in morning and evening sermons, and Dutch is retained for the afternoon sermon only. This development resulted as part of their effort to compete in Canadian society. This increasing presence of the English language in community life is yet another inroad into the citadels of Dutch ethnicity in Holland Marsh.

The growing impact of the mainstream Canadian culture and ideology coupled with the economic process of integration of the Marsh community into the wider Canadian economy, and eventually into the global economy, pose a challenge to traditional Dutch ethnicity and Calvinistic ideology. However, it must be remembered that the Calvinistic ideology is not one sided; it has another individualistic side which can easily be reconciled with the values implied in the Canadianization process. If historical precedents are indicative, it is likely that the Dutch ethnic identity may be modified or even reduced, but it is not likely to be erased from the life of the Dutch-Canadian community in Holland Marsh. Thus, while changes are taking place in various institutional contexts, these changes should not be interpreted as a process in which Canadianization will annihilate the Dutch religiosity and ethnic identity.

Evaluation

The traditional community system of the Dutch Canadians in the Holland Marsh is rooted in two fundamental historical sources – religious ideology and ethnicity. These dimensions mutually reinforce each other to sustain the existence and self-identity of the community. This process may be explained in more than one way. Firstly, it may be interpreted as a consequence of the structural properties of the original Dutch system, historically transplanted to Canadian soil. In this view, continuity, persistence, and tradition are fundamental Dutch qualities, accounting for the relative indestructability of the Dutch identity in Holland Marsh. Secondly, it may be interpreted as a situational necessity. The latter would then be seen to comprise Canadian ecology, the wider Canadian sociocultural environment, and the isolated nature of the farming community. In reality, a combination of both sets of variables may provide a satisfactory key to an understanding of the changing nature of the Dutch-Canadian community in the Marsh.

Given the overall situation, it is not surprising that the evolution of the community has taken the direction it has. The more recent changes in behavioral patterns, both on the individual level and on the institutional level, are the products of one set of compulsions inherent in the existential situation – the pressure of, and the need for Canadianization. Persistence of the traditional pattern as well as the departures from it stem from a common existential and historical situation in which the Dutch Canadians of Holland Marsh find themselves.

While the data are certainly not sufficient to make any large-scale and long-range generalizations and speculation, it would appear that Canadianization will increasingly modifiy the original Dutch patterns, but in the context of a countervailing process of community resistance. There can be no total victory for either side in the ongoing sociological process. There can only be temporary short-term compromises and equilibriated stages. This study has captured merely one stage in this community's long and complicated historical journey.

HUSBANDS AND WIVES

Introduction

The articles in this section focus on some of the important and interesting dimensions of husband-wife relationships which, under the impact of such movements as Women's Liberation and the tremendous increase in participation of wives in the labor force, are undergoing revaluation in modern societies. Consequently, attempts to understand these relationships are also among the most controversial both in popular and social scientific literature.

The article by Brinkerhoff and Lupri deals with the theme of power relations between husbands and wives. Although a great deal has been written on the subject, these authors find that all the prevalent approaches and well-known relevant studies are conceptually and methodologically inadequate. Their chief objection is that most studies, which are based solely on the wives' responses, seriously underestimate the complexity and multidimensional aspects of the power concept. Moreover, family decisions vary in frequency and importance. These authors argue that studies of husband-wife power relations must take such issues into careful consideration.

From their main findings, we learn that: (1) among Canadian couples the husband's socio-economic status is *not positively* associated with the husband's power; (2) in the Canadian context, wives who work for pay have less power vis-à-vis their husbands than the wives who do not work for pay; and (3) even in cases where wives may appear to be equal to, or even more powerful than their husbands, wives make decisions only in those areas in which it is traditionally expected, and these areas are considered less important than those in which husbands make decisions.

Peter Butler's comparative study on single-career and dual-career families also points to conceptual and methodological inadequacies in the existing relevant studies. He finds these studies are deeply influenced by the idea of separation between work and family. This idea, advocated by Talcott Parsons and many of his followers, implies that the husband as wage earner connects the family to the outside world, while the wife's main function is family integration. With the increasing number of working wives, this idea is no longer a useful guide to those who wish to understand the dynamics of husband-wife relations in the context of the occupational world. Butler suggests that a more useful approach is to consider the way each family member is involved in work relative to his or her involvement in family life. Using Walter Buckley's concept of "system" together with data gathered in the Borough of East York in Metropolitan Toronto, Butler reaches several tentative but important conclusions - one being that when more of the family's energies are directed toward work, participation in family life is compromised.

Using data from rural Saskatchewan, Seena Kohl presents the case of wives' dual career in a "hidden sense." Women in farm families make significant contributions both to household services and to the family enterprise. Men, by contrast, make contributions mainly to the enterprise as farm operators; their contributions to household work are minimal. For men, there is a separation between household work and work per se; there is no such separation for women who work both in the farm enterprise and in the domestic sphere. Kohl articulates several formal and informal implications of this situation and their effect on husband-wife relations.

Conjugal Power and Family Relationships: Some Theoretical and Methodological Issues*

Merlin B. Brinkerhoff and Eugen Lupri

Introduction

Two salient dimensions of family structure are division of power and division of labor. Power, under scrutiny here, refers to the potential ability of one spouse to influence the other's behavior and action. It is grounded in the ability to make decisions affecting the life circumstances of the entire family. Power may be divided equally between the husband and the wife or wielded predominantly by one spouse over the other.

The power to make crucial family decisions is highly influenced by the prescribed authority patterns. Weber's classical distinction between power and authority is still a meaningful one. For him authority is legitimated power, or the ability to give orders. Weber states that ". . . patriarchalism means authority of the father, the husband, the senior of the house, the sib elder over the members of the household, the rule of the master. . . ." (Gerth and Mills 1958:195-96) Simmel, too, argues that authority is a form of superordination and subordination. A person may come "to enjoy prerogative decision-making . . . because the family or other social institutions confer authority of decision in a given area upon him." (Simmel 1961:541) According to both Weber and Simmel, then, an authority relation is one person's making decisions that guide and influence the actions of another person. Wolfe (1959:101) puts it succinctly by arguing that authority is a special case of the power structure of the family "having to do with decision-making in social groups."

Ever since the publication in 1960 of *Husbands and Wives* by Robert O. Blood and Donald M. Wolfe, the resource theory of conjugal power has been the focus of considerable cross-national research. Perhaps no other dimension of family organization has enjoyed such extensive cross-national testing.[1] It comes as no surprise, then, that both cogent critiques and a certain disillusionment with the concepts of power and authority emerged rapidly in the international sociological literature. It is precisely the *cross-national*

*Adapted and augmented from M.B. Brinkerhoff and Eugen Lupri, "Theoretical and methodological issues in the use of decision-making as an indicator of conjugal power: some Canadian observations." *Canadian Journal of Sociology,* Vol. 3, 1978. We would like to thank Wendy Weicker for her helpful comments and suggestions.

[1]For a comprehensive review of comparative data and sources, see Lupri (1982), Brinkerhoff and Lupri (1978), and Cromwell and Olson (1975).

testing of propositions derived from the resource theory that has sensitized family sociologists around the world to some of the conceptual and methodological pitfalls in the study of family power as a dynamic process. (Hill 1975)

In spite of such criticisms the concept continues to be widely used. Why? From both theoretical and common sense perspectives it seems reasonable to assume that power, as an explanatory device, should account for the variation in many of those familial characteristics which are often considered under the rubric of "dependent variables." On the other hand, some critics argue that familial power has had "poor success" as a predictor variable, i.e., it correlates weakly, if at all, with many of these dependent variables.

The Problem

A common practice has been to generate an overall power score by calculating the arithmetic average of the responses to a set of items on "who makes various decisions." In so doing, many researchers have given equal weight to all decision-making items, the implicit assumption being that all decisions are of *equal importance* in generating power scores. (Safilios-Rothschild 1970) However, selected decisions may vary in degree of importance across both families and couples.

Another questionable assumption has been that all decisions are made with *equal frequency,* an assumption that can easily be challenged on the grounds of common sense alone. Some decisions are important and frequent; others are important but infrequent; still others are unimportant but frequent; and others are both unimportant and infrequent.

To assume, as most researchers have done, that these decisions are of equal importance for both spouses is unwarranted. Spouses within families may differentially evaluate the importance of selected decisions, thereby distorting the conjugal power score when calculated only on the wife's responses. The problem with such measurement is that conflict is ignored since no differentiation of contested and uncontested decisions is made. (Bahr, Bowerman, and Gecas 1974:358) In addition, there is considerable evidence to suggest that self-reports may contain a bias factor. By examining self-reports from *both* husbands and wives, a more valid description of conjugal decision making may be obtained.

In summary, this paper examines the influence of the evaluative and frequency components of conjugal decision making. In so doing, Canadian findings are compared with those reported for other countries. The husband-wife congruence dimension is also investigated. In order to do so, selected criterion variables, usually thought to be related to decision making or power, will be employed. Hopefully, then, this analysis will contribute to the growing body of cross-national findings of family power.

Methodology

The data for this paper stem from a larger study which investigates the "work-family role system" with special emphasis on the changing roles of women.

The study took place in Calgary, Alberta. A combined systematic, random sample of names and addresses was drawn from a special listing of telephone subscribers. From November 1975 to February 1976 the data were gathered by a two-pronged approach in which 464 couples were interviewed and also required to complete self-administered questionnaires. For this study, "couples" refers to heterosexual pairs currently living together, whether or not officially married. To obtain independent responses, husbands and wives were interviewed simultaneously and separately.

The Canadian Data in Comparative Perspective

The aim of this first section is to report basic findings and to place them in comparative perspective. As indicated earlier, the instrument used in this study was initially developed by Blood and Wolfe (1960). It essentially entails asking respondents – who usually makes the final decision about a number of important family matters. Fourteen decision-making items (Table 2) were selected as important in measuring conjugal power in Canadian families. Each spouse was asked separately:

> *In every family decisions have to be made about such things as where the family will live and so on. Many couples talk such things over first, but the final decision often has to be made by the husband or the wife. Please check (√) the answer that best describes your family situation. WHO USUALLY MAKES THE FINAL DECISION. . . .*

Each decision-making item was measured on a five-point scale where a numerical score of "1" was assigned when the wife "always decides," to a "5" when the husband "always decides." Total scores were calculated by summing the respondent's answers to fourteen family decision-making items, and dividing it by the number of items to which they responded. The possible scores range from 5.00, for the case where the husband always decides, to 1.00, which reflects the wife always deciding. The higher the score, the greater the *husband's* power.

The resource theory of marital power is basically an exchange-model in which power is assumed to derive from resources and needs. Blood and Wolfe state:

> *The power to make decisions stems primarily from the resources which the individual can provide to meet the needs of his marriage partner (1960:14).*

Heer's (1963) criticism prompted Blood to restate the major proposition of the theory as follows:

> *Insofar as marital power is measured in terms of decisions governing transactions between the family and the external system, the comparative participation of the husband and wife in the external systems will determine the balance of power (1963:475-76).*

Replication studies in several countries led to different findings. Attempting to reconcile seemingly contradictory cross-national results, Rodman (1972) modified the conjugal theory of marital power by taking into account the cultural context within which the transactions between the family and the external system take place. The relative power of husband and wife, according to the revised formulation, depends essentially on two factors: the *comparative resources* each spouse brings to the marriage, and the *social norms* regarding the distribution of power. This reformulation is more sensitive to the conceptual distinction between *power* and *authority,* alluded to earlier. However, this has by no means satisfied all critics. (Turk 1975)

While for some propositions of the resource theory empirical support has been reported in the international literature, for others the evidence is highly inconsistent. Undisputed is the observation that the decline of paternal authority is one of the most profound changes in family organization. (Lupri 1976) The Canadian data examined here add further support to this finding.

Controversy, however, centres around three basic propositions. They involve the effects on conjugal power by (1) the employment status of the wife, (2) the socio-economic status of the couple, and (3) the relationship between marital satisfaction and marital power. According to the resource theory, social status, occupational prestige, income, education, and wife's employment are power bases each spouse may use in the marital relationship to gain greater decision-making power. They constitute contributions both may make to the relationship and have often been conceptualized as significant resources each spouse brings to marriage. Here they are considered as independent variables and treated as criterion variables. Marital satisfaction is related to decision making (Corrales 1975; Lupri and Frideres 1981), and also will be used as a criterion variable. Where marital satisfaction is envisioned as a dependent variable, the other criterion variables may be viewed as independent. The following tests each of the three propositions with Canadian data.

1. The Effect of Socio-economic Status on Conjugal Power

Many cross-cultural studies have reported a positive relationship between socio-economic status and the husband's power. *The higher the husband's social status, the greater his power.* It has been argued that the upper-class husband is more likely to transfer to his wife and children such privileges and advantages as security, esteem, money, luxuries, etc. The upper-class position may have been acquired through hard labor, skill, ability, or simply inherited. Such efforts are honored by the wife and children with deference and respect. His power, then, is largely based on what we earlier referred to as legitimate authority.

Comparative data from advanced industrialized nations tend to suggest that paternal authority is more likely to survive in upper social classes. The opposite has been found in less industrialized countries such as Greece and Yugoslavia. What are the Canadian findings? To facilitate comparisions with results reported in the literature, Table 1 presents mean conjugal power scores based on separate reports made by husbands *and* wives, as well as those

Table 1: The Relationship Between Conjugal Power Scores and Selected Criterion Variables for Husbands and Wives

Criterion Variable	Mean Power Score Based on Items *Including* Children as Reported by...			Mean Power Score Based on Items *Excluding* Children as Reported by...		
	Wife	Husband	Both	Wife	Husband	Both
Socio-economic status[1]						
Lower-Lower	2.91	3.07	2.99	3.03	3.06	3.04
Upper-Lower	2.88	2.94	2.91	2.98	3.05	3.02
Lower-Middle	2.89	2.96	2.93	3.01	3.02	3.01
Upper-Middle	2.91	3.02	2.97	2.97	3.11	3.04
Lower-Upper	2.91	2.94	2.93	3.02	3.05	3.04
Upper-Upper	2.92	2.98	2.95	2.99	3.06	3.03
Occupational prestige[2]						
Professional	2.92	2.97	2.95	3.01	3.06	3.04
Lower White Collar	2.92	2.97	2.95	3.02	3.04	3.03
Skilled	2.86	2.98	2.92	2.98	3.08	3.03
Unskilled	2.88	2.94	2.91	3.01	3.02	3.01

For the following sections the "Both" column is reported separately for Husband and Wife:

Criterion Variable	Including — Wife	Including — Husband	Including — Both (Husband)	Including — Both (Wife)	Excluding — Wife	Excluding — Husband	Excluding — Both (Husband)	Excluding — Both (Wife)
Respondent's work status[3]								
Non-Work	2.92	2.70	2.80	2.95	3.04	2.98	2.97	3.06
Part-Time Work	2.88	3.12	2.95	2.92	2.98	3.12	3.05	2.99
Full-Time Work	2.87	2.98	3.03	2.91	2.94	3.06	3.03	2.99
Respondent's marital satisfaction[4]								
Very Happy	2.92	2.98	2.94	2.95	3.00	3.04	3.01	3.03
Happy	2.87	2.97	2.94	2.92	3.00	3.06	3.03	3.02
Unhappy	2.96	2.91	2.89	2.96	3.02	3.12	3.08	3.03
Overall power scores	2.90	2.97	2.94		3.00	3.05	3.03	

[1] Socio-economic status is measured by husband's occupation as classified on the Blishen and McRoberts (1976) scale.

[2] Occupational prestige is measured by husband's occupation as categorized by the Pineo, Porter, and McRoberts (1976) CARMAC scale.

[3] Power scores are reported for work status of wife when she reports, work status of husband when he reports, and work status of each *separately* when combining scores.

[4] Power scores are reported by marital satisfaction of wife when she reports, marital satisfaction of husband when he reports, and by each *separately* when combining power scores.

averaged for both. The scores are broken down by socio-economic status, occupational prestige, wife's work status, and marital satisfaction. Overall power scores are given at the bottom of Table 1.

By and large, the data in Table 1 (left half) show a fairly high degree of egalitarianism among Canadian couples, whether one examines mean power scores based on husbands' or those based on wives' reports. However, the wives' scores suggest that Canadian wives report that they have slightly more power in decision making than do their husbands. Not unexpectedly, the husbands report that they have slightly more power than do their wives. That is, from the husband's perception, he has slightly more say in final decisions than she feels he has. This becomes evident when it is considered that a score of 3.00 indicates complete equality, less than 3.00 that the wife has greater power, and a score greater than 3.00 that the husband has more decision-making power. By examining decision making closely within subgroups, however, one is struck by the absence of any clear, consistent patterns.

What appears to have some consistency in the data is the observation that there is *no* support for the association between social status and the husband's power. Wives from the upper SES levels as well as those whose husbands are professionals tend to report more egalitarian decision making, but so do the wives of the lower-lower socio-economic group. Husbands of the latter group see themselves more powerful than husbands of all higher socio-economic classes. The husbands' self-reported power scores for the four occupational groups listed in Table 1 also reveal no consistent relationship. Hence the Canadian data do *not* lend support to the alleged positive association between the husband's social status and his power. There are a number of reversals in the data. Interestingly they tend to point toward a *curvilinear* relationship between social status and husband's power. Husband-dominance in decision making is more prevalent among couples of both the upper and the lower social classes. Available data need to be re-examined with respect to this notion of curvilinearity in conjugal power relations.

2. Wife's Working Status and Wife's Power

Cross-national findings indicate that wives who work for pay have more marital power than those who do not. Income is a significant resource for both spouses, but especially for wives of the lower classes. (Lupri 1969) The assumption is that the wife's employment not only provides additional income but also other resources that may meet the needs of her husband. Blood and Wolfe state that "the sources of power in so intimate a relationship as marriage must be sought in the *comparative* resources which the husband and wife bring to the marriage. . . ." (1960:12; *our emphasis*)

Again, the Canadian data do *not* fully support the theory: *Working wives have slightly lower scores than do non-working wives.* The scores are summed scores and based on a variety of decisions. Several other studies also found no significant differences between overall conjugal power of working and non-working wives.

The data do, however, show clearly that *lack of job* affects the husband's power considerably. The non-working husbands have the lowest decision-making score of any group. This finding is in agreement with that reported by family sociologists who have examined familial power within the various stages of the family life cycle. (Lupri 1976) Wives whose husbands are retired or without work, generally report higher power scores. Wives, whether they work for pay or not, continue to take their domestic roles seriously. Housework and child-related activities remain within the wife's influence. As the husband retires or becomes jobless, sexual differentiation in the marital power structure increases – with not only the husband and wife making fewer decisions jointly, but the husband making fewer decisions in general.

3. Marital Satisfaction and Marital Power

There is cross-national evidence suggesting that marital happiness and joint decision making go hand in hand. The Canadian data on marital happiness reveal patterns *similar* to those reported for other countries.[2] Canadian couples derive a great amount of satisfaction from joint participation in decision making and sharing in household tasks. That sharing household chores and egalitarian decision making are highly related to marital satisfaction finds additional support from those few couples who report autocratic decision making. Wives who perceive their union as "unhappy" see their husbands as more dominating and powerful, and likewise, husbands who are "unhappy," perceive their wives to be more powerful. It appears that specialization in making decisions tends to prevent the development of companionship between Canadian husbands and wives.

4 Are the Findings Real or Artifacts of the Methodology?

Three basic conclusions emerge from the data presented in Table 1. First, social status and wife's employment appear to be unrelated to the decision-making scores. This is true for wives, husbands, and the combined decision-making scores.

Second, there appears to be a high degree of equality reported. Is the high degree of equalitarianism real or a result of the methodology? For example, it has been suggested that the methodology which relies on self-reports may bias the findings toward greater reports of egalitarianism.

Third, we may conclude from these data that Canadian wives are slightly more powerful than their husbands in making decisions. This finding is contrary to comparable studies in which it was found that husbands overestimate their power while wives underestimate theirs. (Olson 1969) If this is true, wives in our population may be even more powerful than the data seem to indicate.

Perhaps the slight tendency toward "wives' power" is real! Or, alternatively, the finding may be due to the measurement of conjugal power through deci-

---

[2]Marital satisfaction was measured with the general question: "All in all, how happy has your marriage been for you? Please check (√) one. The six-point scale was trichotomized into Very Happpy, Happy (both responses happy and somewhat happy), and Unhappy (responses somewhat unhappy, unhappy and very unhappy were collapsed).

sion making. Although the items employed here are the same or similar to those used in past studies, perhaps their specific content has influenced the overall scores. For example, in the original work on decision making by Blood and Wolfe (1960), and in some subsequent cross-national replications, items containing decisions which involve children were not employed or were used only minimally. This may have had an impact on the averages calculated to arrive at decision-making scores. If wives have major responsibility for the children, the omission of child-related items results in scores which under-estimate her power.

The *right half* of Table 1 contains decision-making scores for the 11 items which *do not* include decisions involving children. While the scores remain relatively equalitarian, one notes that they now tend to exceed 3.00, reflecting a slight increase in the husbands' power. This suggests that at least part of the "wives' power" results from those decisions which relate to their expected duties with the children. Children tend to neutralize the husbands' power in other areas.

The deletion of the child-related items does nothing to clarify the relation-ships with the criterion variables, i.e., there is still no clear, consistent pattern within the subgroups. It is interesting to note that husbands who are "very happy" in their marriages are more equalitarian while those who are "unhappy" report greater husband dominance.

Raven, Centers and Rodriguez (1975:218) stress the importance of analyz-ing the "domains of power." They argue that power can ". . . vary from one domain to the next, with role definitions determining who had power in a given area." Women, in our society, have been expected to take the major responsibility for children. It follows, then, that wives will undoubtedly make many of the decisions about children. Our findings appear to corroborate Turk and Bell's (1972) contention that self-reports are normative responses to perceived cultural expectations. Should culturally expected decision making within domains be considered power? Some have chosen to refer to it by other terms such as authority or policy governance. (Broderick 1975)

Item Variation

A comparison of the means in Table 1 demonstrates that the individual items employed in the overall scale will influence the measurement of conjugal power by decision making. The summation of the various items results in a "levelling effect." By focussing on the mean aggregate scores, much of the variation is masked or hidden. These total scores lack sensitivity to the multidimensionality of conjugal decision making.

One approach to document variation among items, usually lumped togeth-er, is to perform an item analysis with means and standard deviations. This will serve the purpose of demonstrating the problems associated with employing composite scores. Are there certain decisions wives make because they are expected to do so? What are the decisions husbands are expected to make? Should all decisions have the same weight in familial power scores? An item-by-item analysis for husbands and wives separately might clarify these queries.

**Table 2:   Means, Standard Deviations, and Differences Between Means[1]
For Husbands and Wives on Specific Decision Making Items[2]**

Decision making items	Wife		Husband	
	$\overline{X}$	SD	$\overline{X}$	SD
Car to get	3.85	.76	3.86	.74
Spouse change jobs*	3.82	.82	2.95	1.10
Doctor called	2.52	.75	2.60	.72
Friends to entertain	2.88	.52	2.81	.58
Relatives to entertain*	2.86	.55	2.77	.55
Money to spend on food	2.41	.94	2.42	.91
Buy life insurance	3.52	.82	3.52	.85
House or apartment	3.05	.55	3.00	.58
Furniture to buy*	2.81	.60	2.66	.69
Job *you* should take*	2.22	.90	4.00	.82
Go on vacation	3.08	.49	3.03	.48
Children's spending money	2.93	.70	2.85	.66
Children's discipline*	2.68	.65	2.92	.62
Children's clothes	1.88	.68	2.06	.62

[1]The asterisk following the decision-making item indicates that the difference between the wives' $\overline{X}$ and the husbands' $\overline{X}$ is statistically significant at the .05 level or lower, using a two-tailed test.
[2]The Ns varied slightly but were usually about 453 for the wives for the first 11 items and 280 for the last three items; likewise, the Ns for husbands were approximately the same. The last three items were tabulated only for persons with children living at home.

In Table 2 the mean scores and standard deviations for each of the decision-making items are presented for husbands and wives. Both wives ($\overline{X} = 3.85$) and husbands ($\overline{X} = 3.86$) report the husband to be more powerful with respect to decisions about the "car to get." On the other hand, both spouses agree that wives make the decisions regarding "children's clothes" ($\overline{X} = 1.88$ for wives and 2.06 for husbands). Probably the most dramatic finding in Table 2 is the *overall lack of equalitarianism* for each item. Contrary to the observations in Table 1, there is evidence for autocratic decision making. That is, each spouse makes decisions within specific areas. The global scores masked the fact that husbands make some decisions – about car and insurance purchases – and wives make the decisions about children, entertaining, calling the doctor, and buying food. The only decisions which appear to be made jointly (i.e., indicating equalitarianism) concern "going on vacation" and "housing."

Another exploratory approach to comparing husbands and wives is to calculate difference of means tests for each item. By so doing, six of the fourteen decisions show statistically significant differences between the means of husbands and wives at the .05 level or lower. (The argument can be made that direction can be predicted, based on normative expectations, which would result in statistically significant differences on two additional items.) Basically this suggests that where there is some agreement about who makes certain decisions, there is by no means unanimity.

Clearly, the evidence presented here suggests that the responses to the decision-making items more accurately reflect normative cultural expectations than conjugal power. Merely to summate the responses to selected items into global scores masks important variation. Because the specific content of the items dictates the outcome, the approach lacks validity and, therefore, may not tap real differences in conjugal power.

Item Salience and Frequency

As was suggested earlier, not all decisions are of equal salience nor are they made with equal frequency. For instance, decisions about "what relatives to entertain" are probably less salient or important than, "what house or apartment to buy." On the other hand, the former decision is faced much more frequently than the latter. We contend that increased scrutiny must be paid toward matters of salience and frequency. A central question becomes: Should decisions that couples consider highly important be given greater weight in the calculation of conjugal power scores? Similarly, should decisions which are made more frequently, and by which spouses could reaffirm their power, be weighted more heavily?

In Table 3 the average salience or importance and the average frequency of each type of decision are presented for both husbands and wives. In order to measure each item's salience and frequency, the respondents were asked:

Now we would like to know, first, how important *these decisions are for you and your spouse and, second, how* often *you and your spouse make them. Now answer the two questions for each of the decisions in the left column. Please check (√) the answers that best describe your family situation.*[3]

Theoretically, the scores can vary from 1.00, or Very Important, to 3.00, or Not Important.

The data in Table 3 suggest that both spouses evaluate decisions about "children's discipline" as most salient, and those decisions which pertain to "relatives to entertain" as least salient. There is fairly strong agreement among the rankings with regard to the importance of the items. The rank order correlation of .88 indicates fairly strong agreement in evaluating the decisions. However, there is some degree of disagreement between spouses about the relative importance of each item. Where the rank order of the salience of these decisions is similar for husbands and wives, the actual salience scores vary considerably. Difference of means tests, to ascertain whether statistically

---

[3]Salience of decisions was measured on a three-point scale with Very Important weighted 1, Important weighted 2, and Not So Important weighted 3. The higher the importance, the lower the mean score. Frequency of decisions was also measured on a three-point scale with Often assigned a 1, Sometimes assigned a 2, and Rarely given a 3. The more frequent the decision, the lower the score.

Table 3: Salience and Frequency of Decision-Making Items[1] For Husbands and Wives

Decision-making items	Importance Means			Frequency Means		
	Wife	Husband	Difference[2]	Wife	Husband	Difference[2]
Car to get	2.10	2.21	-.11*	2.46	2.49	-.03
Spouse change jobs	1.66	2.05	-.39*	2.68	2.71	-.03
Doctor called	1.70	1.74	-.04	2.41	2.32	-.09*
Friends to entertain	2.34	2.34	.00	1.94	1.92	+.02
Relatives to entertain	2.35	2.43	-.08	2.11	2.13	-.02
Money to spend on food	2.12	2.26	-.14*	1.99	1.96	+.03
Buy life insurance	2.12	2.32	-.20*	2.69	2.74	-.05
House or apartment	1.74	1.86*	-.12*	2.62	2.64	-.02
Furniture to buy	2.07	2.11	-.04	2.40	2.31	+.09*
Job *you* should take	2.02	1.75	+.27*	2.70	2.69	+.01
Go on vacation	2.04	2.05	-.01	2.05	2.03	+.02
Children's spending money	2.15	2.20	-.05	2.34	2.24	+.10
Children's discipline	1.52	1.66	-.14*	1.71	1.84	-.13*
Children's clothes	2.30	2.14	+.16*	2.27	2.00	+.27*
		$\Sigma|d_i|$ = 1.75			$\Sigma|d_i|$ = .91	
		$\Sigma|d_i|/_n$ = .125			$\Sigma|d_i|/_n$ = .065	

[1]The Ns on these items were approximately 450 for the first 11 items and 277 for the last 3 items for the wives, and 435 and 270 respectively for the husbands.

[2]Difference scores merely reflect the wives' average importance score minus the husbands' importance score. The $\Sigma|d_i|$ refers to the absolute difference score and the $\Sigma|d_i|/_n$ refers to the average. These can only be used as crude guides to the "amount of agreement" on these items among husbands and wives. Spearman's rho, a rank order correlation, on the importance means is .88 and on the frequency means is .97. The asterisk following the difference scores indicates that the difference between wives' X and the husbands' X is statistically significant at the .05 level or lower, using a two-tailed test.

significant differences exist between spouses, show that for eight of the four-teen decision areas, the differences are significant at the .05 level or lower. In six of the eight, wives consider the decisions more important than husbands. Importantly, however, there appears to be no pattern with regards to greater disagreement on more important or less important items. That is, the differences appear to be on both types. While the high rank order correlation suggests that husbands and wives evaluate similarly, the difference of means tests indicate wives assign higher overall importance to the decisions.

The greatest amount of disagreement about the salience of the items centres around the area of employment. Whereas wives report the decisions about their "spouses changing jobs" to be very important ($\overline{X} = 1.66$), husbands do not feel their wives' job changes are as important. This finding may not be too surprising in that women's work roles have always taken a back seat in Canadian society. It is not only the husbands, however, who undervalue the importance of the women's work activities relative to their own. Wives also do not report their own job decisions ($\overline{X} = 2.02$) to be as important as their decisions about their husbands' jobs.

When the frequency of decisions is examined (Table 3), the degree of agreement between spouses is even greater. The rank-order correlation for the average frequencies between husbands and wives is .97. Difference of means tests for the frequency of specific decisions show only four to be statistically significant. The item of greatest divergence between wives' and husbands' reports on frequencies is "children's clothes" – a decision considered not very salient by either parent.

Table 3 also contains the average absolute difference scores for the salience and the frequency dimensions. This score indicates less disparity between husbands' and wives' reports on frequency than on salience. We would argue that the salience placed on the various decision-making items is a matter of values, whereas the reports of frequency is more a matter of reported behavior. In short, there seems to be considerable conjugal agreement on the salience and the frequency of the various decisions.

Effects of Salience on Power

Would weighting the decision-making items by their reported degree of salience have any overall impact on the decision-making scores? To illustrate the effect of salience on the conjugal power dimension the items have been placed in an array and ranked from the item deemed most important to that considered least important by both wives and husbands considered separately. The rankings were then trichotomized into three broad groupings of nearly equal size, and the mean power score within each of these groups was calculated.

The results in Table 4 suggest several interesting observations. First, those items found in the "Very Salient" category are the same items for wives and husbands. However, the internal ordering of the two groups do differ somewhat. In the second grouping, termed "Somewhat Salient," there is not as much agreement. Where wives' rankings place "buying life insurance" and "money to spend on food" within this second category, the husband's rankings

Table 4:　The Effects of Salience on Conjugal Power Scores for Wives and Husbands

Wives' Scores	
Items categorized by degree of salience:	Mean Power Score
Very Salient Decisions	
Children's discipline	2.68
Spouse change jobs	3.82
Doctor called	2.52
House or apartment to live in	3.05
Job *you* should take	2.22
Average power score for *Very Salient Decisions*	2.86
Somewhat Salient Decisions	
Go on vacation	3.08
Furniture to buy	2.81
Car to get	3.85
Money to spend on food	2.41
Buy life insurance	3.52
Average power scores for *Somewhat Salient Decisions*	3.13
Not Very Salient Decisions	
Children's spending money	2.93
Children's clothes	1.88
Friends to entertain	2.88
Relatives to entertain	2.86
Average power score for *Not Very Salient Decisions*	2.64

put them in the third grouping. In turn, husbands place decisions about "children's spending money" and about "children's clothes" as more important – in the second group. Similarly, the items within the "Not Very Salient" groupings differ for wives and husbands.

Second, and perhaps more important, according to the average decision-making scores within these broad categories, the husbands report the greatest amount of power ($\overline{X}$ = 3.09) for the grouping of items they consider *most important*. Likewise, the husbands accord the wives the greatest amount of power on what they regard as "Not Very Salient Decisions" ($\overline{X}$ = 2.88). Noteworthy is that wives do not disagree with husbands – they also accord themselves greater power on the least salient items ($\overline{X}$ = 2.64). Earlier it was concluded that wives appear to have slightly greater power than husbands; however, this may have been premature since it was based on composite summary scores of decision-making items. Now it becomes evident that wives' power is based on decisions which they, themselves, and husbands feel are unimportant. While this type of analysis might appear somewhat crude, it does suggest the need to weight decision-making items by their overall importance. In short, we leave the challenge to family researchers to take into

Table 4: The Effects of Salience on Conjugal Power Scores for Wives and Husbands

Husbands' Scores	
Items categorized by degree of salience:	Mean Power Score
Very Salient Decisions	
Children's discipline	2.92
Doctor called	2.60
Job *you* should take	4.00
House or apartment to live in	3.00
Spouse change jobs	2.95
Average power score for *Very Salient Decisions*	3.09
Somewhat Salient Decisions	
Go on vacation	3.03
Furniture to buy	2.66
Children's clothes	2.06
Children's spending money	2.85
Car to get	3.86
Average power scores for *Somewhat Salient Decisions*	2.89
Not Very Salient Decisions	
Money to spend on food	2.42
Buy life insurance	3.52
Friends to entertain	2.81
Relatives to entertain	2.77
Average power score for *Not Very Salient Decisions*	2.88

account the salience dimension in calculating conjugal power based on decision-making items. The weighting method chosen, should serve the particular needs and audience of those researchers.

Couple Congruency

Many scholars assume that valid and reliable data can be gathered from a single member of the family unit. It is usually the wives who are interviewed or observed and their responses are then generalized to the total family. For this reason, family sociology has been disparagingly referred to as "wives' sociology." (Safilios-Rothschild 1969) With respect to the specific area of conjugal power, Eichler (1976:9) raised several critical questions:

In what type of decisions do we find the greatest discrepancy between husband-wife responses? In which decisions do we find the least discrepancy? In what situations does the wife see the husband as more (or less) powerful than he sees himself? In what situations does the wife see the husband as more (or less) powerful than she sees herself?

The data presented in Tables 1 to 4 reveal differences between husbands and wives generally, but *do not* examine the couple as the unit of analysis. Comparisons of means, summated scores and other such rates do not indicate differences and similarities between husbands and wives within their own conjugal unit. They fail to answer the kinds of queries that Eichler raises. When we contrast husbands' and wives' scores, as we have done above, we must be careful not to generalize to couples. Analysis of global comparisons can obscure the variation which may exist within specific couples or dyads because there may be greater variation within the conjugal unit than between husbands and wives generally.

This suggests that the couple may be employed as the unit of analysis and the degree of consistency or homogeneity between spouses may be treated as a variable. A typology has been constructed by cross-tabulating the wife's response with her husband's. The congruency of the couple's responses will be referred to as "intra-couple congruency on decision making." This method yields three broad classes of intra-couple congruency: First, *Mutual Powerlessness* is the type of inconsistency where each reports that the other usually makes the decision; second, *Mutual Powerfulness* refers to the incongruent situation in which each spouse reports he or she usually makes the decision; and, third, *Intra-couple Congruency* exists where spouses basically agree on who makes the specific decision. To facilitate comparisons, a five-fold typology was constructed.[4]

Table 5 contains the degree and type of congruency for each of the decision-making items. We have grouped the intra-couple congruency scores according to the evaluation of the importance of the decision, as presented in the top portion of Table 4. Several patterns emerge. For example, an examination of the middle column, Type III or intra-couple congruency, suggests that overall there is considerable incongruency on many items. Only four of the fourteen decision-making items have congruency scores exceeding 60 percent. The items demonstrating the greatest congruency were decisions involving "going on vacation" and "house to live in." Overall, the incongruency appears highest on decisions relating to jobs, i.e., decisions both with regard to "the job *you* should take" and "spouse changing jobs." Both spouses feel powerful with regard to their own job, but powerless with regard to decisions about their mate's job. Some caution should be exercised with respect to the job items, however, since these are the only items which refer directly to one particular spouse's activities. Other items refer to possible joint or couple decisions. This, of course, does not suggest that couples may not share in

---

[4]When both spouses in a family reported that they made the decision always, the couple was termed *High Mutually Powerful;* in cases where one spouse reports always making the decision while the other reports usually making the decision, and in cases where both spouses report usually making the decision we have termed them *Low Mutually Powerful;* where spouses are in agreement about who makes the decision, the couples are termed *Congruent;* in cases where each reported the other spouse as "always making the decision," the couples are typed *High Mutally Powerless;* and finally, where each spouse reported the other usually made the decision, and in cases where one reported the other always decides while he/she usually does, are termed *Low Mutually Powerless.*

Table 5: Intra-couple Congruency for Specific Conjugal Decisions, by Percent of Each Type*

Decision Making Item	Type I High Mutually Powerful (%)	Type II Low Mutually Powerful (%)	Type III Congruent (%)	Type IV Low Mutually Powerless (%)	Type V High Mutually Powerless (%)	Totals N	(%)
Very Important Decisions							
Children's discipline	1.5	11.5	52.7	29.6	4.6	260	99.9
Spouse change jobs	34.4	20.2	32.7	9.4	3.3	395	100.0
Doctor called	4.1	17.8	49.7	22.4	6.1	443	100.1
House or apartment to live in	3.7	12.4	69.8	12.1	2.1	437	100.1
Job *you* should take	0.2	1.2	16.3	24.3	57.9	411	99.9
Somewhat Important Decisions							
Go on vacation	1.4	13.6	74.7	9.2	1.2	435	100.1
Furniture to buy	4.3	22.3	58.1	13.1	2.2	444	100.0
Car to get	3.6	19.1	52.0	22.1	3.2	444	100.0
Money to spend on food	6.3	19.6	45.8	22.2	6.1	445	100.0
Buy life insurance	7.3	16.2	52.5	18.4	5.6	425	100.0
Not Very Important Decisions							
Children's spending money	3.5	22.2	56.5	13.5	4.4	230	100.1
Children's clothes	0.8	12.3	58.6	23.0	5.4	261	100.1
Friends to entertain	2.2	18.0	65.8	12.6	1.4	444	100.0
Relatives to entertain	2.6	19.5	63.0	13.7	1.2	430	100.0

*For operational definitions of the various types, see footnote 3.

**Decision-making items are grouped according to the evaluation of their importance by the wives.

decisions about jobs; but that the spouse who is directly involved with the activity has greater autonomy to make the decision.

If we take into account the evaluative dimension, we note that decisions about the "job you should take" and about "children's discipline" are both considered among the most important by both spouses *and* are also those in which both spouses feel somewhat powerful. If husbands and wives feel they make decisions on important items, feelings of disharmony and conflict may not result from the incongruency. The items in which the spouses feel most powerless – feel the other makes the decision – appear to be "spouse changing jobs," "furniture to buy," and "children's spending money." These three decisions seem to reflect the greatest intra-couple incongruency of the powerless variety. Only the job item, discussed above, appears among the more important decisions. These findings suggest that intra-couple incongruency may not be related to such variables as marital satisfaction or conflict. Relatedly, there appears to be fairly strong "Intra-couple Congruency" on decisions about "going on vacation," "house to live in," and "friends to entertain." These decisions vary by the degree of importance.[5]

In summary, the focus on intra-couple congruency illustrates the need to collect information from both husband and wife when interested in conjugal decision making, and from all family members when interested in familial decision making. Summed scores based solely on the wives' responses underestimate seriously the complexity and multidimensionality of the "power" concept. Furthermore, it may be concluded that there exists a substantial degree of inconsistency within married couples. Possible implications of this incongruency deserve serious theoretical and research attention.

Summary and Conclusions

The composite summary scores for husbands and wives that have been discussed are not dissimilar to those reported by some other studies. When examined within subgroups of criterion variables, decision-making scores do not appear related to the criterion variables. The composite scores have reflected a high degree of egalitarianism as reported by both husbands and wives.

When the Canadian data on conjugal power were placed in comparative perspective divergent patterns emerged. Among Canadian couples the husband's socio-economic status is *not positively* associated with the husband's power. Furthermore, and contrary to other cross-cultural findings on conjugal power, the Canadian wife's work status does not lead to an increase in her power. Findings indicate that wives who work for pay actually have less power vis-à-vis their husbands than do those who are not in the labor force. The relationship between marital satisfaction and conjugal power was as predicted

---

[5]The evaluative dimension is based on average importance scores over all couples, whereas couple congruency pertains to the pair as the unit of analysis. A better test of this would be to analyze the degree of importance attributed by the couple in relationship to the couple's congruence type. Space precludes such an analysis, but it would seem profitable to do so in subsequent research.

and supportive of findings reported in the international literature. An equal balance of power between couples is more conducive to the development of a happy marriage and companionship than is an autocratic decision-making pattern.

This analysis, then, examined critically the content of the items employed in decision making. One conclusion from the data is that wives appear to attribute their power on the basis of activities that are culturally expected of them. The scores reflect what is "socially desirable" within the context of cultural expectations, but they may not be adequate indicators of conjugal power. Compliance with clear-cut norms pertaining to "who should make a given decision" may do little to enhance one's power. It is a consequence of the normative aspect of the social structure.

The relative salience and frequency of each decision may well be significant for conjugal power. Considerable variation in importance and frequency was reported across items; however, there seemed to be fairly strong agreement between husbands and wives.

Wives acquire most of their conjugal power from items not considered very important by either themselves or by their husbands. For the items they consider more salient, husbands tend to make the decisions. Or, alternatively, for those decisions which are evaluated as highly important, the husband is culturally expected to handle them. If decision making is to continue to be employed as an indicator of conjugal power, much greater attention needs to be paid to weighting the salience or evaluative dimension of the item.

Some exploratory work has been presented on intra-couple congruency. The overriding conclusion to be drawn is that considerable incongruency exists – again confirming the dangers of employing the responses of only one spouse to represent the conjugal unit.

The analysis of these and other data strongly suggests the need for substantial revision of the resource theory of marital power. While the theory is useful in explaining the relative power of husbands and wives in general, power must be related to specific areas of decision making to have predictive value. Moreover, future empirical research would be well advised to explore in detail the multidimensionality of the power concept. This may require a triangulated approach of which decision making is but one aspect. Our data suggest that increased attention must be given to the weighting of relative items in such scales. Furthermore, to rely solely on wives' scores tends to seriously bias the findings. Finally, the Canadian data strongly indicate that future research and theory construction might profit by examining intra-couple congruency on the decision-making dimension.

In sum, according to decision-making scales, wives may appear to be equal to, or even more powerful than, their husbands. But, in reality, wives only make decisions in areas in which it has been traditionally expected – areas of lesser importance.

Husbands, Wives, and Work*

Peter M. Butler

Introduction

Ever since work was moved out of the home philosophers and social critics have been preoccupied with its linkage to the family and its effects upon family life. In sociological analysis it has generally been understood that the development of a modern industrial economy is accompanied by the separation of work from family life. The individual wage earner has replaced the family in our thinking about the basic work unit. The term "occupation," for example, has come to be associated with a specialized and individualized task performance, and family viability has frequently been linked to some amount of job-family insulation.

Yet, there continue to be work-family arrangements that question the appropriateness of this perspective. The continued existence of family enterprise is a case in point. Entire spheres of large and small business organizations have remained family controlled. Moreover, in some professional occupations such as the clergy the demands of work have frequently required the help of unpaid members of the family. Now that married women are becoming wage earners in ever increasing numbers, it is clear that the relationship between the family and work must be closer than had been assumed. This circumstance, while it may not be expected to produce a total integration of family and work activities, makes the complete insulation of the family from the world of work most unlikely.

This paper will examine the ways all family members are involved in work relative to how they are involved in family life. Two family types – single earner and dual earner – will be considered. In dual-earner families both spouses hold jobs; in single-earner families only the husband is employed. The position taken here is that support of dual wage earning is associated with more integrated family and work activity.

Industrialization and Family-Occupational Differentiation

Current macro-sociological theory holds that the Industrial Revolution and the rise of capitalism systematically reorganized labor hastening structural differentiation between the family and the work place. (Smelser 1959) Weber

---

*This paper is based on research from a study conducted by the Family Studies Section of the Clarke Institute of Psychiatry. Support for the study was provided by the Vanier Institute, the Clarke Institute Research Fund, and the Laidlaw Foundation. Full reference to sources cited appears in the bibliography to this work.

(1947), for example, refers to the separation of family from business as a necessary condition for the formal rationality of capital accounting in the emergence of modern enterprise. This position is most fully developed by structural functionalists. Smelser (1959) shows how factory legislation in the British cotton industry, during the period 1830 to 1850, served to bring about the segregation of family and work activities. By removing women and young children from the work place, factory legislation altered socialization practices that had previously been conducted within the boundaries of the apprenticeship system. The net effect was to consolidate the work world under the influence of men and the family under the influence of women.

According to this model then, family system stability rests on an instrumental-expressive balance of sex roles (Parsons 1955) whereby the husband as wage earner occupies a "boundary role" articulating the family to the outside world and the wife is the focal point of family integration. The likelihood of status rivalry between marriage partners is felt to be substantially reduced when only the husband plays a competitive role in the occupational system and the wife assumes the role of homemaker.

There is a considerable body of evidence to suggest that this arrangement may actually be dysfunctional for the family. Some writers have, in fact, seen this as being responsible for perpetuating social inequality, particularly by restricting opportunities for family members to develop as individuals (Epstein 1971; Skolnick and Skolnick 1971), and cite more conflicted marriages (Homstrom 1971) and feelings of alienation from family and community (Gavron 1968) as its concomitants. The contention here is that structural-functional models misrepresent the relations between work and family worlds in contemporary society. While analytically the contrast between them may be recognized, the use of ideal typologies elaborated into general models of behavior masks the reality of the individual's day-to-day relationships in both worlds.

The application of social exchange models to the study of the family is an alternative approach where linkages with the work world are more clearly recognized. According to this approach, transactions with the occupational system are a prime source for the derivation of the resources that govern much of family process and, in particular, the relations between spouses. Exchange models have received most explicit documentation in studies dealing with mate selection (McCall 1966); and marital cohesion. (Scanzoni 1971; Aldous 1969) However, there appear to be several conceptual problems which limit the utility of this perspective as an explanatory tool. One is their failure to specify adequately the nature of resources which are exchanged and how they operate in the interaction process. For example, it is never clear whether such things as skills, education, prestige, or wealth actually direct exchanges in a transaction or merely enhance one's position when one engages in a transaction. Hence, the resource-exchange model has not contributed significantly toward an understanding of the linkages between family life and the world of work. Yet, within the context of this approach many useful questions are raised, particularly with respect to the idea that role expectations in one system may be shaped by performances in other systems.

Rapoport and Rapoport (1965) have interpreted this phenomenon as isomorphism or similarity of behavior patterning between family and occupational roles. Briefly stated, when an individual operates in both worlds simultaneously and the behaviors associated with each are potentially conflicting, he may adopt standards from one sphere in his behavior in the other. It has been shown, for example, that fathers with middle-class occupations tend to evaluate their sons' behavior in terms of their own occupational role demands. (Alberle and Naegele 1968) It has also been shown that wage earners who utilize human relations skills on the job are likely to see many attitudinal and behavioral convergences between their role performance at work and at home. On the other hand, wage earners whose jobs emphasize impersonal problem solving and technical competence are more likely to view their family and occupational lives as being distinct and separate. (Podell 1967)

Unfortunately, the concept of isomorphism in work-family relations has not been extensively researched beyond the level of the individual, yet these examples do illustrate the subtlety of the linkage process. The perspective shows some promise for revealing the mechanisms by which linkages are established, but its application at the level of the whole family is as yet unknown.

Work-Family Linkages and the Study of Maternal Employment

The study of maternal employment is the only area where linkages between the family and the work world have been explored very extensively. And, it is in situations where mothers are wage earners that the intertwining of occupations with the family ought to be most directly observable. The overriding concern of most of this research, however, has simply been to assess the impact on the family of the mother as a job holder. Models developed to assess this usually view participation in the labor force as an independent variable effecting various kinds of disturbance in family life as a forerunner to family change. Generally, existing studies tend to reflect public anxiety rather than scientific curiosity, and as such, often suffer from a paucity of concepts which explain the effects of maternal employment in a family context. Despite these limitations, however, this body of information is instructive because it shows there is no one to one correlation between maternal employment and family pathology.

Maternal employment, for example, has been examined in terms of its effects on the emotional adjustment and social development of children. (Glueck and Glueck 1934, 1957; Stolz 1960; Nye and Hoffman 1963; Myrdal and Klein 1968) In addition, investigations of patterns of family decision making and the distribution of household tasks have been conducted to see if dual involvement in the labor force alters the balance of power in marriage. (Blood and Hamblin 1968; Hoffman 1963; Herr 1963) The most significant finding to this discussion is that when the wife works outside the home her husband appears to exercise less power in family decision making. However, this is not true in all cases. (see Middleton and Putney 1959) It is questionable whether the techniques used in these studies yield an accurate reflection of reality. Turk and Bell (1972) replicated some current measures of power on a sample of Canadian families and found that the overall comparability between the various measures was extremely low.

In seeking to understand the new kinds of family structures that emerge when wives work, some researchers have studied families in which both spouses share a commitment to a full-time work career. (Fogarty 1971; Rapoport and Rapoport 1969, 1971) The behavior patterns that tend to set the dual-career family apart from other more conventionally organized families appear in the lack of segregation between family and occupational activities and relationships with networks. Friendships are often formed by associations through work interests. (Rapoport and Rapoport, 1971)

Despite the multiplicity of research monographs in this area, no clear-cut picture has emerged. These studies are significant because they show that an individual's involvement in an occupation may affect other non-working members of the family. They also make it clear that having dual wage earners is not incompatible with the stability of the nuclear family. However, the findings are not always directly comparable and are often contradictory. In sum, they contribute little to our understanding of how the family adapts when more than one member is a wage earner. It makes little sense to explore the effects of wage earning on the family if the primary variables being considered have reference to individuals, mothers or children, and not to the total family system. There is a need for a more dynamic model, one where the family is the unit of analysis, and relations between wage earners and occupations are seen as interchanges involving the whole family with the work world.

Exploring the Dual-Earner Family as an Adaptive System

The relations between the family and the occupational system may also be explored from an adaptive systems model. A system may be defined as a "... network of elements, such that each component is related to at least some others in a more or less stable way. . . ." (Buckley 1967:41) A viable system is in constant interchange with an environment across some recognizable boundary. To be adaptive to the environment requires that the system maintain boundaries which are relatively permeable and that it be responsive to environmentally induced change. The family's *support* of dual wage earning or single wage earning may be understood as a type of adaptation to the environment.

Drawing upon the general systems perspective then, we contend that families establishing more permeable boundaries are likely to be adaptive to the social environment. Dual wage earning creates a strain on family adaptiveness that requires a crossing of traditional boundaries separating the family from the work world. This is conceptualized as involvement by the family in the occupations of its working members. Involvement is the extent to which occupations pervade family life and encompass all members of the household whether or not they are job holders. The rationale for this is that work roles make demands on time, energy, and other resources of job holders which are normally granted priority over the demands of other institutional spheres. Efforts to define an optimal integration of work and family role demands when both spouses are wage earners bring about involvements by other family members in their jobs. Stated in terms of research design, the support of single wage earning or dual wage earning is viewed as the independent variable and the permeability of the work-family boundary as the dependent variable.

In the analysis that follows, two aspects of family involvement in occupations are operationally considered. The first describes the participation of individuals in work relative to the family, and is labelled *work-related involvement*. The second describes the participation of individuals in family life relative to work, and is termed *family involvement*. These serve as indicators of the boundary-maintaining tendencies of the families studied. When the occupations of wage earners entail involvement by other members of the household possible conflicts between the competing demands of both settings on the time, energy, and other resources of wage earners are prevented. This may influence the levels of family involvement required of individuals as well. Where occupations involve persons other than wage earners they may provide a focal point for all family members which then supersedes their involvement in other kinds of family-centred activity. Hence, we expect an overriding involvement of individuals in work relative to the family, in dual-earner families.

Data

This study of single- and dual-earner families formed part of a larger study of the dynamic properties of family life. The larger study was conducted in Metropolitan Toronto on a representative sample of families drawn from the Borough of East York. Data gathering took place between 1968 and 1969. The East York population was selected because it is representative of the socio-economic composition of Metropolitan Toronto as a whole and is of a size manageable for interviewing. The strategy employed in selecting the sample consisted of stratified random sampling of family households in the borough. A sampling frame was provided by the Metropolitan Toronto Municipal Tax Assessment rolls. The sample comprised 211 families at all stages of the life cycle.

The inquiry involved secondary analysis of these data on a subsample of 124 intact families with children drawn from the larger sample. A sample of sixty-two single earners and sixty-two dual earners was selected and matched on the basis of demographic characteristics believed likely to influence the numbers of wage earners a family might contain. These characteristics included *family structure, life cycle state, socio-economic status, religion, and ethnicity*. Socio-economic status, family intactness, age and number of children are known to be related to the mother's employment status (Hoffman 1963) and by controlling for ethnicity and religion we wished to eliminate the influence of cultural factors that might operate against dual wage earning, such as the endorsement of a traditional ideology.

Findings

One kind of family involvement in the occupational world of its wage earners is having knowledge about the day-to-day activities of wage earners while

Table 1: Single- and Dual-earner Families by Frequency Father's Job is Discussed at Home

Frequency Job Discussed at Home	Single-Earners		Dual-Earners	
	N	%	N	%
Never	26	44.8	15	25.9
Occasionally	17	29.3	21	36.2
Often	15	25.9	22	37.9
Total	58	100.0	58	100.0

Gamma = .31
Tau C = .21
Significance = .0005

they are at work. This was measured by considering the extent that the father's job is discussed with other household members. Fathers were asked: "How much is work and what goes on at work talked about within your family?."

Before recording their answer, fathers were instructed to read it to other members of the family who were present during the interview.

The Table 1 single and dual earners are compared and scored on the family's perception of how frequently the father's job is discussed at home.[1] Essentially, the higher the score, the more a man talks about his work to his family. Looking at this table we find that there was a notable association between having two wage earners in the family and how frequently a man discussed his work at home. In single-earner households 45 percent of fathers reported that they never discuss their work with family members; however, about 35 percent of fathers in dual-earner households reported that they do so often. Differences between samples are statistically significant. Also noteworthy is the fact that less than one-third (15) of all fathers in the dual-earner sample reported that they never discuss work at home, and that so many of the fathers in the total sample (65 percent) do. This is an interesting finding in view of the widely-held assumption that most wage earners believe families shouldn't be burdened with the details of their work lives.

To get a more revealing picture of the intensity of work-related involvement, comparisons were made between single- and dual-earner families on the willingness of individuals to perform tasks related to the jobs of wage earners. *Direct* and *symbolic* patterns of assistance were established for each family by asking fathers: In what ways do family members help you with your job?."[2]

[2]For analytical purposes, collaborative help with a job was interpreted as indexing a type of direct assistance and supportive activities which enhance the wage earner's ability to perform his job, as denoting a type of symbolic assistance.

[1]The degree of association between scores is obtained by using Goodman and Kruskal's gamma. Gamma is the Index of Order Association (Goodman and Kruskal 1954) that tells how much more probable a like order between classes is to an unlike order when the data include large numbers of ties. We also include Kendall's Tau C a similar measure to test for significance of association. (Blalock 1972:421)

Table 2:   Single- and Dual-earner Families by Family Perceptions of Helping Father with Job Regrouped Scores

| | Single Earners | | Dual Earners | |
Help Pattern	N	%	N	%
None	8	12.9	1	2.0
Direct or symbolic	42	67.7	36	70.6
Both direct and symbolic	12	19.4	14	27.4
Total	62	100.0	51	100.0

Gamma = .34
Tau C = .17
Significance = .006

The scoring pattern adopted is based on order: The categories indicate no assistance, either direct or symbolic, or both direct and symbolic types of assistance and the findings are presented in Table 2.

Table 2 indicates a significant association between having dual earners and how much the father perceives he is helped by the family with his job. Clearly the most common forms of helping are symbolic (61.1 percent); however, single-earner fathers tend to perceive direct or both direct and symbolic help. About 40 percent of dual-earner fathers are identified with this pattern. Only one father in the dual-earner sample reported that he is never helped by his family compared with about 13 percent of fathers in the single-earner sample. Also important is the finding that surprisingly few respondents (9 percent) were willing to say they are never helped by their families in any way. The tendency may simply reflect the fact that fathers' responses were subject to the opinions of other family members and norms of solidarity may have prevented many families from describing themselves as giving no help to wage earners. Yet, within the context of role theory, this type of activity has been considered a way in which the wage earner may reduce strain between work and family role performances. (Turner 1970) A man's occupational role is most likely to be in conflict with his role as a spouse and father when his family doesn't identify with his occupation. This, according to Turner, implies that the wage earner and other members of the family are oriented to different reference groups. One method of resolving this type of conflict is for the wage earner to define a role involving other family members in the job in some manner, so that they feel some responsibility for the performance of the job. These data provide some empirical support for this reasoning, suggesting that the boundary between the family and the job is not as rigid as it is often thought to be.

The third way work-related involvement is assessed is to compare the willingness of individuals to recognize the priority of work-oriented activities over family-oriented activities in single- and dual-earner families. When both spouses are wage earners, work may command more of the family's resources than when only one spouse is a wage earner. Therefore, all family members may recognize work demands as having more right to determine what they may or may not do together as a family. In the interview the following questions were addressed to the father and family about his job. "What demands does your work place on your life at home?" "What limitations does this job place on the way you live your lives?" The expectation was that dual-earner families would more likely perceive work as being more demanding of family life than would single-earner families. Simple additive scoring of responses to both questions allows us to rate a father as to whether he and his family view his job as having a high or low priority. Essentially, the inference is that the more demands it makes on family life the higher the priority work is given.

The results of comparing single- and dual-earner families on this measure are presented in Table 3. Clearly this measure yields a rather different picture of work-related involvement than the two previous measures. Both groups viewed the priority of work in a similar way. In fact, virtually identical proportions of families in both groups did not recognize that work has any priority over family life at all. Moreover, the trends of the ratings of work as commanding a high priority were the same for both groups. The overall conclusion here is clear: The number of wage earners in the family did not affect how individuals perceived work as determining family activities; family life was still considered most important even when work received more time and attention; and having two earners in the household provided more incentive for husbands to discuss work with other family members than it did when they were the only spouse employed. Moreover, family members were more likely to help the male with his job when both spouses were employed. But, this condition does not apply to situations that give work priority over family life.

When comparing the salience of family involvement in family life, the first aspect to be considered is the extent the family intends to recognize and encourage individually derived behavior from its members. The index of this phenomenon is derived from seven items related to restriction or control of

Table 3: Single- and Dual-earner Families by Rating Work Priority

Work Priority		Single Earners		Dual Earners	
		N	%	N	%
No priority		13	22.4	13	23.2
Low priority		18	31.0	21	37.5
High priority		27	46.6	22	39.3
	Total	58	100.0	56	100.0

Gamma = .09
Tau C = .06
Significance = .16

Table 4:   Single- and Dual-earner Spouses by Perceptions of Family Restrictions of Individualized Behavior

Restrictiveness	Single Earners		Dual Earners	
	N	%	N	%
High	8	12.9	16	25.8
Medium	28	45.2	18	29.0
Low	26	41.9	28	45.2
Total	62	100.0	62	100.0

Gamma = .07
Tau C = .04
Not significant

an individual's behavior.[3] From the responses to these items, a family-based measure was constructed.

In Table 4, the ordering of spouses on family individualization is related to the number of wage earners there are in the family. As may be seen, no significant differences were found between single- and dual-earner families on this measure. However, the trend was for dual earners to see their families as being less restrictive. The fact that differences for spouses from each group are slight may simply reflect a limitation of the type of questions that were asked. One has the impression, however, that for dual earners the family has considerably less influence over the behavior of individuals since few respondents appear willing to admit that their families never try to influence their behavior; those who do are mainly in single-earner households.

To examine this phenomenon more closely, the amount of time individuals spent with the family was related to the amount of time spent in other systems during weekdays and weekends. The regularity of family activity was also measured.[4] (See Table 5.)

---

[3]The items which were used to construct the measure are: (a) Has your family tried to change the type of friends you have? (b) Has your family tried to change the type of clothes you wear? (c) Has your family tried to change the way you talk? (d) Has your family tried to change the way you wear your hair? (e) Has your family tried to change your manners? (f) Has your family tried to change your personal habits? (g) Has your family tried to change how you handle money? Scores were created first by determining if each individual perceived any attempts on the part of the family to change his or her behavior and then by calculating the ratio of successfully attempted changes to successfully resisted changes KR-20 = .58. A higher score meant a highly restrictive home environment. To obtain a family-based measure on this and other indices of family involvement, spouses scores were summed.

[4]The items used to measure commitments to the family are: (a) About how much of your time on a weekday/Sunday do you usually spend at work or school? (b) About how much of your time on a weekday/Sunday do you usually spend with friends away from work or school? (c) About how much of your time on a weekday/Sunday do you usually spend with your family? (d) About how much time on a weekday/Sunday do you usually spend with other relatives? (e) About how much of your waking time on a Sunday/weekday do you usually spend by yourself?

Table 5: Rank Correlations[a] Between Family Type and Spouses Time Commitment to Family and Non-family Systems on Weekdays and Sundays

	Weekday	Weekend
Work/School	.34[b]	.12[b]
Friends	−.03	0
Family	−.23[b]	−.13[b]
Relatives	−.02	−.01
Self	−.02	0

a. Kendall's Tau C, a negative association indicates a higher time commitment by single-earner spouses.
b. Significant at the .05 level.

On weekdays, the only differentiating factor between single and dual earners was their commitment of time to work and to the family. Standardized for the number of workers in the family, the dual-earner spouses spent more time at their work during weekdays than single-earner spouses. The next most important difference was in the way both groups allocated time to the family; single earners clearly exceeded dual earners here. Interestingly, even on Sundays dual earners clearly exceeded single earners on time committed to work. The conclusion is that having dual wage earners does affect the way spouses commit their time throughout the week. Dual-earner spouses are more committed to work, while single-earner spouses are more committed to their families.

To determine if these differences were true for weekly commitment to the family, relative to all other systems combined, the spouses' time allocation ratios of family time were compared with non-family time. The results of this comparison are presented in Table 6. As predicted, single-earner spouses perceive themselves as being more committed to their families than dual-earner spouses. On weekdays the relationship is unquestionable, on weekends it is not as clear although the differences are in the expected direction.

To get a more revealing picture of involvement in family life, the nature of family activities was considered. To determine if the spouses from single-earner households perceived themselves as doing more things together than dual-earner spouses, they were asked to describe this aspect of family unity by indicating how frequently, if at all, various kinds of joint activities occurred. Then, each spouse's family commitment was rated. Spouses were rated high on family commitment if the total of their scores on the numbers of activities occurring frequently were greater than the total of their scores on the number of activities occurring rarely.

Table 7 shows that when commitment is assessed in this manner, single-earner spouses are still significantly differentiated from dual-earner spouses. The data suggest more clearly that greater commitment to the family as indicated by involvement in joint family activities is typical of single-earner

Table 6: Single- and Dual-earner Spouses by Weekday and Sunday Time Commitment to the Family Relative to Non-family Systems

Time Commitment	Single Earner		Dual Earner		Single Earner		Dual Earner	
	N	%	N	%	N	%	N	%
Low	12	19.4	23	37.1	4	6.5	6	9.7
Intermediate	26	41.9	28	45.2	2	3.2	4	6.4
High	24	38.7	11	17.7	56	90.3	52	83.9
Total	62	100.0	62	100.0	62	100.0	62	100.0

Gamma = .42
Tau C = −.28
Significance = .0001

Gamma = −.35
Tau C = −0.7
Significance = .10

Table 7: Single- and Dual-earner Spouses by Perceptions of Activity Commitment to Family

Commitment	Single-Earners		Dual-Earners	
	N	%	N	%
Low	17	27.4	23	37.1
Intermediate	27	43.6	27	43.5
High	18	29.0	12	19.4
Total	62	100.0	62	100.0

Gamma = −.21
Tau C = −.14
Significance = .01

families. In the single-earner group 27 percent of spouses are marked low but 37 percent of those in the dual-earner group are in this category.

To summarize, the results from comparison data lead to the conclusion that single-earner spouses are more involved with their families than are dual-earner spouses. The relationship appears to be unequivocal, in view of the diversity of the measures of family involvement employed. In spite of the fact that individuals believe that the family has priority over their work lives the data show that when more of the family's energies are directed toward work, involvements in family life are compromised.

Conclusions and Implications

The comparisons have shown that in dual-earner families, occupations are more likely to circumscribe all members of the household and not merely the individual wage earners. Relative to single-earner families, occupations tend to figure prominently in the way individual family members are involved with one another. This is evidence that, as an adaptive response to dual wage earning in dual-earner families, boundaries with the work world are being crossed. What this means for the study of occupations, the family, and society will now be considered.

First, consider the theory informing this paper and the contention that it is inappropriate to think of work and family worlds as being segregated from one another. Arguments have been offered against models that treat work and family systems as interacting but to a very large extent closed; instead the focus has been on the dynamics of inter-system linkages. Clearly, this subtle shift of focus provides some rather different conclusions about the supposed structure of the work world and the supposed structure of the family.

One of the questions arising from this model that warrants consideration both from the perspective of family and occupational sociology is: *Can we conclude that wage earners just represent family units to society?* The family is usually thought of as being connected to the social structure by the wage earner's occupation and his success in it. When the family is considered in the context of the wage earner's job, its contributions may be of a symbolic and supportive nature. Previous research on the Canadian family and its relations with the work world has shown that members of the household are recognized as making indirect contributions to wage earner's jobs through the maintenance of a particular life style. (Seeley *et al.* 1956) This work has identified conditions under which these contributions become more direct and instrumental to the job. Wage earners do not just represent family units; all members of the family, both by their own work and by their support of the work of others, help to locate the family in the social structure, and this must be recognized.

This recognition has implications for stratification theory. Stratification is based, in part, on the premise that status flows from an individual's occupation and is enjoyed by the whole family. *Yet, what happens to the operation of the stratification system when the family and not the individual in the unit is considered?* It is generally accepted that the family forms a unit with respect to rank. However, when the family is the unit of analysis the occupational roles of other individuals can also influence placement. It then becomes theoretically possible for the family to occupy conflicting statuses based on each of their different occupations. It is equally possible for the family to derive its status from the highest ranking occupation, regardless of whether it is the husband or the wife who holds the position.

Consider also the relevance of these findings on the study of women's status in particular. *What might one expect the long-range effects of wage earning on women's status vis-à-vis the family to be?* There is considerable contradictory evidence on power in dual-earner families. Some report that women who work have more power; others report that family power patterns remain unchanged, or that women who work may lose influence over some area of family life. As indicated, one sees a variety of effects on the family life of dual wage earner families, as compared with single wage earner families; all not necessarily power related. Thus, as working becomes more prevalent among women, it might be expected that one of the long-range effects would eventually be a better integration of work into their family lives.

Finally, it needs to be mentioned that a number of statements in the literature suggest that the kinds of linkages that occur between work and non-work areas of life are subject to the overriding effects of variables emanating from the job situation itself. (Dubin 1963; Kohn and Schooler 1973) A more complete analysis of family involvement in occupations would have to consider dimensions of job experience itself such as the basis of the occupational relationship or the type of work setting. These and other job-related variables may govern the extent of opportunities for family involvement. (Butler 1974)

In conclusion the findings indicate that, far from being antithetical to family stability, work may provide an opportunity for intimate interpersonal involvement among individuals which may even supersede involvement in more expressively oriented family activity. There has been a certain readiness to accept ideal typologies that have been formulated in this area as representing the reality of work and family relationships. In short, the ideal types have become stereotypes. The response to this, however, is that individuals do not just represent families in the occupational world. In the sense that occupations affect the lives of other individuals who are not wage earners, they belong to the family and should be investigated as such.

Working Together: Husbands and Wives in the Small Scale Family Agricultural Enterprise

Seena B. Kohl

Introduction

This paper examines the position women hold in small family agricultural enterprises as observed in the southwestern section of Saskatchewan.[1] The agricultural family enterprise is a business as well as a kinship unit where economic demands and expectations are fused with kinship rights and obligations. This is clearly seen when one recognizes that in the family farm the individual proprietor is simultaneously owner, manager, laborer, as well as father, husband, and son; or when one recognizes that marriage partners are also business partners – either *de jure* or *de facto*.

The maintenance of the family agricultural enterprise involves a set of shared agreements among the household members. Among other issues, these agreements include acceptance of the importance of continuity of the enterprise, acceptance of generational authority, and acceptance of deferred consumption agreements which affect allocations of labor, time, and expenditures. In essence, these agreements fall within the domestic sphere – the arena of the wife and mother, and she is of critical importance in both generating and resolving the conflicts or the potential conflicts between the demands placed upon shared resources of family household and enterprise.

The fact that family social roles intersect economic demands of the enterprise and that the means of livelihood are family centred and family held establishes a situation in which the enterprise figures as crucial in the patterning of family life.[2] This integration of family and enterprise gives what we have

---

[1] The data for this paper were collected as part of a larger study of family life and agricultural enterprise development which has spanned more than a decade beginning in 1962. A generalized account of the region and its populations can be found in Bennett (1969). The population on which this discussion is based consists of the adult members of 139 agricultural households. This is the population which is called the Regional Sample. Parts of this paper have appeared in Kohl, 1971; 1976; 1979.

[2] The merged character of family with an economic enterprise means that it is not possible to separate the domestic and private sphere of the household from the public-productive sphere of the enterprise. This establishes a unique set of structural constraints upon the enterprise family members. These constraints are particularly evident when a son attempts to achieve personal independence from the family but

called an instrumental tilt to the farm family and emphasizes the dual expectations held for women in both household and enterprise.

The domestic activities of women are intimately connected to the economic production processes of the enterprise. Women are involved in most of the decisions of enterprise affairs simply by virtue of the fact that household expenses are a rival to the capital needs of the enterprise. Women supply needed labor for enterprise tasks and are involved in the work world of men in spite of the dominant North American ideology that defines agriculture as a male occupation, and in spite of a rigorous and asymmetrical division of labor in which men do not participate in household tasks. These factors would lead one to expect great exploitation of women with concomitant lack of power[3] and restrictions in their alternatives. In fact this does not occur and farm women have important control over their lives and the lives of other family members. This paper will focus on the fusion of family and enterprise and explore the consequences for both men and women.

The Setting: The Jasper Community

The locale of the study is the southwestern region of Saskatchewan to which we have given the pseudonym Jasper, named for the principal town. The livelihood of these residents is based upon small-scale farming and cattle ranching. The region is sparsely populated (1.7 persons per square mile). Often one must drive from one to seven miles from the main road to reach a ranch house. The topography is varied. There are rolling hills intersected by small streams where ranchers settled, and flat plains north and south of the

---

remains economically dependent as occurs during the succession process when economic resources are being transmitted.

Without economic aid and support from one's family a young man could not hope to acquire the capital necessary for entrance into agricultural production. As Jasper farms and ranches increased in value, the son was required to pay a proportionately larger amount to his parents who used it for their retirement, which meant an increasing debt for the young man starting out. Given the land prices prevailing around 1970, a viable ranch in the Jasper region cost anywhere from $300 000 to $800 000; a farm between $50 000 and $350 000. Few young men were able to accumulate the necessary capital for purchase, and all looked to the retiring generation for financial aid. If the son was unwilling to do so, or if financial aid was not available, then his opportunities in agriculture were severely limited.

The young man who desires to farm is, by virtue of situational demands and cultural precedents, encouraged to remain within the family. This is in sharp contrast with the position of the urban middle-class male child who is pushed out and away from the family; his occupational choices lie outside family ownership and control and are mediated, for the most part, by educational and bureaucratic institutions.

Expectations for the daughter's maturity are not tied to the development of continuity of the enterprise. Marriage, rather than an occupation, remains the ideal goal for the female entering adult status. (See Kohl and Bennett 1965.)

[3]Power is defined as the control that is exercised by one party over the physical and social environment of another party. (Adams 1967:32).

range of forested hills, which constitute the region's most prominent natural feature, where the farmers homesteaded.

Settlement of the Jasper region was relatively recent; the earliest settlers, cattlemen, arrived in the 1880s, and the year 1906 witnessed the end of the open range. Districts were established for homesteading around 1900, with the majority of farm homesteaders arriving during the years 1912 through 1916. The agricultural families of the period studied, 1962-1972, are the children and grandchildren of the original homestead population. The struggles of the pioneer generation on the frontier and during the drought and depression were both recent enough and sufficiently vivid to influence the behavior and aspirations of the contemporary Jasper population. (Bennett and Kohl 1975) Continuity of family enterprises is a major goal around which most families organize their expectations, and there is a relatively high rate (68 percent) of father-son succession.

The town of Jasper, population 2400, is a few miles off the major east-west Trans-Canada highway and is the chief service centre for the region. Since 1952, school children have been bussed from the surrounding area (in some cases up to 30 miles) to the central schools in Jasper. In 1964, accepted conveniences such as plumbing, electricity, telephones, and passable roads were still not available in some districts; consequently, where they were available, the occupants made special note of them. By 1970, virtually all urban amenities were available and expected. Despite the geographic isolation, these enterprises and their members are fully integrated into Canadian national economy and society.

The Fusion of Work and Family

The fusion of agricultural enterprise and the family household involves a coalescence of two spheres of activities that North Americans commonly keep separate. The family agricultural enterprise is based upon the availability of labor within the residential group, the domestic household, which ideally[4], as well as most commonly, consists of members of the nuclear family: father, mother, and offspring. As a consequence, the labor resources for the enterprise are limited and depend upon the phase in the domestic cycle.[5]

Availability of labor in the family enterprise is dependent upon the ages and number of children, the physical health of the household members, as well as the kinds of linkages the household has to other agricultural households. The last factor involves the wider kinship (and quasi-kin) network of relationships throughout the region.

---

[4]The small family farm is often presented as a cherished form of institutional life, and this view has been the basis for many governmental policies, both in the United States and in Canada. (See J. C. Gilson 1959; Griswold 1948; Breimeyer 1965).

[5]The span of the family cycle has been divided into different numbers of phases by different writers, although all agree on a minimum of phases: the married couple without children, the couple with preschool children only, the family including school-age children, the couple with no children left at home, and the widow or widower. (Nye and Berardo 1973)

Availability of labor also depends upon psycho-social factors that establish how the "need" for help is viewed and the way in which household members preferentially allocate their time and labor. These involve shared agreements as to priorities in decisions of expenditure of time and labor.

The technological constraints of the enterprise also affect definitions of "need" for household labor. Where the enterprise can substitute machine labor for human labor, as in straight grain farm operations, "needs" for household participation are less and family members have fewer demands on their time: they are freer to organize their time according to their own lights. Where the technological demands of the enterprise are labor-dependent, as in cattle ranching, the organization of the household's time and labor will be more relevant to the success of the enterprise.

The particular phase of the development of the enterprise also sets constraints upon the household and its members.[6] In its initial stages, an enterprise requires deferment of consumption and important labor contributions from the household members. Moreover, during any expansion process, resources must be devoted to the enterprise and consequently away from the household.

Along with the dependence on family labor, the enterprise relies on the shared agreements of the household members as to the definitions of consumption "needs." Where consumption demands on the part of household members are low, a greater proportion of capital can be reinvested in the enterprise. Jasper agrarians are subject to consumption pressures similar to those of members of an industrial society. What is considered "acceptable" has changed; what one generation perceives as luxuries is seen as the next generation's needs. Further, consumption "needs" do not remain stable. Household members are subject to developmental changes in their own individual life cycle, changes that make greater (or fewer) economic demands upon the shared resources of enterprise and household.

The merged character of farm family and economic enterprise was fully recognized by Jasper women, who were acutely aware of the interplay between the two. In contrast, men made a distinction between enterprise and "house." They firmly located the household and the needs of its members in the woman's sphere of action and responsibility. Nevertheless, when discussing enterprise development, virtually all men recognized the need for household support, by using the term "we."

> *We did everything here ourselves ... we didn't get much help from anyone ... we plan to add some land as soon as we can manage it. ...*

In most cases, the enterprise took precedence and the needs of household members were deferred to enterprise needs – something which all household

---

[6]The development phases of the agricultural enterprise are considered as follows: (1) Establishment – what Jasper calles "starting out" or the beginning of establishing an independent enterprise; (2) Development – the expansion and intensification of resources; (3) Maintaining – the period in which a plateau of development has been reached; and (4) Transmission – the period of the transfer of resources.

members learned to accept. (Capener and Berkowitz 1976) As one woman said:

> *The farm comes first, after it the house, but it's from the farm that every-thing comes, so it has to be first.*

Rarely did a woman state that the house came first or was she unwilling to defer her consumption as well as that of her children in favor of investment in the enterprise. For example, one woman remarked:

> *When it comes to spending a dollar I always ask myself, what is it going to make? If you buy a rug, well you have a rug, but if you use the same money and buy a cow, the cow has calves and with the calves you can get the rug but you still have the cow.*

Throughout all phases of household and enterprise development there is a constant juggling of family and enterprise needs. Women who are responsible for household consumption and family activities play critical roles in their resolution. Such juggling is complicated by external factors such as the price of wheat, the availability of credit, the vagaries of weather, the aspirations of children, and the occupational opportunity structure. It is within this context the familiar roles of husband and wife must be considered.

Husbands and Wives

Many aspects of Jasper family life are familiar ones. Jasper men and women share with the larger North American society similar expectations of gender and marital roles, including the traditional view that expects women to consider marriage and raising a family as their main goal, while men are expected to engage in outside occupations.

There is shared agreement in Jasper over the division of labor between husbands and wives: responsibility for the household belongs to the woman; responsibility for the enterprise and its associated activities belongs to the man. The primary responsibility of the farm or ranch wife is that of cook and homemaker. The men eat all meals at home, including "lunch," which is comparable to the urban coffee break. The woman is responsible for ensuring that there is sufficient food to serve all available help. With the aid of a freezer, an invaluable appliance in all Jasper households since the introduction of electricity in the mid-1950s, and a liberal supply of potatoes and bread as staples, she manages nicely. In multiple household enterprises, where there are two women and separate kitchens, the responsibility is shared and dinner chores are alternated.

Dinner, the major meal of the day, is served precisely at noon, and a woman must plan her day around that meal. This set time keeps the woman house-bound and time conscious. If she cannot avoid being away, she must make other arrangements for the men to have dinner. While shopping trips to town often include visiting with friends and family, the woman is always aware of the time, since there is dinner to serve and children to tend. The round of their daily lives is ordered by the clock and the demands of others.

Unlike the male whose work changes according to the season, the female's work remains the same throughout the year.

There's always the kids, cooking and the house. In winter we curl; in the summer I have a garden. But it's pretty much the same all year.

However, women's work does change in terms of the family cycle in that it is dependent upon the demands of the family, which reflect the composition of the household and the ages of its members.

The image of the ideal woman is that of the frontier woman who "does what has to be done," but, aside from this vague prescription which takes for granted the woman's household tasks, there is flexibility in the role which the farm or ranch wife can play in the enterprise. Her participation in the enterprise varies according to her own desires and values, the needs of the enterprise, and the expectations of her husband and other members of the family enterprise. Women's participation spans virtually the entire range of enterprise activities. Women are the "hired hands"; they hay, feed animals, drive trucks, get supplies, mend fences, etc. They are also owner-managers: they provide cash and land, function as accountants, help in business decisions, and serve as labor brokers and personnel counsellors.

While averages are deceptive, in Jasper the time women spend in enterprise activities ranges from about ten hours a week to more than fifty hours, depending upon the seasonal demands of enterprise production. This is similar to other analyses of the contribution of women to the family enterprise; note averages ranging from "half-time" to over 40 hours a week.[7]

The following table indicates the ways in which women contribute to the enterprise:

Table 1: Major Type of Women's Contribution (1970)*

	Number	Percent
**Household organization	6	8.2
Control of consumption	15	20.5
Bookkeeping/literary skills	9	12.3
Agricultural labor	5	6.8
Social relational skills	6	8.2
Women who contribute in all fields	21	28.7
Cash input	9	12.3
Operating head	2	2.7
Total number of women	73	99.7

*This table has been compiled from interviews with a smaller sub-population within the regional sample.

**These women see their primary work as the routine work in the household in contrast with women who see their important activity in the control of consumption along with the routine household tasks.

[7]Saskatchewan Department of Labour (1977) publication *Farm Women* reports similar averages for their Saskatchewan survey population. (Also see W. E. Huffman 1976.)

Although the enterprise is usually given priority over work in the house, household chores still remain; meals to prepare and serve, children to tend, houses to clean – these are all the woman's responsibility, but not priorities in terms of the allocation of shared labor resources. The fact that household tasks are taken for granted as being totally the woman's responsibility means that other chores which she undertakes are added to her basic work load.

The newlywed enters a situation where her husband has been accustomed to a particular style of enterprise participation established by his mother. Often invidious comparisons are made between the mother who had both the energy and organizational ability to participate vigorously in enterprise affairs and the young wife not yet able to match this style. Added to this is the attraction of modern recreational and social alternatives, such as curling or skiing, previously not available to her mother-in-law, but which are often preferred by the young wife who lacks the skills or incentive for enterprise activity. These conflicts are practically resolved as the young wife matures and establishes her own style of participation in the enterprise.

All women share a common means for controlling the expectations regarding their participation in enterprise activities. They simply do not *learn* how to do certain tasks – for example, one woman never learned how to drive: "If I did, it would always be 'mother get this, mother get that.' I have enough to do." Another woman never learned how to milk a cow: "If I did, then it would be my job forever. This way, Joe does it." Men also refrain from performing certain tasks, but when they deny knowing how to cook, bathe a child, or wash clothes, they phrase their lack of learning in terms of the separation of household and enterprise: "It's the wife's job – she's in the house and I'm in the fields."

The degree to which women are able to control household expenditures, freeing income for reinvestment in the enterprise while maintaining shared commitment on the part of the household members who supply the labor for the enterprise, affects the success or failure of the enterprise. Although the manager/father might initiate enterprise activities, the success or failure is dependent upon the organization and consent of the household members. Even those women who are not significantly involved in enterprise tasks – women who see their primary role in the enterprise as one of household activities only – nevertheless, participate in important ways in the economic health of the enterprise, simply by household budgeting and consumption control. While these activities are traditionally considered as part of "housewifely" activities with no "economic" value, they do, in fact, represent important productive value, a fact which only recently has begun to be socially recognized.

Regardless of her desires, the woman's household activities can not be extricated from the enterprise. The control she is able to exercise over the allocation of family members' time is important in terms of available labor for the enterprise. Her decisions either encourage or prevent the children's outside activities: for example, whether they go to 4H camp or help on the enterprise; whether they play on school teams or return home for chores. As one woman said:

Kevin really enjoys hockey and I think he should be able to do it. Of course, it means he can't do his chores when he has a game, but sports are important too.

Women organize the social relationships between the household, the kin group, and the community. They establish reciprocal ties with the larger community, which is vitally important for the exchange of labor. A farm wife with little aptitude for these skills puts the enterprise at a disadvantage since the exchange of labor in Jasper is deeply embedded in social relationships. (Bennett 1968) Hired labor is difficult to find and decidedly not preferred.

Most important, virtually all women are involved in the on-going managerial decisions of the enterprise. Farm and ranch wives have a higher level of education than do their husbands, as indicated in Table 2.

Women also have wider literacy, bookkeeping, and clerical experience. Before marriage, 50 percent of the farm and ranch wives had worked as teachers, in secretarial positions, and in nursing. In contrast, the jobs men held prior to farming (60 percent had work experience outside the region) were, for the most part, in areas that utilized their agricultural skills. These jobs included farm work, construction, factory work, carpentry, and mechanical work. Only 8 percent held jobs based on literacy or organizational skills, such as business, sales, and service occupations. These literacy and bookkeeping skills are crucial for enterprise decision making. Jasper women maintain the breeding records and financial accounts for the enterprise, and attend to the necessary correspondence to national agencies that control the agriculturalists' access to land, water, and credit resources. When interviewed, male agents of the various bureaucracies said they preferred to deal with men on enterprise matters in order to obtain an authoritative response; at the same time, they recognized that to get an authoritative response, the men must check with their wives for an accurate accounting of their enterprise.

During the mid-morning "lunch," the enterprise work tasks, expenditures, market analyses, and crop decisions are discussed and decisions are made. It is a business lunch in the true sense of the word, and it is this feature of agricultural family enterprise life that transforms the role of homemaker.[8]

Conclusion

The work women do in the household through the familiar household tasks make important economic contributions to the enterprise; these household contributions are ignored as they are ignored among non-farm economic

---

[8]D. Hedlund and A. Berkowitz, Department of Education, Cornell University have reviewed farm family research between 1965-1977 (mimeo). They note that both in H. L. Smith, *Work and Authority Patterns as Related to Marital Satisfaction in Wisconsin Farm Families*, Ph.D. thesis, University of Wisconsin, 1969, and in A. Berkowitz, Role Differentiation in 21 New York State Farm Families, unpublished manuscript, Department of Education, Cornell University 1976, wives share more in farm decisions than in farm tasks, although there is considerable involvement in the latter areas. (Also see Capener and Berkowitz 1976.)

**Table 2:   Educational Level of Contemporary Operators
and Wives (1965)**

	Men		Women	
Grade Completed	Number	Percent	Number	Percent
Grade 8	51	50.5	13	14.4
Grades 8 – 11	40	39.6	42	46.6
Grade 12 or more	10	9.9	35	38.8
Total	101	99.0	90	99.8

enterprises. This is a reflection of the larger society's view of housework as "non-work" – that is, the view that homemakers who are not paid do not produce commodities of value to the economy, and are dependants of men. The fact that the non-farm household, in contrast to the farm household, is isolated from the work sphere and that lives are most often distinctly divided into work and non-work segments gives some basis for understanding the disregard of women's economic contributions – what has been called the "hidden factors" of production. (Rowbotham 1974; Oakley 1974)[9]

However, even where farm women perform important enterprise tasks, they are not usually considered as economic contributors since the activities of women outside the wage market are considered "personal services" donated to husbands and children. While both rural sociologists and agricultural economists have recognized the merged character of the farm family and economic enterprise, with few exceptions they have failed to acknowledge the economic contribution of the farm women in both spheres – household and enterprise.[10]

---

[9]The current discussions of the role of the homemaker as involving both work and non-work is a continuation of the problems Marx raised in his analyses of labor as a commodity and the distinction he makes between exchange value and use value. Glazer-Malbin (1976) in an excellent review essay of housework discusses the alternative conceptualization of women's housework and the consequences for women's status.

[10]H. C. Abell (1954) represents one of the few exceptions in which women's labor in enterprise activities such as care of poultry, cleaning of milk equipment is not taken for granted.

For the most part, where there has been recognition of the contribution of farm women the primary emphasis in research concerning women has been concerned with the woman's generalized "homemaking tasks" and the relationship between careful management of such tasks and the interpersonal relationships of the family members, encouraging the woman to expand her concept of household management. (See for example Carl C. Malone and Lucile Holaday Malone 1958:194-95.)

It is noteworthy that although The Royal Commission on Agricultural and Rural Life, Report No. 10, (1956) discussed the unrecognized character of the legal status of the farmwife as an economic partner, in the subsequent recommendations of the Commission there was no proposal for a change in legal status.

The integration of the woman's domestic sphere of the household with the public sphere of the enterprise creates a social situation where women are active participants in what is defined ideologically as the man's world, but not vice versa. Logically, it is possible to conceptualize household and enterprise as a complementary system; each composed of the same personnel but with different directors and tasks. In reality there are dual responsibilities for women – the basis for the women's double burden. However duality also means women have alternatives for gender roles. They may choose to play an active role in the operation of the enterprise or may restrict their attention to the household. (The possibility of women playing an active economic role has not evolved to the point of daughters being considered potential successors.)[11] Men, on the other hand, play only the traditional role, proprietor of the enterprise.

Men do not experience dual expectations. In Saskatchewan as elsewhere, they have no formal (and little informal) responsibility in the household. They are freed from dual sets of expectations and dual work loads. Their "freedom" from dual sets of responsibilities is commonly regarded as an attribute of supremacy. However, what has been only recently appreciated in industrial settings is that men in their "freedom" from household and family tasks are rigidly locked into work roles, and particularly in Jasper, men are locked into a specific work role of agricultural operator. While we commonly think of flexibility in role prescriptions as a "good," and role specificity as a failure of the social system to take into account individual differences, it is important to remember that the flexibility of roles for women has a double-edged character. The sharp side of the blade emerges in the analysis of women's work with its dual work load, a situation which has grave consequences for all women where they are unable to control the dual sets of expectations.[12]

Other research which has looked at the role of farm women has been concerned, for the most part, with the role of the wife in innovation, adoption of new farming techniques and decision making. Most of this research has related value-attitude data of the wife to the profitable operation of the enterprise. This research assumes that production is the unique decision of the male farm operator and the women's part is to serve as an "influence" on management decisions. (For example see: Eugene A. Wilkening and Lakeshmi K. Bharadwaj 1967.)

Delva Hedlund and Alan Berkowitz (see footnote 8) indicate there is beginning to be a change from this model of family-farm research to research which now takes into account more complex interrelations among family members.

[11]Daughters are active participants in the enterprise activities, and they *do* inherit property. Some women are enterprise heads but only by default. (See Kohl 1976.)

[12]Castillo (1977) in her review of the role of women in rural societies cites several instances of the particularly heavy burden rural women carry.

The duality of expectations for women is one aspect of the broader topic concerned with the relative status of women. Analyses of women's position have linked their relative status to their economic contributions noting that where women control land, seed, or distribution of production, their status and associated power has been found to be greater than in these settings where they only contribute labor. (See Brown 1970; Friedl 1975; Sanday 1973.)

COURTSHIP, MARRIAGE, AND DIVORCE

Introduction

One of the social forms that perpetuates itself, generation after generation, is the family. In the context of contemporary western societies, a man and a woman become husband and wife through legally recognized procedures. With the advent of children, whether through biological or adoptive processes, a family emerges. The family, then, is a social artifact in that certain social customs are observed prior to its emergence. Just as certain social conventions are honored to create a family, other social processes, the ultimate being divorce, lead to its dissolution.

The four articles included in this section clarify some of the major aspects of the processes and patterns involved in the generation and the dissolution of the family.

Ramu's article, Courtship and Marriage, indicates that the relevant literature in the Canadian context has focussed largely on the interactional rather than on structural dimensions of this theme. In other words, we know more about the relationship between the courting partners than about the wider structure of social relations within which these relationships occur.

To bridge this gap, Ramu offers a simple, but useful, model based on the concepts of stability and change, and applies it to the available data, identifying some of the social forces that encourage traditional conformity and those that push for change. Ramu concludes that "while Canadian courtship practices continue to reinforce social differences by means of homogamous alliances within most dominant groups, converging trends toward egalitarianism in marital interaction are emerging."

Trigg and Perlman explore the issue of extramarital sex – potentially a set of attitudes and activities that can drastically affect the family as a social form. Under certain conditions, extramarital sex (EMS) puts great strains on the married partners, indeed, even leading to dissolution of particular families.

Trigg and Perlman investigate several interrelated questions about EMS that fit into the wider perspective on the generative and destructive processes of the family. For instance, they ask: What proportion of Canadians approve of, and engage in, extramarital sex? What are the circumstances in which EMS is most likely to be accepted? What types of people are permissive, rather than conservative, about extramarital sex?

One of their major findings is that attitudes toward premarital sex are closely linked to attitudes toward extramarital sex. However, the correlation is by no means equal; a higher percentage of people accept premarital sex.

Moreover, acceptance of premarital sex varies situationally. For instance, premarital sex is acceptable to a larger proportion of people if affection between married partners is missing, but is present between extramarital partners. The authors also suggest that future research would profit from an analysis of cost-reward considerations involved in EMS.

In contrast with family-building processes, divorce is obviously concerned with family-breaking processes, and the last two articles in this section focus on these processes and their implications.

John Peters regards the first marriage as an "engagement" process that involves a connection between two people. Divorce, which is a process of disconnection, is described as a "disengaging, disengaged, and re-engaging" process. By looking at divorce in this context, the author stresses the long drawn-out period to the finality of divorce, while indicating the period of possible rebuilding, in a new context, all that is lost by divorce.

Since the cultural ideal in Canada is to marry and stay married, why do people get divorced? In response to this question, Peters offers an "exchange theory" that conceptualizes the marital relationship as an exchange of rewards. Over a period of time, a couple may discover that the rewards of marriage are not what they had expected. The impact of the Women's Liberation movement, economic and several other factors are considered in relation to the disappointment of reward expectations that often lead to divorce.

However, despite the staggering increase in the divorce rate since the liberalization of Canadian divorce laws in 1968, marriage still remains a positive institution in Canadian society. Many divorced people remarry. Peters considers this re-engagement process in terms of the various characteristics of the couples involved, and the ways in which the re-engagement differs from the engagement marriage.

Maureen Baker considers the consequences and meanings of divorce as they differentially affect men and women when they cease to be husbands and wives. Based on a sample drawn from the population of Metropolitan Toronto, she describes and analyses the data in terms of "support network" and "personal network" models. From the subjects' varying stages of marital dissolution, she is able to trace the processes of divorce as an evolving phenomenon which continues to generate many implications for the parties concerned, even after divorce is legally granted. Baker shows how the implications differ for men and women in terms of legal restrictions, network positions, occupational positions, and so on.

Although women frequently initiate divorce proceedings, they often find themselves at a disadvantage. Child custody, usually granted to the woman, often entails conflict with the divorced husband over child support payments. According to Baker, given the multitude of discriminations against women, divorced mothers with children confront an uphill task, while divorced fathers, on the whole, find it easier to readjust.

Courtship and Marriage

G. N. Ramu*

Any discussion of courtship and marriage in a given society essentially addresses the following questions: Do individuals select their spouses *or* do others? What criteria are used in selection? Once married, how do they interact with their spouses? What personal, practical, and ideological concerns govern such patterns of interaction? Some of these questions will be considered here in light of available sociological data on Canadian society. Because of the relative paucity of Canadian data, the analysis is necessarily tentative and draws upon research conducted in the United States for pertinent comparison and trends.

This chapter is divided into four sections. The first section addresses the guiding perspective which attempts to bring together various findings on Canadian mate selection and marriage. This approach employs the general concepts of *stability* and *change* delineating those social forces that encourage conformity to traditional patterns in contrast to those that are conducive to change. The second and third sections deal respectively with courtship and mate selection, and various aspects of interaction in marriage. The final section offers a brief concluding comment.

A Perspective

A key to understanding courtship and marital behavior in Canada is its culture and social organization. Culture, which constitutes the matrix of social relationships, represents shared meanings about the organization of social life, providing an overarching normative structure for ordering social behavior, including courtship and marriage.

Stability and Pluralism. Canada's unique history of immigration, settlement patterns, language, and religious differences has not succeeded in developing a common cultural focus around which its social and political institutions could achieve coherence. Consequently, over the decades Canada has allowed, and often consciously encouraged "pluralism" as the basis of social organization. Although the full ramifications of pluralism for the development of a national society are unclear, two dimensions of pluralism are pertinent for our consideration here: as a source of structural differentiation; and as an impetus to individual freedom in matters of mate selection and marital adjustment.

*I am deeply indebted to my colleagues, Lawrence F. Douglas and Nicholas Tavuchis, for their comments and editorial advice on an earlier version of this paper.

Pluralism as a source of structural differentiation. By definition, a pluralistic ideology encourages group differences with respect to religion, ethnicity, class, and those characteristics which are specific to one's country of origin – language, literature, arts, food, etc. When a society deliberately encourages various groups to maintain their distinctive characteristics, these groups develop appropriate institutions. A crucial aspect of such institutionalized mechanisms are rules concerning courtship and marriage which become primary means of perpetuating ethnic, religious, or linguistic heritage. Consequently, most social groups seek directly or indirectly to retain control of matters related to mate selection and marriage. The extent to which such control is exercised varies in accordance with importance that the group attaches to the maintenance of its identity. For example, if Catholics or Hutterites have lower rates of intermarriages, this may be interpreted as their exercise of greater control over mate selection than in those groups which have higher rates of intermarriage (e.g. Scandinavians). In this way, pluralism serves to maintain group differences.

Pluralism as a source of individual freedom. Pluralism creates a cultural situation in which individuals can choose alternative courtship and marital patterns to those endorsed by their subcultural groups. It allows a certain measure of personal freedom, in this regard, to adopt a way of life which does not conform to the standards of their original groups. The result of such freedom is not the maintenance of cultural or normative order, but the creation of different, if not deviant, patterns. For example, courtship need not terminate in marriage: the couple may choose to "live together" without a formal marriage contract. In addition, the husband may share the "breadwinner" role with his wife. A pluralistic milieu thus may encourage experiments resulting in changes in the established patterns of marriage.

Change and Convergence. A second parallel set of influences that shapes the nature of courtship and marriage in Canada is the assimilative and cumulative effects of industrialization/urbanization, burgeoning communication technology, secular ideology, democratic egalitarianism, and universal legal codes, all of which tend to undermine subcultural variations. The changes initiated by these forces have been viewed as converging patterns in marriage and family. (Goode 1963; Kalbach 1974:2; Tavuchis 1979) Living in contemporary Canada entails adherence to certain methods of mate selection. For example, generally one cannot depend upon the preferences of parents or kin but has to choose the most eligible person. A Muslim male cannot exercise his religious prerogative of marrying four wives because monogamy is the law of the land. Further, as Elkin (1975) has argued, various technological innovations have brought about common life styles regardless of ethnic, religious, or racial identities of groups. In short, the changes precipitated by objective conditions beyond the control of many groups result in convergent marital patterns as will be demonstrated in the third section dealing with marriage relationships.

In sum, two sets of competing forces representing stability and change are recognized. The former tends toward the persistence of the established social ordering of mate selection and marriage, while the latter facilitates a convergence of patterns with regard to marital interaction and role definitions. It should be noted, however, that the literature on modernization indicates that (cf. Gusfield 1967) such dual and contradictory realities are hardly unique to Canada.

Mate Selection

Courtship in Canada: Controlled Freedom. Although there are various modes of selecting a spouse (whether the analytical focus is on the individual or groups), two general patterns have been identified: assortative and random. Where the maintenance of salient social characteristics, such as religion, race, or ethnicity is deemed important, parents or kinship groups are likely to select mates in accordance with pertinent criteria. The individuals, to be sure, have some freedom but the final decision rests with the group. By controlling who marries whom, the group attempts to maintain its distinctive features, a practice that is referred to as *assortative mating.* (cf. Ramu 1976; Wolf 1972) In *random mating*, on the other hand, there is relatively little interference by the group and individuals are permitted to choose anyone (other than those tabooed for reasons of incest) who meets certain personal criteria such as physical attraction, emotions, and sexual compatibility. Random mating, which is essentially an ideal, encourages social integration which is antithetical to the pluralist basis of social organization.

In Canada, both assortative and random patterns prevail and affect the successive phases of one's courtship career. According to 1976 statistics (Statistics Canada 1976b) over four million persons are potential participants in the marriage market and ideally one can choose anyone from this group. Nevertheless, specific individuals not only live in different kinds of communities but within each community they are further segregated into residential groups based on social class, religion, ethnicity, language, and so on. Thus, the way in which groups are organized allows for the indirect social selection of potential mates, and hence, the first phase of the Canadian mate selection process is essentially assortative.

It would be incorrect, however, to infer that such an assortative marriage market is consciously developed as it is, for example, among certain groups in India or Taiwan. It is basically a concomitant of residential structure and the general tendency of people to live in areas compatible with their socioeconomic status. In most cases, individuals do not fully comprehend these factors that influence their choice mainly because mate selection is a long process (about eight to ten years) that typically involves several partners. Consequently, courtship in Canada is to a large extent controlled. What gives it the appearance of free choice is the fact that the final decision in virtually all cases, rests with the individuals themselves.

Dating. Dating is a form of heterosexual interaction with many objectives including recreation, cultivation of competence in interpersonal relationships, sexual intimacies, and finally, the identification and stabilization of a relationship with the aim of either "living together" or marriage. Earlier research by

Waller (1937) underscored the recreational rather than the mate selection function of dating. Many critics (e.g. Ellis 1954; Mead 1966) consider dating as a game strategy involving deception, exploitation, superficiality, and thrill-seeking – scarcely attributes that would prepare a person for a long lasting relationship. As a result, many observers (cf. Murstein 1980) conclude that dating is not very popular nowadays because of its unreliability as an effective means of spouse selection.

The negative attributes associated with dating stem from Waller's (1937) and Gorer's (1964) assertion that it is a game; an assertion that has recently been challenged by Gordon (1981). Nevertheless, Waller's conception was appropriate for the marital pattern prevalent at the time of his research, i.e., 1930s. Dating behavior of that era merely adumbrated the double standard and male dominance that were likely to follow in marriage. Contemporary perceptions of marriage are gradually being modified in the context of feminism, the increasing number of dual-career families, and egalitarian values. Hence, the dating behavior of the 1950s is passé and current patterns are in tune with changed marital expectations.

Those who argue that dating is now functionally irrelevant do not indicate what has replaced it. Some suggest (Melville 1980:77-86; Murstein 1981:777-81) that group dating is one of the contemporary alternatives. If group dating is widespread – and evidence of this is lacking – it merely indicates that such a collective enterprise acts as a springboard for "pairing" which eventually leads to a more permanent relationship. Such pairing relationships may in fact correspond to the advanced stage of conventional dating – "going steady."

Thus, dating continues to be a common method by which one attempts to select a mate and this appears to be the case in Canada since no clear evidence of alternatives exists. Other than studies by Whitehurst and Frisch (1974) in Ontario and Wakil (1975) in Saskatchewan, information on dating is confined to incidental references (for example, Ishwaran 1980). Whitehurst and Frisch (1974) in their study of a random sample of students in an Ontario university found that dating is not only a common activity but, contrary to Waller's notion, entailed a high component of marriage-preparedness. Most students considered their dating activity as educational, co-operative, and honest in purpose. Wakil (1975) also found dating common on the University of Saskatchewan campus. There a large proportion of students tended to date partners from similar socio-economic backgrounds, a fact which provides support for the notion of stability in courtship patterns. Studies of many ethnic groups (e.g., Ishwaran 1980; Peter 1971; Hostetler and Huntington 1967; Anderson and Driedger 1980; Driedger et al. 1982) allude to dating patterns but discuss them primarily in the context of the maintenance of ethnic identity by controlling dating patterns.

Like their colleagues in the United States, Canadian sociologists have shown little interest in dating patterns and there are no studies later than 1973. The tentative conclusion, therefore, based primarily on incidental references (e.g., Herold and Goodwin 1979) is that despite many academic reservations about dating as an appropriate means of mate selection, most Canadians still continue to engage in it while being selective about their partners. Recent innovations such as computer match-making or videotape introductions are not yet popular and are unlikely to alter the basic pattern through which young people meet.

Living Together. Living together or *cohabitation* may be interpreted either as a contemporary alternative to *steady dating* or *engagement* phase of traditional courtship, *or* as an alternative to marriage. Reiss (1980:106-07) conceptualizes these alternatives as *courtship cohabitation*, and *non-legal marital cohabitation*, respectively. The courtship cohabitation is generally a temporary alliance serving as either an alternative or an adjunct to steady dating and engagement. (Risman et al. 1981; Macklin 1978; Arafat and Yorburg 1973) Courtship cohabitation, which is extremely popular among middle-class college-age youth, is reportedly on the increase in the United States (Glick and Norton 1977) but there is no comparable information available for Canada. Non-legal marital cohabitation is hardly a novel phenomenon and historically has always existed among the lower class (see Liebow 1967), but when it is adopted by the middle class it attracts scholarly attention. In non-legal marital cohabitation, the couples may indeed desire a permanent relationship and parenthood.

In Canada, researchers are now beginning to assess the extent to which living together prevails and its influence on marital adjustment. For example, in the Edmonton area survey, a city-wide sample gathered in the Spring of 1981 included 7.2 percent (29 cases) of respondents who reported living "common law," an almost 100 percent increase within three years (3.6 percent or 16 cases in 1979 Spring). In the Winnipeg Area Study conducted in the Spring of 1981, only 1.8 percent or 6 cases reported living common law.* Given that non-legal marital cohabitation is generally understood as synonymous with common-law marriages, both the Edmonton and Winnipeg data suggest that this type of cohabitation is fairly common. Watson (1981) studied a purposive sample of 84 couples in Victoria who had been married for a year of whom 54 had cohabited and 30 had not. The object of his study was to assess the influence of premarital cohabitation on marital adjustment. He concluded: "The effects of premarital cohabitation/non-cohabitation upon subsequent marital adjustment as measured during the first year of marriage appear, therefore, as somewhat equivocal. While non-cohabiters, on average, obtain higher adjustment scores, neither for men nor women taken separately were their scores significantly above those of cohabiters."

A critical review of the literature on living together suggests that in most cases it is an extension of the courtship process (as in the cases studied by Watson 1981) associated with common residence, a negotiated economic relationship, sexual division of labor and power, intimate sexual and emotional ties, and occasionally even parenthood. With the notable exception of a formal legal contract these features are strikingly similar to those of monogamous marriage. In the past, living together was perceived as a common-law

---

*I am thankful to the directors of these area surveys, Professor Leslie W. Kennedy, Director of Population Research Laboratory, Department of Sociology, University of Alberta, and to Professor Raymond Currie, Department of Sociology, University of Manitoba, for sharing this information.

arrangement that could be terminated without penalty if unforeseen problems were encountered. Such a perception must be challenged in light of recent legal decisions that have supported the female's claim to certain proportion of property accrued during the period of living together. In Canada, provinces such as Manitoba legally recognize the co-ownership of assets accumulated by a couple living together for a period of two or more years.

In conclusion, although contemporary patterns of living together illustrate options available to individuals in mate selection, as a type of heterosexual relationship it is neither new nor drastically different from monogamous marriage, especially in the context of changing property laws applicable to cohabiting couples.

Factors in Mate Selection. It was suggested earlier that Canadian courtship practices involve a certain measure of controlled freedom because individuals are assorted on the basis of certain crucial social characteristics before they date and, ideally, go on to develop mutual attraction and romantic love. This point will be substantiated in terms of *homogamy* and *heterogamy*. Homogamy, used as a synonym to endogamy, refers to the tendency for individuals to marry those with similar social and psychological characteristics. Heterogamy, on the other hand, refers to situations in which individuals marry those with different social characteristics, although common psychological or personal attributes are taken into account. There is considerable sociological evidence suggesting that homogamy prevails in Canada and in the United States, where, as indicated earlier, an initial filtering of eligible couples occurs (see Kerckhoff and Davis 1962; Levinger et al. 1970). The pattern of intermarriages in Canada highlights the prevalence of homogamy.

Intermarriages: Proof of Stability. If, during the last 100 years or so, Canadians had been intermarrying without regard to differences in race, religion, language, ethnicity, or social class, the result would have been, except for the most recent immigrants, a population of "blended Canadians" instead of "hyphenated Canadians" (English-Canadian, Jewish-Canadian, etc.). Intermarriages, in the long run, tend to dissolve subcultural traits. However, such homogenisation never occurred because there is a strong propensity to marry within one's own social group and thus to use marriage as a means to perpetuate the group's identity. The data on intermarriage confirm this assertion. For example, the strict observance of racial homogamy has largely kept Canada a racially monolithic society. The proportion of non-whites in the Canadian population including the Natives is approximately 3 percent. The general sociological assertion is that the smaller the group, the greater the chances of outmarriage (Heer and Hubey 1975) but this does not apply to non-white groups because racial identity is a highly visible and salient criterion in the organization of Canadian social life.

There appears to be greater flexibility with respect to inter-religious marriages. Heer (1962), and Heer and Hubey (1975) found that the percentage of inter-religious marriages rose from 5.8 of all marriages in 1927 to 21.5 in 1972. However, there is variation in the flexibility demonstrated by the three major religious groups in 1972: of those who married outside their own faith,

22.7 percent were Protestants, 20.5 percent were Catholics, and 15.4 percent were Jews. Such variation is seen as a function of the size of the group relative to others in a particular area which affects supply and demand of specific spouses, increased secularization, and the absence of any significant effect of intermarriages on progeny and their identity. (Latowsky 1971; Chimbos 1971; Frideres et al. 1971)

The data on ethnic intermarriages suggest that ethnic homogamy is stronger than religious homogamy in the overall percentage increases although, when broken down by specific ethnic groups, the trends vary. For example, while inter-religious marriages have doubled between 1957 and 1972, the proportion of inter-ethnic marriages rose only marginally: 23.3 percent in 1961 and 24.4 percent in 1971. (Kalbach 1974) Kalbach's (1974) analysis of the trends in inter-ethnic marriages suggest that in 1971 almost one in four marriages represented inter-ethnic alliances. However, some ethnic groups were more homogamous (e.g., Jewish, French, British, and Asiatic) than others (e.g., Scandinavian, Polish, Hungarian, Italian, and German) with no significant variation in recent decades. (Kalbach 1974) Most case studies of inter-ethnic marriages (cf. La Coste 1966; Carisse 1976; Berman 1968; Boissevan 1976; Driedger et al. 1982; Anderson and Driedger 1980; Campbell and Niece 1979) suggest that conditions conducive to ethnic homogamy in Canada include the perceived importance of ethnic identity, persistent family patterns, kinship control of mate selection, fear of assimilation, and a social milieu supportive of pluralism.

Residential Propinquity. Another factor which encourages homogamy is *residential proximity*. Catton (1964:529) aptly pointed out that since people with similar social characteristics tend to cluster together residentially, one effect of propinquity is to increase the likelihood of such categorical homogamy. If one accepts Shevky and Bell's (1955) social area analysis, then residential arrangements reflect social class, and according to Porter (1965), social class is correlated with ethnic status in Canada. Therefore, residential propinquity acts as an initial filtering device in mate selection.

Summary and Conclusions. Thus far various aspects of courtship and mate selection have been examined mainly on the basis of Canadian evidence which is often sketchy and tentative. The main theme of the argument has been that there is more social control of mate selection than is commonly recognized and admitted, and that mate selection in Canada is both assortative and random. Such an argument does not, however, neglect the changes that have introduced uniformity in the interpersonal aspects of courtship behavior. These changes transcend the limits of social criteria. Within the homogeneous marriage market prevalent among most social groups, factors such as physical attraction (Walster et al. 1966), romantic love (Goode, 1959; Greenfield 1965; Reiss 1980:V), value consensus (Murstein 1970), similar personality traits, and common assumptions about marriage and family life in general are significant for individual choice. Nevertheless, the ways in which these forces influence mate selection within the various social or ethnic groups in Canada have not yet been sociologically documented.

Because of the pluralistic emphasis on social organization in Canada and because marriage is considered one of the important means of maintaining a group's identity, mate selection for the vast majority of Canadians tends to be homogamous. Such changes as have occurred in the direction of heterogamy are slow and uneven. The greatest degree of convergence seems to have taken place in the method of courtship in that, regardless of their national origin and subcultural emphasis, most groups encourage some form of dating as the means by which to initiate the mate-selection process.

Marriage in Canada: Some Structural and Interactional Aspects

Whether the marriage is homogamous or heterogamous, the issue confronting the couple centres not on the perpetuation of their group identity but on the quality of their interpersonal relationships. It is generally believed that the couple can take for granted such matters as role performance, decision making, division of labor, sexual adjustment, and marital satisfaction, as well as the problems and pleasures of parenthood. However, despite the prevailing normative guidelines, couples are faced with the challenging task of defining and negotiating mutually satisfying marital relationships over a period of time. The dynamics of such definition and negotiation are too complex to be dealt with here; therefore, this section will focus on certain objective conditions that guide these processes.

Dual Realities. In analysing the literature, one encounters a widespread ambivalence toward marriage. The statistics on marriage and remarriage rates underscore the fact that most Canadians marry (see Peter's article in this volume). In 1965, 43.6 percent of the population was married and, in 1976, this rose to 47.7 percent. In 1976, almost two-thirds of the adult population was married compared with just over half in 1901. (Statistics Canada 1979a) Furthermore, many of those who divorce remarry within three years and the rate of remarriage has tripled during the ten years following 1966. (Statistics Canada 1979b) What these statistics suggest are that: (1) not only do most Canadians get married, but most also remain married, and (2) of those who divorce most remarry.

While the statistical evidence confirms the popularity of marriage, increasing divorce rates indicative of problems in stabilizing the relationship together with continuing search for alternatives, present contradictory trends. For example, Whitehurst and Plant's (1971:84) study of a sample of Ontario university students suggests that, compared with their American counterparts, "Canadians significantly more often agreed that 'marriage is passé' as an institution and should be done away with." Henschel's (1973) discussion of couples who "swing" (exchange spouses for sexual purposes) and Whitehurst's (1975, 1979) account of emerging alternatives to contemporary marriage and family further illustrate parallel but counter trends. Many American analyses have offered variations on the same theme. (Otto 1970; The O'Neills 1972; Bernard 1972) In essence, these accounts argue that marriage in North America is being found unnecessary, irrelevant, redundant, and, that as a consequence, many individuals are seeking functional alternatives. (Kanter 1973; *The Humanist* 1974; Sussman 1975; Libby and Whitehurst 1977)

This duality with regard to marriage in Canada appears to be consistent with the perspective outlined earlier in terms of stability and change. Many, if not most, Canadians continue to live according to the conceptions of marriage and family relationships exemplified in their parents' marriage, and supported by their ethnic subcultures. Many of the case studies in Ishwaran's (1980) anthology on ethnic families in Canada support this view. The emphasis in these cases is on continuity rather than change. However, one will also have to recognize the pressures for change stemming from the changing economic position of women, recognition of values as embodied in feminist ideology within the legal system and in interpersonal relationships. These dimensions are examined next.

Stability in Marital Relations. One of the ways in which stability in marital patterns can be understood is by examination of factors that determine conformity to traditionally defined marital roles. Customarily, marital relations have been patriarchal stressing male dominance. The support for patriarchy is derived from notions of gender identity and perceptions of biological differences that are seen as determining the social and psychological competence of males and females in relation to various activities including marriage. This kind of traditional approach to marriage and family is legitimized by such sociological explanations as offered by Parsons and Bales (1955).

Patriarchy versus Egalitarianism. Most couples tend to take their marital roles for granted seldom discussing, for example, how decisions will be made and authority exercised in matters of common concern. Furthermore, hardly any such discussion or negotiation *precedes* marriage. Instead, most couples depend upon customary definitions, at least initially, and such innovations as occur come about gradually after marriage in response to the exigencies of everyday living. Generally, the husband tends to retain much of the *formal authority* although he may frequently delegate it to his wife either because of his other preoccupations, his incompetence, or unwillingness to deal with certain matters. Such a patriarchal stance is generally derived from the husband's role as the breadwinner. If the wife is limited to domestic chores, it is not because she cannot perform an economic role but because she is perceived as being biologically and psychologically more suited to perform a homemaker's role than is the husband.

There is strong evidence that such a patriarchal pattern prevails in Canada both attitudinally and behaviorally although some shift in the direction of egalitarian relationships seems to be under way. In a poll conducted in 1978, a sample of Canadians in thirty-one of the largest urban centres was questioned concerning the kinds of marital forms preferred. Over 60 percent preferred a traditional legal marriage with children, and the wife as homemaker as the most satisfying arrangement. Only 23 percent wanted a dual-career marriage with children. (Weekend Magazine, Winnipeg Free Press 1978 02 11) Men are reluctant to accept egalitarian values in their marital life as Hobart (1975:175-76) found in a study of post-secondary school students in Alberta and Quebec.

Men were not only less egalitarian, they were also less willing than women to accept this possibility in their future marriages. What is interesting in Hobart's findings is that French-Canadian men were more egalitarian, and favorable to the emancipated roles of women than their English counterparts in Alberta. Similar tendencies have been noted in the area of marital adjustment by Carisse (1976:193). She found that in French-English intermarriages in Montreal the mode of adjustment favored the husband at the expense of the wife's culture, suggesting masculine dominance in the choice of the culture to be transmitted to children of inter-ethnic marriages.

The situation is summed up by Eichler (1975:230), who after an examination of egalitarianism in Canadian families states that, " . . . there is no egalitarian family in Canada at the present time, because our society does not as yet, provide for equality of opportunity for men and women because of legal, socio-economic distinctions in the rights and duties of husbands and wives."

Legal Aspects of Marriage. In Canada, as in most Western societies, marriage is a contractual relationship entered into usually within a religious context. When legally formalized, marriage becomes an agreement between the spouses on a set of complex mutual rights and obligations concerning the division of labor and power, economic interdependence, child rearing, sexual services, and so on. However, unlike other contracts, a marriage contract is not drawn up by the contracting parties, and the terms of contract are typically unknown to the contracting parties. (Weitzman 1975) The main reason for this anomaly is that most rights and duties are supposed to be commonly understood because there are part of a cultural heritage rooted in centuries of religious, moral, social, economic, and ideological histories that have come to shape female-male relationships in Canada as elsewhere.

The origins of the Canadian marriage law may be traced to the 400-year-old British Common Law and the Napoleonic code (for Quebec only). Because these legal norms are unwritten and based on values and norms relevant for pre-industrial Europe, most interpretations have been conservative, favoring a patriarchal system. For example, Weitzman's analysis of the legal aspects of marriage in the United States suggests that there are four key provisions in the unwritten marriage contract based on the assumption that certain obligations and privileges should be assigned to men and women, regardless of individual preferences and capabilities. These are: (1) the husband is the head of the household; (2) the husband is responsible for support; (3) the wife is responsible for childcare; and (4) the wife is responsible for domestic services. Corresponding provisions are found in Canada as is shown by Wuster (1975), Zuker and Callwood (1971), and Cameron (1977). Eichler's analysis further confirms the persistence of the traditional characteristics cited by Weitzman. It is therefore important to recognize that the legal aspects of marriage reflect the most formal conceptions of husband-wife relationships and that these remain essentially patriarchal in nature although in recent years there have been partially successful efforts to alter this situation.

In sum, there is evidence supporting the stability of marital roles in relation to traditional assumptions about what men and women can and should do in their marital life. However, these assumptions are being seriously challenged and attempts to revise or replace them are meeting with some success. A discussion of such changes follows in the next section.

Factors Precipitating Changes in Marital Relations. Regardless of the structural control of marriage through homogamy, traditional roles, and legal underpinnings of patriarchy, marriage continues to be the most enduring dyadic relationship spanning over fifty years of an individual's life. Such a relationship cannot remain static when the social milieu within which it operates undergoes continuous changes. The following discussion will identify some of the changes evident in the Canadian marital patterns and examine certain factors that have precipitated these changes. The main contention is that marital relations are slowly moving in the direction of egalitarianism and the forces contributing to this move are feminist ideology, the increasing participation of married women in the labor force, and changes in the matrimonial property laws.

Feminist Ideology. The modern feminist movement started in the mid-1960s in response to various discriminatory practices against women including patriarchy and the continuing denial of societal rewards in terms of education, occupation, income, prestige, and power. The movement itself is complex not only in its organization but also in its varying ideologies and means. (cf. Frieden 1963; Millet 1970; Thompson 1970; Royal Commission 1970; Mitchell 1971) In this regard, Adams (1980:276-78) identifies several foci within the diversified feminist movement three of which are: (1) feminist-humanist; (2) radical feminist; and (3) socialist feminist.

The *feminist-humanist* position emphasizes the liberation of both men and women who are seen as oppressed by the traditional sex role ideology. This calls for reforming most social institutions beginning with the family where gender roles are initially defined. The *radical feminist* perspective defines men as oppressors of women because they are the immediate beneficiaries of women's institutionalized servitude. Hence, liberation stands for freedom of women from activities which benefit men even if these entail certain personal sacrifices for women. The *socialist feminist* camp shifts the focus from men to the more abstract industrialist capitalist system because not all men are oppressors but only those with bourgeois characteristics. As a result the object is not only to overthrow male dominance but the totality of class relations that engender inequality.

In Canada, it appears that the main objective of feminism, equality of sexes, is politically accepted and efforts are being made to implement programs which would ameliorate women's position. (Royal Commission 1970, 1971, 1979; CBC Task Force 1975; Bennett and Loewe 1978) However, it is difficult to assess the long-term effects of various feminist movements on the marital relations. Nevertheless, it seems clear that attitudes toward egalitarianism, women and work, and marriage laws have been influenced by feminism.

From Patriarchy to Egalitarianism. There are recent indications of a trend toward egalitarianism. Some patriarchal tendencies may be continuing among certain isolated groups but as an ideology it is no longer universally nor automatically accepted. Studies suggest that women have begun to look for different ways to shape their lives both within and without marriage. For example, a majority of students studied by Whitehurst and Plant (1971) held negative attitudes toward marriage and one of the reasons cited was that the belief that "marriage is based on inferior women and superior men" was wrong. Most students suggested changes in the marital system to make it more egalitarian.

Hobart's (1976:175-76) attitudinal survey of a sample of secondary school students in Alberta and Quebec further highlights the emerging egalitarian trend. Fewer than a third of the males and a small proportion of females thought that the wife's role should be limited to that of homemaker and caretaker of children, although a majority of the men preferred that their wives leave the labor force upon motherhood. At the behavioral level, Hobart (1975:451) found tangible evidence of the prevalence of egalitarianism in matters related to matrimonial property rights. In a Calgary study of 464 couples, Brinkerhoff and Lupri (1978) found a generally high degree of egalitarianism in matters of decision making and exercise of power, although wives tended to be slightly more powerful than husbands when children-related factors were included for analysis. When these were excluded husbands gained in power, but the couple still maintained a high degree of egalitarianism.

While some of these studies indicate that changes are occurring in the direction of egalitarianism, one must be cautious in making generalizations because there is no consensus among sociologists on either the definitions of authority, power, and influence in marital relations or the techniques of their measurement. Despite these problems it seems clear that egalitarianism in varying degrees has entered marital relations. Whether it is more or less than what it was several decades ago cannot be easily established.

Women, Work, and Marriage. Historically, women as a group have demonstrated competence in work both within and outside the home despite the problems of *role overload.* For example, some women on farms participate in farm chores while also performing the roles of mother and wife. Similarly, lower-class women have always been "co-breadwinners" in addition to their domestic roles. In stressful periods such as wars, urban middle-class women have shown that they too can efficiently handle the dual responsibilities of home and work. It appears that it is only during peace and prosperity that women, especially middle-class women, are confronted with a choice between being a wife and mother and pursuing a career. However, evidence on married working women suggests a definite shift toward the latter.

Married women are entering the labor force at an unprecedented rate – 60.4 percent of all the female workers in Canada in 1979. (Women's Bureau, Labour Canada 1979) In a penetrating analysis of the changing roles of women in Canada, Lupri and Mills (1981, *in press*) observe that:

> *Indeed the single most dramatic and pervasive trend in the status of women since World War II has been the increase in proportion of married women who work for pay. The five-fold increase of married women entering the labor force has been increasing almost twice as fast as that*

for all women. But more important, the largest increase in labour force activity has occurred for the group generally viewed as least likely to work – mothers of pre-school age children . . . In fact, married women with preschool children have the greatest growth rate between 1967 and 1973; their participation showed an overall increase of 73 percent in these few years.

It is no accident that the increase in married women's participation in the labor force corresponds with the social and political recognition of women's rights in Canada during the last fifteen years, as well as measures introduced for improving these rights.

In brief, the financial contributions that married employed women make, the contacts they develop outside home, the sense of accomplishment and self-fulfillment they experience obviously have a bearing on redefinition of marital roles and on the readjustment process. Meanwhile, along with the increasing economic importance of women there is a growing concern about inflexible marriage and family laws, and considerable pressure is now being exerted to have them changed.

Changing Legal Structure. As indicated earlier, according to the British and French legal traditions, when Canadian women marry they have limited independence in matters of property, personal identity, freedom, and non-familial options in life. For example, once a woman marries her identity merges with that of her husband's in that she takes his surname and social status. Norms of residence call for her to reside with her husband regardless of her wishes. Most financial institutions treat her as a legal minor in that they would grant her credit only after the husband provides a guarantee even when she has independent income. In the event of divorce, she cannot claim an equal share of the matrimonial assets receiving only what the husband chooses to give in terms of alimony and child support. (Time 1974 03 05; Zuker and Callwood 1971; Wuster 1975; Chapman 1968; Weitzman 1975)

In recent years, however, because of pressure from women's groups together with the increasing economic independence of women and their significant contributions to the household economy, marriage laws are being amended to give women equality on most matters. The BNA Act of 1867 placed marriage within provincial jurisdiction, therefore most provinces were pressured to change relevant laws and nearly all have moved in this direction at this writing. For example, in Manitoba, women now need not assume their husband's surname or take up residence upon marriage with their husbands if such a change would interfere with their careers. They also retain considerable freedom in matters related to consumer credit, control of their premarital assets, and are entitled to equal share of the matrimonial assets in the event of divorce.

Such changes are indicative of a shift in marital relations in the direction of egalitarianism. To be sure, these changes are not generally accepted as legitimate because widespread awareness of the intricate legal aspects involved would depend upon massive changes in public opinion.

Summary and Conclusions. Three factors – the feminist ideology, increasing participation of married women in the labor force, and a changing legal structure – are seen as generally contributing toward the shaping of egalitarian marital relations. There are many other developments which would exert considerable influence on this process that have not been discussed here. For example, the educational system has become more accommodative in that married persons can upgrade their skills by attending evenng classes or in mature student programs. These changes allow married women to upgrade their qualifications for re-entering the labor force once their children attain school age. There has also been an increase in governmental assistance to employed women by subsidies to day-care programs for their preschool children. Further, there appears to be changing perceptions of parenthood in that most women complete childbearing at a relatively early age so that they can return to the workforce, *or* they postpone parenthood until they are established in their careers. (Macleans 1981 05 04) Some couples are avoiding parenthood altogether in favor of careers. (Veevers 1980; Ramu *forthcoming*) These trends together will likely sooner or later contribute to the development of egalitarian marriage and family life in Canada.

Consequences of Change: Rewards and Costs

The general impact of the changes described earlier on marriage is becoming increasingly apparent. As one would have anticipated, the changing socio-economic status of women has in many cases necessitated the redefinition of male and female roles, ultimately calling for marital re-adjustment. Women, when gainfully employed, are in a better position to bargain for advantages in their domestic life in exchange for their contributions to the economic well-being of the family. Such a bargaining process and the ensuing exchange patterns have been carefully documented by many sociologists. (Blau 1964; Scanzoni 1970; Osmond 1978; Nye 1978) Furthermore, in a milieu which is supportive of egalitarianism and legal changes, men tend to experience difficulty as evidenced by their unfavorable response to changes in the roles that their wives play. In any event, the changes in married life, as elsewhere, entail both rewards and costs.

One of the features of traditional marital roles has been the pre-eminence of the husband as the sole provider for the family and the authority in all matters. In order to perform this role efficiently men tended to place greater emphasis on their employment and its associated activities. This had a visible effect on marriage as well as on the responsibilities of parenthood. As Aldous et al. (1979:229) point out, ". . . the man who is an occupational success is a marital failure." As Adams (1980:281-84) notes, "The problem that the modern male faces is how to balance between work and family, between getting ahead and domestic peace." The cost of playing this instrumental role has been heavy as Melville (1980:216) points out: "Most health statistics, as well as the criminal records, demonstrate that males are more vulnerable to stress and they commit more serious crimes. Men have more heart attacks than women; they die younger; they are more likely to develop ulcers, commit suicide, and to become alcoholics. Perhaps these are symptoms of the pressure that males feel as they try to meet masculine expectations." Although some of these problems may be alleviated by marriage, as Bernard (1972) suggests, the recent changes do seriously increase the costs of the transition to egalitarian marital roles.

As Nye and Berrardo (1973:X) suggest, marital roles are continuously changing in response to social changes. Consequently the husband's role tends to be less authoritarian, more conciliatory, more recreational, and more companionate. Inflation correlated with rising costs of maintaining the family have encouraged women to become co-breadwinners and this seriously erodes the power base of the male. Komarovsky's (1973:873-74) study shows that there is a continuing ambivalence among the majority of men regarding their wives' employment. Nye (1972:279) and Burke and Weir (1976) further suggest that husbands of employed wives tend to be less satisfied with their lives and often manifest symptoms of physical illness. But whatever their problems in accepting the changing status of their wives, men are forced to come to terms with it because alternatives such as separation or divorce bring even more problems (Gilder 1975). Consequently, men will eventually adapt because in the words of Booth (1977:649), "The added income and the greater personal fulfillment the wife and probably the husband eventually enjoy far outweigh the short-term disadvantages which female employment may bring to the conflict."

The Canadian data on male roles tend to be more inconclusive in that some studies confirm the continuity of male dominance while suggesting beginnings of changes (c.f., Hobart 1976; Carisse 1976a; Meissner et al. 1975) while others suggest a fairly dramatic shift toward egalitarianism in marital relations (Brinkerhoff and Lupri 1978; Lupri and Frideres 1981; Hobart 1975). Gallup Polls conducted in 1966 and 1976 showed considerable change in attitude toward the role of the father. Of the 1011 Canadians questioned, 49 percent agreed that the father should be the boss of the family while in 1966 almost two-thirds (63 percent) held a similar attitude. What is interesting is that a majority of women (51 percent) in 1976 did not agree that fathers should have the final word. This demonstrates a gradual shift in the perceptions of the ideal role of the male in marriage and the family.

The women who seek employment outside the home do so because their income is essential for the maintenance of the household or it enhances the standard of living of the family. Regardless of the motives, employment confers mixed blessings on women. As one would expect, women's co-breadwinner role alters the balance of power within marriage and many American studies support this although one Canadian study found the opposite to be the case: " . . . working wives report slightly lower power scores than non-working wives." (Brinkerhoff and Lupri 1978:6) The fact remains that when women are not totally economically dependent on men, their own self-concept improves and this, in turn, will be reflected in increased marital happiness. An American study (Burke and Weir 1976:284) reports that working women tended to be in better physical and emotional health and held more positive views about life in general and marriage in particular. This is corroborated in

Canadian study of marital happiness. Lupri and Frideres (1981) found that "... a wife's employment status has an important and positive effect on both wives' and husbands' marital satisfaction. Employed wives are slightly more likely to be 'very satisfied' with their marriage than are housewives (53% versus 48%)."

The Canadian data further suggest that the newly acquired financial independence of women has enabled them to obtain more resources for personal care and comfort (Hobart 1975) and that for many employed married women, children do not pose obstacles to their careers. (Bruce 1978) It is important, however, to recognize that these gains have been made at an enormous cost to both men and women, especially the latter.

The evidence suggests that a majority of Canadian women conform to their traditional role expectations – homemakers, caretakers of children, and sexual companions to their husbands. For example, in 1976, the number of married women in the population was approximately 5.5 million of which approximately 2.4 million were in the labor force (Statistics Canada 1979a, b) thus confirming that most married women continue to be homemakers. Those who are in the labor force are there either in place of their conventional homemaker role or as an adjunct to it. The evidence suggests that regardless of which options these women exercise, numerous re-adjustments are inevitable in their marriage and in their lives in general. Carisse (1976b) in a study of 149 innovative French-Canadian women in Montreal found that 51 had never been married so that they could pursue orderly and highly successful careers, whereas 41 combined their careers with marriage with many sacrifices in their personal lives and career achievement. Some 33 had to relinquish their professional roles in order to fulfil their marital and maternal responsibilities before returning to non-familial roles, and the remaining 33 women waited to complete their marital and motherhood roles before involving themselves in voluntary work or in the labor force. Carisse's study illustrates that responses to the changes do not necessarily take a single predictable course but vary in relation to the biographical contexts of the couples.

Finally, most married women tend to experience much more than men, at least initially, what the Rappoports (1971) refer to as the *role overload* because in addition to their normal household responsibilities they also are breadwinners. This is evident from a study conducted in Vancouver by Meissner and his colleagues (1975) showing that equality in the marital/familial division of labor does not automatically result when wives hold paying jobs. Their data indicate (p. 433) "... that most married women do the regular necessary and most time-consuming work in the household every day. In view of the small and selective contribution of their husbands, they can anticipate doing it for the rest of their lives." Based on a detailed log of contributions to housework by the spouses, the authors show that generally husbands do not share household work as most studies have pointed out. They conclude instead that "... paid work offers to married women the potential of at least some financial independence from their husbands but, at the same time, confirms their domestic dependency in the menial and subordinate character of much of their paid work." (Meissner et al. 1975:437-38)

Summary and Conclusions. A review of Canadian sociological literature on marriage suggests that, in general, attention has not been focussed on the structural but on the interactional dimensions. For example, there is little indication of subcultural variations such as those frequently considered in the analysis of courtship and mate selection. The statistical evidence indicates that a large majority of marriages tend to conform to the traditional models in that the husband is the sole breadwinner and the wife is the homemaker. However, about 2.4 million couples (this number is increasing) can be viewed as participating in dual-worker marriages in which the wife has assumed the role of co-breadwinner.

The concepts of stability and change have been employed to interpret the manner in which marital relations function. There is a very strong tendency, both attitudinally and behaviorally, to conform to traditional role definitions which established patriarchy, or male dominance, in crucial marital concerns. At the same time, there are some indications that marital relations are heading toward egalitarianism. Such competing trends seem to characterize the duality of Canadian marital life.

Conclusions

An assessment of the field of courtship and marriage in Canada reveals that serious gaps in our knowledge of this field continue to persist. As a consequence, any attempt to draw systematic generalizations will be premature. The sketchy evidence evaluated here suggests that while Canadian courtship practices continue to reinforce social differences by means of homogamous alliances within most dominant groups, converging trends toward egalitarianism in marital interaction are emerging. In short, at present, courtship and marriage in the Canadian context reflects a continuing, if not conflicting, duality in terms of stability and change or pluralism and convergence.

Extramarital Sex:
The Standards of Canadians

Linda J. Trigg and Daniel Perlman

In the 1940s, Kinsey (Kinsey et al. 1948) collected information on the frequency of extramarital sex (EMS). But, it was not until the 1970s that theoretically based investigations of extramarital sexual attitudes and their determinants began. Byrne (1977:3) described research on sexual behavior as a "progressive evolution from less taboo concerns (animal behavior, studies of primitive cultures, and abnormality) to the succession of 'shocks' that attended the extension of sexual knowledge to the normal, contemporary human sphere with Freud, Kinsey and Masters and Johnson."

Within the normal sphere, the sociological and psychological issues involved in premarital sex (PMS) have been studied extensively for over two decades. (Reiss 1967; Reiss and Miller 1974, 1979) Yet more intensive systematic research on EMS is a relatively new phenomenon.

Given the increasing tendency of the general public to accept PMS, does this mean that EMS is also becoming an acceptable phenomenon? Do those individuals who endorse premarital sex also endorse extramarital relations? What are the circumstances under which EMS is sanctioned? What are the variables that influence or predict attitudes toward EMS?

This paper attempts to answer these and similar questions by reviewing recent studies of EMS and by reporting data pertaining to the attitudes of Canadians toward extramarital relations. Only one other study (Edwards and Booth 1976) reports information obtained from a Canadian sample. Specifically, it assesses sexual behavior in and out of marriage with data from a sample (N=507) of Toronto husbands and wives.

The data for this paper came from two sources: a nation-wide poll, and a more in-depth survey of Winnipegers. The national poll was conducted by the Canadian Institute for Public Opinion (CIPO) in August of 1977. The sample consisted of 1039 respondents representative of Canada's non-institutionalized, adult population. These respondents were asked their opinion on seventeen questions that covered a variety of issues, plus an additional twelve demographic and background questions.

The in-depth study was based on a structured forty minute interview, during which respondents were asked 127 questions pertaining to their background, social relationships, and attitudes toward EMS. More personal questions were presented in a self-administered, confidential questionnaire.

The interviewers, students from a social psychology class, were instructed to interview only people who were (or had been) married; they were not permitted to interview friends. Quota sampling was used; in all, 147 interviews were completed. The sample included a balance of males and females and an equal number of respondents in three age categories - under 35, between 35 and 50, and over 50.

Attitudes Toward Extramarital Sex

Attitude toward EMS was assessed in the national opinion poll by the question:

> *There has been a lot of discussion about the way morals and attitudes about sex are changing in this country. What is your opinion about a married person having sexual relations with someone other than the marriage partner - is it always wrong; almost always wrong; wrong only sometimes; or not wrong at all?*

In the Winnipeg study, a modified version of this question was asked in reference to a married *man,* and then repeated in reference to a married *woman.* Both answers were combined to form a scale score used in correlational analyses.

In the national opinion poll, 66 percent of the respondents claimed extramarital sex is "always wrong." Only 2 percent answered that it is "not wrong at all." Winnipegers were slightly more reconciled to EMS. However, their responses may have been influenced by the fact that the question followed a series of questions examining circumstances under which EMS might be sanctioned. A reply that EMS is sometimes acceptable may have been made to achieve consistency with their earlier answers.

Using data from representative samples of respondents in the United States, Glenn and Weaver (1979) examined attitudes towards PMS, EMS, and homosexual relations. In general, reported attitudes toward EMS were highly restrictive with about 70 percent of respondents indicating that extramarital relations were "always wrong." In comparison, then, the representative sample of the population in the United States was more conservative in their attitude toward EMS.

Circumstances Surrounding Extramarital Sex

With few exceptions, past research on EMS has used a general measure of acceptability. To broaden the scope of response to extramarital sexual standards, the dependent measure was supplemented with conditions under which extramarital sex might be acceptable. Given a list of fourteen situations originally developed by Sponaugle (1977), Winnipeg respondents were asked how strongly they agreed with extramarital sex under each circumstance. From this, the percentage of acceptance was calculated for each situation.

The results shown in Table 1 indicate that the circumstances surrounding EMS do influence attitudes. For many respondents, being in love with the extramarital partner or having a physically handicapped spouse incapable of sexual relations justifies EMS. However, other circumstances, for example that the extramarital relationship will never be detected, do not justify EMS in the respondents' minds.

Table 1: Percentage of Positive Responses to Extramarital Sex Under Various Circumstances

Circumstance	Percentage
The person is in love with the extramarital partner.	29%
The spouse is unable to have sex because of a physical handicap.	26%
The spouse is having sex with another person.	22%
The spouse is unaffectionate.	21%
The spouse approves.	18%
The spouse is incapable of satisfying his/her spouse sexually.	17%
There is a separation because of military service, extended business trips, etc.	13%
The person has little or no affection for the extramarital partner.	10%
The other person is not married.	10%
The spouse is physically unappealing.	7%
There is no possibility of the spouse or anyone else ever finding out about this relationship.	7%
The person and his/her spouse have no children.	6%
The spouse does not know the other person.	5%
The other person is married.	5%

Sample: 147 Winnipeg Respondents

The total number of circumstances in which respondents approved of EMS correlated .67 with respondents' general attitude toward EMS. Thus, these two measures are highly related, although they reflect slightly different aspects of the underlying construct.

Attitudes Toward EMS Compared With Attitudes Toward PMS

There is no similarity between the degree of acceptance of extramarital sex and that of premarital sex. The Canadian public is much more liberal in their attitudes toward PMS than they are toward EMS. A national poll in 1980 tapped the public's attitude toward PMS patterns. Of 1051 people interviewed, 52 percent considered premarital sex acceptable, 15 percent were undecided, and 33 percent felt premarital sex was unacceptable. In the United States, data from 1974 analysed by Snyder and Spreitzer (1976) also revealed more liberal attitudes toward PMS than toward EMS.

Prior to the mid-1960s, there was no documentation of sexual standards or changes in attitude. Nevertheless, a historical view of Canadian literature and sex manuals suggests, not surprisingly, that puritan forces played an important role in shaping sexual attitudes. The data collected since the mid-1960s shows a trend toward increasing acceptance of PMS. Between1970 and 1980, there was a 21 percent increase in Gallup Poll respondents who considered premarital sex acceptable. (Perlman, *in press*) To date, however, this trend has not emerged in attitudes toward extramarital relations.

Extramarital Sexual Behavior

Data on the incidence of extramarital sex in Canada is sparse. In Edwards and Booth's (1976) Toronto study, 22 percent of males and 5 percent of females reported having extramarital sexual relations. In the Winnipeg study, approximately 17 percent of all respondents (regardless of gender) reported having engaged in extramarital sex. The proportion of Canadians engaging in extramarital sex appears to be lower than the proportion of those doing so in the United States. For example, a recent survey in the United States (Glass and Wright 1977) found that the incidence of EMS was 36 percent for females and 40 percent for males.

Theoretical Perspectives for Understanding Extramarital Sexual Standards

While it has not reached the most advanced stages of theory development, research during the 1970s has identified several factors useful in predicting attitudes toward extramarital sex. These predictive variables can be roughly classified into three categories: demographic factors, dyadic influences, and individual attitudes or differences. The Winnipeg survey incorporated all three types and generally expected them to be associated with acceptance of EMS as in past studies. The present investigation also assessed supplementary variables such as friendship patterns and leisure activities. In the following summary, social factors are grouped with dyadic influences under the category of interpersonal determinants.

Sociodemographic Factors

Social characteristics such as age and gender have intuitive appeal in predicting extramarital sexual standards. This area of research has been categorized by Davis (1974) as "sexual-demography."

In a relatively comprehensive study, Singh, Walton, and Williams (1976) examined some of the conditions and contingencies of extramarital permissiveness. Among the demographic factors, they found that religious conviction was inversely related to extramarital permissiveness (i.e., religious individuals were less accepting of EMS). They also found that membership in certain groups was directly related to extramarital permissiveness (e.g., older people were less likely to approve of EMS than younger people; males were more likely to approve than females; blacks were more likely to approve than whites; and unmarried persons were more likely to approve than married persons). In general, the predictive strength of these demographic factors was low to moderate, and findings for social class were insignificant, although complex offsetting trends may exist depending upon the intervening variables.

Snyder and Spreitzer (1976) found support for the proposition that different age cohorts would view EMS differently – respondents over 65 years being more conservative than those under 65 years. Gender, social status, church attendance, marital status, and parenthood were predictors of general attitudes toward EMS, PMS, and homosexuality for both age groups.

In another study of attitudes toward PMS, EMS, and homosexual relations, Glenn and Weaver (1979) found that Jews, persons with no religion, young adults, and persons with more than twelve years of school were more permissive than the general adult population.

In the Canadian opinion poll, attitudes toward extramarital sex were associated with several demographic variables (see Table 2). Single respondents, younger people, and those with more education were all more accepting of extramarital sex. Men and women did not differ.

Several additional predictors emerged from this data set. As in the United States (Glenn and Weaver 1979), Jews and people listing "other" religious affiliations were more accepting of EMS than were Protestants or Catholics. However, somewhat unexpectedly, acceptance of EMS was related to income: higher income respondents were more permissive. Community size was also a factor: people from larger communities were more accepting of EMS than those from smaller communities. With regard to region, people living in Alberta and British Columbia were the most liberal, while people on the Prairies were the most conservative.

Interpersonal Determinants

In recent years few studies have focussed solely on demographic variables as predictors of EMS. Rather, researchers have studied sexual behavior outside of marriage as being influenced by a combination of background variables, social factors, and interpersonal needs.

In addressing the latter two dimensions, dyadic factors have been examined by several researchers. (Edwards and Booth 1976; Glass and Wright 1977; Reiss, Anderson and Sponaugle 1980) Specifically, the influence of marital happiness on either attitudes or behavior has been explored under the assumption that the unhappily married would be more accepting of EMS than the happily married. Despite some inconsistencies, this generalization has been largely supported. For example, based on their Toronto study, Edwards and Booth (1976:73) conclude:

it appears that the more severe the marital strain ... the lower the frequency of marital coitus; and as the latter becomes more infrequent, the more likely is extramarital involvement to occur.

Table 2:   **Percent of Respondents Claiming Extramarital Sex is "Always Wrong" by Selected Demographic Variables**

	Number	Percentage
Age		
Under 30	317	54.9
30-39	196	63.3
40-49	151	63.6
50-59	127	75.6
Over 60	153	85.6
Marital Status		
Single	221	51.1
Widowed, Separated, Divorced	82	64.6
Married	648	70.8
Education		
Grade School only	144	78.5
Secondary School	582	65.1
University	142	55.6
Religious Affiliation		
Protestant	381	70.1
Catholic	445	65.4
Jewish	18	44.4
Other	103	56.3
Income		
Under $10 000	197	74.6
$10 000-$14 999	256	67.1
$15 000-$19 999	148	63.5
Over $20 000	207	57.5
Community Size		
Under 1000	232	62.5
1000-9999	107	80.4
10 000-29 999	78	73.1
30 000-500 000	235	65.1
Over 500 000	300	61.7
Region		
Maritimes	98	63.3
Quebec	269	61.3
Ontario	350	69.7
Prairies	92	81.5
West	143	55.9
Party Preference		
Liberal	332	59.9
NDP	102	59.8
Progressive Conservative	160	64.4
Undecided	233	78.5

NOTE: All analyses are based on the 1977 Canadian Institute of Public Opinion Survey.

In a somewhat more complex analysis, Glass and Wright (1977) postulated that length of marriage and gender moderated the relationship between EMS and marital satisfaction. In fact, they found that extramarital sexual behavior was generally associated with lower marital satisfaction, but the strength of the relationship between these two measures varied within different subgroups. Essentially, EMS was associated with lower marital satisfaction among all respondents, except for wives in young marriages and for husbands in old marriages. While the results for young women are perplexing, the male findings are easier to interpret. Glass and Wright argue that young male newlyweds who engage in EMS may be dissatisfied with their relationships, whereas, older males who engage in affairs do so mainly for sexual gratification and not for emotional involvement.

Overall, the attempt in the Winnipeg study to predict attitudes toward EMS via dyadic factors met with mixed success. (For selected correlations see Table 3.) To assess marital satisfaction, six questions from Spanier's (1974) scale were selected.

The general measure of attitudes toward EMS was not significantly correlated with such factors as marital satisfaction, free time spent with spouse, or the proportion of mutual friends. However, the first two were related to the number of circumstances in which respondents considered EMS acceptable. The less satisfied respondents were with their marriages, and the less free time they spent with their spouses, the greater the number of circumstances in which they would accept EMS. Also, less satisfaction with one's overall family life was associated with having a more permissive attitude.

Turning to past relationships, respondents who reported a larger number of premarital sexual partners were more accepting of EMS. This correlation was fairly strong and held for both measures. Similarly, respondents who had engaged in premarital sex with their spouse were somewhat more tolerant of EMS.

A variety of information was obtained on friendship patterns, the ways respondents spent their free time, and the like. Only two of these correlated with either EMS measure. People who rarely engaged in community activities would accept EMS under more circumstances, while people who frequently attended cultural activities had more restrictive general feelings toward EMS.

In summarizing these patterns, three points can be made: (1) the dyadic factors worked less well than expected in predicting answers to the single-item, general measure of attitudes toward EMS; (2) these factors did, however, predict the number of circumstances in which EMS would be deemed permissible; and (3) premarital sexual behavior and current family life satisfaction were useful predictors of both EMS measures.

Overall, interpersonal needs and social factors bear consideration in any theory of extramarital permissiveness. Marital satisfaction, for example, tends to be related to extramarital sexual standards. However, other variables such as length of marriage, gender, perceiving divorce as an option, reasons for EMS, and circumstances surrounding EMS may moderate any direct relationship between marital happiness and EMS permissiveness.

Table 3: Correlation Coefficients for Interpersonal and Social Predictors of Attitudes Toward Extramarital Sex

Predictor	Scale End Points[a]	Measure of EMS	
		General[b]	Circumstances[b]
Marital satisfaction	6=satisfied; 37=dissatisfied	.11[c]	.31
Free time with spouse	1=most; 5=none	.08[c]	.21
Satisfaction with family life	1 = satisfied; 7 = dissatisfied	.21	.30
Premarital sex with spouse	1=No; 2=Yes	.14[c]	.25
Number of premarital sexual partners		.34	.39
Frequency of engaging in community/volunteer activities	1=often; 5=never	.14[c]	.22
Frequency of attending cultural activities	1=often; 5=never	−.23	−.10[c]

Note: Results are based on the Winnipeg sample.
[a]Scale endpoints are provided for descriptive purposes but are not the exact wording used in the survey.
[b]For both EMS measures, higher numbers reflect greater acceptance of extramarital sex.
[c]This correlation is not signficant at the p <.05 level.

Attitudinal Factors

A number of individual differences or attitudes have been associated with attitudes toward EMS. Reiss, Anderson and Sponaugle (1980) focussed on attitudes toward women, premarital sex, and politics. All three proved important: people supporting gender equality, accepting premarital sex and political liberality were all more accepting of EMS.

The Winnipeg study incorporated all of these variables and generally expected them to be associated with attitudes accepting extramarital sex, as in past studies. Gender equality was measured by four items previously used by Reiss et al. (1980). Several supplementary variables were added to the attitudinal set of predictors including attitudes toward divorce, family, and community, and right-wing authoritarianism. Authoritarians typically espouse conventional moral standards and have conservative views regarding premarital behavior. (Perlman, *in press*) Given this, it was expected that more highly authoritarian people would have restrictive attitudes toward EMS. Authoritarianism was measured by six items from Altemeyer's (1981) very carefully developed, right-wing authoritarianism scale.

The attitudinal factors proved to be strong predictors of extramarital standards (see Table 4). Of these authoritarianism and attitudes toward premarital sex were the best predictors. As expected, nonauthoritarians and people with permissive attitudes toward PMS were more accepting of EMS. Acceptance of extramarital sex was also related to attitudes favoring more liberal divorce laws, gender equality, and the belief that family stability is less essential for the well-being of society. Finally, those who were dissatisfied with their lives were also more accepting of EMS.

Overall, attitudinal factors appear to be related to extramarital permissiveness. These factors all have a liberal quality in common. That is, more liberal political attitudes plus more liberal attitudes toward women's roles, PMS, marriage, and family directly predict more liberal attitudes toward EMS. In addition, some of these factors moderate the correlations of social charateristics and demographic variables, suggesting that a comprehensive theory of extramarital permissiveness must systematically incorporate individual differences associated with attitudes toward EMS.

The Best Set of Predictors

To determine the best combination of predictors in the Winnipeg study, stepwise regression analyses were performed on the data. These analyses were repeated twice; once for the general measure, and once for the number of circumstances under which EMS might be acceptable. A total of twenty-four predictive variables were used. These included all the major variables in the data hypothesized or found to relate to EMS.[1]

---

[1]As is recommended (Nie, Hull, Jenkins, Steinbrenner and Bent 1975) for such analyses, listwise deletion of missing data was employed. For those unfamiliar with regression analyses, predictors having insignificant simple correlations with the criterion variable can still add small amounts of useful information in a regression equation depending upon their relationship with the set of predictors. Conversely, some predictors with high simple correlations may be redundant in the total set.

Table 4: Correlation Coefficients for Attitudinal Predictors of Extramarital Sexual Standards

Predictors	Scale End Points[a]	Measure of EMS	
		General[b]	Circumstances[b]
Attitude toward PMS	1=wrong; 4=all right	.38	.37
Authoritarianism	6=nonauthoritarian; 24=very authoritarian	-.42	-.30
Political view	1=conservative; 7=liberal	.14[c]	.25
Should divorce laws be ——?	1=easier; 3=harder	-.30	-.26
Importance of family stability for well-being of society	1=important; 4=not important	.20	.33
Gender equality	4=sexes unequal; 16=sexes equal	.17	.06[c]
Life satisfaction	4=satisfied; 16=sexes equal	.03[c]	.19

Note: Results are based on the Winnipeg sample.
[a]Scale endpoints are provided for descriptive purposes but are not the exact wording used in the survey.
[b]For both EMS measures, higher numbers reflect greater acceptance of extramarital sex.
[c]This correlation is not significant at the p < .05 level.

For the general acceptance of EMS measure, a regression equation with nine predictors appeared optimal. This equation had a multiple *r* of .72 accounting for 50 percent of the variance in scores. The nine predictor variables, starting with the most important, were: attitude toward premarital sex, authoritarianism, proportion of mutual friends, premarital sexual experience with spouse, frequency of engaging in community activities, frequency of engaging in cultural activities, number of children, attitude toward gender equality, and gender.

For the circumstances measure, a regression equation with seven predictors had a multiple of *r* of .68. This accounted for 47 percent of the variance. Attitude toward premarital sex, as in the first regression equation, was the first variable entered. The next six were: attitude toward the importance of family stability, gender equality, life satisfaction, religious affiliation, number of premarital sexual partners, and gender.

For both measures, variables from the attitudinal and interpersonal needs categories were better predictors than variables from the demographic set. Certainly, these findings were consistent with the trend away from conceptualizing sexual attitudes solely as a function of one's religious background, education, income, etc.

Reiss, Anderson, and Sponaugle (1980) used "path analysis" to develop a causal model of extramarital permissiveness and to explore theoretical issues concerning extramarital relations. This analytic technique is used to identify the causal patterns among a set of variables. In essence, it permits the investigator to establish a chain of events, although it is, of course, dependent on the variables being measured.

Working with eight measures, Reiss et al. (1980) found that all eight were significantly correlated with extramarital permissiveness. Yet, only three variables – happiness of marriage, attitude toward premarital sex, and education – demonstrated a "direct" causal path. Three other variables – religious conviction, gender equality, and political liberality – were shown as important antecedents of marital happiness and attitudes toward PMS. (Religious conviction was positively associated with happiness of marriage and negatively associated with attitude toward PMS. Political liberality and gender equality were negatively associated with happiness of marriage and positively associated with PMS.) Finally, gender and age helped predict both the direct and the once removed indirect causes of extramarital permissiveness. Thus, their model portrays a sequence of causes starting with demographic factors, followed by attitudes, and finally to the three factors – education, marital happiness, and attitudes toward PMS – as being the most immediate "causes" for accepting EMS.

Reiss et al. (1980) suggested the inclusion of a few other variables in future work. Some of these were designed to improve the measurement of the quality of marriage. These included marital sex satisfaction, diffuse intimacy conception, emphasis on pleasurable aspects of sex, and autonomy of heterosexual interaction. People with diffuse intimacy conception satisfy their needs via several, rather than one, interpersonal relationships. Autonomy of heterosexual interaction, a key predictor of attitudes toward PMS, is freedom from the control of such social institutions as the family and the church. Reiss et al. believe that emphasizing sexual pleasure, having poor marital sexual relations, having a diffuse conception of intimacy, and having heterosexual autonomy, all foster extramarital sex. Although proof of these hypotheses awaits further testing, the model is very plausible.

Conclusions

Relationships of Attitudes Toward PMS and EMS. Extramarital sex is not an accepted phenomenon by the majority of adults in the general population; yet, there are circumstances under which engaging in EMS would be sanctioned by close to 30 percent of the individuals polled.

An interesting question concerns the relationship between accepting premarital sex and accepting extramarital sex. Attitudes toward PMS are the best predictors of attitudes toward EMS, yet the absolute figures of acceptance are markedly different for the two phenomenon. Premarital sex is much more widely accepted. Over the past fifteen years, there has been a considerable change in societal attitudes in the area of PMS; however, this same change is not evident in attitudes toward EMS. Whether or not this divergence of opinion will continue is unknown. However, there is another interesting aspect to be considered.

Although attitudes toward PMS may be changing, most individuals still believe in certain prevailing conditions. Specifically, they tend to endorse PMS for persons who are in love or deeply committed to one another. (Perlman, *in press*) As a general rule, the data do not support casual "swinging" PMS. Moreover, the conditions under which EMS was sanctioned included being in love with the extramarital partner. The variable tying the two attitudes together may reflect attitudes about sex *with love* rather than simply attitudes about sex. Thus, what at first appars to be a divergent view toward PMS and EMS may actually reflect an underlying *permissiveness with affection* standard, in contemporary society.

Reconceptualization of the Dependent Measure of EMS

Insight into the relationship between EMS and other attitudes was the result of supplementing the dependent measure with conditions under which EMS might be accepted. In the general attitude measure, one either accepts or rejects EMS; there are no qualifying circumstances. For some individuals an "all-or-none" position is all that is required, but for many people, behavior and attitudes are influenced by situational factors, societal ideals, and, perhaps, by expected costs, benefits, and consequences. These issues that influence judgments and choices are not explored if one views EMS (or PMS) as an "all-or-none" phenomenon. Reconceptualizing the measure of EMS to include variables that might influence judgments seems essential for better understanding of the nature of these human relationships.

Extramarital Sex: The Product of Motivations and Circumstances

Some of the variables involved in predicting attitudes toward extramarital sex indicate that extramarital sexual standards are subject to modification by circumstantial events. It would appear that general attitudes toward EMS and actual EMS behavior are also modified by motivational factors. Thus, it can be argued, extramarital sex reflects a classic assumption of social psychologists, namely that behavior is a function of the person and the environment.

The study by Glass and Wright (1977) alludes to different motivations of men and women involved in EMS. These authors suggest that, particularly among older men, EMS may be solely sexually motivated with no intent to detract from or to replace the emotional attachments in the marriage. The opposite may be true for younger individuals who are dissatisfied with their primary relationships and seek emotional satisfaction elsewhere. These observations are still fairly hypothetical.

Since costs and rewards are associated with marital and extramarital relationships, a better understanding of EMS may be gained from a reward-cost type analysis. A decision to engage in extramarital sex involves economic and psychological rewards and costs. There are three factors that may influence extramarital relations: first, the rewards of the extramarital relationship itself must appear favorable compared with its costs; second, the reward-cost ratio of the extramarital relationship must favorably outweigh the reward-cost ratio of the marital relationship; and finally, there must be no insurmountable barriers to the establishment of an extramarital relationship.

According to this view, the satisfaction of sexual and emotional needs within the marriage may preclude extramarital sex, whereas unfulfilled sexual needs may be a cost/debit in the marriage and may reinforce the reward/attraction of extramarital sex.

Obviously, the pleasures and frustrations directly related to sex itself are not the only rewards and costs to be calculated. There are financial expenses, psychological factors such as guilt feelings, damage to one's reputation, and the like. Indeed, the application of this framework involves the task of specifying and measuring the specific rewards and costs involved.

Several common consequences of engaging in extramarital relations have been identified. (Blood and Blood 1978) Negative consequences include jealousy and divorce. (Although divorce is generally regarded as a cost, there are undoubtedly cases when this is not so.) A positive consequence is marital enrichment resulting from improved conjugal sexuality, a greater sense of personal independence, or increased marital intimacy and fulfillment. Obviously, such outcomes should be considered in attempting to determine the rewards and costs of extramarital sex.

Summary

1. Over the last decade, there has been a gradual increase in the research on extramarital sex as a legitimate scientific enquiry. Research has focussed on both attitudes and behavior. Although there is no comprehensive model of

extramarital relationships, some progress has been made toward defining the parameters, issues, and motivations involved.

2.   Extramarital sex is not a behavior accepted by the majority of Canadian adults. In most surveys, approximately 65 to 70 percent of respondents feel that EMS is "always wrong." Moreover, it appears to be even less widely practiced, with less than a quarter of respondents in a Toronto survey admitting to having engaged in extramarital relations.

3.   For the most part, general attitudes are subject to modification by the circumstances or conditions surrounding EMS. While there is no circumstance that leads to acceptance by more than 30 percent of the population, EMS is more widely accepted in cases where one is in love with the extramarital partner or when one's spouse is unable to engage in sexual relations. These findings indicate the value of identifying specific complex circumstances surrounding EMS behavior.

4.   Even though attitudes toward premarital sex are a strong predictor of attitudes toward extramarital sex, increasing acceptance of PMS has not been paralleled by a similar trend toward EMS. Whether or not Canadian attitudes toward extramarital sex will become more accepting in the 1980s is unknown.

5.   The three categories of variables for predicting extramarital standards were: demographic factors, interpersonal needs and social factors, and attitudinal or individual differences. The first category is the least useful in predicting attitudes, although such factors as age and religious orientation were associated with acceptance of EMS. Not surprisingly, at the interpersonal level having an unsatisfactory marriage leads to extramarital involvements. In the Winnipeg study, being nonauthoritarian and being accepting of PMS went hand-in-hand with acceptance of EMS. Several studies have attempted to synthesize these different sets of predictor variables in order to form a more comprehensive perspective of EMS. Reiss et al.'s (1980) path analysis is a noteworthy example of these efforts.

6.   A better understanding of EMS attitudes and behavior requires more extensive investigation into the impact of these relationships upon the marriage, and an examination of the individual perceptions of the meaning and consequences of EMS and the various motivational issues within and without a marriage that lead to involvement in EMS. A cost-reward analysis is a recommended method for future research in this area.

Divorce: The Disengaging, Disengaged, and Re-engaging Process

John F. Peters

Every society has some means whereby heterosexual partners in marriage may become detached from one another. In the modern world, broken marriages are usually dissolved legally by a process known as divorce. Some societies such as those in Argentina and Spain may not permit statutory termination of the marriage; nevertheless, married couples sometimes do permanently cease living with one another.

A study of separation and divorce in Canada reveals considerable variation in frequency by region, religion, ethnicity, age, and social class. The concern of the sociologist in this field of research is to recognize the statistical as well as the actual degree of separation and divorce, and to investigate the social reasons and consequences of this aberration in the historical institution of marriage. It is not the social scientists' concern to morally evaluate the divorce experience; such judgments are left to the citizen, who may effect changes on a regional or national level if he or she so wishes.

Many theoretical frames of reference can be applied to this subject. This analysis will focus on the "Exchange" or "Choice and Exchange" theory. In a few instances brief references will be made to structural functionalism and to symbolic interaction. To establish a base for this chapter, the reader will first be presented with pertinent Canadian statistical data.

As with much social science research, there are certain limitations with this data: many partners live together but are not legally married, many married couples live apart from one another, yet are not legally divorced. Such cases are not shown in the statistics used for this study. Nevertheless, there is much to be gained in studying divorce despite the recognized limitations, particularly in noting difference of divorce patterns by region, as well as variation over time. This information in itself will hint at sociopsychological and political implications.

Demographic Perspectives and Trends

Until recently, Canada's divorce rate was considered low for a western country in the modern world. Residents of Newfoundland and Quebec could obtain a divorce only through Ottawa, whereas people in other parts of Canada were granted divorces within their own provinces. Divorce was granted primarily on grounds of adultery. In 1968, divorce laws were changed to include separation, mental and physical cruelty, as well as drug or alcoholic addiction. In the following year, the divorce rate escalated by 130 percent (some provinces as much as 566 percent) and since 1969 it has risen an average of 7 percent annually.[1] In absolute numbers divorces have increased five times their number in 1968.

Unlike the United States, where every state has different divorce laws, Canada's divorce laws apply to the entire country. This has simplified matters for divorce research in Canada. There is, however, considerable variation in the divorce rate from one province to another as indicated in Table 1. Alberta has the highest divorce rate, a characteristic it frequently shares with British Columbia. The provinces of Newfoundland, Prince Edward Island, New Brunswick, and Saskatchewan consistently show a comparatively low rate. Until about 1972, Quebec had one of the lowest rates in Canada but now maintains, as does Ontario, a rate close to the national figure. The Yukon and Northwest Territories have a figure twice that of the federal divorce rate. Almost all provinces are showing a consistent gradual annual increase in divorce.

Divorces can only occur out of legal marriages. Canada is a country where the institution of marriage is socially, religiously, and politically encouraged. Of the adult population, 90 percent marry at some point in their lifetime. In the early and mid-1940s, there was an unusually high marriage rate. Since 1972 there has been a slight decline in the number of annual marriages.

Table 1:   Divorces by Province, in Number and Rate, per 100 000 Population, 1980

Province	Number	Rate
Canada	62 019	259.1
Newfoundland	555	95.8
Prince Edward Island	163	131.0
Nova Scotia	2 314	271.3
New Brunswick	1 326	187.4
Quebec	13 899	220.2
Ontario	22 442	261.7
Manitoba	2 282	221.7
Saskatchewan	1 836	189.3
Alberta	7 580	364.2
British Columbia	9 464	358.5
Yukon and Northwest Territories	158	559.5

(Vital Statistics, Vol. II, Marriages and Divorces, 1980, Table 10, pp. 16, 17)

---

[1]Unless otherwise indicated, the statistics are from 1980. Divorce rates are based upon 100 000 population in Canada.

There were 191 069 marriages in 1980. (VS: Table 1,2)[2] Taking the average age of those who enter their first marriage, Canadians are marrying about half a year later than they did a decade ago. The current average age is 23.3 for women and 25.5 for men.

The ages of married couples, the duration of marriages, and the ages at which divorces take place have always been of interest to researchers. At the time of their divorce in 1980, 38 percent of women were under 30 years of age. The 25 to 29 age cohort made up 25 percent of all cases. (VS: Table 14, 22) Of all men divorcing in 1980, 26 percent were under 30 years of age. The 30 to 34 age cohort was fairly evenly distributed for divorcing men and women. The median ages for the divorcing wife and husband in Canada were 32.4 and 35.0, respectively. This shows a gradual trend to divorce at a younger age. (VS: Table 1, 2)

The median duration of marriages before divorce was 9.9 years in 1980. This figure shows a gradual decline throughout the past years which is expected to continue. Canada's rate has not reached the 7-year median (popularly referred to as the 7-year itch) found in divorces in the United States. The number of divorces occurring between the fourth and seventh years of marriage is fairly constant between 6.8 to 7.2 percent (see Table 2). The frequency of divorce after 10 years, although it declines each year thereafter, has a sufficiently high frequency to move the median to 9.9 years.

Most western countries, including Canada, show a very close relationship between early marriage and the possibility of divorce. Comparisons of the frequency of age cohort marriages and divorces show a disproportional representation amongst those who marry young.[3] In 1980, 4.2 percent of all men who married were under 20 years of age. (VS:Table 3, 5) However, 12.1 percent of all divorced men had married when under 20 years of age. (VS:Table

Table 2:   Divorces by Duration of Marriage, in Percent, 1980

Duration in Years	Percent	Duration in Years	Percent
Under 1 year	0.2	8 years	6.0
1 year	1.8	9 years	5.5
2 years	3.8	10-14 years	19.3
3 years	5.0	15-19 years	11.1
4 years	6.8	20-24 years	8.1
5 years	7.2	25-29 years	5.5
6 years	7.2	30 + years	5.4
7 years	6.8	not stated	0.1

(Vital Statistics, Volume II, Marriages and Divorces, 1980, Table 16, p. 24)

[2]When reference is made to (VS) see Vital Statistics 84-205, Volume II, Marriages and Divorces, 1980.

[3]Although the usage of only 1980 marriage statistics is not a true comparison, the relationship between the two percentages is significant for illustrative purposes.

18, 26-30) Women under 20 years represented 17.0 percent of all marriages, yet had a 38.7 percent representation of all divorces. These percentages show a close correlation between those who marry young and those who divorce.

At one time, children were considered a deterrent to separation and divorce. Most counsellors are quick to point out that a single-parent home is often better for a child than a home in which there is constant verbal and physical tension. Of all divorces, 53 percent of the couples had children: about 22.6 percent of divorcing couples had one child and 20.8 percent had two children (377 couples had five or more dependent children). Over 59 450 dependent children were affected by divorce in 1980. (VS:Table 17, 26)

Most of those who divorce remarry, particularly those under 35 years of age. Of the 191 069 brides in 1980, 14.7 percent had been divorced at least once before, while 16.2 percent of the bridegrooms had been married previously. (VS:Table 5, 8) The percentage of divorcees remarrying has increased consistently for both men and women over the past forty years, and quite substantially in the past few years.

Among wives and husbands who divorced in 1980, 8.1 percent had been previously divorced. (VS:Table 11, 18) Moreover, the number who divorce for a second or third time is showing an increase, thus affecting a large number of adults and children.

Legal Considerations

In Canada, a marriage cannot be terminated because the relationship has stagnated or because one or both partners wishes a change. Neither can a legal separation be obtained for these reasons. Divorce is granted only in accordance with Canadian law. That law finds its origin in the English Matrimonial Causes Act of 1857 which remained unchanged until 1925. (Pike 1975) A man could file for divorce if his wife was adulterous. However, a woman could only request a divorce if her husband had deserted her or been physically cruel: a husband's adultery was not, in itself, sufficient grounds. This medieval double standard viewed a woman as a husband's property!

Despite social and economic development in the mid-twentieth century, Canada moved rather slowly in changing its archaic divorce laws. The structure of our society, particularly the influences of the institutions of religion, polity, and family, opted for a status quo despite some attempts for change. The federal government did not want to offend the Roman Catholic church nor the Roman Catholic majority in Quebec. At the same time, smaller interest groups lobbied for change in the divorce laws, so various studies were made. The Roman Catholic hierarchy finally recognized that its specific beliefs should not necessarily restrict the larger society, and the door for change was opened slightly. The final outcome was The Divorce Act, 1968.

Grounds for divorce comprised marital offenses and marital breakdown. Marital offenses were divided into three basic categories: adultery, physical cruelty, and mental cruelty; marriage breakdown consists of: addiction to drugs separation of not less than three years, and desertion of not less than five years (see Table 3). In marriage breakdown, neither husband nor wife is judicially blamed for the deterioration of the marriage.

Table 3: Alleged Grounds for Divorce, by Type of Offence and Reasons for Marital Breakdowns, Canada 1980

Alleged Grounds	Number	Percent
Marital Offense		
Adultery	25 521	30.9
Physical cruelty	12 316	14.9
Mental cruelty	16 617	20.2
Other	173	.2
Marriage Breakdown		
Addiction to drugs	1 508	1.8
Separation	24 689	30.0
Desertion	1 267	1.5
Other	423	.5
	82 514	100.0

(Vital Statistics, Volume II, Marriages and Divorces, 1980, Table 20, p. 30)

In more recent years, the Canadian Bar Association and some women's groups have argued that the marriage breakdown grounds are too stringent, particularly the length of the separation period. They advocate a reduction to six months or a year. Others contend that the institution of the family will be seriously threatened by such a law, that people need a longer period of time in which to evaluate themselves and their marriage relationship before officially terminating the marriage. Canadian society is not prepared to accept a law similar to that in Sweden where a couple may divorce when either partner wishes.

Two matters closely related to divorce are child custody and the division of assets. The jurisdiction of these concerns is in the hands of the provincial court. (Some cities, such as Hamilton and Edmonton, have sought to simplify this system by establishing a Unified Family Court.) Provincial laws regarding assets after a divorce have changed or are in the process of change in several provinces. The unequal distribution of assets was widely publicized in the 1974 Murdock versus Murdock case, in Alberta. The Supreme Court of Canada ruled that Irene Murdock was not entitled to half interest in the family's prosperous ranch, even though she had contributed to its growth and operation during twenty-four years of marriage.

In 1978, the Family Law Reform Act, which provides for an equal division of family assets, was passed in Ontario. Under this law, no financial penalty is imposed on the transgressor. Clients and relatives of the alleged offended partner, however, often feel some financial penalty should be levelled against the "guilty" party. It has been suggested that where financial equality is a legal reality, women are more likely to file for divorce, since they are ensured a share of the assets – a resolution that was rare before the act was passed.

The terminology, formality, and the reverberation of the spacious courtroom often inhibits and frightens citizens, particularly those caught in the emotional turmoil of a divorce case. Possibly that is why 90 percent of all divorces involve a lawyer, whose fee in the simplest non-contested cases ranges between $500 and $1000. However, divorce kits are available for approximately $100 and, in British Columbia, the court registry has published a practical divorce guide, available at cost.

Two-thirds of all divorces in Canada are filed by the wife. (VS:Table 1, 2) The person who files is known as the petitioner, the other as the respondent. After the petition is filed, the respondent is notified and a date is set for a court appearance, usually within 30 to 90 days. In Canada, 90 percent of all divorce cases are not contested and, contrary to popular belief, often take as little as three minutes of the court's time to execute. (Protracted proceedings account for less than 10 percent of all divorce cases, and usually involve only the more wealthy of our society.) If the case is successful, a decree nisi is granted, and the respondent is again notified. Ninety days later, the court reconvenes, and in non-contested cases a decree absolute is granted. Of all decrees nisi granted, 99 percent result in decrees absolute. Almost 80 percent of all divorce cases are completed within twelve months of filing. (Reed 1975) Reed's study shows that cases based on alleged adultery are processed more quickly than those based on physical or mental cruelty.

Adultery and separation have always been the most prominent grounds for divorce, 31.0 percent and 30.0 percent of all cases respectively (see Table 3). Until 1977, the number of cases filed on grounds of separation exceeded the number filed on grounds of adultery. It is anticipated that grounds of separation will be used less in the years ahead. In cases of both mental cruelty (20.0 percent) and physical cruelty (15.0 percent), medical evidence is often requested by the court. Adultery, however, need not be witnessed. A friend's testimony supporting the couple's three-year separation is often sufficient evidence for separation suits. Attempts to reunite within the three-year period are permitted, however, cohabiting in excess of three months nullifies the separation.

Some Theoretical Perspectives

Most Canadians expect that every adult will marry sometime in his or her life. Marriage has been characterized as almost instinctual. Almost everyone is born into a family, reared by a father and/or a mother, and usually has at least one sibling. Early childhood influences portray families as good and marriage as a natural state for adults. Further socialization from the family, school, and, in many cases, the church reinforces the value of the family. Most teenagers have friends of the opposite sex in high school, and before the age of twenty, many have experienced some degree of intimacy in such a relationship. People are told, and in many cases shown, that a fuller expression of intimacy is possible in marriage.

From a social structural point of view, the economic and political systems have reinforced the institution of marriage. As people grow older and die, they must be replaced for the social system to continue. Reproduction usually takes place in the context of marriage.

Our capitalistic system places much emphasis on consumerism, and families are very acquisitive consumers: hence, they are encouraged. The religious system also reinforces values pertaining to marriage: love and care of married partners, sex only when married, sex between heterosexual partners, and the birth and nurture of children. All the institutions mentioned have overtly or covertly socialized individuals to consider marriage as a way of life. Marriage is one of many traditions that conjointly contributes to the continuity of our social system.

Once they have decided to marry, the couple spend more time together, thereby socializing one another for their new life. Discussions between them cover such topics as life goals, number and timing of children, careers, finances, and areas of mutual interest. Each becomes the "significant other," and their friends become the reference group. With increased intimacy between the two, language becomes important as do gestures, posture, tone and pitch of voice, and facial expressions. The interaction becomes a continual process of knowing and becoming known. Partners not only act but react with one another. All these processes are basic to a symbolic interactionist framework in the study of marriage.

An increasing number of married couples in Canada find that wedded life does not approximate the model they were socialized to expect. Differences of opinion, repeated disagreements, tensions, arguments, and sometimes even mental and physical abuses tarnish the ideal model. Indeed, partners once seen as symbols of youth, beauty, and trust are regarded as threatening, ugly, and untrustworthy, and wedded life is described as disappointing, confining, and stagnating. The relationship between husband and wife referred to as primary group is no longer appropriate. The couple may adopt a pretense of well-being, but this is only to satisfy social norms of expected behavior. In reality, each partner may be seeking happiness with another, and mutual friends no longer serve as a reference group.

The decision to separate often involves a return to the family nest where the mother resumes her nurturant role, soothing, caring, protecting, and supporting the adult son or daughter during the emotional trauma of separation. The separated person vacilates between experiences of high and low self-esteem; sometimes filled with hope and confidence, at other times filled with despair.

The once married person returns to the single life. If there are children, however, one parent assumes the custodial role of wage earner, mother, and father, while the visiting parent is unsure whether to be parent, friend, helper, and/or entertainer. Since there are insufficient role models and inadequate social support systems from the community, both parents falter in such situations.

The social exchange or choice and exchange theory will broaden our understanding of the process of disengaging, and why people choose such a traumatic alternative.

"All contracts among men rest on the schema of giving and returning the equivalence." (Simmel 1950) In an economic system, the exchange of currency for goods is easy to understand. An object is purchased with an appropriate payment in dollars and cents. If payment is considered inadequate, the exchange is not made. Both parties must be satisfied with the exchange.

Simmel (1950), Homans (1961), Thibaut and Kelley (1959), Blau (1964), and others have applied this method of exchange to the costs and rewards involved in social life. People select those with whom they wish to socially interchange, almost every action involving some expectation of reciprocity. If the action yields no return, it is seldom repeated; or if the action fails to yield a reward comparable to one's expectations, the exchange will be re-evaluated and possibly terminated. Rewards in this context are not economic but social: a smile of approval, a kiss, or the prestige gained from association with a specific person.

"The Comparison Level (CL) is a standard by which the person evaluates the rewards and costs of a given relationship in terms of what she/he feels she/he deserves." (Thibaut and Kelley 1959:21) The executive might expect his secretary to bring him coffee, while the factory laborer has no such expectation. Reciprocated expectations vary from person to person over status, time, and circumstance. The value of any social act may change with time. Where holding hands was once a substantial reward for a dating couple, a warm and lengthy embrace may be viewed as only marginally rewarding at a later date. "Levels of alternatives" refers to lowest exchange level acceptable in light of alternative opportunities. (Thibaut and Kelley 1959:21) In other words, each choice has a level below which no exchange is possible. An example is the wife who agrees to perform the duties of a homemaker in an unhappy marriage, only as long as the spouse refrains from engaging in extramarital affairs.

In the disengaging process, the perceived value of specific conjoint behaviors such as close eye contact, long quiet conversations, and sexual intimacy may have depreciated to a point of minimal or no reward for either partner. Similarly, the value of a partner's household tasks, positive habits, and courtesies may no longer seem important.

The disengaging process is not abrupt but gradual. It may begin with a casual but rewarding friendship that may become more important than the marriage. Over a period of time, the marriage is evaluated by comparing the costs and rewards involved. The suburban homemaker may weigh the cost of the unsatisfactory marriage with the reward of a spacious house and ample time to pursue pleasurable activities. The husband similarly considers the rewards of a well-kept home and attention to his domestic needs in relation to the cost of living with a partner whom he no longer loves. Initially this exchange may appear satisfactory but, after a time, the costs may exceed the rewards. Research indicates that men who provide above average financial rewards to their families have a lower incidence of marital dissolution than average. (Nye 1979:26) Women in occupations with remuneration above the average are more likely to be single or divorced. (Ross and Sawhill 1975:56) It would appear that for some women a career offers greater rewards and fewer costs than marriage.

Costs and rewards between partners in a strained marriage are always weighed with perceived alternatives. (Levinger 1976) If the homemaker fears the loneliness or insecurity of separation, she will not readily choose divorce. A wife with a profession that provides economic stability and social interaction, however, is more likely to choose divorce than the wife who is unemployed. The cost of violating religious convictions and separation from one's children are often considered too high and divorce is avoided. On the other hand, those who see the alternative of new heterosexual relationships, and particularly remarriage, may more readily opt for disengagement. Although divorce is not desirable, it is viewed as a transitional step necessary for remarriage. (Nye 1979:26)

Some professions carry less social stigma toward divorce than others. For example, a rural minister considering divorce will undoubtedly be more socially affected than a performer considering the same alternative.

Further Considerations

Many social factors can be associated with the increased divorce rate in Canada. As noted earlier, marriage is highly regarded in our society and most people seek such a union. At the same time, however, personal goals and individual rights are also valued. A balance between these two cultural values when they conflict in the marital bond has not been achieved as yet in our society.

Four general types of marriage are found in Canada: (i) a traditional marriage in which the wife submits to the husband's authority; (ii) a passive, congenial relationship, in which the marriage is secondary to other interests of both partners, such as their careers; (Cuber and Haroff 1965) (iii) an egalitarian marriage in which decision making is shared; or (iv) an unhappy and/or unstable marriage. The traditional union which was common at the turn of the century no longer satisfies most members in modern society. Some couples have opted for the passive, congenial relationship by default: In a marriage that did not meet their expectations, other priorities assumed increased importance until the marriage became secondary. While many aspire to some form of egalitarianism, few achieve it. Such a marriage involves considerable flexibility and negotiation which many partners find either too difficult or too time consuming to execute. An unhappy and/or unstable marriage may continue for many years, or the couple may seek a physical and/or legal separation fairly quickly. Occasionally, an unstable marriage may gain relative stability through counselling, economic assistance, or community/group support which enables the partners to resolve their differences.

The Women's Liberation movement has contributed significantly to the altered perception of marriage. Personal awareness, particularly among women, has focussed on social inequalities and institutional exploitation, and marriage has not escaped this scrutiny. A few women have been quick to demand immediate change to rectify the inequalities in their marriages, while many more have pondered the implications of their subordinate positions and cautiously sought more gradual changes in their relationships. The rejection of the once accepted relationship and the disregard for his role as provider have frustrated and confused many husbands. However, with mutual negotiation and understanding, most husbands and wives can learn new respect and regard for one another. Many, of course, will view this struggle to adapt as too strenuous when other alternatives appear easier and more immediate.

The pursuit of economic gain and success is a threat to marital relationships. Research consistently shows that individuals in geographical regions experiencing much social mobility or economic prosperity encounter a higher divorce rate. Currently the relatively prosperous cities of Calgary and Edmonton have an unusually high divorce rate for Canada.

Divorce and desertion are also prevalent at the opposite end of the pole among those in the lower economic strata. Here, low levels of education coupled with limited economic resources puts a strain on the partners and the marriage. These couples, who tend to marry young, lack the coping mechanism necessary to deal with problems such as unemployment, poor health, a large number of children, or inadequate housing. (Ambert 1980:70) A husband may feel frustrated in his inability to provide for his family, while the wife may experience the stress of overcrowding and limited funds for the family's needs.

Demographic factors also affect marriages today. On the average, couples now live together for thirty-five years, a figure which includes the termination of the relationship by either death or divorce. (Bell 1979:528) Marriages often last fifty or even sixty years, and include several life stages. The couple experience young adulthood, middle age, retirement, and the senior citizen stages together. (Ambert 1980:68) Critical points in this long age span may be employment, career changes, employment of the wife, geographic relocation away from the immediate family, rejection of parental values by the children, family versus societal dependency for familial needs, and declining or failing health.

The institution of marriage is becoming more secularized. Although the majority of weddings in Canada still take place in a church or synagogue, this is usually for ostentation or to placate the parents. Even the sacred vow – till death do us part – in pragmatic secular terms has come to mean – as long as we love one another.

Divorce also has a contagious aspect in that a couple in a strained relationship may choose divorce more readily if they have friends that have already done so. Almost every Canadian living in an urban environment knows someone who has divorced. This familiarity tends to increase the incidence of divorce.

It can also be argued that divorce is more frequent because divorce laws are more relaxed. Canadian divorce rates did escalate following the Divorce Act of 1968, and some fear that further relaxation, such as a bona fide "no-fault" clause, might spell the end of the institutions of marriage and the family, and possibly even our society. Pike (1975) has argued that Canadians have always sought other means of dissolving a marriage, even when divorce laws were strict. Some had their marriages annulled, others divorced in the United States, and many more simply chose to separate. There is ample statistical evidence indicating that the incidence of legal divorce has increased and continues to increase. There is also reason to believe that broken marriages occur more frequently today than in the past. There is no doubt that expectations in marriage have changed, however, there is not substantive evidence that marriages today are any more or less satisfactory than a generation ago.

Re-engaging

In Canada, it is estimated that more than 50 percent of divorced women and over 60 percent of divorced men remarry. Indeed, remarriage of a divorced woman under thirty-five is more likely to occur than is marriage for a single woman of the same age. Of the total annual marriages, the percentage of the divorced who remarry is rising: 14.7 percent of the brides and 16.2 percent of the bridegrooms in 1980. (VS:Table 5, 8) At the same time, the percentage of widows and widowers who remarry remains constant, while the percentage and number of single women and single men who marry is declining. British Columbia, which has the largest proportional divorce population, also has the highest percentage of marriages by women and men with divorce status (20.5 percent and 21.5 percent respectively), while Newfoundland has the lowest (3.8 percent and 5.9 percent respectively). (VS:Table 7:19-24)[4]

It is not surprising that many who divorce remarry. The majority are not against marriage per se, they simply wish to sever an unsatisfactory relationship. It is estimated that possibly one-third of all marriages dissolve because of an attachment to a third person, and many of these relationships result in marriage after the divorce. Most people seek a trusting and permanent relationship with a person of the opposite sex, and marriage makes this socially acceptable and legally possible.

Studies indicate that divorced women from the lower economic strata are more likely to remarry than divorced women from any other group. (Carter and Glick 1976:269) On the other hand, men in the lower strata are less likely to remarry and those in the upper economic bracket are most likely to remarry. Upper strata men can provide financial security, whereas those of the lower income group have little to offer. Fewer economically independent women choose to remarry, while those in the lower income strata stand to gain considerably in remarriage.

The younger the age at divorce, the greater the likelihood of remarriage. In 1977, brides who were previously divorced made up 11 percent, 27 percent, and 23 percent of all brides in the 20-24, 25-29, and 30-34 age cohorts, respectively. Bridegrooms who had been previously divorced made up 3.4 percent, 19 percent, and 24 percent in the same age cohorts, respectively. (VS:Table 6:12-18)[5] There is no reliable Canadian data showing the span of time between divorce and remarriage, but it is believed that the majority remarry within three years. Coincidently, about one-third of all Canadian divorces are granted on the grounds of separation – a three-year period.

The disengaging experience entails disillusion, erosion, detachment, physical separation, grief and anger, second adolescence and rebuilding. Should remarriage occur before the rebuilding stage, it will likely be unsuccessful.

Most popular literature seems to imply that the divorced person who

---

[4]1977 data.

[5]1977 data.

remarries is likely to divorce a second or even a third time. However, there is no evidence to support this. Most remarriages remain intact until the death of one of the spouses. The marriage of a divorced person, however, is more likely to end in divorce when compared with the marriage of a single person. In 1980, over 8 percent of all men and women who divorced had divorced at least once before. (VS:Table 11, 18)

There are some differences in selecting a mate for a second or third marriage. (Peters 1976) Individuals are older and more experienced regarding relationships, sex, work, and life in general; in many cases, children are involved.

In a first marriage the couple normally has little in terms of debts or assets, whereas both partners usually bring some financial aspects into a second marriage. Partners who feel they have been treated unfairly in the former marriage may be less likely to disclose their financial assets. Furthermore, monies from a former marriage may justly belong to children from that marriage.

Another frequent problem in remarriage is the ready-made family. Patterns of discipline, routine schedules, and expectations between parent and child are often changed in the reconstituted family. Such adaptations must include the parent and the step-parent.

Conclusion

Long intimate heterosexual relationships generally lead to marriage in Canadian society, a pattern that will likely continue. However, due to social, economic, political, religious, and psychological influences, expectations in marriage are changing. Some who are married wish to terminate the union to pursue other interests or to find another partner. Others simply want to dissolve an unhappy marriage. Although children are disrupted by divorce, they adapt quickly providing they are given assurance of care and security.

The disengaged always experience an abrupt role change, often into roles which are ill defined. Some adapt readily, others more slowly, and still others bear the scar of a severed intimate married relationship for many years.

Canadian society is in transition. While accepting the historic institution of the family, Canadians are adapting to greater flexibility in marriage. Our society is attempting to make the disengaging/re-engaging process more normative and less destructive to the persons involved. Such a shift from previous patterns of socialization will demand considerable effort on the part of our educational, religious, familial and community systems and networks. This is the challenge of the 1980s.

Divorce: Its Consequences and Meanings

Maureen Baker

In the past ten years, the rate of marriage dissolution has increased considerably in a number of western industrialized countries. Since 1968 when the
Canadian divorce laws were liberalized, the divorce rate in Canada has soared
to such an extent as to lead to speculation about the future of the family as an
institution. Although social services such as separation counselling are available to those experiencing marital dissolution, our society has developed few
institutionalized ways of dealing with the social reality of widespread divorce.
Whereas bereavement entails elaborate social rituals, separation and divorce
are often surrounded by confusion concerning acceptable behavior. The norm
of non-involvement in other people's marriages is stronger than active assistance. Consequently, many people in this transition period do not know where
to turn for assistance, and receive few guidelines on on how to cope with
their loss of partner.

In 1979-1980, 150 personal interviews with separated and divorced people
residing in Metropolitan Toronto were conducted by the author, with the
assistance of graduate students in the Faculty of Social Work at the University
of Toronto. We were interested in three areas of marriage dissolution: (1) to
whom they turned for assistance at the "critical time"; (2) how their "personal
networks" changed throughout the stages of marriage breakdown; and (3)
the problems they experienced throughout this transitional period.

Because the status of men and women differs in both marriage and public
life, we assumed that their experiences in separation and divorce would also
be dissimilar. We therefore concentrated on sex differences in personal and
support networks after marriage dissolution.

The theoretical framework of the study was based on network analysis and
the sexual inequality literature. Network analysis has focussed on the links
between units rather than on the units themselves. (Collins and Pancoast
1976:17) We felt that people's social links throughout the process of marriage
dissolution would have some effect on how they adjusted to their new single
role. Therefore, not only were "support networks" analyzed, but also their
"personal networks." "Support networks" referred to those people to whom
the subject turned for any kind of assistance at the most difficult or traumatic
time of their marital dissolution. We defined "personal networks" as those
people to whom the subjects felt emotionally close at the time of the interview. Since the subjects were at different stages of marital dissolution, we
were able to observe how personal networks changed throughout the various
stages. For the sake of expediency, we limited the number of personal network members to six per subject.

Numerous studies have indicated that the experiences of men and women within the family differ. For example, Irving (1972) and Spicer and Hampe (1975) revealed that women retain closer ties with their families and in-laws both during and after marriage. Schlesinger (1979) has reiterated that 90 percent of custodial single parents are women. However, Brandwein et al. (1974) and Hetherington et al. (1976) have suggested that custodial fathers are perceived differently than custodial mothers. Men with custody are perceived more sympathetically than women with custody, and are given more outside support from friends and relatives.

The sexual inequality literature certainly leads us to believe that men and women's experiences after marriage will differ. Women in Canada (and most other countries) have a lower earning potential than men when they enter the labor force. (Armstrong and Armstrong 1978) Although women have been entitled to support payments after separation, studies tell us that about 70 percent of men default at some time on these payments. (Brandwein et al. 1974) In other words, although mothers usually receive custody of the children, they are less able to care for them financially than are the fathers.

The literature related to the sexual double standard also leads us to believe that women's post-marital dating and sexual activity may differ from men's. Men are more likely to experience extramarital affairs than women. (Duberman 1977) Men are more likely to remarry after divorce and widowhood than women. (Kuzel and Krishnan 1973; Ambert 1980) This latter point is partially related to age-specific death rates and the fact that men usually marry down in age, but it is also affected by the fact that men have been granted the initiative in dating situations and have more leeway in non-marital sex. In the larger society, men and women's different occupational status and sex roles grant them different social experiences.

Bernard (1972) has popularized the idea that marriage may have different consequences and meanings for men and women. Contrary to popular belief, Bernard argues that men find the institution of marriage more desirable because it enables them to pursue their occupational and leisure interests free from the worry of domestic responsibilities. Women, on the other hand, must accommodate their work and leisure pursuits with their domestic responsibilities. Therefore, after marital dissolution, men more often and more quickly move back into marriage.

Huber and Spitze (1980) reinforce this notion when they conclude that women consider divorce as an option more often than men. Using Becker's utilitarian theory of marital instability, they suggest that the division of labor is changing in many American marriages. More wives are entering the labor force and sharing their husband's breadwinner role. However, husbands seldom reciprocate by sharing the responsibility of the housework. (Clark and Harvey 1976; Meissner et al. 1975). This creates dissatisfaction in wives and leads them to contemplate life on their own.

Using these studies as a theoretical basis, we decided to investigate the transition from separation to divorce through semi-structured interviews. All the subjects were between the ages of twenty-five and forty-five. They could have been separated for any length of time, but none were divorced for longer than two years. We limited the time-span of the divorced segment of the sample, because we assumed that the longer the time since the divorce, the greater the possibility of reinterpretation of the details. We viewed the legal divorce as more final than the physical separation, and therefore placed no limit on the number of years separated.

Because it is impossible to acquire a list of separated people in any community, we were forced to use non-random sampling. Beginning with numerous different sources, we used a snowball sampling technique, asking each interviewee for an additional name. Two organizations catering to separated and divorced people and several social service agencies provided us with some of the potential interviewees. The final sample of 150 contained more women than men, a higher proportion of people with children than we might expect, and a higher proportion of people with university education than the proportion that exists in the Canadian population. However, we were able to interview a wide variety of people, from different religious and ethnic groups. The incomes ranged from $2500 per year to $70 000. Most of the interviews were carried out in the subject's home, which gave the interviewer an opportunity to make some observations on lifestyle. Each interview lasted about one to two hours, and concentrated on their networks as well as their perceptions of their problems.

Findings

Canadian statistics indicate that women who work full time in the labor force earn about three-fifths of what men earn. In 1977, the average earned income of female employees who worked 50 to 52 weeks was $9143 compared with $15 818 for men. (Labour Canada 1977:41) In our sample, the men also earned considerably more than the women. The gross income of male subjects was $24 577, and the gross income of women (including support payments) was $14 771 in 1979. This discrepancy between men and women can partly be explained by the fact that males in the sample had higher educational qualifications than the females, and were more likely to be working full time. But the difference is fairly consequential when we realize that the children were living with their mothers in 87 percent of cases.

Although we did not explicitly ask how much support payments women obtained from their husbands, we received some indication. One man who was a medical doctor paid his wife $20 000 per year, but several working-class men paid nothing at all. An American study recently suggested that about 70 percent of ex-husbands default on their support payments or pay only sporadically. (Brandwein et al. 1974)

The most common living arrangements for separated and divorced women was with the children (50.5 percent); the men were most likely to be living alone (45.3 percent). This living arrangement tended to affect the subjects' social and sexual lives, as men were freer to date in the evening or bring their companions home.

Although we know that women file for divorce more often than men, little information about who initiates the separation is available. From those interviewed, however, 62 percent of the female subjects and 42 percent of the males reported that the wife initiated the separation. Although most men said that their wife initiated the separation, men were more likely than women to say that it was a "joint decision" (25 percent of males and 13 percent of females).

When we asked about extramarital relationships, we found that men were more likely than women (64 percent of men and 47 percent of women) to say that neither they nor their spouse had been involved in a serious extramarital relationship at the time of the separation. Both sexes were more likely to say that their spouse had been involved, but women especially made this accusation. Women were also more likely than men to see this "affair" as the "cause" of the break-up (21 percent of women and 17 percent of men). Of the sample, 42 percent viewed the extramarital relationship as merely a catalyst to a marriage which was already dissolving.

Of the 150 subjects, 71 percent had children. In 87 percent of the cases, the children lived with their mother. Although several respondents reported joint custody, this was restricted to a few highly educated couples. Most people with children felt that their children had been affected or changed in some way by the separation. However, not all saw this change as permanent or negative.

About 18 percent argued that their children were now better off than prior to the separation. They related this to lack of tension in the household and increased opportunity for the children to learn independence. Twenty-four percent said that their children had not been affected at all by the separation. Either the children were too young at the time, or had already left home. Some women said that their husband had seldom stayed home, and had had little interaction with the children throughout the marriage. Therefore, his absence was barely missed.

About 58 percent of those with children cited a number of behavioral and emotional problems experienced by their children at the time of the physical separation. But most felt that these were temporary problems. Those who had been separated for longer periods of time related fewer behavioral problems with the children. It was the male subjects, rather than the females, who expressed more concerns about the children's welfare. Part of this could have been motivated by guilt about leaving the family or not sharing custody. At any rate, one of the most common worries that men expressed was that their ex-wife was not providing adequate care and discipline for the children.

The separated and divorced subjects with children were far more likely to maintain some form of a relationship with their former spouse than those without children. Of those with children 29 percent compared with 72 percent of those without children saw their ex-spouse twice a year or never. Those with children who were not custodial parents usually saw their children every week or two, although some virtually lost contact. It seems that people not only stay married "for the sake of the children," but they also maintain contact with each other after separation for the same reason. Most of the contacts between ex-partners took place within the context of visiting the children.

Support Networks. The most difficult or traumatic time of the marriage dissolution for most people seemed to be just *before* the separation. What made this a difficult time depended on whether the subject initiated the separation or whether his or her partner did. Those who initiated often felt extreme guilt about leaving their partner or children and breaking their marriage vows. Since most of the women retained custody, it was more often the men who expressed guilt feelings about leaving the children. The initiators also worried about whether they could cope alone, although some of them seemed to already have developed close relationships.

For those whose partner initiated the break-up, anxiety about the future seemed to be the major problem. Some of the subjects had married in their teens or early twenties, and their marriage had lasted from ten to twenty-four years. Whether they could cope alone was a major concern, especially for the women in their forties who had not been gainfully employed. Although much of the concern related to being alone for the first time, many people worried about being able to find a job, support their children, repair their damaged self-esteem, and build a new lifestyle outside of marriage.

To ascertain their support networks, we gave the subjects a list of categories of people who may have given them assistance at the critical time of their marriage breakdown. They were asked to verbally indicate if they had turned to any of these people, and if so what kind of assistance they received from them. This list included several categories of friends, kin members, and professionals.

Men were most likely to turn to same sex friends (77.4 percent), opposite sex friends (60.4 percent), and then were equally divided between parents and family counsellors (37.7 percent). On the other hand, women turned to same sex friends (84.5 percent), parents (60.8 percent) and their siblings (53.6 percent). A review of the responses indicated that women were more likely to rely on kin than were men at the critical period. But both sexes turned mainly to their friends. The first person and most important helper that men turned to were friends, while women were split between friends and kin. Men were more likely than women to turn to lovers and professionals.

Although 77 percent of men who first turned to their friends turned to male friends, only 55 percent said that their male friends were most helpful. In other words, a sizable proportion of men turned to men for help and did not get it. They claimed that they were more likely to recieve nurturance and emotional support from their women friends. On the other hand, women overwhelmingly agreed that same sex friends were most helpful.

Only about 10 percent of the sample listed specific professionals as being the most helpful during their crisis period. This is despite the fact that between 24 and 35 percent turned to doctors, family counsellors, psychiatrists, and lawyers. Only 7 percent turned to the clergy, and most of these agreed that they were not very helpful. More people turned to lawyers than any other group of professionals, and more complaints were voiced about lawyers. These included the expense and lengthy procedures of obtaining a legal divorce, and the idea that the adversary system creates problems by pitting husband and wife against each other. Some argued that their lawyers were too harsh on their spouse, and some argued that the lawyers were not demanding enough. People with lower education seemed more likely to complain about legal procedures and lawyers.

Personal Networks. One of the major goals of the study was to examine how personal relationships change throughout the transition from separation to divorce. We gathered information about people's "personal networks," or to whom they felt close at the time of the interview. An analysis of variance was carried out on these network variables by "stage of breakdown," controlling for sex. The sample was divided into four stages of breakdown, depending on the length of separation and their legal status (separated versus divorced). Stage one included those who were separated twelve months or less. Stage two included those separated from thirteen to twenty-four months. Stage three included those separated for more than two years, but not divorced. And stage four included those who had obtained a legal divorce.

An analysis of variance led us to conclude that men and women pass through similar stages of separation and divorce. However, men seem to become socially and sexually active much earlier than women. For example, men include more people whom they recently met in their personal networks, more opposite sex people, more lovers, and more unmarried people. Men begin to meet new people within the first year of separation, and are most sexually active after the first year. Although women are less sexually active than men, after two years of separation their sexual activity reaches a peak. However, they become more socially active *after* they are legally divorced.

The problems cited by separated and divorced people also varied by stage of breakdown. The twenty potential problems given to the subjects for rating in terms of seriousness to them were divided into three categories. With a Pearson Correlation Matrix we found that the problems within each group correlated highly with one another. Those who reported high emotional problem scores tended to be women, those without lovers in their personal networks, those who rated their sex life as "poor," those with low income, and those whose children lived with them. Subjects with high scores in practical problems tended to be women, low income earners, Catholics and Jews, custodial parents, and those with a poor relationship with their former spouse. Those who reported high scores on child-related problems were also likely to report high anxiety and unhappiness. We must reiterate that we are not talking about causation here, but merely correlation.

Although the differences between men and women were not statistically significant on child-related problems, women reported more emotional and practical problems than men. Both sexes reported the most serious practical problems within the first year. This is to be expected, as finding new accommodation, adjusting to a divided income or finding a new job, and establishing a new lifestyle often occurs with the physical separation. Interestingly enough, the emotional problems and child-related problems correlated with each other, but seemed to be most severe after the practical problems were solved. Men cited the most serious emotional and child-related problems after two years of separation, but women did after the legal divorce. People seem to go through a period of elation after the first year when the mundane practical problems are straightened out. But a year later, many go into a slump. One of the major complaints for women is loneliness, or lack of meaningful heterosexual relationships. Both sexes reported anxiety about the children and shortage of money.

There was some relationship between people's networks and the problems they cited. Those who included lovers in their networks, those who were cohabitating with the opposite sex, those living with people they considered emotionally close, frequent visits with network members, and long-term relationships reduced the scores on the "loneliness" problem. Those who retained a majority of married network members cited problems meeting new dating partners.

Although most problems were rated as less serious by those who were legally divorced, the behavior of children and finding adequate child care continued to be a problem for a minority. There was a weak tendency (but not statistically significant) for personal networks to become more interconnected (i.e. more people know each other) with advancing stages of marriage dissolution. But the anticipated connection between closely-knit networks and problems scores was not found. It seems that "recovery" from marriage breakdown is only partially related to the structure of social networks. Other structural variables – both social and economic – also seem to affect one's experience in separation and divorce.

Most of the subjects felt that their lives had improved since the last few months of their marriage, which was seen as a low point. Both sexes felt that they were now happier, more independent, more confident, and had developed personally as a result of the marriage dissolution. Divorced people most often mentioned that their friendships were stronger and more meaningful, their sex lives were more enjoyable, and that they were generally happier.

When asked about their concerns with being separated or divorced, men focussed on worries about their children. Most men lost custody of their children, and remained ambivalent about the custody issue for some time. Women were more likely to worry about lack of financial stability. The longer people remained separated without divorcing, the *less* likely they were to desire remarriage. However, these people who had obtained a legal divorce were more favorable to the idea of remarriage. There were no significant differences between men and women in desire to remarry.

Discussion

Although support networks at the most critical time of marriage breakdown, and changes in personal networks with stages of marriage dissolution were the main concerns of the study, we were also interested in the post-marital adjustment problems of men and women at different stages of marriage breakdown, seeking potential connections between personal networks and post-marital adjustment.

American studies (Levinger 1979; Goode 1956) have shown that women most often file for divorce. But both men and women subjects in our study reported that women first suggested the separation. Yet, the women usually claimed that they did this as a result of the misbehavior of their husbands. Female subjects were more likely than males to report that their spouse had been involved in a "serious extramarital relationship" at the time of separation, and also more likely to say that this was the "cause" of their separation.

On the other hand, male subjects were more likely to say that neither they nor their wives were involved in an extramarital affair. Although the men and the women in the study were not married to each other and therefore could have had quite different experiences, we suggest that men and women interpret extramarital sex differently. Women are more likely to see it as a betrayal or an indication of a serious marital problem. Men, who more often are involved in extramarital relationships (Duberman 1977:65; Ambert 1980:98), rationalize this behavior as less serious. Although we did not ask explicitly why they decided to leave, this information sometimes came out of open-ended questions. Women provided far more unsolicited details about their marriages and why they failed than did the male subjects. Although most people seemed to blame their spouse for the marriage dissolution, a minority of people parted by mutual consent, and spoke kindly of their spouses. A minority of subjects also said that their relationship with their spouse had actually improved since separation.

Support Networks. We found that the most critical or traumatic time of the marriage dissolution process for most people was just before the physical separation. However, many people also experienced serious difficulties for several months after separation. Most people relied on their friends for support through the difficult periods, although women also received assistance from their parents and siblings. This close relationship between women and their families has also been found among married women. (Irving 1972) Spicer and Hampe (1975) further found that divorced women maintained more contact with their in-laws than divorced men did, as the women were eager to maintain a relationship between their children and the grandparents. However, aside from this explanation, women have traditionally been seen as responsible for the maintenance of family relationships.

Despite the fact that separated and divorced people relied mainly on friends and kin for support at the time of their separation, about one-third of the sample also turned to such professionals as family counsellors, lawyers, and psychiatrists. Yet they seldom turned to these people first, or deemed them most helpful.

A number of the male subjects mentioned that although they first turned to men friends for assistance, their women friends were far more supportive. They claimed that their male friends were more reluctant to discuss the separation and were not willing to spend much time talking to them. Both sexes agreed that women friends provided greater emotional support. This may relate to sex role socialization, in which women are encouraged to be more expressive and supportive, and to play a more nurturant role in interpersonal relationships.

Personal Networks. Personal networks also varied by sex. Men were more likely to have what we would call "open-networks." This means that they included more people whom they met within the past year. Women were more likely to include people whom they knew at the time of separation. After the first year of separation, men were most socially and sexually active and seem to have a relatively easy time moving back into the "dating scene."

Men included more opposite sex people in their personal networks; more lovers; more separated, divorced and single people; and more people whom they met within the past year. Women also went through a stage in which their sexual and social activity increased, but it came later than for men – after legal divorce. This network material implies that men make the transition from married to single status more easily and faster than do women. This is probably related to the fact that women have to solve their more serious practical problems before they can begin to think about dating and making new social contacts. They often need to find employment, child care, and sufficient money before they are emotionally calm enough to feel sociable. Having custody of children restricts their social and sexual lives. And being a woman implies fewer socially acceptable opportunities to initiate relationships, unless she is unusually aggressive. Because of the higher mortality rates and higher remarriage rates of men, the separated or divorced woman often experiences difficulty meeting men. If she has custody of several children, this may further discourage men from developing a serious relationship with her. Consequently, separated and divorced men tend to date and remarry younger, childless women. (Ambert 1980)

Reported Problems. Women at all stages of marriage dissolution cite more problems than men. Problems were divided into three types: emotional, practical, and child related. Pearson Correlation Coefficients showed differences between men and women that were statistically significant in emotional problems (.002) and practical problems (.001). Although men reported slightly more serious child-related problems than women, the differences were not statistically significant.

The problems reported by the separated and divorced vary with the stage of marriage dissolution. In the first year of separation, both men and women reported having their most serious practical problems. These included shortage of income, legal problems, getting financial support from their spouse, inadequate housing, and property disputes.

In the second year of separation, both men and women reported the least serious emotional problems. Having sorted out some of the practical worries, both sexes felt less anxious and depressed. This is also the period in which men are most socially and sexually active.

But after two years of separation, men report the most serious emotional and child-related problems. Emotional problems include loneliness, depression, anxiety about the future, sleepless nights, finding dating partners, problems with relatives, and wanting reconciliation. Perhaps after an initial period of dating a number of different women, men long for some security and domestic life. Child-related problems include: arguments about child rearing, verbal abuse from their spouse, losing contact with their children, their spouse's relationship with the children, the behavior of the children, finding adequate care for the children, custody disputes, and visitation problems. Perhaps because men seldom have custody of the children, their lack of control over the children's lives is worrisome. Many men in the study did not feel that they could handle custody themselves, yet they felt that their wives could not cope with the children alone. Some men actually said that they had "ruined" their children's lives or at least caused their children hardship by leaving the marriage. This guilt about leaving the family followed some men for several years.

Women seemed to go through a similar stage or "relapse" after legal divorce. Although they were most sexually and socially active at this time, they reported the most serious emotional and child-related problems. It seems that women who find new partners experience a decrease in problems, but those who do not, tend to be lonely. A minority of women also report an increase in behavioral problems of their children. Further analysis has indicated that there is a correlation between those with emotional problems and those with child-related problems. Goode (1956) found that divorced women who experienced the most emotional trauma with marriage breakdown also reported the most behavioral problems with their children. Children seem to become more upset when the mother has difficulty coping, and this in turn augments the mother's anxiety. But we also found that there was a correlation between the absence of a lover in one's personal network, and serious emotional problems. It is difficult to know whether experiencing emotional problems prevents the attraction of a lover, or whether those who cannot find a lover are consequently depressed and lonely. Again we suspect that they reinforce each other.

While the more tangible problems of marriage breakdown - such as finding a new home, finding adequate financial resources, arranging visitation rights for the children, solving property disputes - tend to be settled within the first year of separation, other problems persist. People seem to experience emotional ups and downs for years after the separation. The "highs" come after the first year, to both sexes, but later they become less optimistic about life without a partner. Because this study did not include those who had remarried, we may have interviewed a disproportionate number of people who wanted to remain independent or who were experiencing adjustment problems.

Conclusion

The varying experiences of men and women in marriage dissolution relate to sex role socialization and sexual inequality in the larger society. Many of the social services provided for separating people focus on the female with children, as she is most often in need of financial assistance. But there are numerous other problems for both sexes which are less often dealt with by professionals.

Although there is a slight trend toward joint custody, lawyers still do not encourage men to even try for it. Many men stay in unhappy marriages or experience severe emotional problems because they feel that the system favors the woman with respect to custody. It seems that the more educated men make a greater effort to retain their children, share custody, and visit their children at regular intervals. Although absence of any children reduces the problems of both men and women, giving up guardianship of one's children often engenders guilt and anxiety.

The fact that women are usually granted custody regardless of their eco-

nomic situation means that many women experience serious economic problems. Reliance on support payments is not feasible as most men do not pay
their ex-wives enough or at regular intervals. (Brandwein et al. 1974) Furthermore, women's incomes are considerably lower than men's even when they
work full time. If married women concentrated more on job training and
experience throughout their marriages, they would have fewer problems upon
marriage dissolution. Yet, our society does not wholeheartedly support the
full-time employment of married women. Lack of child care, viewing domestic labor as "women's work," and employment discrimination discourages
some women from seeking paid labor. And many husbands find it easier if
their wives stay at home with the children. Viewing marriage and child rearing
as a full-time career for women not only leads to a decrease in power in
family decision making (Blood and Wolfe 1960; Gillespie 1971), but also leads
to economic problems upon marriage dissolution.

Although 82 percent of the sample relied on same sex friends for support
throughout the process of marriage dissolution, women also lean heavily on
their parents. A minority of women move back with their mothers or take an
apartment in her house. This is especially true of the working-class woman
with children, but is increasingly being perceived as an undesirable and temporary solution to economic and child-care problems. Parents are much more
likely to offer assistance to their female children upon separation, but are
apparently also more likely to "interfere" with the lives of their separated
daughters. A number of women who relied on their parents for support
commented that this assistance has "strings attached." Their parents now provided frequent advice. A few women in the study replaced dependence on
their husbands with dependence on their parents after marriage breakdown.

The fact that men had more open social networks meant that they made
the transition in marital status more easily than women. Those women who
were not employed outside the home or who worked with women only experienced serious difficulties in meeting new partners. Making new social
contacts is related to psychological readiness, but also to the opportunity
structure. Full-time employment and freedom from child care in one's spare
time (or money to pay a baby-sitter) are essential ingredients to meeting new
people. The combination of custody, low income, and the age gradient in
dating work against separated and divorced women. Older women with children are considered by many men to be potential problems as dating partners.

The fact that women and men's personal networks differ throughout the
stages of marriage breakdown is consequential to their problems. But network characteristics are influenced by sex roles. The fact that women are
often encouraged to be career homemakers, retain custody of their children,
administer to the needs of others rather than their own, maintain a close
relationship with their parents, feel responsible for holding the family together,
make a connection between love and sex, wait for men to ask them out, and
emphasize their physical attractiveness in dating situations affects their personal networks and their post-marital problems.

These interviews have led us to view marriage dissolution as a process
which takes place over a series of several years after the physical separation.
Sex, age, income, education, presence of children, and custody of children

seem to be important variables in discussing the characteristics of people's personal and support networks at various stages of marriage dissolution. Women seem to experience more problems recovering from marriage breakdown, especially because they usually have lower incomes, the custody of the children, and because there exists a sexual double standard. The older woman is more likely to experience problems finding a well-paying job and a new partner. Older men also experience more emotional problems than younger men, but financially they have fewer problems than younger men or women.

In providing social services for those experiencing separation and divorce, we must take into consideration the fact that men and women do not have equal opportunities to support themselves or explore new relationships. A trend toward joint custody and increased employment opportunities would be a step in the direction of alleviating some of the problems. But we also have to work on eliminating the double standard of sexual behavior and the age gradient in dating in order to allow men and women to enjoy similar lifestyles after the dissolution of their marriages.

FAMILIES IN CRISIS

Introduction

While divorce is a form of family disruption, family life also involves various kinds of crises. The four articles in this section consider the nature of such crises, and focus on various socioculutral coping devices that some situations may generate.

Henry Radecki's article deals with the crisis situation created by a prolonged period of work stoppage (261 days) at the INCO plants in Sudbury. In light of the extreme hardships the families experienced, it is surprising to learn that the crisis, instead of disrupting family life, greatly enriched it. Fewer than 5 percent of the wives interviewed believed that their marriages had deteriorated, 50 percent reported that their family life was not affected, while 40 percent reported that their family ties grew closer during the strike period. Radecki notes several reasons for this: The very fact that husbands were present at home; that, anticipating a strike, some had saved enough to support their families; and that, as long-time residents of the community, most were homeowners. The author draws attention to the network of friends and relatives whose support was available to these strikers.

Mary Van Stolk deals with a very different kind of crisis situation – battering and abusing children. Her point of departure is that, although families are generally considered to be nonviolent toward their members, empirical data and relevant theory indicate that violence among family members is so common as to be universal. The author's implicit question is: How can we account for this anomaly between belief and practice?

Not only unwanted children but also wanted children may be battered. We learn that rules of behavior and absolute obedience are of utmost importance to abusive parents. Moreover, a battered child is likely to become an abusive parent, regardless of social, economic, and religious backgrounds.

The author presents some cross-cultural information to show what is being done to deal with the widespread problems of child battering and abuse, and she offers suggestions for futher improvement that include changes in the legal system, parenting instruction, sex education, and specialized police training.

Benjamin Schlesinger focusses on the single-parent family – a crisis situation in a society that expects a "proper" family to have both parents present. However, according to the 1976 Census of Canada, 9.8 percent of the families in Canada were one-parent families; of these, 83 percent were fatherless and 17 percent were motherless. A significant twist to this article is that its basic data were collected from the children of single-parent families, with an average age of fifteen years. Schlesinger indicates many of the coping devices that these children develop, and suggests several dimensions in which further studies are necessary.

The article by Jacqueline Massé et al. is concerned with the question why some unwed mothers keep their children while others give them up for adoption. While the authors are not directly concerned with a crisis situation as such, it is possible to see that retention of children by unwed mothers is the incunabulum of single-parent families, which could lead to the kinds of crisis indicated in Schlesinger's article. Once the article by Massé et al. is thus located within this general perspective of crises, attention may be shifted to what the authors have accomplished in terms of their own objective.

The exploration suggests that the young unwed mothers in a supportive environment tend to keep their children. The authors extend the interactionist ideas of G.H. Mead into the labelling theory of deviant behavior. In a society where mothers are expected to be married, unwed motherhood is deviance. Keeping one's child in such a situation necessitates coping with the social consequences of this kind of deviance. It depends, then, on the extent to which the unwed mother is labelled a deviant by the various social groups, and the influence that this labelling has had on her developed self-perception as a deviant. The authors' data and analysis confirm the hypothesis that an unwed mother who is not destructively labelled a deviant tends to keep her child, while those who are so labelled do not.

Families In Crises

Henry Radecki

Introduction[1]

Economic factors such as job security, level of remuneration, and regularity or dependability of income have potential for family and marital crises. A review of general literature indicates that the family commonly experiences increased hostility and fragmentation as economic hardships increase. (Hansen and Hill 1964) This position is supported by sociological research dealing, for example, with factors related to marital separations. At the same time, "a general principle of sociology indicates that certain events outside a group such as wars, floods, and depression tend to solidify the groups." (Eshleman 1978:621) Drawing on Burr (1973:199), a prolonged strike could be included among these outside events.

In the context of economic variables, views differ since "for most categories of men, family is a greater source of both involvement and satisfaction . . . than is work," but this satisfaction is derived from being a good provider for the family. (Corfman 1979:388) When this role is no longer fulfilled due to unemployment or work instability, and where no clearly identifiable outside force can be assigned responsibility, the resulting economic hardship may well have negative effects on the family. On the other hand, a prolonged strike situation falls clearly within the definition of economic hardship, but family structures and relationships may not be threatened since the forces responsible for the economic hardship are recognizable. In this case, even a prolonged strike is seen as a temporary situation – a stage toward an improved family income.

The prolonged inability to provide for the family has been the subject of many studies, especially focussing on the 1930s. (Eisenberg and Lazarsfeld 1938; Komarovsky 1940; Rainwater 1974) Some interest in the effects of unemployment and layoffs continues. (Jones 1972) Typically, the literature shows that the reaction to unemployment, layoffs, and the accompanying loss of the breadwinner's role and status is closely related to a variety of family and community problems.

In a review of data dealing with termination of employment and layoffs among selected major industries in Ontario, it was argued that when a worker is unemployed for six months or longer, his standards of living deteriorate and

[1]This paper draws on research data and anlaysis that was financed by Social Service Division, Social Services Program Branch, Health and Welfare Canada and the Youth Employment and Immigration Commission. Additional funding was received from the office of Mr. F. A. Sorochinsky, Vice-President, Ontario Division, INCO Metals, and Local 6500, United Steel Workers of America (USWA).

he enters the ranks of the improverished. "Those less skilled, those with lowest seniority and those at the bottom of income scale . . . suffer the most" (Eleen and Bernardine 1971:41) The study in Thompson, Manitoba, where INCO Thompson Division permanently laid off almost one-third (650) of its hourly-paid employees, established that "during the first quarter of 1978, there appears to have been a signficantly greater number of marital breakdowns resulting in separate single parents with children requiring some support services." (McKenzie et al. 1978:30) Another study found that laid-off workers showed a marked decrease in social drinking, frequenting taverns and seeing old friends. Of the fifty-two subjects studied in Seattle, Washington, 38.3 percent experienced increased tensions and conflicts after being laid off, but also "more enjoyable moments which tended to overshadow the trying times." (Briar 1979:43) The workers laid off by General Electric in St. Catharines, Ontario, experienced "a loss of voluntary interaction." (Crysdale 1968:275)

In comparison with the literature on unemployment and layoffs, little is known about the social costs of long-term strikes. The studies and articles tend to limit themselves to the dynamics of contract negotiations (Smith 1978) or other processes related to strike action, and to income losses and gains. (Imberman 1978) The financial aspect was the primary concern for the researchers of the forty-eight-day strike at the British Post Office in 1971, and the ninety-one-day strike at Chrysler Corporation of Great Britain in 1973. The authors did not find any significant changes in family structures and relationships as a result of these strikes. (Gennard and Lasko 1975) A review of studies dealing with relationships among jobs, incomes, and family life depicts work as a "validating activity" that takes place largely within the family or with family members. "When husbands cannot bring home that level of income which would provide the family with the kind of income it needs to have a mainstream existence, both husbands' and wives' sense of identity is diminished." (Rainwater 1974:364-65)

Discussing the costs and benefits of strikes, it was argued that a brief spell of unemployment or strike may be initially attractive but, over time, there emerges a pattern of increasing marginal costs, especially the loss of goodwill in labor-management relations. (Reynolds 1977:23)

It is most likely that prolonged strike situations everywhere elicited some interest and coverage by the mass media in the past, and family experiences or accounts by individuals were discussed in magazines or newspapers. (Hyman 1973; Kossick 1979; Ross 1979a; 1979b) However, the validity and generalization of such accounts are not high. There does not seem to be other sources that deal more systematically with the impact of strikes on the family beyond the references indicated above.[2]

The dearth of relevant comparison studies is accentuated further in that the research on families subjected to unemployment or layoffs cannot be readily comparable to the strikers' situation. Among the more obvious dis-

---

[2]A search through the holdings of Newman Industrial Relations Library at the Centre for Industrial Relations University of Toronto, and at other industrial relations libraries in Ontario failed to locate studies dealing with the impact of prolonged strikes on the families.

tinctions is the projection for the future; the striker expects to return to work with improved working conditions, while the unemployed or the laid-off worker is faced with limited income and an uncertain work future, especially if over forty years of age.

In Canada, the laid-off or unemployed worker is eligible for Unemployment Insurance benefits up to $159.00 weekly (1979 figures) for a period of one year. When this support ends, (s)he can apply for provincial welfare.

The striker and his family suffer heavier economic costs for the duration of the strike as they are not eligible for Unemployment Insurance or Welfare, but must rely on their own savings and strike pay. Monies available to the strikers from their labor unions varied across Canada in the past and the amounts differ substantially at present. In the case of Local 6500, United Steel Workers of America, those who performed picket duty were given weekly food vouchers of $25 for a single member, $30 for those who were married, and $3 for each dependent child. It has been estimated that, in 1978-1979, a family of four would require between $200 and $250 weekly to meet basic needs. Thus, while the unemployed or laid-off workers face a sharp decline in their resources and may eventually be defined as "poverty striken," strikers often face disaster once the strike exhausts their financial reserves.

The review article of studies on families in crises notes the difficulty of formulating and applying a comprehensive theoretical framework which could encompass the range of serious difficulties or crises that may apply to the family under certain conditions or emergencies. (Burr 1973:199-217; Hansen and Hill 1964) For the purposes of this paper, only a few selected variables will be examined in greater detail to inquire into their relationship to the effects of strikes on families. It may be hypothesized that the factors of ethnicity, size of the family, and the length of marriage are important variables affecting intra-family experiences during a prolonged strike.

Background

According to the 1971 Census of Canada, metropolitan Sudbury is a northern Ontario city with an ethnically mixed population of over 150 000; the French segment is the largest (37.4 percent), followed by the Anglo-Celtic (36.6 percent), the Italian (6.6 percent), the Ukrainian (3.6 percent), the German (3.2 percent), and the Polish (1.9 percent). There are over 50 other smaller ethnic minority groups in the Sudbury area. The composition of INCO hourly-paid employees reflects the ethnic diversity of Sudbury.

Mining for nickel ore began in this area in 1883 and, for many decades, the mining and smelting occupations constituted the largest single segment of the Sudbury work force. In 1971, these jobs represented 25.9 percent of the total labor force; another 21.3 percent were in service industries and only 14.7 percent of Sudbury's work force was employed in the manufacturing occupations. The total income derived directly from the mining and smelting jobs represented nearly 20.0 percent of the total earnings in the region, but this proportion is higher if mining and smelting dependent or related earnings are considered.

Organization of the INCO's hourly-paid work force began in the 1910s, but it was not until 1944 that the company officially recognized the union. Since 1958, contract negotiations have taken place every three years and have been characterized by confrontation and related strikes of shorter or longer duration. The strikes of 1958 and 1969 were especially significant. The eighty-six-day strike action in 1958 realized very few gains for the union members, but created opposition and hostility toward this strike among the strikers' wives. The shorter strike of 1969 was considered a victory for the union, and was termed "the revenge for '58." The adversary union-management positions were accentuated further by other strikes, layoffs, and disputes. The last strike began on September 15, 1978 and lasted 261 days. This was the longest strike in INCO's history and, in terms of lost man-hours (2.2 million), the longest strike in Canadian labor history. The union-management negotiations were reportedly hostile and bitter. Throughout the strike, the image of INCO was largely negative among the strikers and their families and this attitude was, in time, shared by the larger community.

Methodology

The planning for the Strike Impact Study (SIS) started during the strike and interviewing began during the first week that the hourly-paid workers returned to work. The study, conducted between June and August, 1979, consisted of three closely-related projects: face-to-face interviews with the wives of the striking INCO workers; face-to-face interviews with wives randomly selected from the 1979 voters' list; and contacts through telephone and mail with all known organizations and services in the community to establish and explore their role in relation to families affected by the strike.

In the case of families directly affected by the strike (the focus of this discussion), the complete list of 11 700 members of Local 6500 USWA was used to extract the respondents. Selecting every ninth member, over 1200 names were drawn, but because of refusals,[3] ineligible cases, inability to locate the selected cases, or conduct interviews within the time available, the SIS produced 569 useable interviews. An additional 80 strikers' families were part of the sample extracted from the 1979 voters' list, making the total number of strikers' families interviewed 649.

The researchers used a standardized questionnaire consisting of 454 questions of which over 80 were open ended. Two major issues were addressed: the economic coping experiences of the families during the 1978-1979 INCO strike; and husband-wife, parents-children relationships during that period. The gathered data provided the basis for the first report (Radecki 1979) and also serves as the source for this discussion. Additional sets of relationships were considered to accentuate certain experiences of the strikers' families during the work stoppage.

---

[3]The actual proportion of refusals was 36.8 percent.

Findings: Matters of Economy and Finance

From 649 interviews, 52.0 percent had resided in Sudbury between 11 and 29 years, another 33.5 percent had lived there for 30 years or more, while only 14.6 percent had been there for ten years or less. An overwhelming majority of the sample (84.7 percent) were home owners, while 14.8 percent, the majority of whom were younger people, rented their accommodation. Only 20.2 percent of the strikers considered in the SIS were employed by INCO for nine years or less, while 44.8 percent worked for the company between 10 and 24 years, and the remaining 35.0 percent had at least 25 years seniority with the company.

Prior to the strike, 34.5 percent of the strikers' wives had worked for wages full-time; this proportion increased to 40.4 percent during the strike period. Interestingly, only 33.8 percent intended to remain in the labor force once their husbands returned to work. During the strike, 41.9 percent of the husbands worked either full-time, part-time, or part of the time.

For over half (57.3 percent) of the strikers' families, the weekly income was under $100. With this, 61.2 percent of them purchased less meat, fruit, fresh vegetables, and so-called "junk foods." There were also cutbacks in the purchase of packaged or convenience foods, alcoholic beverages, and frequenting of restaurants. A majority of the strikers' families cut down on the purchase of new clothing and reduced spending on entertainment. In addition, various strategies were used to save money; 17.9 percent swapped things, such as clothing, 22.6 percent traded labor, 74.0 percent took better care of their possessions, and 47.1 percent practised energy conservation.

Nearly two-thirds (64.3 percent) of the families had expected a lengthy strike and over three-quarters of all families had made some preparation, including additional savings and special food stocks. The fact that 72.0 percent had previously experienced a strike was considered very helpful in coping with the 1978-1979 strike. While nearly all the families began the strike with some amount of savings, 43.6 percent had no savings left when it ended in June 1979. Moreover, for half of this group, savings were exhausted five months before the strike ended. While this was undoubtedly a severe economic crisis, only 2.3 percent of these families admitted that they had sold things to "make ends meet," and an insignificant proportion reported that they had had to move to less expensive accommodation. While 2.4 percent considered applying for financial assistance from social agencies, only 1.3 percent actually sought such help. Over one-quarter of the strikers had had to borrow money to tide them over the strike, and 29.1 percent ended the strike with debts.

Nearly all the strikers' families reported losses in wages (which the majority did not expect to recover) ranging from $1000 to $20 000. Where savings were not exhausted, they were often seriously depleted, or undermined – a serious problem for those INCO workers nearing retirement.

Financial losses and the sharp reduction of income affected families differently. Just over 10.0 percent reported that they were not at all affected by the strike conditions, while nearly 20.0 percent were affected severely. A majority, over 70.0 percent, were only somewhat affected. In over half of the families, confidence and pride were not affected; while confidence and pride did suffer for about 15.0 percent, it apparently increased for a slightly larger proportion.

Approximately one-third considered the strike a bad, or a very bad experience. Nearly 40.0 percent found the experience both good and bad, and over one-quarter considered the strike period a good, or a very good experience. The strength and resilience of the family is clearly indicated in that hopes and plans for the future did not change for almost half of them; fewer than 5.0 percent saw future prospects as poor. Nearly two-thirds regarded their future prospects as good, or very good.

Those who experienced severe ecoomic hardships were generally younger families with little seniority at INCO, and with relatively little savings prior to the strike. These were often families where both the husband and the wife did not work for wages full-time during the strike, and they tended to have incurred debts through credit purchases. Interestingly, an often voiced comment was that they knew of other families who were "really suffering," but that they, themselves, were "not too badly off."

The Radecki report (1979:71) hypothesized that the 1978-1979 strike experience would not have long-lasting economic effects for a majority of the strikers' families. At the time of writing (1981), there did not appear to be any widespread economic difficulties, and no significant problems were discovered in the analysis of the follow-up data gathered in 1980. (Radecki 1981)

Previous strike experience and advance preparation emotionally prepared most families (70.7 percent) for the work stoppage. Still, the prolonged strike with the ensuing economic hardships and uncertainties affected their earlier attitudes and nearly 70.0 percent of both husbands and wives reported experiencing strike-related stress.

Table 1:   Amount of Stress Experienced During the Strike*

	Wife	Husband	Children
		(in percentages)	
A great deal more	21.9	25.3	6.9
More	47.0	43.9	29.6
No change	26.7	25.3	40.7
Less	3.7	3.5	1.7
A great deal less	0.5	0.8	0.2
Don't know/No answer	0.4	1.2	21.0

N=649

*As compared with before the strike.

Findings: Intra-Family Concerns

The SIS research found that 11.9 percent of the respondents were married less than five years and 39.6 percent were married twenty-one years or longer. Only 9.8 percent of the married couples were childless, while 43.9 percent had one or two children, 34.7 percent had three or four, and 11.5 percent had five or more children. As in the case of the larger community, the largest single ethnic group represented in the SIS findings was the French with 30.4 percent, followed by the Anglo-Celtic with 17.9 percent, the Slavic groups with 7.9 percent, the Finnish group with 3.2 percent, and the "Other" ethnic groups with 13.7 percent. Further, the field survey allowed for an additional ethnic category "Canadian," for those who did not wish to, or could not, define themselves in some ethnic category; this group made up 19.1 percent of the total.[4]

The husband-wife and parents-children relationships were also affected by the 1978-1979 INCO strike. While a significant proportion of the wives enjoyed having their husbands at home for prolonged periods, this was not appreciated by all, and over one-quarter saw their husbands' presence as interfering with their routine and chores.

About one-fifth of the strikers found work outside the Sudbury area. Their absence from the home and family was generally evaluated by the wives as undesirable, and was related to some negative consequences for the wives and children in about 15.2 percent of the cases. The consequences were seen largely as emotional problems stemming from the absence of the husband/father, but also included some minor disobedience problems among the children.

It was expected that the economic hardships and changed work patterns would increase marital problems. This expectation was confirmed by one-

Table 2:   Wife's Evaluation of Husband's Presence in the Home

	(in percentages)
Increased family cohension	7.5
Enjoyable to wife and children	31.2
Some positive, some negative effects	12.4
No difference	14.0
Husband was a nuisance	22.9
Husband disrupted routines	2.7
Other positive or negative opinions	9.4

N=649

[4]According to the field researchers, the category "Canadian" was chosen primarily by the French-Canadian and Anglo-Celtic groups.

Table 3:   Husband's Behavior During the Strike*

	Marital Quarrels	Husband's Swearing	Husband's Use of Physical Force
		(in percentages)	
Never took place	14.3	45.6	89.2
Less often	12.8	4.5	1.5
No change	52.5	40.4	6.3
More often	16.6	6.0	0.8
Much more often	2.8	1.5	0.2
No answer	0.9	2.0	2.0

N=649
*As compared with before the strike.

third of the wives who reported some marital difficulties, primarily involving increased quarreling and swearing.

In general, only 4.3 percent of the marriages deteriorated because of the strike; positive and negative changes were reported by 6.3 percent, 26.7 percent of the respondents saw no change, and another 14.5 percent claimed their marital relationships were good before the strike and remained good throughout this period. The largest segment, 42.9 percent, saw improvement in their marital relationships during the strike.

As indicated in Table 4, a small proportion of the respondents indicated decreases in certain relationships, while a significantly greater proportion experiences an enrichment in marital relationships through increases in activities in all four categories listed. To examine these relationships further, factors of length of marriage and husband's ethnicity were introduced as controlling variables (see Table 5).

Those couples married between six and twenty years tended to be drawn closer together under the impact of strike conditions. This was especially pronounced for the French and the Anglo-Celtic groups. For specific years of marriage categories in all but one ethnic group, a small proportion of husband-wife relationships became less close during the strike; only within the Finnish group did husband-wife relationships remain stable or improve. The pattern (all under 5.0 percent except for the 6–20 years married category for the Canadian group) is not sufficiently pronounced to draw more valid inferences, but there are clear differences in husband-wife relationships that can be related to the husband's ethnicity.

To test the degree that the intimate husband-wife relationships were affected by the strike, two additional variables were introduced.

Table 6 shows that the frequency of sexual relations increased for nearly all ethnic groups in all years married categories; surprisingly, these increases

Table 4: Husband-Wife Relationship During the Strike*

	Talk Together	Spend Time Together	Try to Please Each Other	Have Sexual Relations
	(in percentages)			
Much more often	12.9	15.3	9.2	5.7
More often	42.8	50.5	30.7	16.9
No change	39.0	26.2	54.5	64.4
Less often	3.5	5.4	3.7	7.9
Much less often	0.9	2.0	0.9	2.2
Don't Know/ No Answer	0.8	0.6	0.9	2.9

N=649
*As compared with before the strike.

were generally lowest for those in the 0 – 5 years married category. Further, for Italian and Finnish groups within this category, sexual relations remained stable throughout the strike. There are two possible explanations: Intimate relations for this years married category may have already been at their peak and the availability of more free time and rest may not have basically altered those relationships; or younger workers, lacking previous strike experience, may not have been prepared for the long work stoppage and, therefore, may have been under greater stress which, in turn, might have affected their intimate relations.

As noted earlier, about one-third of the wives reported some marital problems, primarily increases in quarreling and swearing, but fewer than 3.0 percent of the marriages experienced more serious problems such as separation or divorce; about half of these serious problems could be traced to conditions which existed prior to the strike. Fewer than 5.0 percent believed that their marriages deteriorated because of the strike, but for every marriage that weakened, ten improved or were strengthened.

Shared family activities increased for three times as many families as for those in which such activities decreased. For 42.5 percent of the respondents, the family was closer, or much closer, intra-family relationships remained the same for 50.1 percent, and the internal family cohesion became less, or much less evident during the strike for 6.3 percent of the total sample.

Data in Table 7 indicates that there is generally a stronger tendency toward closer family relationships for those with no children, or families with one to three children in the 6–20 years married category, and for those families with four or more children in the 21+ years married category. Although further tests are required for corroboration, it would seem that the presence of children is not a contributing factor to the fragmentation or the weakening of family relationships under stress.

Table 5: Husband-Wife Closeness During the Strike

Controlled for Years Married and Husband's Ethnicity

Ethnicity	Canadian		Anglo-Celtic		French		Italian		Slavic		Finnish		Other	
Distance	Closer*	Less Close	Closer	Less Close	Closer	Less Close	Closer	Less Close	Closer	Less Close	Closer	Less Close	Closer	Less Closer
Years Married														
0 – 5	10.4	—	7.0	0.9	7.2	2.1	2.3	—	5.9	—	9.5	—	5.7	1.1
6 – 20	28.0	5.6	33.0	1.7	35.1	3.1	11.4	2.3	17.6	—	33.3	—	13.8	1.1
21 +	9.6	0.8	18.3	0.9	11.9	1.5	11.4	2.3	13.7	3.9	9.5	—	18.4	2.3
	N = 125		N = 115		N = 194		N = 44		N = 51		N = 21		N = 87	

*Other category - No difference

Table 6: Frequency of Sexual Relations During the Strike

Controlling for Years Married and Husband's Ethnicity

Ethnicity	Canadian		Anglo-Celtic		French		Italian		Slavic		Finnish		Other	
Frequency	More Often*	Less Often	More Often	Less Often	More Often	Less Often	More Often	Less Often	More Often	Less Often	More Often	Less Often	More Often	Less Often
Years Married														
0 – 5	4.8	2.4	2.7	1.8	3.1	2.1	—	—	2.2	—	—	—	1.2	3.5
6 – 20	15.3	6.5	16.8	6.2	20.7	5.2	7.0	2.3	10.9	4.3	9.5	—	8.1	9.3
21 +	3.2	1.6	11.5	1.8	3.6	3.1	7.0	2.3	2.2	6.5	4.8	—	4.7	3.5
	N = 124		N = 113		N = 193		N = 43		N = 46		N = 21		N = 86	

*Other category - No change

Table 7: Family Relationships During the Strike

Controlling for Years Married and Number of Children

N. of Children	None		1 – 3		4 – 5		6 +	
Relationships	Closer*	More Distant	Closer	More Distant	Closer	More Distant	Closer	More Distant
Years Married								
0 – 5	15.0	—	8.1	1.4	1.7	—	—	—
6 – 20	20.0	—	33.3	3.1	14.5	3.4	12.1	—
21 +	13.3	1.7	9.8	1.4	23.1	2.6	21.2	—
	N = 60		N = 420		N = 117		N = 33	

*Other category - No change

Table 8: Family Relationships During the Strike

Controlling for Years Married and Husband's Ethnicity

Ethnicity	Canadian		Anglo-Celtic		French		Italian		Slavic		Finnish		Other	
Relationships	Closer*	Less Close	Closer	Less Close	Closer	Less Close	Closer	Less Close	Closer	Less Close	Closer	Less Close	Closer	Less Close
Years Married														
0 – 5	9.7	—	3.5	—	3.6	2.6	4.5	—	3.9	—	9.5	—	9.0	1.1
6 – 20	28.2	4.8	25.7	2.7	29.5	5.2	15.9	2.3	17.6	3.9	19.0	—	10.1	3.4
21 +	7.3	—	18.6	—	11.9	1.0	15.9	9.1	9.8	3.9	4.8	—	20.2	2.2
	N = 124		N = 113		N = 193		N = 44		N = 51		N = 21		N = 89	

*Other Category - No change

Closer family relationships are especially pronounced for the 6-20 years married category, but this is affected, in turn, by the factor of ethnicity. Only in French and Other ethnic groups did primary relationships become less close during the strike in the 0-5 years married category. Only for the Finnish group was there no loss of family relationships registered. Less close family relationships for the 21+ years married category are either not registered or less pronounced than for the 6-20 years married category, except for the Italian group. There does not appear to be a ready explanation for the relatively sharp difference registered by this ethnic group.

Just over 12.0 percent of the strikers' wives reported that their children developed problems within the family and with the outside environment. The problems ranged from confusion over parental role changes - where the mother worked while the father remained at home - to conflicts involving the striking father's status in peer group interaction. More generally, minor problems stemmed from the reduction or total elimination of spending money, especially during the latter stages of the strike. The SIS researchers attempted to ascertain if any unusual trends in juvenile problems were observed or noted by the local police, by school officials, and by various service groups and agencies concerned with youth problems in general. None of these groups noted any significant or unusual patterns of juvenile problems or delinquency during the strike or during the twelve months following its resolution.

Controls for ethnicity and the number of children within the family are indicated in Table 9. The French group shows the most consistent behavioral problems for children, while the Finnish group reported none. The "immigrant" groups - Italian, Slavic, Finnish, and Other - reported proportionately fewer problems with children than the more "established" groups - Canadian, Anglo-Celtic, and French. The hypothesis that families of Eastern or Southern European heritage maintain more traditional family patterns and tend to adhere to parental authority over generations tends to be supported by the SIS findings.

Conclusions

The 1978-1979 INCO strike was economically disastrous for about 20.0 percent of the families directly involved, and it was a period of hardship for another 70.0 percent; but the financial difficulties did not bring about large-scale disruptions in family structures and relationships. In general, 50.0 percent of the wives reported that their family relationships were not affected, while over 40.0 percent reported that their families grew closer during this period. The positive evaluation of the husbands' presence at home was reflected in that over half of the couples communicated more and spent more time together, nearly 40.0 percent tried to please each other more, and nearly 20.0 percent engaged in sexual relations more often. Only 5.0 percent of the wives became pregnant and, of these, over half were planned. Marriage and family relationships remained unchanged or were enriched for an overwhelming majority of the respondents despite the long strike and ensuing economic hardships, and fewer than 5.0 percent of the wives believed that their marriages had deteriorated because of the strike.

Table 9: Childdren's Behavior at Home During the Strike

Controlling for Number of Children and Husband's Ethnicity

Ethnicity	Canadian			Anglo-Celtic			French			Italian			Slavic			Finnish			Other		
No. of Children	1-3	4-5	6+	1-3	4-5	6+	1-3	4-5	6+	1-3	4-5	6+	1-3	4-5	6+	1-3	4-5	6+	1-3	4-5	6+
Behavior Improved	13.3	7.1	—	8.5	16.0	—	11.3	17.2	—	16.0	28.6	—	20.8	22.2	—	18.2	—	100.0	6.7	8.3	—
Got worse	13.3	14.3	—	11.9	4.0	—	19.8	13.8	6.7	8.0	—	—	4.2	—	—	—	—	—	6.7	8.3	—
Different for different children*	1.3	—	—	—	—	—	0.9	3.4	6.7	4.0	—	—	—	—	—	—	—	—	2.2	—	—
N =	75	14	5	59	25	5	106	29	15	25	7		24	9		11	2	1	45	12	2

*Other category – No change

The ability of the families to cope for an extended period with very limited outside financial resources is related to several factors. Because the majority of the strikers had had strike experience, they had accrued the necessary savings to meet their needs during the strike. It would seem that the hourly-paid INCO workers' families defined strikes as problematic, but not necessarily crisis events; thus, they were able to accept the hardships of the strike as part of the worker's life in this community. Also, a majority of the strikers were home owners and long-time residents. Generally, they were stable families with networks of relatives and friends in the community who provided some support for the strikers. A significant proportion of the strikers were of ethnic backgrounds whose cultures emphasize family ties and traditional family interdependence, thereby allowing the family members to be more resilient to the outside problems. Here, the immediate family served as a cushion against adversities created by the strike. While not discussed in this paper, there was overwhelming support for the husband's position and his decision on the strike from his wife and family. In this sense, there was a "common family front" which assured a degree of harmony and precluded a more hostile husband-wife relationship as was the case during the 1958 strike at INCO.

The results of the SIS research and the discussion presented in this paper should be considered bearing in mind two factors: First, the research was conducted immediately following the settlement of the 261-day strike. While the respondents had had little time to reflect on their experiences, the information provided is likely more accurate than if the study had been carried out six months or a year later. At the same time, a follow-up study would be highly desirable to establish the long-term effects of a strike of such duration. Secondly, the responses were restricted to the wives of the strikers on the assumption that they could report more accurately the various effects of the strike on their families. It is recognized, however, that the husbands' evaluations of the strike effects are missing.

A Harder Look at the Battered and Abused Child

Mary Van Stolk

Any act of commission or omission by individuals, institutions, or society as a whole, and any conditions resulting from such acts or inaction, which deprive children of equal rights and liberties, and/or interfere with their optimal development, constitute, by definition, abusive or neglectful acts or conditions.[1]

The Child and Society

"The family is generally seen as a social group committed to nonviolence between its members. Yet the empirical data and relevant theory leaves no doubt that violence between family members is so common as to be almost universal."[2] A large segment of society believes in the need to scare, abuse, and terrorize children; convinced that all manner of paddles, belts, wooden spoons, fly swatters, and electric cords are standard equipment for the job. These forms of abuse are often interspersed with threats of one kind or another. "You will be taken to the police station if you are not good." "The bogeyman will get you." "You will be put in the cellar, in the alley, in the closet." Terror and solitary confinement, as well as physical abuse, are used to break the spirit and ensure obedience.

These routine, culturally-sanctioned punishments, spankings, slaps, shakings, screaming sessions, and threats are not classified as child battering but as child abuse. Often, the only difference between the battering home and the so-called normal home, is the *degree* of physical or emotional abuse used. (Steinmetz and Straus 1974)

To the battering and abusive parent alike the rules are all important and the child is punished in relation to the rules. Differences over obedience to rules cause one parent to beat, while another spanks, slaps, or screams. The battering parent simply takes North American "normal child-rearing practices" to the furthest point. (Goode 1971; Gil 1971; Terr 1970)

---

[1] David G. Gil, "Unraveling Child Abuse," in *Child Abuse and Violence*, ed. David G. Gil (New York: AMS Press Inc., 1979), p. 4.

[2] Murray A. Straus, "A General Systems Theory Approach to a Theory of Violence Between Family Members," *Social Science Information* 12, 3 (1973 06): 105. *See also*, Suzanne K. Steinmetz and Murray A. Straus, "The Family as Cradle of Violence," *Society* 10, 6 (1973): 50-56.

At one time, almost all the major institutions of our society had the right to use violence. Corporal punishment was the rule of the day in the courts and prisons; masters used physical punishment on apprentices. Today, only the police, parents, and teachers have a clear legal mandate to use violence as a means of social control. (Steinmetz and Straus 1974)

Wertham (1972) pointed out an important factor in the "inter-relation of psychological and social factors in the Battered Child Syndrome. The idea that human violence is an eternal, inborn instinct amounts to a biological justification for violence, and this attitude carries over to the abused and battered child."[3] This belief also strongly sanctions continued support for the use of force and corporal punishment in the home and school. (Prescott 1979; Gil 1971)

The first legal challenge to the absolute rights and control of parents over children occurred in New York City in 1874. While visiting an aged woman in a tenement house, a church worker learned that a child was being inhumanly treated by her adoptive parents. This little girl was badly beaten daily. The child was also seriously malnourished and neglected. After appeals to protective agencies including the police and the district attorney's office proved futile, the church worker, in desperation, appealed to the American Society for the Prevention of Cruelty to Animals (SPCA). She pointed out that this child was being treated as an animal and was certainly a member of the animal kingdom. It was on this basis that the SPCA brought action that resulted in the child's removal from her parents. (Fontana 1964) One year later, the New York Society for the Prevention of Cruelty to Children was organized. It is a sad commentary that it took the persistence of an unnamed church worker and the SPCA to instigate action in one of the first recorded cases of a maltreated child. (Allen and Morton 1961)

In *The History of Western Philosophy*, Bertrand Russell outlines the philosophical and historical foundation of society's attitude toward parental rights:

> *Aristotle's opinions on moral questions are always such as were conventional in his day. On some points they differ from those of our time, chiefly where some form of aristocracy comes in. We think that human beings, at least in ethical theory, all have equal rights, and that justice involves equality. Aristotle thinks that justice involves, not equality, but right proportions, which is only 'sometimes' equality. "The justice of a master or a father is a different thing from that of a citizen,* for a son or slave is property, and there can be no injustice to one's own property."[4]

The belief that there can be no injustice to one's own property still allows and sanctions the abuse of children under the guise of punishment. Today, society

---

[3]Frederic Wertham, "Battered Children and Baffled Adults," *Bulletin of the N.Y. Academy of Medicine* 48, 7 (1972): 887-98.

[4]Bertrand Russell, *History of Western Philosophy* (London: George Allen and Unwin Ltd., 1969), p. 186. Reprinted with the publisher's permission.

says that a man or woman who strikes a child is committing assault if the child is not his or her own, but rarely interferes in the assault of a child carried out as punishment by a parent.

Society's covert sanction of the use of violence is confirmed by the lack of support for the battered child. A very large portion of battering incidents occur with the full knowledge of family members and neighbors. It is also reaffirmed by the failure of society to recognize or help these child victims. (Gil 1970; Elmer 1967)

Although it is often only one child who is singled out as the recipient of these crippling, maiming, and sometimes lethal assaults, (Gil 1970) all the children in these families are witnesses to and experience abuse, and hence grow up with the experience of abuse as the dominant child-rearing method in the enforcement of rules and the maintenance of discipline. (Gelles 1973)

Because both child abuse and battering are carried out as punishments and because punishment is a righteously-loaded word in society, it is sometimes easy to ignore the actual physical acts carried out by battering and abusive parents within the concept of punishment. Children are punched, kicked, pinched, bitten, scratched, and flung against hard objects. They are beaten with tree branches, heavy books, building materials, garden tools, furniture, coat hangers, and high-heeled shoes. They are stabbed, locked for days in closets, put out of the house in their night clothes in zero weather, chained to bed posts, placed in scalding baths, or given boiling enemas. Boiling water and hot coffee are the most common causes of scalds. Infants are fed boiling milk, and children are forced to eat their own feces and vomit. Contact burns are inflicted by placing children on hot stoves or surface heating units. They are thrown on the grates of floor furnaces and commonly are burned by cigarettes. (Weston 1974; Gillespie 1965)

> *A three-year-old girl was admitted with second and third degree burns on her feet, buttocks and perineum. She also had a bruise on her left arm and a pinch mark on her neck. While the mother was at work, her boyfriend was bathing the child. Allegedly, he answered the phone and the child turned the hot water on herself. Because the story and the burn did not match, and because bruises were present, the proper authorities were notified. In the hospital, the child showed no fear of the staff and interacted well with her mother. She refused, however, to look at the boyfriend and became wide-eyed and fearful when he entered the room. He, on the other hand, encouraged her to call him "Daddy" but she refused. When he left she told a nurse, "he burned me." When her real father arrived, she immediately smiled, wanted to be held, and asked him to take her home. The mother's reaction was one of anger and defensiveness with the staff. When she was told that her child had lost parts of eight toes, she shed no tears and said nothing.*[5]

---

[5]Patricia S. Phillips, Elaine Pickrell, and Thomas S. Morse, "Intentional Burning: A Severe Form of Child Abuse," *Journal of the American College of Emergency Physicians* (November-December 1974): 388.

Almost all child abuse leading to death or permanent injury is associated with a fanatical belief in the need for absolute obedience. "He would not stop wetting his bed so we had to beat him," goes the rationale. "She would not stop crying so I threw her across the room to show her I meant business." "I told him not to touch the stove but he would not obey, so I took his hand and held it over the burner. Next time I say don't touch, he'll obey."

Wright, in a ten-year follow-up of abused children, found that 40 percent were emotionally disturbed and 50 percent had below normal intelligence. Some failure in physical growth was evident in 60 percent of the cases. (Wright 1970; Elmer and Gregg 1979)

The Battered Child As Battering Parent

A child who grows up in a battering or abusive household has a high risk of growing up to batter or abuse in turn. This cycle of abuse is continued with a terrible certainty and is confirmed in the case histories of child batterers and child abusers alike. (Sherriff 1964; Curtis 1963; Paulson and Blake 1967; Jenkins et al. 1970) Professional opinions of the past decade on the psychological characteristics of the child-abusing parent reveal that: (1) the abusing parent was himself raised with some degree of deprivation; (2) the abusing parent brings to his role as parent mistaken notions of child rearing; (3) there is present in the parent a general defect in character structure allowing aggressive impulses to be expressed too freely; and (4) while socio-economic factors might sometimes place added stresses on basic personality weakness, these stresses are not of themselves sufficient or necessary causes of abuse. (Spinetta and Rigler 1972)

The link between a battering university professor with an IQ of 150 and a battering mother with a grade six education and an IQ of 100, lies in the physical and emotional brutalizing they each *experienced* in their childhood.

Battering, therefore, occurs in all walks of life and in all combinations of social, economic, and religious backgrounds. (Steinmetz and Straus 1974) One basic factor in the etiology of child abuse draws unanimity: Abusing parents were themselves abused or neglected, physically or emotionally, as children. (Spinetta and Rigler 1972)

As a result of their childhood exposure to violence, battering parents have a deep emotional commitment to the use of a high degree of force in their interactions with children. One severe incident of battering, therefore, usually means that there will be more. (Atkinson et al. 1965; Boardman 1962; Gil 1979; Kreindler 1976) Failure to protect a child who has once been severely battered means exposing that child to a high risk of death or permanent injury. (Helfer 1974; Earl 1965; Fisher 1958; Fontana 1966; Paulson and Blake 1967; Roberts 1968; Shaheen et al. 1975)

Once a child has been severely abused by his parents the chances are one in five that he will be injured again. Child victims of such repeated abuse are also likely to sustain permanent crippling injuries or risk dying at an early age. This is a major finding of the study of child abuse in Ontario. American studies of abuse report that risk of repeated injury may go as high as thirty to fifty percent.[6]

Who Batters The Child?

Almost anyone to whom an infant is exposed is a potential child batterer, and 90 percent of the people who abuse their children are mentally and intellectually normal. Unwanted children are more likely to be battered, but many battered children are desperately wanted. (Prescott 1979; Zalba 1971; Wasserman 1967; Bennie and Sclare 1969; Resnick 1969, 1970; Gil 1979; Lowry and Lowry 1970) No one social class tends to batter more than any other. However, the upper classes can afford to take their children to private physicians who will keep quiet, while lower-class parents must take their children to public clinics. (Caffey et al. 1972)

A significant new finding is that alcoholism is a major problem related to child abuse. (Solomon 1970; MacMurray 1978) It is apparent from British reports that alcohol also plays a significant role in the battered wife-child syndrome, whether among the rich or the poor.[7] American studies of interpersonal violence report a high association between alcohol and violence. One important feature of these findings was that alcohol-related violence is almost exclusively male violence. (Gelles 1972)

Battering and abusive parents grew up in homes that were cold, unloving, and punitive. These parents experienced little love or empathy for their needs when they were children. The three key elements involved in child battering are: (1) battering parents are likely to have had poor nurturing; (2) such parents tend to look to a young child to give them the love and understanding that they never had, and then react violently when this unrealistic desire is not fulfilled; and (3) the batterer is involved in some major or minor crisis which precipitates the abuse. (Caffey et al. 1972)

Each discipline has a vital role to play in the protection of the child. Society, represented by the neighbor, teacher, public health nurse, physician, dentist, or other family members, must report to a protective agency all suspected cases of abuse. Social agencies must investigate these reports with a high degree of skill and competence, and seek diagnosis from medical practitioners who understand the diagnostic techniques available to them in assessing the extent of injury sustained by the child. Lawyers, magistrates, and jurists must then assess this information, not from the position of parental rights, but from the primary concept that a safe environment is the legal right of all children, and on that basis formulate a responsible judgment on the relative safety or lack of safety of the child's environment. If at any point one discipline fails to

---

[6]Ellen Rosenblatt and Cyril Greenland, "The Early Identification of Child Abuse" (Paper presented to the Annual Meeting of The Canadian Public Health Association, 1974 06 20), p. 1.

[7]Great Britain, House of Commons, *The Select Committee on Violence in Marriage, Minutes of Evidence* (London: 1975 02 26).

maintain its responsibility in the chain of events from the original report to final legal assessment, the opportunity to protect the child and help the parents may be lost.

Violence In The Home Is A Crime Against The Child

Family and domestic violence is increasingly recognized as a national problem. It affects millions. Its victims – children and adults – suffer emotional, physical, and sexual abuse. Family violence exists at all socio-economic levels. Generally the violent incidents are vastly underreported because of fear, shame, guilt, or a feeling of hopelessness by the victim.

In North America, domestic violence comprises one of the largest areas of complaints to law enforcement agencies (Parnas 1967) and at that only a fraction of the actual incidents are reported. Of those reported, only a fraction are responded to and from those only a few charges are laid. (Levens and Dutton 1977)

In 1977, the Second World Conference of The International Society on Family Law was held in Canada. The subjects under discussion were child abuse, interspousal violence, sexual offences within the family, suicide among children, and violence in the family in general.

Findings in the field of family violence disclose that the most likely place for a person to be murdered or seriously assaulted is at home, by family members. (Parnas 1977; Bard 1973, 1974) Canadian statistics on homicide show that between 1967 and 1971, 37.5 percent of murder victims (675 persons) were classified as "domestic" and that of these nearly three out of every four victims were members of the immediate family of the suspect.[8] In 1975, 52 percent of homicides in Canada were domestic homicides.[9] As for police intervention in domestic violence, a police officer is more likely to be killed or assaulted while performing in this line of duty than in any other category of police activity. (Parnas 1967; Levens and Dutton 1977; Bard 1973, 1974)

The U.S. National Center on Child Abuse and Neglect lists child abuse as the fifth killer of children in the United States, after accidents, cancer, congenital abnormalities, and pneumonia.[10] If all accidental deaths in Canada and the United States were properly investigated and the numbers of children who committed suicide, were murdered, or died of pneumonia brought on by parental neglect were correctly assessed, the figures would place child abuse much closer to the top of the list.

The past reluctance to become involved in domestic violence has been shared by all of society's helping agencies for a variety of reasons: lack of information as to the nature and extent of the problem; poor training in recognition and treatment procedures; inadequately trained personnel; interagency empire building; lack of co-ordination and respect between the

---

[8]Canada, Statistics Canada (Ottawa: 1973)

[9]Canada, Statistics Canada (Ottawa: 1976)

[10]*Newsweek*, 1977 10 10, p. 112.

various disciplines, plus general confusion as to what child abuse and violence in the family really means. All of these problems have led to a situation of gross mismanagement and outright despair among those whose work takes them face to face with the victims.

The recent world-wide recognition of the nature and scope of domestic violence,[11] the numbers and kinds of victims it creates, the cost to society in crimes not only against persons and property within the home but its effect on the numbers of crimes against persons and property beyond the family proper in the school, street, and society at large has prompted a much more realistic look at family crime. (Bard and Zacker 1974)

The belief that a man's home is his castle has hindered the enforcement of law and order by allowing the most grievous assaults and atrocities to be perpetrated on the weakest and most vulnerable members of North American society, while the attackers remain invulnerable by tradition and custom.

The belief that the child is the property of the parents provides a situation whereby the kings and queens of millions of North American castles matter of factly attack, kill, rape, and maim their children. Most commonly they do this under the righteous banner of discipline and parental authority. (Gil 1970) Relatives, friends, neighbors, medical and legal agencies shake their heads and speak of the need for treatment and parental education. For the victims, treatment is often too late and for the attackers treatment is too often only a word. (Hoshino and Yoder 1973)

In almost all cases of child battery not only did other family members know of prior attacks of a grossly serious nature, but often so did a variety of adults from all areas of community life. (Gil 1968; Lero and de Rijcke-Lollis 1979) The single most common impediment to protection for children is that the community believes the parents have more right to assault their child than the child has the right to protection from the community. (Fraser 1974)

The result of this delusion is that crime in the home is virtually unpunished, thereby creating a community double standard of national proportions. Only now, as the state begins to count the cost of maintaining the delusion that there could be law and order in the land but not in the home, has the state realized that there cannot be something called federal and provincial law and at the same time proceed as if these laws did not apply to parents and relatives within the family. The community is more likely to indict a woman for shoplifting than they are for breaking a child's leg, while a man may face the court for cavorting with a prostitute but not for raping his daughter.[12]

---

[11]For example, the interdisciplinary Second World Conference of The International Society on Family Law dealing with "Violence in the Family," which took place in Montreal from June 13-17, 1977.

[12]The national statistics on incest in the United States reported in 1977 indicate that 41 percent of the victims are seven years old or less, and the age of the male perpetrators ranges from seventeen to sixty-eight. The attacker is known to the victim in 75 percent of the cases, and in over 25 percent of the cases the man resides in the child's home. Of all cases of sexual abuse of children, 20 percent involve incest. *See* G. D. Kane, "The Word That Must Be Spoken," *American Humane* 65, 12 (1977): 13.

The best kept secrets are family secrets. But the cost to the taxpayer in maintaining the victims of those secrets has risen to the point where a clear look at violence of all categories within the family is necessary. Juvenile crime,[13] teenage pregnancies, teenage alcoholism, and childhood suicide[14] (Rood-de-Boer 1977) have only just begun to surface, but already the numbers of adolescents and children who cannot bear to continue life in their homes speaks of the despair and hopelessness of a childhood population who exist as the subjects of violent and brutalizing parents.

Violence is not endemic to humanity. Childhood experiences are the major cause of crime[15] and this will continue to be so until an interdisciplinary approach to child advocacy promotes an awareness of North American child-rearing practices in the light of world data on the care and feeding of the young. North Americans do not consider their own practices weird, only those of other people with funny-sounding names and funny-sounding customs. When so-called primitive peoples are told about our common practices of child birth and child care they cannot believe that adults would act in so terrible a fashion toward human life.

Early life experiences as causes of crime mean more, however, than just the physical abuse and/or neglect of the child. Sexual abuses of the infant and child are the direct cause of adult crimes of sexual violence. In North America, sex and violence are linked in the constant bombardment of television propaganda depicting violent male behavior as rewarded by sexual favors from women, either given or taken. The legal bias that supposed that women liked to be raped is only now being understood in terms of crime and violence.[16]

Because there is no scientific evidence to support the Judeo-Christian concept that all children are born bad, victims of original sin, imps of Satan or evil, the inborn tendency-to-aggression theory, as put forth either in religious or quasi-scientific form by Lorenz, Ardrey, etc., has not been able to withstand current interdisciplinary findings in anthropology, psychology, and neuro-psychology. (Prescott 1975; Montagu 1968, 1972)

A new field theory on aggression is emerging. Quite simply stated, it would appear that violence is of our own making. Where culture stands between the

---

[13]*Time,* 1977 07 11, p. 12.

[14]Since the 1950s, Canada's rate of suicide among the young has almost quadrupled, making it second to automobile accidents as the leading cause of death of fifteen- to twenty-four-year-olds. It is estimated that in 1979 close to 1000 Canadian youths died by their own hands, and it is generally conceded that the number based on projections of reported cases is light. The actual figure could be anywhere from 25 to 100 percent higher – many cases never finding their way into the records. *See Maclean's,* 1979 07 30, p. 20.

[15]Canada, Senate of Canada Standing Committee on Health, Welfare and Science, *Minutes of Proceedings of the Subcommittee on Childhood Experiences as Causes of Criminal Behaviour* (Ottawa: 1977-78).

[16]In 1976, there were an estimated 56 730 forcible rapes in the United States – 52 for every 100 000 females, according to the FBI's annual Uniform Crime Reports. This figure is recognized as only a fraction of the actual rapes committed.

child and its biological needs, a high degree of illness, impairment, aggression, and crime result.

Babies are not born with a predisposition toward violence or crime. (Genoves 1970; Gorer 1968; Montagu 1968) They will, however, soon adopt all kinds of ways and means of surviving and coping in a violent and destructive environment. As soon as capable they will push, shove, hit, poke, attack, and kill. They will also lie and steal. Monkey see, monkey do is a firm principle. The human child learns from example. And if the home does not expose the child to a violent atmosphere, then the school ground and television do.

The child in the home and school sees the bully. Fathers, mothers, sisters, brothers, aunts, uncles, cousins, teachers, and babysitters impose a lawlessness of multiple dimensions upon children. In observing these crimes the child notes, not without bitterness, that there are few laws in society and no laws in the family to protect them.

The British Columbia Royal Commission on Family and Children's Law states: "A reason for introducing the legal rights of children arises from the existing legal position of the child in our system of justice. In a word, the child's legal position is non-existent."[17]

The reluctance to call a crime a crime if a relative has committed it causes mental illness, violence, and despondency among the children of such homes. The child who dies a grisly death at the hands of the assaulting parents is a murdered child. It is not an abused child any more than the police officer shot while intervening in a domestic argument is an abused officer. Family violence is violence.

If crime is to be dealt with, then the family must be made safe for citizens of all ages.[18] By failing to support family law, the family is abandoned to the psychopathology of the incorrigible, the violent, the depraved, the disturbed, the deranged, and the savage.

For those whose work it is to study violence, the sights and sounds of family carnage are equal only to the hush of denial. In a very real sense, domestic crimes have been and continue to be the perfect crimes. As in all crimes, the cover up is a vital factor. As in other crimes, the same principles hold true. Violence or the threat of violence is used on the victim or the victim's associates. Financial reprisals, the ignorance or vulnerability of the victim are also used to support unlawful behavior. Behind the closed doors of North American domiciles the child is taught the rudiments of crime in the raw, where the law is often the law of the bully, the deranged, and the ignorant. To enforce family law is to protect all citizens from the lawless, whether they be young or old. To enforce family law is to stop the breeding of criminals at its source. Can legislators expect the police officer to enter into the armed camp of domestic violence to protect citizens who are being assaulted if the governing body, through its judiciary, does not punish familial criminal assaults?

---

[17]Canada, The British Columbia Royal Commission on Family and Children's Law, *Children and the Law, Part III, Children's Rights* (Vancouver: 1975 03), p. 2.

[18]"Sweden Leads," in *Where. The Education Magazine for Parents* (London: 1978 10) p. 3.

Either the law is the law or it is not. The question is: Can men and women within the home remain above the law and continue to rule on the basis of whim, ignorance, mental illness, and outright arrogant brutality? Or is there one standard of behavior for all citizens?

Sweden is one country whose citizens believe that it is more efficient, in terms of services to the family and reduction of costs to the taxpayer, to adopt a "one standard of behavior for all" attitude in its application of the law. In 1920, when "husaga," the master's right to flog his servant, was abolished in Sweden, the law still stipulated that parents had the right to punish their children. In 1949, the word "punish" was replaced by "reprimand," and parents were entitled to some extent to use corporal punishment as a means of education. In 1966, however, this section was excluded from the Swedish Family Code. Thereby the last parental right to intentionally inflict bodily harm on children vanished and the general provision about assault came into force within the field of Family Law. This implied that only the slightest forms of corporal reprimands fell outside the offence of assault. (Nelson 1977)

Effective July 1, 1979, Sweden enacted legislation on subjecting children to physical punishment or other degrading treatment, stating explicitly that children may not be punished by means of blows, beatings, boxing the ears, and by other similar means, and that children may not, for any other reason or cause, be subjected to acts of physical or mental coercion.

The Swedish Commission on Children's Rights maintains that physical punishment is a form of degrading treatment. Mentally humiliating and dismissive treatment is another. Their effects can be identical, that is to say, lack of self-esteem, and a personality change that may leave its mark on the child throughout its childhood and adolescence, and affect it as an adult.

The primary purpose of the provision is to make it clear that beating children is not permitted, and to create a basis for general information and education for parents as to the importance of giving children good care.[19]

In 1977, California, the most treatment-oriented state in the world, moved to determinate sentencing. California found while investigating deaths of women and children that in almost all cases where a victim met a violent death the police had been called in on a number of occasions for serious assaults – assaults which had they happened outside of the home would have resulted in charges being laid. California's law has changed from a treatment response to family crime to a position of protection for the victim and punishment for the attacker.[20]

---

[19]Abuse of elderly persons in their own homes and by their own families has been documented in a Massachusetts' study that cites various forms of mistreatment, including repeated battering, malnutrition, unreasonable forced confinement, intentional over-sedation, and sexual abuse. One of the most significant findings of the study is that elder abuse is a recurring event. The study also reports that, in most cases, the elderly victim of abuse is a woman. *See* "Elder Abuse in Massachusetts: A Survey of Professionals and Paraprofessionals." Boston: Legal Research and Services for the Elderly, 1979.

[20]*See* California Rules of Court, New Sentencing Rules for the Superior Court, Effective 1977 07 01.

Does that mean putting people in jail? Yes. It means that if you attack your relatives you are also attacking a citizen of the State of California and the state does not allow assaults on its citizen no matter what their family relationship. Therefore, as a first offence a person may be charged and sentenced to imprisonment for a period not exceeding one year. What will this mean? No one knows, but what it says is that the State of California no longer condones a double standard of law.

In October, 1978 the New York City Police Department implemented a new spouse abuse policy, instructing officers to arrest any man who is accused of assaulting his wife. Upon receiving a complaint call from a woman who reports that her husband has beaten her, at least one police officer must answer the call promptly and must arrest the man unless there is proper justification not to do so. This means that the officer must arrest the man if he finds reasonable evidence that a felony has been committed. The officer must also remain with the woman and assist her in getting to a shelter or receiving proper medical attention. Previously, police limited their intervention in domestic disputes to informal mediation. Under the new policy, the police must treat spouse assault incidents as they treat violence among strangers.[21]

Family Law in Canada

Canada needs to implement and enforce its existing laws. Children will be best protected when the Magna Charta has been extended into North American homes. One standard of law for all members of the community.

Protection for all citizens means removing Section 43 from the Canadian Criminal Code, which says: "Every schoolteacher, parent or person standing in the place of a parent is justified in using force by way of correction toward a pupil or child, as the case may be, who is under his care, if the force does not exceed what is reasonable under the circumstances."[22]

In his summation to the Second World Conference of The International Society of Family Law, the first international interdisciplinary examination of violence in the family, the distinguished trial judge of the Third Judicial Circuit of Detroit, Michigan, Judge Victor J. Baum, stated: "Certainly one of the highlights of this Conference is a consensus, which is even now gathering momentum, that to eliminate violence within the family, we must first eliminate corporal punishment of children."

Corporal punishment in the home, in the school, and in the prison is not the answer to family violence and crime. (Feshbach 1979; Luker 1978; Zigler 1979; Gil 1979; National Ad Hoc Advisory Committee Report on Child Battering 1973; Goode 1979; Straus 1971; Eron et al. 1971; Gelles and Straus 1979; Bailey 1975; Bedau and Pierce 1976) Punishment and fines, however, are consistent with management of unlawful behavior and can be conducted in a manner appropriate to the concepts of modern medical and mental health

---

[21]*See* "New Spouse Abuse Policy for New York Police," in *Response to Violence and Sexual Abuse in the Family* (Washington, D.C.: Center for Women Policy Studies, 1978 10), p. 3.

[22]Canada, Criminal Code of Canada, Section 43.

treatment. Of course we wish to see parents and relatives restored to society and to the home at such time as they are able to restrain their behavior and maintain themselves as lawful citizens living in consort with others in dignity and camaraderie.

As things stand in 1982, the child who is abused today is highly unlikely to receive help or protection from the many agencies operating to serve it. (Needham 1975) Police are commonly forced to return youngsters who run away from homes too terrible to bear, (Brenton 1978; Runaway Youth, A Status Report and Summary of Projects 1976) knowing that these youngsters will again be beaten, humiliated, and often sexually assaulted. Battered children are also routinely returned to homes by agencies that are going to do referrals and going to provide treatment for the parents, only to find the children have been assaulted again and are either permanently damaged or dead.

Education for Parenting

The necessity to teach good parenting is obvious.[23] Citizens within and outside of the home must learn how to settle their problems without attacking or murdering one another. All citizens owe their allegiance to the laws of the land over and above the laws of the home. Of course, the government has no place in the bedrooms and kitchens of North America so long as the laws of the land are not broken. Murder, assault, and character assassination, however, often take place in the nation's bedrooms, where children are killed for sucking their thumbs or wetting their beds.

If Canada were to adopt a standard definition of abuse and enforce its laws accordingly, then all educational faculties would be mandated to instruct their personnel and student bodies in the full understanding of the law and its implications. For instance, if David Gil's definition of abuse was adopted, which reads "Any act of commission or omission by individuals, institutions, or society as a whole, and any conditions resulting from such acts or inaction, which deprive children of equal rights and liberties and/or interfere with their optimal development, constitute, by definition, abusive or neglectful acts or

---

[23]In his December 16, 1975 presentation to the Canadian Parliamentary Standing Committee on Health, Welfare and Social Affairs investigating Child Abuse and Neglect, the Minister of National Health and Welfare recommended that increased emphasis in our educational system be placed on "realistic and practical courses for young persons, both male and female, on subjects such as child rearing and child care, family life, marriage, responsibilities of parenthood, homemaking and management of finances." *See* Report to the House of Commons by the Standing Committee on Health, Welfare and Social Affairs, *Child Abuse and Neglect* (Ottawa: 1976 07) pp. 55-56.

In their August 1976 *Committee Report on the Abused and Battered Child*, the Federation of Women Teachers' Associations of Ontario stated: "Many professionals involved in the treatment of problem children now believe that the only way to insure better parenting in the coming generations is to offer a course in parenting at all levels in the school system. Here, the greatest number of prospective parents could be influenced. To our knowledge, a course of this type has not yet been developed in Canada."

conditions,"[24] then it can be argued that a full curriculum on child care explaining what constitutes an act of commission or omission or an abusive or neglectful act or condition would be obligatory as well as logical. The adoption of such a definition as part of Canadian legislation would require all schools to immediately teach parenting. Such a curriculum can be constructed in consultation with the International Pediatric Association, the World Federation for Mental Health, the World Health Organization, or any other appropriate sources. The need is imperative.

As to the need for sex education, in February 1980 the New Jersey State Board of Education gave preliminary approval to a plan requiring school districts to establish mandatory sex education from kindergarten classes through the 12th grade. The plan would require school districts to provide instruction in reproductive systems, dating, child abuse, sexual assault, incest, parenting, social and emotional growth, family planning, child rearing, and preparation for marriage and childbirth.[25] This is consistent with numerous Canadian recommendations, including a Vanier Institute of the Family survey which reported that 90 percent of educators thought that sex education should be offered by schools.[26]

What Has Been Done?

In 1946, radiologist John Caffey was the first to diagnose fractured skulls and fractures of the long bones in infants and declare them to be the result of trauma. Prior to Caffey, radiologists examining infants with such fractures refused to recognize this evidence of assault and simply labelled these as injuries of unknown causes.

In 1955, a team of doctors in Detroit were the first to state that parental uncontrollable aggression was the cause of such injuries. Finally, in 1962, a team of physicians at the University of Colorado School of Medicine led by Henry Kempe identified and labelled such assaults as the battered child syndrome.

In 1972, *The Battered Child in Canada* was published. In 1973, the Canadian government convened a National Ad Hoc Advisory Committee on Child Battering. In 1974, a Background Paper on Child Abuse and Neglect was prepared by the Solicitor General of Canada. In 1975, The Canadian Council on Social Development prepared a report on Services for Abused and Battered Children. Also in 1975, the British Columbia Royal Commission on Family and Children's Law presented its Final Report. In 1975-1976, the Canadian Parliamentary Standing Committee on Health, Welfare and Social Affairs investigated the problems of child abuse and neglect in Canada. In 1977, the Second World Conference of The International Society on Family Law, dealing with

---

[24]David G. Gil, "Unraveling Child Abuse," in *Child Abuse and Violence*, ed. David G. Gil (New York: AMS Press Inc., 1979), p. 4.

[25]*The New York Times,* 1980 02 08, p. B2.

[26]*See Report of Family Life Education Survey, Part II, Family Life Education in the Schools* (Ottawa: Vanier Institute of the Family, 1971 04), p. 11.

"Violence in the Family," was held in Canada. In 1977-1978, the Canadian Senate Standing Committee on Health, Welfare and Science undertook an inquiry into Childhood Experiences as Causes of Criminal Behaviour. In 1978, the International Association of Youth Magistrates Tenth Annual Congress was held in Canada, the theme of the Congress being "The Magistrate in the Face of Environmental Pressures on Youth and the Family." In 1979, the Canadian government commissioned a study on "Child Abuse and Neglect in Canada: An Analysis of Past Research and Demonstration Projects." The International Year of the Child was declared in 1979.

What Can Be Done?

Comprehensive family violence programs are needed in the following areas: police – crisis intervention training, protection for victims, and social service referrals by police agencies; prosecution – vigorous prosecution of serious cases and special services to encourage victim and witness co-operation, use of pre-trial counselling and social service referrals for some offenders; legal services – when necessary, to obtain restraining orders protecting victims; courts – extended court hours, including weekends, to obtain temporary restraining orders; corrections – court ordered community-based treatment and confinement for selected offenders; family services – including 24-hour hotline telephone service, shelters, day care centres, mental health and social services, employment counselling, training, job placement, and self-help groups; public education – to increase reporting and reduce community tolerance toward family violence; training – at universities and in the field, special emphasis to be placed on training interdisciplinary personnel, including doctors, nurses, hospital administrators, psychiatrists, social service workers, teachers, principals, police officers, lawyers, prosecutors, magistrates, and others who are likely to encounter family violence cases; education for parenting – including information on nutrition, life skills, sex education, human development, mental health, the effects of physical and emotional deprivation on the growing child; collection of data – to determine the response of criminal justice and social service agencies to these cases and to assist interdisciplinary personnel in handling family violence cases. In addition, the establishment of a full medical record on each child, to prevent medical abuse in the form of over exposure to medication or x-rays.

Survival

Today, the North American child receives more protection and attention to its health and welfare than ever before. Yet at the same time, for a multitude of reasons, it is very possible that the child's survival has never been so threatened. Clearly there are only two priorities that cut across all other political, religious, economic, moral, and ethical issues. They are the health and welfare of the human child.

Living in One-Parent Families: The Children's Viewpoint

Benjamin Schlesinger

Introduction

The 1976 Census of Canada (Wargon 1979), indicated that 9.8 percent of Canada's families were one-parent families; of these 83 percent were fatherless and 17 percent were motherless. There were 898 040 children aged 0–24 years living in these families constituting 10.5 percent of all children in Canada aged 0–24 living at home. Children in these families increased from 6.6 percent of all children living at home between the ages of 0–24 years in 1956 to 10.5 percent in 1976. The median age of these children declined slightly from 13.7 years in 1956 to 13.3 years in 1976. (In 1976, the median age of children in husband-wife families was 11.2 years.)

Focussing on one-parent families, the census found that 42.6 percent were in the 6–14 year old age group; 42 percent were in the 15–24 year age group, and 15.4 percent were in the 0–5 year old group. The average one-parent family had 1.6 children, whereas the two-parent families had 1.5 children.

The fastest growing type of one-parent families is the single mother and her child. It is estimated that 80 to 90 percent of the single mothers who gave birth during the 1975-1978 period have kept their children. The ratio of births to single mothers has increased from 3.9 percent of all births in 1956 to 6.8 percent in 1976, and 10.4 percent in 1978.

The increasing trend toward one-parent families is also evident in divorce and separation statistics. The only decline is among the widowed one-parent families. In 1978, there were 57 155 divorced couples (Statistics Canada 1980); they had a total of 59 140 children. The average number of children per divorced couple was 1.04 children; of the couples divorced in 1978, 45 percent were childless.

During 1978, there were also 36 149 births to single women. Of these births, 47 percent were to women aged 19 years and under. About 90 percent kept their babies.

Literature Trends

From a review of the literature (Schlesinger 1981), the following trends emerged related to children in one-parent families.

American Studies

Existing data do not provide sufficient evidence to assess the effects of fatherlessness on children in one-parent families. Although in the 1980s there tend to be more studies related to children in fatherless rather than motherless families. Most studies appear to emphasize the problems encountered in raising the children, rather than the coping mechanisms employed in one-parent families. Longitudinal studies following up the lives of children growing up in one-parent families are non-existent.

In studies of motherless families, emphasis has been on middle-class educated fathers. Except for the financial aspect, fathers appear to experience similar problems in the area of child care, social life, parenting and home-making skills, personal problems, and community support as do mothers in one-parent families.

The literature also indicates that most children undergo stress following a separation, death, or divorce in their own families, suggesting that it takes about two years for the average child to adjust to the new one-parent situation. It has also become evident that parents who are unhappy, anxious, fearful, angry, and hostile at the time of the marriage breakup will produce problems in their children. Caution should be exercised in analysing studies that examine children of one-parent families in clinical settings, since this has a built in bias involving children with problems.

Canadian Studies

In the past, studies related to children in one-parent families asked the parent living at home about the child's adjustment, it is only recently that investigators have actually queried the children about their feelings.

Ercul, Goldenberg, and Schlesinger (1979) interviewed fourteen children in one-parent families living in Toronto. Most of the children with younger siblings felt that it was difficult for the youngsters to understand the situation. Those with older siblings felt that most of them were coping well. The children cited a number of responsibilities of the missing parent that their older siblings had assumed. These included giving advice, disciplining, teaching sports, discussing sex, sitting at the head of the table, giving sister away at her wedding, cooking, cleaning, and telling the younger child when to go to bed.

The children themselves took on additional responsibilities such as: fixing things around the house, shopping for food, cooking, cleaning, paying for their own clothes, playing a father role, caring for younger siblings, working part time, and serving as a listening post for the parent. Most of the children felt that they would have fewer responsibilities in a two-parent family.

Robson (1979), a child psychiatrist, interviewed 28 adolescents aged 11–18 years of whom 14 were boys and 14 were girls. The parents had separated 1–5 years prior to the study. The young people felt that their experiences had given them insight into their situations and they offered advice to those children of potential one-parent families. This book is a good insight into the lives of adolescents of separated parents. Troyer (1979), a journalist, interviewed children from divorced families and discovered that hurt and anger were the emotions most often experienced by these children after the divorce. Some of the major issues were: dual loyalties, the use of children as pawns and spies, the need for support from the extended family, and the need for personal help on the part of the children of divorce.

The Study

During March and April of 1980, a research seminar, consisting of 13 students[1] and the author, completed a study of 40 children aged 12–18 years, living in one-parent families. After receiving the approval of the Review Committee on the Use of Human Subjects, Parents Without Partners and One-Parent Families Association of Canada were approached for volunteer subjects.

The questionnaire consisted of 87 structured questions and four open-ended questions. Each child was interviewed alone, for about one hour. They were middle class, white, urban dwellers, living primarily in fatherless homes for an average of 5 years. Their parents had been either separated or divorced, and the average age of children was 15 years. Of the 40 children interviewed, 23 were girls and 17 were boys. All of their parents at home were working.

Personal Characteristics of the Sample

The average age of the total sample of 40 children was 14.87 years. The males were a little older, the average being 15.05 years; the average age of the females was 14.7 years. The age range of the respondents was 12–18 years. Of the 40 children, 17 were Protestant, 8 were Roman Catholic, 4 were Jewish, and 8 did not give any religious affiliation. Of our total sample, 14 were first born, 17 were last born, and 9 were middle children. It is of interest that all the children had at least one sibling. In a range of 1–13 years, on the average, the subjects were living for a period of 4.7 years in a one-parent family. The three most frequent housing situations in which the children found themselves were (1) rented housing (37.5 percent); (2) own home (32.5 percent); and (3) rented apartment (22.5 percent).

Of the 36 mothers living at home, 60 percent were employed in clerical/sales positions. Ten mothers were professionals (nurses, social workers, accountants), and five were in semi-professional occupations (day care workers, managers, etc.). All four of the fathers at home had semi-skilled occupations.

---

[1]The students who participated in this study were:

Gary Brooks	Gail Greenberg
Glenn Bruder	Gia Levin
Cindy Clarke	Mary Anne McEvenue
Pat Evans	Janet Miniely
David Feder	Sophia Papahariss
Leslie Glennie	Sylvie Thibault
	Joyce Tremmel

They received their Master of Social Work degree from the University of Toronto, in June 1980.

Of the 36 non-custodial fathers, a third were professionals, a third were in the managerial/executive category, and the rest were semi-skilled. The four non-custodial mothers were in the secretarial field.

Findings: Some Personal Factors

The questions asked in this section related to personal aspects of life in a one-parent family. Eighteen of the subjects (40 percent) had moved to a new neighborhood after the separation. This, in turn, meant changes in schools and friendships. Over 70 percent of the children had contact "less than once a month" with paternal uncles, paternal grandparents, paternal cousins, maternal cousins, and maternal aunts. Maternal grandparents were seen more frequently by about 5.0 percent. Most of the contact was with visits, followed by telephone calls, and letters. It is of interest that since separation contact with maternal grandparents and maternal cousins has increased, and with paternal aunts and paternal cousins it has decreased.

The non-custodial parent was seen once a week by eight of the children, several times a month by nine, several times a year by eleven, once a month by five, and not at all by seven. Time with the non-custodial parent was spent (in order of frequency) going out for a meal, visiting friends and relatives, outdoor activities, watching television, going to the movies, and shopping. Of the children 70 percent (28) stated that they felt they had enough contact with their custodial parent, while 30 percent felt they did not. The residence of the non-custodial parent was in the same province (Ontario) for eighteen, in the same city (Toronto) for seventeen, in another province for four, and another country for one.

When asked with whom they had discussed the separation, the five most important persons, in order of frequency, were mother, friends, sister, brother, and father. The most helpful of these persons were the mother and friends. Of all the children, 55 percent (22) stated that the parents *had not talked to them about the separation, before it actually occurred*. When asked how they felt about the separation (in order of frequency) they felt upset, unhappy, confused, sad, worried and, in at least half of the situations studied, relieved. When asked how they preferred to spend their free time, they responded (in order of frequency) with a friend, in organized activities, by themselves, at home, and with the absent parent. When they had a problem, the subjects indicated that they talked most frequently with a friend, mother, and other persons; only four consulted the father.

At least half of the children indicated the following as advantages and disadvantages of living in a one-parent family: more household jobs; feeling closer to their mother; feeling closer to their sister; more friends from one-parent families; more independence; missing the absent parent; unpleasant chores; more self-confident; more freedom; spending more time alone; and an increase in baby-sitting duties. Some of the more salient disadvantages were that they came home to an empty house, they were not closer to their father, and their relocation to a new neighborhood.

The Voices of Children

The most interesting findings were the result of four open-ended questions in which the children had an opportunity to voice their opinions.

The following are some of the responses to the question – *If you had a friend whose parents were about to separate, what advice would you give him/her?*

Boys: age 12
- try to see the other parent off and on;
- don't feel guilty; try to take it calmly.

age 15
- go on with your life;
- forget about the separation, there is nothing you can do about it.

age 16
- helps child grow up more quickly.

age 17
- every separation is unique;
- stay out of parents' way and let parents make own decisions.

age 18
- look for the best side of it that you can;
- try to understand patiently what your parents are going through.

Girls: age 12
- get your say in about visiting arrangements with the parent not living at home;
- the absent parent will always love you;
- you will worry, but speak to father or mother.

age 13
- do not get mad at parents 'cause they need their own freedom;
- don't pity yourself;
- keep in touch with the parent you are not living with.

age 14
- it hurts at first and takes a long time to get over, and then it doesn't hurt so badly;
- you should think of both parents, and the "good times" that you had with the parent who's leaving and not only think of the bad times. This is because your sores have to heal ... you have to get over it.
- it doesn't mean they don't love you if they separate.

age 15
- don't feel guilty if your parents separate;
- try and look at both sides of the situation, mother's and father's;
- try not to get too bitter about it;
- tell them you are not the cause of their separation;
- don't accept any blame;
- it's okay to get upset but it's not the end of the world.

age 17
- don't take sides;
- try to be understanding;
- let parents work out own problems, don't get in the middle;
- go out if things at home are unpleasant, like fighting.

From their comments, these children seem to be very sensible and perceptive. Some are protective of their parents and realize that it is up to the adults to work things out. They also feel that they are not to blame for the separation of their parents, and that life must go on despite a change in family status. For some, the change means growing up quickly with disruptions in their regular routines. The hurt of the separation is evident and they especially do not want to be blamed for their parents' actions. They want to have a definite say about the visiting arrangements. They also feel trapped by double loyalty to the now separated parents.

The next question was – *If you were asked to talk to a group of parents who were about to separate, what advice would you give them?*

Boys: age 12 • keep calm, get the pain over with fast.

age 15 • would go to absent parent and tell them not to be too sweet, don't keep giving money and candy;

• to parent at home, don't lean too heavily on the child.

age 16 • to realize whom they could be hurting if they go through with separation.

age 17 • tell them whatever they do, to act their age;

• remember that the kids are going through times which are as tough or tougher.

age 18 • consider what it will do to your marriage in the future.

Girls: age 12 • to try and work out your problems and to try to agree on things;

• ask kids if they have problems;

• you should talk to each other;

• explain to your children exactly what is about to happen, what the custody arrangements are to be.

age 13 • don't ignore kids through this 'cause they'll feel rejected; they'll think it's their fault;

• make sure you are doing the right thing (make sure that you are doing what you think is best).

age 14 • I'd ask them why they were splitting up. Then I'd tell them to always explain fully to the kids because they are always the last to know and the people who suffer and are hurt the most. Tell the whole and not half-truths.

Children want to be told the truth about the separation; they do not want to be ignored at the time of family crisis. This is probably the most difficult part for parents, since they themselves may not really understand why the separation took place. In these situations the children often counsel their parents. It is evident from these interviews that parents fail to realize that their children are also experiencing the pain and anxiety of separation.

The third question was – *A friend at school asks you to tell him/her what life in a one-parent family is like, what would you tell him/her?*

Boys: age 12 • much like any other family, but you are minus a parent.

       age 15 • lots of time alone, convenience.

       age 16 • more freedom in a one-parent family, less rules and the child gets away with more the child becomes more self-sufficient.

       age 17 • it has its ups and downs, one hell of a lot harder than growing up in a regular family;
               • kids have to grow up much more quickly.

       age 18 • it's closer, more jobs, more responsibility.

Girls: age 13 • not so bad, I got used to it after a few months, I know my parents better;
               • more responsibility;
               • don't see other parent as much;
               • cannot talk to both parents about the same problem at the same time.

       age 14 • you miss the quality of the parent who is not living with you.

       age 15 • not really different from two-parent family, I still see both of my parents;
               • a lot more freedom.

       age 16 • get lonely at times without the other parents;
               • I don't want other people to know that I am from a single parent family.

       age 18 • at first it's hard to accept that your father or mother is gone, and if you don't go to as many places or do as many things without both parents being there;
               • still get to see dad and speak to him;
               • it's different you have to adjust to the absence of the non live-in parent, to the busy schedule of the other parent, and the lack of free time that he/she has to spend with you.

These children definitely feel the absence of the missing parent, and adjustment to the parent not living at home is a major change for them. While it takes some time to adjust to the many changes of a one-parent family, most children eventually become accustomed to the new family patterns.

The last question was – *Is there anything else you feel you want to add to this interview which might be of help to children in one-parent families?*

      Boys: age 17 • divorce or separation is something that just happens;
               • kids must understand that separation is not their fault;
               • kids no longer have to please both parents to avoid parents fighting;
               • kids should know that things will be hard at first, but kids should remain the same and keep trying.

age 16 • some children think it's the end of the world when parents split up;
  • they must realize that life in a single-parent family can be more rewarding than in a two-parent family;
  • while there are some losses, there are some gains;
  • it's not as bad as it first may seem.

age 18 • make your own way through your own problem;
  • don't let problems roll over you;
  • don't be afraid to have someone to talk to;
  • be careful but don't be afraid;
  • be more dependent on yourself.

Girls: age 16 • try behaving yourself, because your parents are going through a lot with this separation;
  • do not get involved in your parents' conflicts;
  • it's good to get involved in a group;
  • help each other along;
  • then meet other people.

age 12 • don't always complain or keep trying because it just puts more pressure on the parent who remains with you and try to help him/her as much as you can.

age 14 • take each day as it comes and don't worry; you're going to feel hurt and think that your parents split up because it was your fault. But take one day at a time and it will all blow over;
  • you won't forget your memories but you'll feel better eventually with time.

age 15 • children should realize that parent has more responsibility and should try to help out more and not cause extra hassles;
  • accept the fact;
  • don't let absent parent drift out of your life;
  • kids have to reach out to their parents as well as parents reaching out to the kids;
  • try to understand parents you are living with;
  • if something is bothering you, don't keep it for yourself, talk about it with friends or relatives.

This advice of these "veterans" to other children facing parental separation is to avoid involvement in their parents' conflicts and anxieties. These children are quite self-reliant and stoic in their attitude toward life in a one-parent family. For some, the new family form is even considered an improvement over the two-parent family situation. Perhaps most important of all is their realization and acceptance of extra household chores and added responsibilities.

Emerging Themes

From the open-ended questions, it is clear that these children understand that they are not responsible for their parents' separation. Moreover, they feel their parents' quarrels and disagreements are not their concern. On the other hand, they advocate empathy and understanding for their parents' experience at the time of the separation; and they want to know why their parents are separating. Despite their painful experiences, these children have a realistic outlook toward their situation and that of their parents throughout the separation struggle.

Included in their advice to parents is the fact that children want to be consulted regarding custody arrangements. Further, they want their parents to reconsider the separation, and stay together as long as possible. It is the adults who are separating, not the children, and they do not want to be placed in the middle of the adult fights; indeed, they tell parents to "grow up and act their age."

The responses to questions regarding life in a one-parent family indicate that children have less supervision, more freedom with fewer rules, and less discipline. It appears that children grow up more quickly in one-parent families, becoming more independent and assuming more responsibilities. They miss the absent parent and want to keep contact with him/her. In many cases, the family is drawn closer together as the children adjust to the new one-parent situation.

Conclusions

In reviewing previous studies related directly or indirectly to children in one-parent families, the following issues emerge: there are only a handful of studies; almost no study examines the longitudinal aspects of living in a one-parent family; most are based on interviews with parents; the samples used are small, primarily middle class, white, and urban, more studies are needed that address sociocultural, racial, and economic differences of children growing up in one-parent families; the majority of studies focus on children in divorced families, more studies are needed of widowed and unmarried one-parent families; it is also important to investigate more "coping" one-parent families and to understand the dynamics of child rearing in order to obtain a balanced picture; comparative studies of children in temporary versus permanent one-parent families are helpful.

Many children move into reconstituted families, while others remain in one-parent families; what effect does growing up in a one-parent family have on subsequent marriages of these children? Are one-parent families producing divorce-proof children?

This paper is an exploratory study into the lives of children in one-parent families from the children's viewpoint. It is hoped that this study will encourage other investigators to follow up on some of the issues suggested in this discussion. Only the children can tell us what it means to grow up in a one-parent family.

The last word is left to one of the children in this study – "separation and divorce for children is not the end of the world."

An Unwed Mother's Decision to Give up Her Child as a Consequence of Labelling[1]

Jacqueline C. Massé, Micheline St-Arnaud,
Marie-Marthe T.-Brault

The Problem

A lot of things have changed in Quebec over the last twenty years. From a cultural as well as a structural point of view, Quebec society has experienced a number of changes. These overall transformations have been accompanied by changes in attitudes and behaviors.

Thus, despite the diffusion of effective new contraceptives, the rate of births out of wedlock in Quebec went from 5.2 percent in 1965 to 7.4 percent in 1973, the national rate was 6.7 percent and 9 percent, respectively.[2] Moreover, the proportion of these children that were kept by their mothers increased: in the early 1960s, about two-thirds of the unwed mothers gave the child up for adoption and a third kept the child; however, in the early 1970s, the proportions were reversed.

There has been an increase in the number of unmarried women who decide to give birth to a child and to assume responsibility for it. Nevertheless, a good number of births outside wedlock are unplanned and occur among young adolescents who are very upset to learn they are pregnant. (In 1974, in Quebec, 34.2 percent of unwed mothers was less than twenty years of age.)[3] These adolescents, who do not abort their pregnancy, must decide whether to keep the child or to give the child up for adoption. This choice is surely a very important decision for them.

A number of factors, including medical, judicial, economic, psychological, and social, no doubt influence their decision. However, this article focusses

---

[1]This article has used data gathered in a study conducted in 1972-1975 and titled "Le dilemme de la mère célibataire: garder son enfant ou le confier pour adoption." Begun by the Ville-Marie Social Work Agency (today The Social Work Agency for Unwed Parents attached to the CSSMM), this study was subsequently carried out in the Sociology Department of the University of Montreal and was funded by the Canadian Minister of Health and Social Welfare. This article was translated by Ruth Ann Pitts.

[2]Statistiques de l'Etat civil.

[3]Centre des Services sociaux du Montréal métropolitain.

on the social factors that influence their decision, particularly the attitude of the surrounding groups toward unwed mothers.

Principal Studies of the Subject

A number of studies have dealt with the decision of unwed mothers to keep or give up their child. Researchers[4] have tried to explain this decision by establishing empirical relations between assorted social factors and the choice of the young women. Of all these factors, the relationships with the family, the natural father, and the opinions and prejudices of other social groups are of central importance. In general, these studies indicate that when these relationships are good the unwed mother tends to keep her child.

Just why this is so is difficult to explain since there are very few social theories that support the empirical studies on the subject. Hence, the purpose of this study is to provide a theoretical scheme to understand the link found by a number of studies between keeping the child and good relations with surrounding social groups.

Theory and Hypotheses

In so far as the unwed mother's situation is considered abnormal in relation to the traditional family, it is seen as a form of deviance. Labelling theory, which concerns non-criminal deviance, comes from the interactionist hypotheses of G. H. Mead (1934) and his students. Indeed, labelling theory was elaborated from a vision of society based mainly on relations among individuals inside institutions or relations between individuals and institutions. These relationships defined as a gestalt of interactions linked one to the other in a process of psychological and social interdependence. The principal authors of this theory[5] move the centre of interest from the individual and his/her personality to the social milieu, by making the social groups who create the norms and decide which individuals will be labelled deviant responsible for this deviance.

This theory is based, in part, on the fact that deviant behavior is tolerated by certain groups or sub-groups and penalized by others, that there are cultural differences between societies, and that judgments of deviance and social control vary from one epoch to another. This perspective implies a dynamic analysis of the phenomenon.

The first step in this theoretical elaboration is the social dimension of *perception*. Our perception of things and of persons is influenced by the constant interaction that forms the basis of social life. This interaction not only colors our attitudes and our daily behavior guiding our actions, it also influences the perception we have of ourselves. This perception of ourselves

---

[4]Costigan 1964; Festinger 1971; Grow 1969; Lincourt 1965; Meloche 1957; Meyer, Borgatta, and Fanshel 1959; Meyer, Jones, and Borgatta 1956; Sister Ste-Madeleine-du-Sauveur 1952; Vincent 1960; Yelloly 1965.

[5]Becker 1963; Erikson 1968; Goffman 1963; Kitsuse 1964; Lemert 1951, 1967; Sagarin 1977; Schur 1971; Scott 1969; Sheff 1966; Simmons 1969.

is intimately linked to the role that the individuals around us attribute to us and expect us to assume. According to Gerth and Mills (1967:186), "What we think of ourselves is decisively influenced by what others think of us." Meltzer (1967:10), commenting on the theories of G. H. Mead, affirms "The self is formed in the same way as other objects – through the 'definitions' made by others." Also, "One of the major variables which influence our behavior vis-à-vis another person is the sort of impression we have formed of him and the dispositions we have attributed to him." (Hastorf 1970:17) Thus, for the interactionists, an individual is deviant not because (s)he has performed a certain act, but because the persons around him/her react negatively to that act by judging it as deviant. This judgment of deviance is a process of interaction between the individual and the groups to which (s)he belongs that takes place in a given time and place.

To better understand this process of deviance, one must consider certain social processes, such as the formation of *stereotypes,* the progressive implication in a new role, and all the mechanisms of negotiation between the deviant individual and those who conform to the norm – the normals. As Schur (1971) points out, stereotypes play a primary role in the social process that creates deviance. When certain personality traits or behaviors are selected to globally identify a group of persons, stereotypes are created which are later very difficult to change. The stereotyped image which is conveyed through interaction with others becomes part of the psychological process of accepting the role that others expect us to assume. Erikson (1968) called this process "role commitment," or progressive implication in an attitude which conforms to the role assigned to us by the group.

Goffman (1963) studied this phenomenon and named it "moral career." He observed that interaction between stigmatized persons and so-called normal people caused a disturbance (generally non-pathological) in the personality of the former who then must seek an equilibrium between the normal person ego and the stigmatized person ego. He emphasized the importance of the other's behavior in this psychological process. He concluded that generally the person has great difficulty in perceiving him/herself as other than through the imposed stigmatized judgment.

Even having described the role of the social-psychological process of perception in the emergence of deviance, the following questions still beg investigation: Why are certain acts and/or certain individuals rather than others stigmatized? Who decides in a society what norms are to be followed and what categories are deviant?

It seems that the phenomenon is the result of *power relations* between certain values and certain groups. "Social groups create deviance by making rules whose infraction constitutes deviance and by applying those rules to particular people and labeling them as outsiders. From this point of view, deviance is *not** a quality of the act the person commits, but rather a consequence of the application by others or rules and sanctions to an *offender*.*" (Becker 1963:9) Those who dictate standards of behavior are in positions of power that command compliance. Becker cites adults who impose their norms

---

*Author's emphasis.

on youths, whites on blacks, men on women. Clearly, this political aspect of the phenomenon of deviance which is limited to conflicts of value and interests continually present in the society cannot be ignored.

Hypotheses. The purpose of this description of theories of deviance was to expose aspects which are most relevant to the data analysis of the present research. The principal ideas evolved are the social characteristics of deviance seen as the result of a sequence of interactions involving mainly the phenomenon of perception.

First, the perception of oneself is inevitably linked to the perception that others have of one and communicate to one by way of stereotypes. Thus, an individual is perceived and perceives him/herself as deviant, not because (s)he has committed a certain act, but because the persons surrounding him/her have reacted negatively by labelling him/her as deviant in the face of this act.

Unwed mothers, then, will perceive themselves as deviant if they feel rejected or are labelled as different by those around them; hence, the first hypothesis: *An unwed mother's perception that she is labelled deviant by the surrounding groups will lead her to label herself as deviant.*

Second, this perception that others have of an individual influences praxis and implies a role that is attributed to and expected of that person. Often the stigmatized individual will assume the role that the group has attributed.

This being the case, the attitude of surrounding groups with regard to the child as well as the unwed mother's feelings of acceptance or rejection by them will influence her decision to either keep the child or give the child up for adoption. The second hypothesis follows: *the unwed mother's perception that she is labelled deviant by her surrounding groups and the resulting self-labelling will influence her to give up her child, the symbol of her deviance.*

Methodology

Selection of Subjects. This research was undertaken with the collaboration of the Ville-Marie Social Work Agency of Montreal,[6] whose clientele is almost exclusively unwed mothers. The subjects for this study were selected from this clientele. Thus, it is not representative of all unwed mothers in the Montreal region, but of those who addressed themselves to this agency at that time.

Subjects selected were French Canadians living on the Montreal Island, who had given birth between March 1970 and March 1971, and whose child was living at the time of the interview. Of the 396 eligible persons, 180 (45.5 percent) completed the interview. Those interviewed were fairly representative of the total sample with regard to age, education, occupation, father's occupation, place of residence, and even their decision regarding the child.

Collection of the Data. In an interview averaging two and a half hours, data were collected using a questionnaire. Three factors were considered in the design of this questionnaire: a review of the pertinent literature; a composite

---

[6]Today, this agency is known as the Social Work Agency for Unwed Parents (CSSMM).

portrait of the typical young unwed mother from the experience of about twenty social workers; and anonymous biographical sketches from about fifteen unwed mothers.

From this information a questionnaire was constructed that covered the following sociological areas: (1) socio-economic characteristics; (2) social activities; (3) family relations; (4) sexual experiences; (5) information about the father of the child; (6) relations with the child's father; (7) history of the pregnancy; (8) relations with surrounding groups and help received from them; (9) factors influencing the decision concerning the child; (10) perception of the acceptance or rejection of unwed mothers; (11) future plans; and (12) information on the child.

Research Techniques. Indices were constructed according to the theoretical constructs to operationalize the concept of labelling central to the study. These indices were then linked to the decision in order to test both the theory and the empirical conclusions of the other researchers who had studied the link between the decision and relations with surrounding groups.

The dependent variable in this study was the mother's decision concerning the child, while the independent variables were the different levels of deviant labelling.

The labelling indices were constructed in light of the importance accorded perception. In particular, Lemert (1951) and Becker (1963) insisted that perception is at the heart of the emergence of deviance. Thus, they affirm that deviance is not the result of a particular act, but the result of the perception that one has of this act. In other words, deviance is born in peoples' minds, and the labelling that results is what is apparent.

Accordingly, construction of the indices that operationalize the labelling of the deviance surrounding unwed mothers was based on the perception of the respondents. Following Gerth and Mills (1967), Meltzer (1967), and Hastorf et al. (1970), two levels of perception were established: (1) one's self-image, and (2) the image that one believes others have of her. One of the poles of the first level is the perception of oneself as deviant, or the labelling of oneself as deviant. One of the poles of the second level is the perception that others judge one as deviant, or perception of deviant labelling by others.

Others were divided into two groups – the primary and secondary. Indeed, these two groups have very different characteristics. The primary group has a direct effect on the individual. Comprised essentially of family members, they are a part of her immediate surroundings and continue to have a certain authority over her. The influence of secondary groups is more diffuse. These are persons who are more removed, but who have the power – due to age, class or status – to make a judgment about her.

Thus, three indices of perception of deviant labelling were established: (1) the respondent's perception that she was deviant, or self-labelling; (2) the respondent's perception that the primary group labelled her as deviant; and (3) the respondent's perception that secondary groups labelled her as deviant.

Then, a certain number of indicators for each index was assigned. The first index (self-labelling) was made up of ten indicators, of which the most important were the way the respondent saw herself as a woman (the same or different from others); her fears (little or great) of losing the affection of others; and her estimate of the number (large or small) of unwed mothers in the society. The second index comprised twelve indicators, of which the most important were the respondent's mother's position (favorable or unfavorable) with regard to keeping the child, and the respondent's impression as to whether her decision was more or less influenced by her mother. The third index was composed of seventeen indicators, of which the most important were the social worker's position (favorable or unfavorable) with regard to keeping the child; the respondent's impression of having been more or less influenced by the social worker at the moment of the decision; and the attitude of age- and class-power people toward unwed mothers. All testing of the hypotheses was based on regression analysis.

Description of the Population Studies

The population of 180 unwed mothers interviewed had a median age of 20.8 years; the majority came from Montreal; half had completed at least ten years of education; and more than two-thirds were from working-class families.

When they became pregnant, one fourth of the respondents (27.8 percent) were students and two-thirds (65 percent) were employed. Over half (52.9 percent) of those employed had a semi-skilled or unskilled job, whereas 39.4 percent of the workers had either a white collar job or were skilled workers. At the time of the interview, there were few students in the group (9.4 percent), the proportion of workers had diminished also (to 48.9 percent), and two-fifths of the respondents (41.7 percent) stayed at home. Of the total, 67 percent had decided to keep the child.

The majority of the respondents did not label themselves as deviant, nor did they feel that they were labelled as deviant by their families. Nevertheless, more than half perceived that the secondary groups labelled them as deviant.

Results

Relationship Between Self-labelling and Labelling by Surrounding Groups. Labelling theory emphasizes individual perception. Thus, self-perception is intimately linked to the image that others project onto us and expect to see us reflect. Several authors have insisted on this aspect of social interaction. In particular, Lemert (1951), Gerth and Mills (1967), Becker (1963), Meltzer (1967), Hastorf et al. (1970) emphasized it. Indeed, they confirmed the strict interdependence between our self-image and the image that we think others have of us. In this context, deviance and the feelings we have about it are the result of others' judgments. According to these authors, an individual is deviant and perceives him/herself as such not because (s)he committed a certain act, but because, given the act, people in surrounding groups react negatively by labelling him/her as deviant.

The assumption was that this aspect of labelling theory would be revealed when applied to the population under study. Indeed, given that unwed mothers

Table 1:   The Gross Effect of Each of the Indices Measuring Labelling by Primary and Secondary Groups on Self-labelling

Indices	Zero-order Correlation Coefficients	Percentage of the Variance of the Dependent Variable Explained by the Independent Variable	Level of Significance
	(R)	(R^2)	(P)
Labelling by the Primary Group	.257	.066	.001
Labelling by Secondary Groups	.131	.017	.078

are rejected by certain persons, their feeling of deviance should increase when they perceive this normative rejection, or deviant labelling. This is the basis for the first hypothesis. Table 1 shows the relationship between labelling by primary and secondary groups and self-labelling. Only labelling by the primary group is significantly linked to self-labelling. This means that the influence of the primary group on the individual is primordial in this domain.

Table 2 presents the net effect of the two dimensions of labelling by surrounding groups on self-labelling. In Table 2, the regression coefficients are smaller than the correlation coefficients in Table 1, which indicates that there is a relationship between the two labelling indices. Table 2 shows that when the relationship between the two indices is eliminated, once again labelling by the primary group has a primordial effect on self-labelling. This relationship continues to be very significant, confirming the discovery made by analysing the gross effect of labelling by surrounding groups on self-labelling. Finally, labelling by surrounding groups explains 7.1 percent of the variance in self-labelling which is statistically significant.

Thus, the findings confirm that unwed mothers who perceive that they are stigmatized by the group immediately surrounding them are more likely to label themselves as deviant, while labelling by more distant groups has much less effect. Hence, the first hypothesis is supported, but only in part, by the study.

Relationship Between the Decision and Labelling. According to labelling theory, the individual conforms to the role that surrounding groups expect him/her to assume. The theories of Erikson (1968) and Goffman (1963) referred to earlier offer insight into the decision question. Indeed, perhaps the decision of these unwed mothers represents the acceptance of a role attributed to them by others. Perhaps those who feel that they have been labelled as deviant by others try to conform to their expectations by rejecting the child that the others have also rejected. Those who do not perceive

Table 2: Net Effect of Labelling by the Primary and Secondary Groups on Self-labelling

Indices	Regression Coefficient	Level of Significance
	(Beta)	(P)
Labelling by the Primary Group	.239	.002
Labelling by Secondary Groups	.077	.300

Multiple Correlation Coefficient: .267
Percentage of Variance Explained by all the Variables: .071
Level of Significance: .001

stigmatization by others would be more likely to keep their child. Thus, each would conform to the role attributed to her by the surrounding groups. This reasoning led to the second hypothesis.

Table 3 gives the gross effect (obtained by regression) of each labelling index on the decision. In this table, the three dimensions of deviant labelling that were considered are significantly related to the decision in the expected direction. Further, labelling by surrounding groups explains more of the variance in the decision (18.8 percent for secondary groups and 15 percent for the primary group) than self-labelling (7.3 percent). This supports the theory on which the study was based, namely, that individuals adopt their roles as a function of images projected from surrounding groups.

Thus, those unwed mothers who feel more stigmatized by the group immediately surrounding them and by more distant groups are those who are more likely to define themselves as deviant and to give their child up for adoption.

Table 3: The Gross Effect of the Indices of Labelling on the Decision

Indices	Correlation Coefficient	Percentage of the Variance of the Dependent Variable Explained by the Independent Variable	Level of Significance
	(R)	(R²)	(P)
Self-Labelling	.269	.073	.000
Labelling by the Primary Group	.388	.150	.000
Labelling by Secondary Groups	.434	.188	.000

Table 4:   Net Effect of Deviant Labelling on the Decision

Indices	Regression Coefficient	Level of Significance
	(Beta)	(P)
Self-labelling	.146	.031
Labelling by the Primary Group	.252	.000
Labelling by Secondary Groups	.365	.000

Multiple Correlation Coefficient: .538
Percentage of Variance Explained by all the Variables: .289
Level of Significance: .000

The net effect of the three dimensions of labelling on the decision is indicated in Table 4. In this table the regression coefficients are smaller than the corresponding zero-order correlation coefficients in Table 3, indicating that there are indeed certain relationships between the indices. Nevertheless, even when the mutual influence between indices is eliminated, each continues to have an effect on the decision in the same direction as found previously, and the relationships continue to be statistically significant. In addition, labelling by surrounding groups is still more strongly related to the decision than is self-labelling. All this supports earlier findings of the gross effects of labelling on the decision.

Finally, the three levels of labelling explain 28.9 percent of the decision, and this is statistically significant.

Thus, the findings confirm that an unwed mother's perception of deviant labelling by others and the perception of herself as deviant influence her decision to give up the child, the symbol of this deviance.

Summary and Conclusion

The goal of this study was to discover why certain unwed mothers keep their children while others give them up for adoption. Related literature indicated that those young women who continue to have good relations with their milieu after their pregnancy is disclosed are more likely to keep the child. To understand this conclusion, research was conducted within a conceptual scheme taken from the labelling theory of interactionists.

Two hypotheses were postulated: (1) an unwed mother's perception that she is labelled as deviant by the surrounding groups will lead her to label herself as deviant; and (2) an unwed mother's perception that she is labelled as deviant by her surrounding groups and the resulting self-labelling will influence her to give up her child, the symbol of her deviance.

The empirical results support these two hypotheses. There is a statistically significant relationship between self-labelling as deviant and labelling from the family. In addition, giving up the child is significantly linked to the respondents' feelings of deviance and their perception of being labelled as deviant by primary and secondary groups. Results confirm that there is definitely a correlation between keeping the child and the relationship with surrounding groups; those who tend to keep their child are generally on better terms.

These conclusions support the importance of the milieu for unwed mothers. Thus, the fact that two-thirds of unwed mothers gave up their children in the early 1960s while the same proportion kept their children in the early 1970s can be largely attributed to the change in attitude toward unwed mothers.

References

Abell, H. C. "The Women's Touch in Canadian Farm Work." *The Economic Annalist* 24 (1954):37-38.

Aberle, D., and Naegele, K. D. "Middle-class Fathers' Occupational Role and Attitudes Toward Children." In *Sourcebook in Marriage and the Family*, edited by M. B. Sussman, pp. 219-28. Cambridge, Mass.: Houghton Mifflin, 1955.

Aboud, Frances E. "Ethnic Self-Identity." In *A Canadian Social Psychology of Ethnic Relations*, edited by R. C. Gardner and R. Kalin, pp. 37-56. Toronto: Methuen, 1981.

Abu-Laban, Sharon. "Arab-Canadian Family Life." In *An Olive Branch on the Family Tree: The Arabs in Canada*, edited by Baha Abu-Laban, pp. 158-80. Toronto: McClelland and Stewart, 1980.

Adams, Bert N. *The Family: A Sociological Interpretation*. 3d rev. ed. Chicago: Rand McNally, 1980.

Adams, R. N. *The Second Sowing*. San Francisco: Chandler Publishing Co., 1967.

Aldous, Joan. "Occupational Characteristics and Males' Role Performance in the Family." *Journal of Marriage and the Family* 31 (1969):707-12.

Aldous, J.; Osmond, Marie W.; and Hicks, Mary W. "Men's Work and Men's Families." In *Contemporary Theories About the Family*, Vol. 1, edited by Wesley R. Burr and Reuben Hill. New York: The Free Press, 1978.

Allen, A., and Morton, A. *This Is Your Child: The Story of the National Society for the Prevention of Cruelty to Children*. London: Routledge and Kegan Paul, Ltd., 1961.

Altemeyer, R. A. *Right-wing Authoritarianism*. Winnipeg: University of Manitoba Press, 1981.

Ambert, Anne-Marie. *Sex Structure*. 2d rev. ed. Don Mills: Longman Canada, 1976.

—————————. *Divorce in Canada*. Don Mills: Academic Press, 1980.

Anderson, Alan, and Driedger, Leo. "The Mennonite Family: Culture and Kin in Rural Saskatchewan." In *Canadian Families: Ethnic Variations*, edited by K. Ishwaran. Toronto: McGraw-Hill Ryerson, 1980.

Anderson, Grace, and Higgs, David. *A Future to Inherit: The Portuguese Communities of Canada*. Toronto: McClelland and Stewart, 1976.

Antoniou, C. *Greek Family Life*. Ontario Ministry of Culture and Recreation: Multicultural Development Branch, 1974.

Arafat, I., and Yorburg, B. "On Living Together Without Marriage." *Journal of Sex Research* 9 (1973).

Armstrong, Pat, and Armstrong, Hugh. *The Double Ghetto. Canadian Women and Their Segregated Work*. Toronto: McClelland and Stewart, 1978.

Asch, S. E. "Effects of Group Pressure Upon the Modification and Distortion of

Judgements." In *Readings in Social Psychology*, edited by G. E. Swanson et al., pp. 2-11. New York: Holt, Rinehart and Winston, 1952.

Asch, S. E.; Bloch, H.; and Hertzman, M. "Studies in the Principles of Judgements and Attitudes: I. Two Basic Principles of Judgement." *Journal of Psychology* 5 (1938):210-51.

Association on American Indian Affairs. *Indian Family Defense* 11. New York, 1979.

Atkinson, R. G.; Clark, M. N.; Lucas, M. G.; and Wickett, G. S. "The Battered Child Syndrome." Master's thesis, University of British Columbia, 1965.

Axelrod, Morris. "Urban Structure and Social Participation." *American Sociological Review* 21 (1956):17.

Bahr, S.; Bowerman, C. E.; and Gecas, Viktor. "Adolescent Perceptions of Conjugal Power." *Social Forces* 52 (1974):357-67.

Bailey, Wm. C. "Murder and Capital Punishment: Some Further Evidence." *American Journal of Orthopsychiatry* 45, 4 (1975):669-88.

Balakrishnan, T. R.; Ebanks, G. E.; and Grindstaff, C. F. *Patterns of Fertility in Canada, 1971.* Ottawa: Statistics Canada, Minister of Supply and Services, 1971.

Baldus, B., and Tribe, V. "The Development of Perception and Evaluation of Social Inequality Among Public School Children." *Canadian Review of Sociology and Anthropology* 15 (1978):50-60.

Bandura, A.; Ross, D.; and Ross, S. A. "Imitation of Film – Mediated Aggression." *Journal of Abnormal and Social Psychology* 66 (1963):3-11.

Bard, Morton. *Family Crisis Intervention: From Concept to Implementation.* U.S. Department of Justice Monograph. Washington, D.C.: U.S. Government Printing Office, 1973.

––––––––––. "The Study and Modification of Intra-Familial Violence." In *Violence in the Family*, edited by Suzanne K. Steinmetz, and Murray A. Straus. New York: Dodd, Mead and Co., 1974.

Bard, M., and Zacker, J. "The Prevention of Family Violence: Dilemmas of Community Intervention." *Journal of Marriage and the Family* 33, 4 (1974):677-82.

Bardwick, Judith. *Psychology of Women.* New York: Harper & Row, 1971.

Barth, F. *Ethnic Groups and Boundaries.* Boston: Little, Brown, 1969.

Baxter, E. "Children's and Adolescents' Perceptions of Occupational Prestige." *Canadian Review of Sociology and Anthropology* 13 (1976):229-38.

Beattie, C.; Desy, J.; and Longstatt, S. *Bureaucratic Careers: Anglophones and Francophones in the Canadian Public Service.* Ottawa: Information Canada, 1972.

Becker, Howard S. *Outsiders. Studies in the Sociology of Deviance.* New York: The Free Press, 1963.

Bedau, Hugo, and Pierce, Chester M., eds. *Capital Punishment in the United States.* New York: AMS Press Inc., 1976.

Bell, Norman W., and Vogel, Ezra F. *A Modern Introduction to the Family*, 2d rev. ed. New York: The Free Press, 1968.

Bell, R. R. *Marriage and Family Interaction.* 5th rev. ed. Homewood, Ill.: Dorsey Press, 1979.

Bell, Wendell, and Boat, Marion D. "Urban Neighbourhoods and Informal Social Relations." *American Journal of Sociology* 62 (1957):395.

Bennett, J., ed. *The New Ethnicity.* Boston: West Publishing Co., 1975.

Bennett, James E., and Loewe, Pierre M. *Women in Business: A Shocking Waste of Human Resources.* Toronto: Financial Post Books, 1977.

Bennett, John W. "Reciprocal Economic Exchanges Among North American Agricultural Operators." *Southwest Journal of Anthropology* 24 (1968):276-309.

——————— . *Northern Plainsmen: Adaptive Strategy and Agrarian Life.* rev. ed. Arlington Heights, Ill.: AHM Publishing Co., 1976.

Bennett, John W., and Kohl, Seena B. "Characterological, Institutional, and Strategic Interpretations of Prairie Settlement." In *Western Canada Past and Present*, edited by A. W. Rasporich. Calgary: McClelland and Stewart West and the University of Calgary, 1975.

Bennett, John, and Tummin, Melvin M. *Social Life: Structure and Function.* New York: Alfred A. Knopf, 1948.

Bennie, E., and Sclare, A. "The Battered Child Syndrome." *American Journal of Psychiatry* 125, 7 (1969):975-79.

Berman, Louis A. *Jews and Intermarriages.* New York: Thomas Yoselaff, 1968.

Bernard, Jessie. *The Future of Marriage.* New York: Bantam Books, Inc., 1973.

Besanceney, P. H. "On Reporting Rates of Intermarriage." *The American Journal of Sociology* 70 (1965):718-19.

Blalock, Hubert M. Jr. *Social Statistics.* 2d rev. ed. Toronto: McGraw-Hill Ryerson, 1972.

Blau, Peter. *Exchange and Power in Social Life.* New York: John Wiley, 1964.

Blishen, B. "A Socio-economic Index for Occupations in Canada." *Canadian Review of Sociology and Anthropology* 4 (1967):41-53.

Blood, B., and Blood, M. *Marriage* 3d rev. ed. New York: The Free Press, 1978.

Blood, Robert O., and Hamblin, Robert L. "The Effects of the Wife's Employment on the Family Power Structure." In *A Modern Introduction to the Family*, 2d rev. ed., edited by W. Norman, and Ezra F. Vogel, pp. 182-87. New York: The Free Press, 1968.

Blood, R. O., and Wolfe, D. M. *Husbands and Wives: The Dynamics of Married Living.* New York: The Free Press, 1960.

Boardman, H. E. "A Project to Rescue Children From Inflicted Injuries." *Social Work* 7, 1 (1962):48.

Bobiwash, Libby, and Malloch, Lesley. *A Family Needs Survey.* Toronto: Native Canadian Centre, 1980.

Boissevain, Jeremy. *The Italians of Montreal. Social Adjustment in a Plural Society.* Ottawa: Queen's Printer, 1970.

——————— . "Family and Kinship Among Italians of Montreal." In *The Canadian Family Revised*, edited by K. Ishwaran. Toronto: Holt, Rinehart and Winston, 1976.

Booth, Alan. "Wife's Employment and Husband's Stress: A Replication and Refutation." *Journal of Marriage and the Family* 39 (1977).

Boyd, M.; Eichler, M.; and Hofley, J. R. "Family: Functions, Formation and Fertility." In *Opportunity for Choice: 1976,* edited by Gail Cook, pp. 13-52. Ottawa: C. D. Howe Research Institute, 1976.

Brabant, Sarah. "Sex role stereotyping in the Sunday Comics." *Sex Roles* 2 (1976):331-37.

Bradway, J. W. "What Family Members Should Know About the Law." In *Family, Marriage and Parenthood*, edited by H. Becker, and R. Hill. Boston: D. C. Heath, 1948.

Brandwein, R. A.; Brown, C. A.; and Fox, E. M. "Women and Children Last: the Social Situation of Divorced Mothers and Their Families." *Journal of Marriage and the Family* 35 (1974):498-514.

Breimeyer, Harold. *Individual Freedom and the Organization of Agriculture.* Urbana, Ill.: University of Illinois Press, 1965.

Brenton, M. *Runaways – Children, Husbands, Wives and Parents.* Boston: Little, Brown, 1978.

Breton, Raymond. "Institutional Completeness of Ethnic Communities and the Personal Relations of Immigrants." *American Journal of Sociology* 70 (1964):193-205.

_____. "Academic Stratification in Secondary School and the Educational Plans of Students." *Canadian Review of Sociology and Anthropology* 7 (1970):17-34.

_____. "The Structure of Relationships Between Ethnic Collectivities." In *Canadian Ethnic Mosaic*, edited by Leo Driedger, pp. 55-73. Toronto: McClelland and Stewart, 1978.

Breton, R.; Burnet, J.; Harmann, N.; Isajiw, W. W.; and Lennards, J. "The Impact of Ethnic Groups on Canadian Society: Research Issues." In *Identities*, edited by W. W. Isajiw, pp. 191-213. Toronto: Peter Martin, 1976.

Brettell, Carol. "Ethnicity and Entrepreneurs: Portuguese Immigrants in a Canadian City." In *Ethnic Encounters: Identities and Contexts*, edited by G. L. Hicks, and P. E. Leiss, pp. 169-80. Belmont, Calif.: Wadsworth, 1977.

Briar, Katherine H. *The Effect of Long-Term Unemployment on Workers and Their Families.* San Francisco: R. & E. Research Associates, Inc., 1978.

Brim Jr., Orville G., and Wheeler, S. *Socialization After Childhood.* New York: John Wiley, 1966.

Brinkerhoff, M. B., and Lupri, Eugen. "Theoretical and Methodological Issues in the Use of Decision-Making as an Indicator of Conjugal Power: Some Canadian Observations." *Canadian Journal of Sociology* 3 (1978):1-20.

Brown, D. G. "Masculinity-femininity Development in Children." *Journal of Consulting Psychology* 21 (1957):197-202.

Brown, J. K. "Economic Organization and the Position of Women Among the Iroquois." *Ethnohistory* 17 (1970):151-67.

Bruce, Christopher J. "The Effect of Young Children on Female Labour Force Participation Rates: An Exploratory Study." *Canadian Journal of Sociology* 3 (1978).

Buckley, Walter. *Sociology and Modern Systems Theory.* Englewood Cliffs, N.J.: Prentice-Hall, 1967.

Burgess, Ernest W. "The Family as a Unit of Interacting Personalities." *Family* 7 (1926):3-9.

Burke, Ronald J., and Weir, Tamara. "Relationship of Wive's Employment to Husband, Wife and Pair Satisfaction and Performance." *Journal of Marriage and the Family* 38 (1976).

Burr, Wesley R. *Theory Construction and the Sociology of the Family.* New York: John Wiley, 1973.

Butler, Peter M. "Involvement in Work and Family Worlds: A Study of Work-Family Linkages in Single-Earner and Dual-Earner Families." Ph.D. dissertation, University of Toronto, 1974.

Byrne, D. "Social Psychology and the Study of Sexual Behaviour." *Personality and Social Psychology Bulletin* 3 (1977):3-30.

Caffey, John; Silverman, Frederic N.; Kempe, C. Henry; Venters, Homer; and Leonard, Martha. "Child Battery: Seek and Save." *Medical World News* 13, 22 (1972).

Cameron, Silver D. "The State of the Union." *Weekend Magazine, Winnipeg Free Press,* 1977 05 07.

Campbell, Douglas F., and Neice, David C. *Ties That Bind - Structure and Marriage in Nova Scotia.* Port Credit, ON: The Scribblers' Press, 1979.

Campbell, J. K. *Honour, Family and Patronage.* Oxford: Clarendon Press, 1964.

Canada. Department of Manpower and Immigration. Canadian Immigration and Population Study. Green Paper, Volume 2, The Immigration Program. Ottawa: Minister of Manpower and Immigration, 1974.

Canada. Royal Commission of Agriculture and Rural Life. Report No. 10, The Home and Family in Rural Saskatchewan, Regina, 1956.

Canada. Royal Commission on the Status of Women in Canada. Ottawa: Information Canada, 1970.

Canada, Statistics Canada. *Dictionary of the 1971 Census Terms.* Ottawa: Minister of Industry, Trade and Commerce, 1972.

_____ . 1976 Census of Canada. *Lone-Parent Families.* Catalogue 93-833. Ottawa: Minister of Supply and Services, 1978.

_____ . 1976 Census of Canada. *Families: Introduction to Volume 4.* Catalogue 93-820. Ottawa: Minister of Supply and Services, 1979.

Capener, H., and Berkowitz, A. "The Farm Family: A Unique Organization." *New York State Food and Life Sciences Quarterly* (1976):8-11.

Carisse, Colette. "Cultural Orientations in Marriages Between French and English Canadians." In *The Canadian Family in Comparative Perspectives,* edited by Lyle E. Larson, 1976a.

_____ . "Life Plans of Innovative Women: A Strategy for Living Feminine Role." In *The Canadian Family in Comparative Perspectives,* edited by Lyle E. Larson, 1976b.

Carter, H., and Glick, P. C. *Marriage and Divorce: A Social and Economic Study,* rev. ed. Cambridge, Mass.: Harvard University Press, 1976.

Castillo, Gelia T. "The Changing Role of Women in Rural Societies: A Summary of Trends and Issues." *Seminar Report No. 12,* Agricultural Development Council Inc., New York, 1977.

Catton, W. R. "A Comparison of Mathematical Models for the Effect of Residential Propinquity of Mate-Selection." *American Sociological Review* 29 (1964).

Chafetz, Janet Saltzman. *Masculine/Feminine or Human?.* Itasca, Ill.: Peacock, 1974.

Chapman, F. A. R. *Everything You Should Know About Law and Marriage.* Toronto: Pagurin Press, 1968.

Chimbos, Peter D. "Immigrants' Attitudes towards Their Children's Interethnic Marriages in a Canadian Community." *International Migration Review* 5 (1971):5-7.

_____ . "The Greek-Canadian Family: Tradition and Change." In *Canadian Families - Ethnic Variations,* edited by K. Ishwaran. Toronto: McGraw-Hill Ryerson, 1980.

_____ . *The Canadian Odyssey: The Greek Experience in Canada.* Toronto: McClelland and Stewart, 1980.

Clark, Susan, and Harvey, Andrew. "The Sexual Division of Labour: The Use of Time." *Atlantis* 2 (1) (1976).

Clement, W. *The Canadian Corporate Elite: An Analysis of Economic Power.* Toronto: McClelland and Stewart, 1975.

Cohen, Anthony P. "The Political Context of Childhood: Leaders and Anti-Leaders in a Changing Newfoundland Community." In *Socialization and Values in Canadian Society: Volume One - Political Socialization,* edited by Elia Zureik, and Robert M. Pike, pp. 161-84. Toronto: McClelland and Stewart, 1975.

Coleman, James S. *The Adolescent Society.* New York: The Free Press, 1961.

Collins, Alice, and Pancoast, Diane. *Natural Helping Networks.* Washington, D.C.: National Association of Social Workers, 1976.

Cook, Gail C. *Opportunity for Choice: A Goal for Women in Canada.* Ottawa: Information Canada, 1976.

Coombs, L. C.; Freedman, R.; Friedman, J.; and Pratt, W. F. "Premarital Pregnancy and Status Before and After Marriage." *The American Journal of Sociology* 75 (1970):800-20.

Corbett, J. T. "Psychiatrist Reviews the Battered Child Syndrome and Mandatory Reporting Legislation." *North-West Medical* 63 (1964):920-22.

Corfman, Eunice. "Married Men: Work and Family." In *Families Today* Vol. 1 (HIMH Science Monographs 1), edited by Eunice Corfman. Rockville, Md.: National Institute of Mental Health, 1979.

Corrales, R. G. "Power and Satisfaction in Early Marriage." In *Power in Families,* edited by R. Cromwell, and D. Olson, pp. 197-216. New York: John Wiley, 1975.

Corrigan, Samuel W. "A Note on Canadian Indian Marriage Law." *Western Canadian Journal of Anthropology* 4 (1974):17-27.

Coser, Lewis A. *Continuities in the Study of Social Conflict.* New York: The Free Press, 1967.

Costigan, Barbara H. "The Unmarried Mother: Her Decision Regarding Adoption." Ph.D. dissertation, University of Southern California, 1964.

Counts, G. S. "The Social Status of Occupations: A Problem in Vocational Guidance." *School Review* 33 (1925):16-27.

Cromwell, R., and Olson, D. eds. *Power in Families.* New York: John Wiley, 1975.

Cruikshank, Julie. "Matrilocal Families in the Canadian North." In *The Canadian Family Revised,* edited by K. Ishwaran. Toronto: Holt, Rinehart and Winston, 1976.

————————. *Athabascan Women: Lives and Legends.* Ottawa: Canadian Ethnology Service. Paper no. 57, 1979.

Crysdale, Stewart. "Workers' Families and Education in a Downtown Community." In *The Canadian Family Revised,* edited by K. Ishwaran. Toronto: Holt, Rinehart and Winston, 1976.

————————. "Social Effects of a Factory Relocation." In *Canada: A Sociological Profile,* edited by W. E. Mann. Toronto: Copp Clark Publishing Co., 1968.

Cuber, John F., and Haroff, Peggy B. *The Significant Americans.* New York: Appleton-Century, 1965.

Cuneo, C. J., and Curtis, J. E. "Social Ascription in the Educational and Occupational Status Attainment of Urban Canadians." *Canadian Review of Sociology and Anthropology* 12 (1975):6-24.

Curtis, G. C. "Violence Breeds Violence - Perhaps." *American Journal of Psychiatry* (1963):120-386.

Dahl, Robert A. *Who Governs?* New Haven: Yale University Press, 1975.

Damas, D. "The Problem of the Eskimo Family." In *The Canadian Family*, edited by K. Ishwaran. Toronto: Holt, Rinehart and Winston, 1971.

Danziger, Kurt. *The Socialization of Immigrant Children*. Ethnic Research Programme, I.B.R., York University, 1971.

——————. "Differences in Acculturation and Patterns of Socialization Among Italian Immigrant Families." In *Socialization and Values in Canadian Society*, Volume II, edited by R. M. Pike, and E. T. Zureick. Toronto: Carleton Library, 1975.

——————. "The Acculturation of Immigrant Italian Girls." In *The Canadian Family Revised*, edited by K. Ishwaran. Toronto: Holt, Rinehart and Winston, 1976.

——————. "Attitudes to Parental Control and Adolescents' Aspirations – A Comparison of Immigrants and Non-Immigrants." In *Childhood and Adolescence in Canada*, edited by K. Ishwaran. Toronto: McGraw-Hill Ryerson, 1980.

Darroch, Gordon. "Urban Ethnicity in Canada: Personal Assimilation and Political Communities." *Canadian Review of Sociology and Anthropology* 18 (1981):93-100.

Darroch, Gordon A., and Marston, Wilfred G. "An Examination of the Social Class Basis of Ethnic Residential Segregation." *American Journal of Sociology* 77 (1971):491-510.

Davis, A. F. "Prestige of Occupations." *British Journal of Sociology* 3 (1952):134-47.

Davis, Kingsley. *Human Society*. New York: Macmillan, 1952.

Davis, P. "Contextual Sex – Saliency and Sexual Activity: The Relative Effects of Family and Peer Groups in the Sexual Socialization Process." *Journal of Marriage and the Family* 36 (1974):196-202.

Dawson, Richard E., et al. *Political Socialization*. 2d rev. ed. Boston: Little, Brown, 1977.

Driedger, Leo. "Urbanization of Ukrainians in Canada: Consequences for Ethnic Identity." In *Changing Realities: Social Trends among Ukrainian Canadians*, edited by W. R. Petryshyn, pp. 107-33. Edmonton: Canadian Institute of Ukrainian Studies, 1980.

Driedger, Leo, and Church, Glenn. "Residential Segregation and Institutional Completeness: A Comparison of Ethnic Minorities." *Canadian Review of Sociology and Anthropology* 11 (1974):30-52.

Driedger, Leo; Valle, Frank; and De Vries, John. "Towards an Ecology of Language Characteristics in Canada." In *Language and the Politics of Accommodation: Comparative Studies in Educational Socio-Linguistics*, edited by Robert N. St. Clair, and Moshe Nahir. Louisville: University of Kentucky Press, in Press, 1982.

Duberman, Lucile. *Marriage and Other Alternatives*. New York: Praeger, 1976.

Dubin, Robert. "Industrial Workers' Worlds: A Study of the Central Life Interests of Industrial Workers." *Social Problems* (1956):131-41.

Dunning, R. W. "Rules of Residence and Ecology Among the Northern Ojibwa." In *The Canadian Family*, edited by K. Ishwaran. Toronto: Holt, Rinehart and Winston, 1971.

Dyer, W. G. "Parental Influence on the Job Attitudes of Children from two Occupational Strata." *Sociology and Social Research* 42 (1958):203-06.

Earl, G. H. "Ten Thousand Children Battered and Starved." *Today's Health* (September, 1965):51.

Eaton, J. W. "Controlled Acculturation." *American Sociological Review* 17 (1952).

Edwards, J. N., and Booth, A. "Sexual Behaviour In and Out of Marriage: An Assessment of Correlates." *Journal of Marriage and the Family* 38 (1976):73-81.

Eichler, Margrit. "The Equalitarian Family in Canada." In *Marriage, Family and Society: Canadian Perspectives*, edited by S. Parvez Wakil. Toronto: Butterworths, 1975.

_____ . "Power, Dependency, Love and the Sexual Division of Labour." Unpublished. Toronto: Ontario Institute for Studies in Education, 1976.

Eisenberg, Phillip, and Lazarsfeld, Paul F. "The Psychological Effects of Unemployment." *Psychological Bulletin* 35 (1938):358-90.

Eleen, John W., and Bernardine, Ashley G. *Shutdown: The Impact of Plant Shutdown, Extensive Employment Terminations and Layoffs on the Workers and the Community.* Toronto: Ontario's Federation of Labour, CLC, 1971.

Elkin, Frederick. *The Family in Canada.* Ottawa: Vanier Institute of the Family, 1964.

_____ . "Life Styles of Canadian Families." In *Marriage, Family and Society*, edited by S. Parvez Wakil. Toronto: Butterworths, 1975.

Elkin, Frederick, and Handel, Gerald. *The Child and Society.* New York: Random House, 1978.

Ellis, Albert. *The American Sexual Tragedy.* New York: Twayne, 1954.

Elmer, Elizabeth. "Child Abuse: The Family's Cry For Help." *Journal of Psychiatric Nursing* 5, 4 (1967):332-41.

Elmer, Elizabeth, and Gregg, Grace. "Developmental Characteristics of Abused Children." In *Child Abuse and Violence*, edited by David G. Gil, pp. 295-307. New York: AMS Press Inc., 1979.

Epstein, A. L. *Ethos and Identity.* London: Tavistock, 1978.

Epstein, Cynthia Fuchs. "Law Partners and Marital Partners (Strains and Solutions in the Dual-Career Family Enterprise)." *Human Relations* (1971):549-64.

Ercul, D., Goldenberg, N., and Schlesinger, B. "Children in One-Parent Families." In *One in Ten – The Single Parent in Canada*, edited by B. Schlesinger. pp. 16-20. Toronto: University of Toronto, 1979.

Erikson, Kai T. "Patient Role and Social Uncertainty." In *Deviance: The Interactionist Perspective*, edited by Earl Rubington, and Martin S. Weinberg, pp. 337-43. New York: Macmillan, 1968.

Eron, L.; Walder, L. O.; and Lefkowitz, M. M. *Learning of Aggression in Children.* Boston: Little, Brown, 1971.

Eshleman, J. Ross. *The Family: An Introduction.* 2d rev. ed. Boston: Allyn and Bacon, Inc., 1978.

Fagot, B. I., and Patterson, G. "An in vivo analysis of reinforcing contingencies for sex role behaviours in the preschool child." *Developmental Psychology* 1 (1969).

Farber, Bernard. *Family: Organization and Interaction.* San Francisco: Chandler Publications, 1964.

Farner, O. *Huldrych Zwingli.* Zuerich: Zwingli – Verlag, 1954.

Fels, Julie. *Ontario Native Women: A Perspective.* Thunder Bay, ON: Ontario Native Women's Association, 1980.

Fernandez, Ronald. *The Social Meaning of Being Portuguese Canadian.* Toronto: Multicultural Historical Society of Ontario, 1979.

Feshbach, Norma D. "The Effects of Violence in Childhood." In *Child Abuse and Violence*, edited by David G. Gil, pp. 575-85. New York: AMS Press Inc., 1979.

Festinger, Trudy B. "Unwed Mothers and their Decisions to Keep or Surrender Children." *Child Welfare* 50, 5 (1971):253-63.

Firth, Raymond. *Two Studies of Kinship in London.* London: University of London, 1956.

Firth, Raymond; Herbert, Jane; and Forge, Anthony, eds. *Families and Their Relatives.* London: Routledge & Kegan Paul, 1969.

Fisher, S. H. "Skeletal Manifestations of Parent-Induced Trauma in Infants and Children." *Southern Medical Journal* 51 (1958):956-60.

Fogarty, Michael P., et al. *Sex, Career and Family.* London: George Allen and Unwin Ltd., 1971.

Fontana, V. J. *The Maltreated Child. The Maltreatment Syndrome in Children.* Springfield, Ill.: Charles C. Thomas, 1964.

_____. "Recognition for Maltreatment and Prevention of the Battered Child Syndrome." *Pediatrics* 38 (1966):1078.

Forbes, H. D. "Conflicting National Identities Among Canadian Youth." In *Foundations of Political Culture: Political Socialization in Canada*, edited by Jon H. Pammett, and Michael S. Whittington, pp. 288-315. Toronto: Macmillan, 1976.

Forcese, Dennis, and Richer, Stephen. "Socialization: Becoming Canadians." In *Issues in Canadian Society: An Introduction to Sociology*, edited by Dennis Forcese, and Stephen Richer, pp. 21-53. Scarborough: Prentice-Hall, 1975.

Fraser, B. G. "A Pragmatic Alternative to Current Legislative Approaches to Child Abuse. *American Criminal Law Review* 12 (1974):103-24.

Freedman, J. D. "On the Concept of the Kindred." *Journal of the Royal Anthropological Institute* 91 (1961):192-220.

Friedan, Betty. *The Feminine Mystique.* New York: Dell, 1963.

Frideres, J.; Goldstein, Jay; and Gilbert, R. "The Impact of Jewish-Gentile Intermarriages in Canada: An Alternative View." *Journal of Comparative Family Studies* 2 (1971).

Friedl, E. *Men and Women: An Anthropological View.* New York: Holt, Rinehart and Winston, 1975.

Friedmann, Robert. *Hutterite Studies*, edited by H. S. Bender. Goshen, Ind.: Mennonite Historical Society, 1961.

Furstenberg, Frank F. Jr. "Work Experience and Family Life." In *Work and the Quality of Life*, edited by James O'Toole, pp. 341-60. Cambridge, Mass.: The MIT Press, 1974.

Garbin, A. P., and Bates, F. L. "Occupational Prestige and its Correlates: A Re-examination." *Social Forces* 44 (1966):295-302.

Garigue, Philippe. "French-Canadian Kinship and Urban Life." *American Anthropologist* 58 (1956):1090-101.

_____. *La Vie Familiale des Canadiens Francais.* Montreal: Presses de l'Université de Montreal, 1962.

_____. "Change and Continuity in Rural French Canada." In *French Canadian Society* Vol. 1. Carleton Library No. 18, edited by Marcel Rioux, and Yves Martin. Toronto: McClelland and Stewart, 1964.

_____. "The French-Canadian Family." In *Canadian Society*, edited by Bernard R. Blishen, et al. Toronto: Macmillan, 1968.

Gaskell, Jane S. "Sex-role ideology of working class girls." *The Canadian Review of Sociology and Anthropology* 12 (1975):453-61.

Gavaki, Efie. "The Greek Family in Canada: Continuity and Change in the Process of Adjustment." *International Journal of Sociology of the Family* 9 (1979):1-16.

Gavron, Hannah. *The Captive Wife: Conflicts of Housebound Mothers.* Middlesex: Pelican Books, 1968.

Gelles, Richard J. *The Violent Home: A Study of Physical Aggression between Husbands and Wives.* Beverly Hills, Calif.: Sage Publications, 1972.

——————. "Child Abuse as Psychopathology: A Sociological Critique and Reformulation." *American Journal of Orthopsychiatry* 43, 4 (1973):618.

Gelles, Richard J., and Straus, Murray A. "Family Experience and Public Support of the Death Penalty." In *Child Abuse and Violence*, edited by David G. Gil, pp. 530-57. New York: AMS Press Inc., 1979.

Gennard, John, and Lasko, Roger. "The Individual and the Strike." *British Journal of Industrial Relations* 13, 3 (1975):346-70.

Genoves, Santiago. *Is Peace Inevitable?.* New York: Walker and Co., 1970.

Gérin, L. "The French-Canadian Family: Its Strength and Weaknesses." In *French Canadian Society* Vol. 1. Carleton Library No. 18, edited by Marcel Rioux, and Yves Martin. Toronto: McClelland and Stewart, 1964.

Gerth, H., and Mills, C. W., eds. *From Max Weber.* New York: Oxford University Press, 1958.

————. "Institutions and Persons." In *Symbolic Interaction*, edited by Jerome G. Manis and Bernard N. Meltzer. Boston: Allyn and Bacon, 1967, pp. 185-89.

Gil, David G. "Incidence of Child Abuse and Demographic Characteristics of Persons Involved." In *The Battered Child*, edited by R. E. Helfer, and C. H. Kempe, pp. 24-25. Chicago and London: University of Chicago Press, 1968.

————. *Violence Against Children.* Cambridge, Mass.: Harvard University Press, 1970.

————. "Violence Against Children." *Journal of Marriage and the Family* 33, 4, (1971):637-48.

————. "Unraveling Child Abuse." In *Child Abuse and Violence*, edited by David G. Gil, p. 4. New York: AMS Press Inc., 1979.

Gilbert, S., and McRoberts, H. A. "Academic Stratification and Education Plans: A Reassessment." *Canadian Review of Sociology and Anthropology* 14 (1977):34-47.

Gilder, George. *Naked Nomads: Unmarried Men in America.* New York: Times Books, 1974.

Gillespie, Dair. "Who Has the Power? The Marital Struggle." *Journal of Marriage and the Family* 33 (1971):445-58.

Gillespie, R. "The Battered Child Syndrome: Thermal and Caustic Manifestations." *Journal of Trauma* 5 (1965):523-34.

Gilson, J. C. "Family Farm Business Arrangements." Agricultural Economics Bulletin 1, Faculty of Agriculture and Home Economics, University of Manitoba, 1959.

Glass, S. P., and Wright, T. L. "The relationship of Extramarital Sex, Length of Marriage, and Sex Differences on Marital Satisfaction and Romanticism: Athanasiou's Data Reanalyzed." *Journal of Marriage and the Family* 39 (1977):691-703.

Glazer, N., and Moynihan, D., eds. *Ethnicity: Theory and Experience.* Cambridge, Mass: Harvard University Press, 1975.

Glazer-Malbin, Nona. "Housework." *Signs: Journal of Women in Culture and Society* 1 (1976):905-22.

Glenn, N. D., and Weaver, C. N. "Attitudes Toward Premarital, Extramarital, and Homosexual Relations in the U.S. in the 1970's." *The Journal of Sex Research* 15 (1979):108-18.

Glick, P. C. "The Life Cycle of the Family." *Marriage and Family Living* 17 (1965).

Glick, Paul C., and Norton, Arthur J. "Marrying, Divorcing, and Living Together in the U.S. Today." *Population Bulletin* 32 (1977).

Glueck, Sheldon, and Glueck, Eleanor. *One Thousand Juvenile Delinquents.* Cambridge: Harvard University Press, 1934.

——————. "Working Mothers and Delinquency." *Mental Hygiene*, (1957):327-52.

Goffman, Irving. *Stigma.* Englewood Cliffs, N.J.: Prentice-Hall, 1963.

Gold, Dolores. "Full-time employment of mothers in relation to their 10-year-old children." Paper presented at Research for Women: Current Projects and Future Directions, An Interdisciplinary Conference, 1976, at Mount Saint Vincent University, Halifax, Nova Scotia.

Goldberg, Philip A. "Are men prejudiced against women?" *Transaction* 5 (1968):28-30.

Goldenberg, Sheldon. "Kinship and Ethnicity Viewed as Adaptive Responses to Location in the Opportunity Structure." *Journal of Comparative Family Studies* 18 (1977):149-65.

Goldlust, John, and Richmond, Anthony. "Factors Associated with Commitment to and Identification with Canada." In *Identities*, edited by W. W. Isajiw, pp. 132-53. Toronto: Peter Martin, 1978.

Goode, William J. *After Divorce.* New York: Macmillan, 1956.

——————. "The Theoretical Importance of Love." *American Sociological Review* 24 (1959).

——————. "The Sociology of the Family." In *Sociology Today*, Vol. I, edited by Robert K. Merton, et al., p. 179. New York: Harper & Row, 1959.

——————. "A Theory of Role Strain." In *Selected Studies in Marriage and the Family*, edited by Robert F. Winch, et al., pp. 82-101. New York: Holt, Rinehart and Winston, 1962.

——————. *World Revolution and Family Patterns.* New York: The Free Press, 1963.

——————. "The Protection of the Inept." *American Sociological Review* 32 (1967):3-18.

——————. "Force and Violence in the Family." *Journal of Marriage and the Family* 33, 4 (1971):624-36.

Gordon, Michael. "Was Waller Ever Right? The Rating and Dating Complex Reconsidered." *Journal of Marriage and the Family* 43 (1981).

Gorer, Geoff. *The American People: A Study in National Character.* New York: Norton, 1964.

Gorer, G. "Man Has No 'Killer' Instinct." In *Man and Aggression*, edited by Ashley Montagu. New York: Oxford University Press, 1968.

Goyder, J. C., and Curtis, J. E. "Occupational Mobility in Canada over Four Generations." *Canadian Review of Sociology and Anthropology* 14 (1977):303-19.

Greenfield, Sydney. "Love and Marriage in Modern America." *Sociological Quarterly* 4 (1965).

Greenglass, Esther R. "A Comparison of Maternal Communication Style between

Immigrant Italian and Second Generation Italian Women Living in Canada." *Journal of Cross-Cultural Psychology* 3 (1972):185-92.

Gregg, Allan, and Whittington, Michael S. "Regional Variation in Children's Political Attitudes." In *The Provincial Political Systems: Comparative Essays*, edited by David J. Bellamy et al., pp. 76-85. Toronto: Methuen, 1976.

Griswold, Whitney. *Farming and Democracy.* New York: Harcourt, Brace and Co., 1948.

Grow, Lucille J. "The Unwed Mother Who Keeps Her Child." In *The Double Jeopardy, The Triple Crisis: Illegitimacy Today*, pp. 115-25. New York: National Council on Illegitimacy, 1969.

Gunn, B. "Children's Conceptions of Occupational Prestige." *Personnel and Guidance Journal* 42 (1964):558-63.

Gusfield, Joseph R. "Tradition and Modernity: Misplaced Polarities in the Study of Social Change." *American Journal of Sociology* 72 (1967).

Haller, A. O.; Holsinger, D. B.; and Savaiva, H. U. "Variations in Occupational Prestige Hierarchies." *American Journal of Sociology* 77 (1972):941-56.

Haller, A. O., and Lewis, D. M. "The Hypothesis of Intersocial Similarity in Occupational Prestige Hierarchies." *American Journal of Sociology* 72 (1966):210-16.

Hansen, D. O., and Converse, J. W. "Cultural Milieu and Isolation as Sources of Intra-societal Variation in Occupational Prestige Hierarchies; Recent Brazilian Data." *Rural Sociology* 41 (1976):371-81.

Hansen, Donald A., and Hill, Reuben. "Families Under Stress." In *Handbook of Marriage and the Family*, edited by Harold T. Christensen, pp. 782-819. Chicago: Rand McNally, 1964.

Harney, Robert F. "The Italian Community in Toronto." In *Two Nations, Many Cultures: Ethnic Groups in Canada*, edited by J. L. Elliott, pp. 220-36. Scarborough, Ont.: Prentice-Hall, 1979.

Harvey, E., and Harvey, L. R. "Adolescence, Social Class and Occupational Expectation." *Canadian Review of Sociology and Anthropology* 7 (1970):138-47.

Hastorf, Albert H. et al. *Person Perception.* Reading, Mass.: Addison-Wesley, 1970.

Hatt, P. K. "Occupation and Social Stratification." *American Journal of Sociology* 55 (1950):533-43.

Hedlund, D., and Berkowitz, A. "A Review of Farm Family Research 1965-1977." Mimeo, Department of Education, Cornell University, n. d.

Heer, David M. "The Trend of Interfaith Marriages in Canada: 1922-1957." *American Sociological Review* 27 (1962).

_____. "The Measurement and Bases of Family Power: An Overview." *Marriage and Family Living* 25 (1963):133-39.

Heer, David M., and Hubey, Jr., Charles A. "The Trend of Interfaith Marriages in Canada: 1922 to 1972." In *Marriage, Family and Society*, edited by S. Parvez Wakil. Toronto: Butterworths, 1975.

Helfer, R. E. "The Responsibility and Role of the Physician." In *The Battered Child*. 2d rev. ed., edited by R. E. Helfer, and C. H. Kempe, p. 33. Chicago: University of Chicago Press, 1974.

Henripin, J., and Légaré, J. "Recent Trends in Canadian Fertility." *Review of Canadian Sociology and Anthropology* 3 (1971).

Henshel, Ann Marie. "Swinging: A Study of Decision-Making in Marriage." *American Journal of Sociology* 78 (1973).

Hepworth, H. Philip. *Services for Abused and Battered Children.* Ottawa: The Canadian Council on Social Development, 1975.

_____ . *Foster Care and Adoption in Canada.* Ottawa: Canadian Council on Social Development, 1980.

Herold, Edward S., and Goodwin, Marilyn R. "The Adoption of Oral Contraceptives Among Adolescent Females: Reference Group Influence." In *Childhood and Adolescence in Canada*, edited by K. Ishwaran. Toronto: McGraw-Hill Ryerson, 1979.

Hetherington, E. M.; Cox, M.; and Cox, R. "Divorced Fathers." *Family Co-ordinator* 25 (1976):417-28.

Hill, R. Foreword. In *Power in Families*, edited by R. Cromwell and D. Olson. New York: John Wiley, 1975.

Hill, Reuben, and Hansen, Donald A. "The Identification of Conceptual Frameworks Utilized in Family Study." *Marriage and Family Living* 22 (1960):299-311.

Hobart, C. W. "Attitudes Toward Parenthood Among Canadian Young People." *Journal of Marriage and the Family* 35 (1973):93-101.

_____ . "Ownership of Matrimonial Property." *The Canadian Review of Sociology and Anthropology* 12 (1975).

_____ . "Orientations to Marriage Among Young Canadians." In *The Canadian Family in Comparative Perspective*, edited by Lyle E. Larson. Scarborough, Ont.: Prentice-Hall, 1976.

_____ . "The Changing Family Patterns among Ukrainian-Canadians in Alberta." In *The Canadian Family in Comparative Perspective*, edited by L. E. Larson, pp. 351-65. Scarborough, Ont.: Prentice-Hall, 1976.

Hodge, R. W. et al. "A Comparative Study of Occupational Status." In *Class, Status and Power*, edited by R. Bendix and S. M. Lipset, pp. 309-34. New York: The Free Press, 1960.

Hodge, R. W.; Seigel, P. M.; and Rossi, P. H. "Occupational Prestige in the United States, 1925-63." *American Journal of Sociology* 70 (1964):286-302.

Hodgetts, A. B. *What Culture? What Heritage?.* Toronto: Ontario Institute for Studies in Education, 1968.

Holmstrom, Lynda Lytle. *The Two-Career Family.* Cambridge, Mass.: Schenkman Publishing Company, 1972.

Homans, George C. *Social Behaviour.* New York: Harcourt, Brace and World, 1961.

Horowitz, Donald L. "Ethnic Identity." In *Ethnicity: Theory and Experience*, edited by N. Glazer and D. P. Moynihan, pp. 111-40. Cambridge, Mass.: Harvard University Press, 1975.

Hoshino, G., and Yoder, G. H. "Administrative Discretion in the Implementation of Child Abuse Legislation." *Child Welfare*, 52, 7 (1973):414-24.

Hostetler, John A., and Huntington, Gertrude. *The Hutterites in North America.* New York: Holt, Rinehart and Winston, 1967.

Hruby, F. *Die Wiedertaeufer in Maehren.* Nachfolger: Leipzig M. Heinius, 1935.

Huber, Joan, and Spitze, Glenna. "Considering Divorce: An Explanation of Becker's Theory of Marital Instability." *American Journal of Sociology* 86 (1) (1980):75-89.

Huffman, W. E. "The Value of the Productive Time of Farm Wives: Iowa, North Carolina and Oklahoma." *American Journal of Agricultural Economics* (1976):836-43.

Hughes, Everett H. "Industry and the Rural System in Quebec." In *French Canadian*

Society Vol. 1. Carleton Library No. 18, edited by Marcel Rioux, and Yves Martin. Toronto: McClelland and Stewart, 1964.

The Humanist. "New Forms of Marriage." Volume 34 (1974).

Hunter, A. A. "A Comparative Analysis of Anglophone-Francophone Occupational Prestige Structures in Canada." *Canadian Journal of Sociology* 2 (1977):179-93.

Hurtig, Mel. *Never Heard of Them. . .They Must Be Canadian.* Toronto: Canadabooks, 1975.

Hyman, R. "Living With Strikes." *New Society* 25 (1973).

Imberman, Woodroof. "Strikes Cost More Than You Think." *Harvard Business Review* (May/June, 1978).

Indian and Northern Affairs. *Indian Conditions: A Survey.* Ottawa, 1980.

Irving, Howard. *The Family Myth.* Toronto: Copp Clark, 1972.

Isajiw, W. W. "The Process of Maintenance of Ethnic Identity." In *Sounds Canadian*, edited by P. M. Migus, pp. 129-38. Toronto: Peter Martin, 1975.

Ishwaran, K. *Family Life in the Netherlands.* The Hague: Van Keulers, 1959.

_____ . *The Canadian Family.* Toronto: Holt, Rinehart and Winston, 1971.

_____ . "The Canadian Family: Variations and Uniformities." In *Social Process and Institution: The Canadian Case*, edited by J. E. Gallagher, and R. D. Lambert. Toronto: Holt, Rinehart and Winston, 1971.

_____ . *The Canadian Family Revised.* Toronto: Holt, Rinehart and Winston, 1976.

_____ . "Family and Community Among the Dutch Canadians." In *The Canadian Family Revised*, edited by K. Ishwaran, pp. 266-88. Toronto: Holt, Rinehart and Winston, 1976.

_____ . "Family, Church and School in a Dutch-Canadian Community." In *The Canadian Family Revised*, edited by K. Ishwaran, pp. 356-79. Toronto: Holt, Rinehart and Winston, 1976.

_____ . *Family, Kinship and Community.* Toronto: McGraw-Hill Ryerson, 1977.

_____ . *Canadian Families: Ethnic Variations.* Toronto: McGraw-Hill Ryerson, 1980.

Ishwaran, K., and Chan, K. B. "The Socialization of Rural Adolescents." In *Childhood and Adolescence in Canada*, edited by K. Ishwaran, pp. 97-118. Toronto: McGraw-Hill Ryerson, 1979.

_____ . "Time, space, and Family Relations in a Rural Dutch Community." In *Canadian Families – Ethnic Variations*, edited by K. Ishwaran, pp. 198-220. Toronto: McGraw-Hill Ryerson, 1980.

Jabbra, Joseph G., and Landes, Ronald G. *The Political Orientations of Canadian Adolescents: Political Socialization and Political Culture in Nova Scotia.* Halifax: Saint Mary's University, 1974.

_____ . "Political Orientations Among Adolescents in Nova Scotia: An Exploratory Study of a Regional Political Culture in Canada." *Indian Journal of Political Science* 37 (1976a):75-96.

_____ . "Support for Maritime Union Among Nova Scotian Adolescents." *Dalhousie Review* 56 (1976b):70-82.

Jansen, Clifford. "Community Organization of Italians in Toronto." In *Canadian Ethnic Mosaic*, edited by L. Dreidger, pp. 310-26. Toronto: McClelland and Stewart, 1978.

Jaros, Dean. *Socialization to Politics.* New York: Praeger Publishers, 1973.

Jenkins, Richard L.; Gants, Robert; Shoji, Takeshi; and Fine, Edna. "Interrupting the Family Cycle of Violence." *Journal of the Iowa Medical Society* 60, 2 (1970):85-89.

Johnstone, John C. *Young People's Image of Canadian Society: An Opinion Survey of Canadian Youth 13 to 20 Years of Age.* Ottawa: Queen's Printer, 1969.

Jones, F. E. "Some Social Consequences of Immigration to Canada." In *Canadian Society – Sociological Perspectives*, edited by B. R. Blishen; F. E. Jones; K. D. Naegele; and J. Porter. Toronto: Macmillan, 1968.

Jones, Mervin. *Life on the Dole.* London: Davis Poynter, 1972.

Kalbach, Warren E. "Propensities for Intermarriage in Canada." Paper presented at the annual meeting of The Canadian Sociology and Anthropology Association, 1974, at the University of Toronto.

——————. "The Demography of Marriage." In *Marriage, Family and Society*, edited by S. Parvez Wakil, pp. 59-84. Toronto: Butterworths, 1975.

Kalbach, W. E., and McVey, W. *The Demographic Bases of Canadian Society.* Toronto: McGraw-Hill Ryerson, 1971.

Kallen, E. *Spanning The Generations: A Study In Jewish Identity.* Don Mills: Longman, 1977.

Kallen, Evelyn, and Kelner, Merrijoy. "Parents and Peers: Who Influences Student Values?." In *The Canadian Family Revised*, edited by K. Ishwaran, pp. 213-26. Toronto: Holt, Rinehart and Winston, 1976.

Kane, G. D. "The Word That Must Be Spoken." *American Humane* 65, 12 (1977):13.

Kanter, Rosabeth M. *Communes: Creating and Managing the Collective Life.* New York: Harper & Row, 1973.

Kayfetz, B. "The Evolution of the Jewish Community in Toronto." In *A People and Its Faith*, edited by Albert Rose, pp. 14-29. Toronto: University of Toronto Press, 1959.

Kelner, M. "Ethnic Penetration into Toronto Elite Structure." *Canadian Review of Sociology and Anthropology* 7 (1970):128-37.

Kerckhoff, Allan C., and Davis, Keith E. "Value Consensus and Need Complementarity in Mate Selection." *American Sociological Review* 27 (1962).

Kinsey, A. C.; Pomeroy, W.; and Martin, C. *Sexual Behaviour in the Human Male.* Philadelphia: Saunders, 1948.

Kitsuse, John I. "Societal Reaction to Deviant Behavior: Problems of Theory and Method." In *The Other Side. Perspectives on Deviance*, edited by Howard S. Becker, pp. 87-103. London: The Free Press of Glencoe, 1964.

Klassen, P. S. *The Economics of Anabaptism 1525-1560.* The Hague: Mouton and Co., 1964.

Knight, G. "Work Orientation and Mobility Ideology in the Working Class." *Canadian Journal of Sociology* 4 (1979):27-41.

Kohl, Seena B. "The Family in a Post-Frontier Society." In *The Canadian Family*, edited by K. Ishwaran. Toronto: Holt, Rinehart and Winston, 1971.

——————. *Working Together: Women and Family in Southwestern Saskatchewan.* Toronto: Holt, Rinehart and Winston, 1976.

——————. "Women's Participation in the North American Family Farm." *Women's Studies International Quarterly* 1 (1978):47-54.

_____ . "The Making of a Community: The Role of Women in an Agricultural Setting." In *Kin and Families in America*, edited by A. J. Lichtman, and J. R. Challinor. Washington: Smithsonian International Symposia Series, 1979.

Kohl, Seena B., and Bennett, J. W. "Kinship, Succession, and the Migration of Young People in a Canadian Agricultural Community." *International Journal of Comparative Sociology* 6 (1965):96-115.

Kohn, Melvin L., and Schooler, Carmi. "Occupational Experience and Psychological Functioning: An Assessment of Reciprocal Effects." *American Sociological Review* (1973):97-118.

Komarovsky, Mirra. *The Unemployed Man and His Family.* New York: Dryden Press, 1940.

Kornberg, Allan et al. *Citizen Politicians - Canada: Party Officials in a Democratic Society.* Durham, N.C.: Carolina Academic Press, 1979.

Kosa, John. *Land of Choice: The Hungarians in Canada.* Toronto: University of Toronto Press, 1957.

Kossick, Don. "Labour: The INCO Strike." *Canadian Dimension* Vol. 13, No. 6 (1979):14-18.

Kralt, J. *Ethnic Origins of Canadians.* Profile Studies, Demographic Characteristics. Bulletin 5, Catalogue 99-790. Ottawa: Census of Canada.

Kreindler, Simon. "Psychiatric Treatment for the Abusing Parent and the Abused Child." *Canadian Psychiatric Association Journal* 21, 5 (1976):278.

Kurelek, William. "Development of Ethnic Consciousness in a Canadian Painter." In *Identities*, edited by W. W. Isajiw, pp. 46-56. Toronto: Peter Martin, 1977.

Kuzel, Paul, and Krishman, P. "Changing Patterns of Remarriage in Canada, 1961-1966." *Journal of Comparative Family Studies* 4, 2 (1973):215-24.

Labour Canada. *Women in the Labour Force.* Ottawa: Women's Bureau, Labour Canada, 1979.

Lambert, Ronald D. *Sex Role Imagery in Children: Social Origins of Mind.* Studies of the Royal Commission on the Status of Women in Canada. Ottawa: Information Canada, 1969.

Lambert, Wallace E. "Social Influences on the Child's Development of an Identity." In *A Canadian Social Psychology of Ethnic Relations*, edited by R. C. Gardner and R. Kalin, pp. 57-75. Toronto: Methuen, 1981.

Lamy, Paul G. "Political Socialization of French and English Canadian Youth: Socialization into Discord." In *Socialization and Values in Canadian Society: Volume One - Political Socialization*, edited by Elia Zureik, and Robert Pike, pp. 263-80. Toronto: McClelland and Stewart, 1975.

Landes, Ronald G. "Socialization to Political Culture: A Comparative Study of English-Canadian and American Schoolchildren." Ph.D. dissertation, York University, 1973.

_____ . "The Use of Role Theory in Political Socialization Research: A Review, Critique, and Modest Proposal." *International Journal of Comparative Sociology* 17 (1976):59-72.

_____ . "Political Socialization Among Youth: A Comparative Study of English-Canadian and American School Children." *International Journal of Comparative Sociology* 18 (1977a):63-80.

_____. "Pre-Adult Orientations to Multiple Systems of Government." *Publius: The Journal of Federalism* 7 (1977b):27-39.

Landes, Ronald G., and Jabbra, Joseph G. "Partisan Identity Among Canadian Youth: A Case Study of Nova Scotian Adolescents." *The Journal of Commonwealth and Comparative Politics* 17 (1979):60-76.

Landes, Ruth. *The Ojibwa Woman.* New York: Norton, 1971.

Larson, L. L. *The Canadian Family in Comparative Perspective.* Toronto: Prentice-Hall, 1976.

Latowsky (Kallen), Evelyn. "Three Toronto Synagogues: A Comparative Study of Synagogues in Transition." Ph.D. dissertation, University of Toronto, 1969.

_____. "The Family Life Styles and Jewish Culture." In *The Canadian Family*, edited by K. Ishwaran. Toronto: Holt, Rinehart and Winston, 1971.

Lee, Danielle J., and Lapointe, Jean. "The Emergence of Franco-Ontarians: New Identity, New Boundaries." In *Two Nations, Many Cultures: Ethnic Groups in Canada*, edited by J. L. Elliott, pp. 99-114. Scarborough, Ont.: Prentice-Hall, 1979.

Lehman, H. C., and Witty, P. A. "Further Study of the Social Status of Occupations." *Journal of Educational Sociology* 5 (1931):101-12.

Lemert, Edwin M. *Human Deviance, Social Problems and Social Control.* Englewood Cliffs, N.J.: Prentice-Hall, 1967.

_____. *Social Pathology.* New York: McGraw-Hill, 1951.

Lero, Donna S., and de Rijcke-Lollis, Susan. *Report on Early Childhood Educators' and Private Home Day Care Providers' Knowledge, Attitudes and Experiences Related to Child Abuse, A Summary.* Ontario Ministry of Community and Social Services, Children's Services Division, July 1979.

Levens, Bruce, and Dutton, Donald G. "Domestic Crisis Intervention – Citizens' Requests for Service and Vancouver Police Department Response." *Canadian Police College Journal* 1, 1 (1977):29-50.

Levinger, George. "A Social Psychological Perspective on Marital Dissolution." In *Divorce and Separation*, edited by G. Levinger, and O. Moles. New York: Praeger, 1979.

Levinger, George; Senn, David; and Jorgenson, Bruce. "Progress Toward Permanence in Courtship: A Test of the Kerckhoff-Davis Hypothesis." *Sociometry* 33 (1970).

Libby, Roger W., and Whitehurst Robert N. *Marriage and Alternatives: Exploring Intimate Relationships.* Glenview, Ill.: Scott Foresman, 1977.

Liebow, Elliot. *Tally's Corner: A Study of Negro Street Corner Men.* Boston: Little, Brown, 1967.

Lincourt, Solange. "Garde ou abandon de l'enfant." Master's thesis, Département de Service Social, Université de Montréal, 1965.

Lipmen-Blumen, Jean, and Tickamyer, Ann R. "Sex roles in transition: a ten-year perspective." *Annual Review of Sociology* 1 (1975):297-337.

Litwak, Eugene. "Occupational Mobility and Extended Family Cohesion." *American Sociological Review* 25 (1960a):9-21.

_____. "Geographic Mobility and Extended Family Cohesion." *American Sociological Review* 25 (1960b):385-94.

Lowry, T. P., and Lowry, A. "Abortion as a Preventive for Abused Children." *Psychiatric Opinion* 8, 3 (1970):19-25.

Luker, Samuel R. "Childhood Experiences as Causes of Criminal Behaviour."

Presentation to the Canadian Senate Subcommittee. *Minutes of Proceedings*, 1978 11 28.

Lumsden, Ian, ed. *Close the 49th Parallel: The Americanization of Canada.* Toronto: The University of Toronto Press, 1970.

Lupri, E. "Contemporary Authority Patterns in the West German Family. A Study in Cross-National Validation." *Journal of Marriage and the Family* 31 (1969):134-44.

————. "Gesellschaftliche Differenzierung und Familiale Autorität." In *Soziologie der Familie*, edited by Eugen Lupri, and Günther Lüschen, pp. 323-52. Zweite Auflage. Köln: Westdeutscher Verlag, 1976.

Lupri, Eugen. "The Changing Position of Women and Men in Comparative Perspective." In *The Changing Positions of Women in Family and Society: A Cross-National Comparison*, edited by Eugen Lupri, pp. 8-32. Leiden: E. J. Brill, 1982.

Lupri, E., and Frideres, J. "Marital Satisfaction and The Family Life Cycle: The Canadian Case." Paper presented at the 1976 Annual Meetings of the Canadian Sociology and Anthropology Association, Quebec City, 1976 05 26-29.

————. "The Quality of Marriage and the Passage of Time: Marital Satisfaction over the Family Life Cycle." *Canadian Journal of Sociology* 6 (1981):283-305.

Lupri, Eugen, and Mills, Donald L. "The Changing Roles of Canadian Women in Family and Work: An Overview." In *The Changing Positions of Women in Family and Society: A Cross-National Comparison*, edited by Eugen Lupri. Leiden: E. J. Brill, 1982.

Lysenko, Vera. *Men in Sheepskin Coats.* Toronto: Ryerson Press, 1947.

Maccoby, Eleanor Emmons, and Jacklin, Carol Nagy. *The Psychology of Sex Differences.* Stanford, Calif.: Stanford University Press, 1974.

————. "What We Know and Don't Know About Sex Differences." In *Contemporary Issues in Educational Psychology*, edited by H. F. Clarizio et al., pp. 84-89. Boston: Allyn and Bacon, 1977.

Mackie, Marlene. "The Accuracy of Folk Knowledge Concerning Alberta Indians, Hutterites, and Ukrainians." Ph.D. dissertation, University of Alberta, 1971.

————. "Gender Socialization in Childhood and Adolescence." In *Childhood and Adolescence in Canada*, edited by K. Ishwaran, pp. 136-60. Toronto: McGraw-Hill Ryerson, 1979.

Macklin, E. D. "Non-marital Heterosexual Co-habitation: A Review of Research." *Marriage and Family Review* 1 (1978).

Maclean's. "The Finishing Touch: Postponed Parenthood: Babies after Thirty," pp. 45-51. 1981 05 04.

Maetjko, Alexander. "Multiculturalism: The Polish Canadian Case." In *Two Nations, Many Cultures: Ethnic Groups in Canada*, edited by J. L. Elliott, pp. 237-49. Scarborough, Ont.: Prentice-Hall, 1979.

Malone, Carl C., and Malone, Lucile Holaday. *Decision Making and Management for Farm and Home.* Ames: The Iowa State College Press, 1958.

Margin, Harry W. "Correlates of Adjustment Among American Indians in an Urban Environment." *Human Organization* 23 (1964):290-95.

Margolin, G., and Patterson, R. "Differential Consequences Provided by Mothers and Fathers for their Sons and Daughters." *Developmental Psychology* 12 (1975):537-38.

Markle, Gerald E. "Sex Ratio at Birth: Values, Variance, and Some Determinants." *Demography* 11 (1974):131-42.

Maykovich, Minako Kurokawa. "Acculturation versus Familism in Three Generations of Japanese-Canadians." In *Canadian Families: Ethnic Variations*, edited by K. Ishwaran. Toronto: McGraw-Hill Ryerson, 1980.

——————————————. "Japanese and Mennonite Childhood and Socialization." In *Childhood and Adolescence in Canada*, edited by K. Ishwaran. Toronto: McGraw-Hill Ryerson, 1979.

——————————————. "The Japanese Family in Tradition and Change." In *The Canadian Family Revised*, edited by K. Ishwaran. Toronto: Holt, Rinehart and Winston, 1976.

Mazur, Allan, and Robertson, Leon S. *Biology and Social Behavior.* New York: The Free Press, 1972.

McKenzie, B. D.; James, V. P.; Check, Linda; and Penning, Yvonne. *Thompson and Cutbacks: A Social Impact Assessment.* Winnipeg: University of Manitoba, 1978.

Mead, G. H. *Mind, Self and Society.* Chicago: The University of Chicago Press, 1934.

Mead, Margaret. "Marriage in Two Steps." *Redbook.* 1966 07.

Meissner, Martin; Humphreys, Elizabeth; Meis, Scot M.; and Scheu, William J. "No Exit for Wives: Sexual Division of Labour." *The Canadian Review of Sociology and Anthropology* 12 (1975).

Meloche, Denise. "Garde ou abandon de l'enfant illégitime." Master's thesis, Département de Service Social, Université de Montréal, 1957.

Meltzer, Bernard N. "Mead's Social Psychology." In *Symbolic Interaction*, edited by Jerome G. Manis, and Bernard N. Meltzer, pp. 5-25. Boston: Allyn and Bacon, 1967.

Melville, Keith. *Marriage and Family Today* 2d rev. ed. New York: Random House, 1980.

Merton, Robert K. *Social Theory and Social Structure.* New York: The Free Press, 1957.

Meyer, Henry J.; Borgatta, Edgar F.; and Fanshel, David. "Unwed Mothers' Decisions about their Babies: An Interim Application Study." *Child Welfare* 38, 2 (1959):1-6.

Meyer, Henry J.; Jones, Wyatt; and Borgatta, Edgar F. "The Decision by Unmarried Mothers to Keep or Surrender their Babies." *Social Work* 1, 2 (1956):103-09.

——————————— . "Social and Psychological Factors in Status Decisions of Unmarried Mothers." *Journal of Marriage and the Family* 24 (1962):224-30.

Middleton, Russell, and Putney, Snell. "Dominance in Decisions in the Family, Race and Class Differences." *American Journal of Sociology* 65 (1959):605-09.

Millet, Kate. *Sexual Politics.* New York: Avon Books, 1970.

Mindel, C. H. and Habenstein, R. *Ethnic Families in America: Patterns and Variations.* New York: Elsevier, 1976.

Miner, Horace. *St. Denis.* Chicago: Chicago University, 1939.

Mitchell, Juliet. *Women's Estate.* Baltimore: Penguin, 1971.

Money, J., and Ehrhardt, A. *Man and Woman, Boy and Girl.* Baltimore: John Hopkins University Press, 1972.

Montagu, Ashley, ed. *Man and Aggression.* New York: Oxford University Press, 1968.

——————————— . *Touching: The Human Significance of the Skin.* New York: Harper & Row, 1972.

Morgan, W. R.; Alwin, D. F.; and Griffin, L. J. "Social Origins, Parental Values, and the Transmission of Inequality." *American Journal of Sociology* 85 (1979):156-66.

Murdock, G. P. *Social Structure.* New York: The Macmillan Co., 1949.

_____. "Kin Term Patterns and Their Distribution." *Ethnology* 9 (1970):165-207.

Murstein, Bernard L. "Stimulus-Value-Role: A Theory of Marital Choice." *Journal of Marriage and the Family* 32 (1970).

_____. "Mate Selection in the 1970s." *Journal of Marriage and the Family* 42 (1980).

Mussen, Paul H. "Early sex-role development." In *Handbook of Socialization Theory and Research*, edited by David A. Goslin, pp. 707-31. Chicago: Rand McNally, 1969.

Nagata, Judith A. "Adaptation and Integration of Greek Working Class Immigrants in the City of Toronto, Canada: A Situational Approach." *International Migration Review* 4 (1969):44-67.

_____. "One Vine, Many Branches: Internal Differentiation in Canadian Ethnic Groups." In *Two Nations, Many Cultures: Ethnic Groups in Canada*, edited by J. L. Elliott, pp. 173-81. Scarborough, Ont.: Prentice-Hall, 1979.

Native Canadian Centre of Toronto. "Our Position on Native Child and Family Welfare in Toronto." 1980.

Needham, H. G. "Child Abuse and Neglect. A Background Paper," pp. 13-17. Ottawa: Solicitor General of Canada, 1974 08 22.

Nelson, Alvar. "Legal Responses to Child Abuse." Paper presented to the inter-disciplinary Second World Conference of The International Society on Family Law dealing with Violence in the Family, 1977 06 13-17, in Montreal.

Nett, Emily M. "Socialization for Sex Roles." In *Courtship, Marriage and the Family in Canada*, edited by G. N. Ramu, pp. 78-95. Toronto: Macmillan, 1979.

Newman, Peter. *The Canadian Establishment*. Toronto: McClelland and Stewart, 1975.

Nie, N. H.; Hull, C. H.; Jenkins, J. G.; Steinbrenner, K.; and Bent, D. H. *Statistical Package for the Social Sciences*. New York: McGraw-Hill Book Company, 1975.

Niemi, Richard G. "Political Socialization." In *Handbook of Political Psychology*, edited by Jeanne N. Knutson, pp. 117-38. San Francisco: Jossey-Bass Publishers, 1973.

Nye, F. Ivan. "Marital Interaction." In *The Employed Mother in America*, edited by F. Ivan Nye, and Lois Hoffman. Chicago: Rand McNally, 1972.

_____. "Is Choice and Exchange Theory the Key?." *Journal of Marriage and the Family* 40 (1978).

_____. *Role Structure and Analysis of the Family*. Beverley Hills, Calif.: Sage, 1976.

_____. "Choice, Exchange and the Family." In *Contemporary Theories About the Family*, edited by W. Burr; R. Hill; F. I. Nye; and I. Reiss, pp. 1-41. New York: The Free Press, 1979.

Nye, F. Ivan, and Berardo, Felix M. *Emerging Conceptual Frameworks in Family Analysis*. New York: Macmillan, 1966.

_____. *The Family: Its Structure and Interaction*. New York: Macmillan Publishing Co. Inc., 1973.

Nye, F. Ivan, and Hoffman, Lois W. *The Employed Mother in America*. Chicago: Rand McNally, 1973.

Oakley, Ann. *Women's Work: A History of the Housewife*. New York: Pantheon Books, 1974.

O'Bryan, K. G.; Reitz, J. G.; and Kuplowska, O. M. *Non-Official Languages: A Study in Canadian Multiculturalism.* Ottawa: Supply and Services Canada, 1976.

Ogburn, William F. *Social Change.* New York: Huebach, 1923.

—————————. "The Changing Family." *The Family* 19 (1938):139-43.

Ogmundson, Rick. "The Sociology of Power and Politics: An Introduction to the Canadian Polity." In *Introduction to Canadian Society: A Sociological Analysis*, edited by G. N. Ramu and Stuart D. Johnson, pp. 157-211. Toronto: Macmillan, 1976.

Olson, D. "The Measurement of Family Power by Self-Report and Behavioral Methods." *Journal of Marriage and the Family* 31 (1969):545-50.

O'Neill, N., and O'Neill, George. *Open Marriage: A Synergic Model.* New York: M. Evans Company, 1972.

Osmond, M. "Reciprocity: A Dynamic Model and Method to Study Family Power." *Journal of Marriage and the Family* 40 (1978).

Ossenberg, R. J., ed. *Canadian Society: Pluralism, Change and Conflict.* Scarborough, Ont.: Prentice-Hall, 1971.

Osterreich, Helgi. "Geographical Mobility and Kinship: A Canadian Example." In *The Canadian Family Revised*, edited by K. Ishwaran. Toronto: Holt, Rinehart and Winston, 1976.

Otto, H. Ed. *The Family in Search of Future.* New York: Appleton-Century-Crofts, 1970.

Oxnam, Desmond W. "Cost and Benefits of Industrial Conflict." *Economic Activity* (Australia) 2, 4 (1968):41-47.

Pammett, Jon H. "The Development of Political Orientations in Canadian School Children." *Canadian Journal of Political Science* 4 (1971):132-41.

—————————. "Adolescent Political Activity as a Learning Experience." In *Foundations of Political Culture: Political Socialization in Canada*, edited by Jon H. Pammett, and Michael S. Whittington, pp. 160-94. Toronto: Macmillan, 1976.

Pammett, Jon H., and Whittington, Michael S. *Foundations of Political Culture: Political Socialization in Canada.* Toronto: Macmillan, 1976.

Parnas, Raymond I. "The Police Response to the Domestic Disturbance." *Wisconsin Law Review* 1 (1967):914-60.

—————————. "The Relevance of Criminal Law to Inter-spousal Violence." Paper presented to the interdisciplinary Second World Conference of The International Society on Family Law dealing with Violence in the Family, 1977 06 13-17, in Montreal.

Parsons, Talcott. "The Kinship System of Contemporary United States." *American Anthropologist* 45 (1943):22-38.

—————————. *The Social System.* Glencoe: The Free Press, 1951.

—————————. "The Social Structure of the Family." In *The Family: Its Function and Destiny*, edited by Ruth N. Anshen. New York: Harper and Brothers, 1959.

—————————. "The Forces of Change." In *Man and Civilization: The Family's Search for Survival*, edited by Seymour M. Farber et al. New York: McGraw-Hill, 1965.

Parsons, Talcott, and Bales, Robert F., eds. *Family, Socialization and Interaction Process.* New York: The Free Press, 1955.

Parsons, Talcott, and Shils, Edward A., eds. *Toward A General Theory of Action.* New York: The Free Press, 1952.

Patterson, James G. *The Romanians of Saskatchewan: Four Generations of Adaptation.* Ottawa: National Museums of Canada, 1977.

Paulson, M. J., and Blake, P. R. "The Abused, Battered and Maltreated Child: A Review." *Journal of Trauma* 9, 4 (1967):56-57.

Pavalko, R. M. "Socio-economic Background, Ability, and the Allocation of Students." *Canadian Review of Sociology and Anthropology* 4 (1967):250-59.

_____ . *Sociological Perspectives on Occupations.* Ithasca, Ill.: Peacock, 1972.

Pellegreno, D. D., and Williams, W. C. "Teacher Perception and Classroom Verbal Interaction." *Elementary School Guidance and Counselling* 7 (1973).

Perlman, D. "The Premarital Sexual Standards of Canadians." In *Marriage and Divorce in Canada*, edited by K. Ishwaran. Toronto: McGraw-Hill Ryerson, 1979.

Peter, Karl A. "Factors of Social Change and Social Dynamics in the Communal Settlements of Hutterites 1527-1967." Ph.D. dissertation, The University of Alberta, 1967.

_____ . "The Hutterite Family." In *The Canadian Family*, edited by K. Ishwaran. Toronto: Holt, Rinehart and Winston, 1971.

_____ . "The Instability of the Community of Goods in the Social History of Hutterites." In *Western Canada Past and Present.* Calgary, Alta.: McClelland and Stewart West Ltd., 1975.

_____ . "Childhood and Adolescent Socialization Among Hutterites." In *Childhood and Adolescence in Canada*, edited by K. Ishwaran, pp. 344-65. Toronto: McGraw-Hill Ryerson, 1979.

Peter, K. A. and Peter, F. *Der Gemein Ordnungen.* Reardan, Wash.: Paul Gross, 1980.

Peters, John F. "A Comparison of Mate Selection and Marriage in the First and Second Marriages." *Journal of Comparative Family Studies* 7:3 (1976):483-90.

_____ . *Divorce.* Toronto: University of Toronto Press, 1979.

Petryshyn, W. R. *Changing Realities: Social Trends Among Ukrainian Canadians.* Edmonton: The Canadian Institute of Ukrainian Studies, 1980.

Phillips, Patricia S.; Pickrell, Elaine; and Morse, Thomas S. "Intentional Burning: A Severe Form of Child Abuse." *Journal of the American College of Emergency Physicians* (November-December, 1974):388.

Piaget, J. *The Psychology of Intelligence.* London: Routledge, Kegan Paul, 1947.

Piddington, Ralph. "A Study of French-Canadian Kinship." In *The Canadian Family Revised*, edited by K. Ishwaran. Toronto: Holt, Rinehart and Winston, 1976.

Pietrofesa, J. K., and Schlossberg, N. K. "Counselor Bias and the Female Occupational Role." In *Counselor Bias and the Female Occupational Role*, edited by N. Glazer-Malbin, and H. Y. Waehrer, pp. 219-21. Chicago: Rand McNally, 1972.

Pike, R. M. *Who Doesn't Get to University – And Why.* Ottawa: Runge Press, 1970.

Pike, Robert. "Legal Access and the Incidence of Divorce in Canada: A Socio-historical Analysis." In *The Canadian Review of Sociology and Anthropology* 12, 2 (1975):115-33.

Pineo, Peter C. "The Extended Family in a Working-Class Area of Hamilton." In *The Canadian Family Revised*, edited by K. Ishwaran. Toronto: Holt, Rinehart and Winston, 1976.

Pineo, P. C., and Porter, J. "Occupational Prestige in Canada." *Canadian Review of Sociology and Anthropology* 4 (1967):24-40.

Podell, Lawrence. "Occupational and Familial Role-Expectations." *Journal of Marriage and the Family* 29 (1967):492-93.

Podoluck, J. R. *Incomes of Canadians.* Ottawa: Dominion Bureau of Statistics, 1968.

Porter, J. *The Vertical Mosaic.* Toronto: University of Toronto Press, 1965.

Pratt, David. "The Social Role of School Textbooks in Canada." In *Socialization and Values in Canadian Society: Volume One - Political Socialization*, edited by Elia Zureik, and Robert M. Pike, pp. 100-26. Toronto: McClelland and Stewart, 1975.

Prescott, James W. "Body Pleasure and the Origins of Violence." *The Futurist* (1975).

_____. "Deprivation of Physical Affection as a Primary Process in the Development of Physical Violence." In *Child Abuse and Violence*, edited by David G. Gil, pp. 76-77. New York: AMS Press Inc., 1979.

_____. "Abortion or the Unwanted Child." In *Child Abuse and Violence*, op. cit., pp. 560-74.

Presthus, R. *Elite Accommodation in Canadian Politics.* Cambridge: Cambridge University Press, 1973.

Price, C. A. "Report on the Greek Community in Toronto." Master's thesis, York University, 1958.

Price, John A. *Native Studies: American and Canadian Indians.* Toronto: McGraw-Hill Ryerson, 1978.

_____. *Indians of Canada: Cultural Dynamics.* Scarborough, Ont.: Prentice-Hall, 1979.

Propper, Alice Marcella. "The Relationship of Maternal Employment to Adolescent Roles, Activities, and Parental Relationships." *Journal of Marriage and the Family* 34 (1972):417-21.

Proudfoot, Stuart B., and Pammett, Jon H. "Children, Television and Politics: Is the Medium the Message?." In *Foundations of Political Culture: Political Socialization in Canada*, edited by Jon H. Pammett and Michael S. Whittington, pp. 134-48. Toronto: Macmillan, 1976.

Pryor, E. T. "Family Income and Stratification in Canada." In *Marriage, Family, and Society*, edited by S. Parvez Wakil. Toronto: Butterworths, 1975.

Public Service of Canada. *Implementation Report on Status of Women Report Recommendations.* Ottawa: Public Service Commission.

Pyke, S. W. "Children's Literature: Conceptions of Sex Roles." In *Socialization and Values in Canadian Society* 2, edited by Robert M. Pike and Elia Zureik, pp. 51-73. Toronto: McClelland and Stewart, 1975.

Radcliffe-Brown, A. R. *Structure and Function in Primitive Society.* Glencoe: The Free Press, 1952.

Radecki, Henry. "Polish-Canadian, Canadian-Polish or Canadian?." Mimeographed, York University, 1970.

_____. *Ethnic Organizational Dynamics.* Waterloo: Wilfrid Laurier University Press, 1976.

_____. *The 1978-79 Strike at INCO; The Effects on the Families: A Report.* Sudbury: SIS Analysis (Laurentian University), 1979.

_____. *One Year Later; The 1978-79 Strike at INCO; The Effects on Families.* Sudbury: SIS Analysis (Laurentian University), 1981.

Radecki, Henry, and Korn, Benedykt Heyden. *A Member of a Distinguished Family: The Polish Group in Canada.* Toronto: McClelland and Stewart, 1976.

Rainwater, Lee. "Work, Well-Being, and Family Life." *Work and the Quality of Life*, edited by James O'Toole, pp. 361-78. Cambridge, Mass.: The MIT Press, 1974.

Ramu, G. N. *Family and Caste in Urban India.* New Delhi: Vikas Publishing, 1976.

――――――. "Kinship Networks." In *Courtship, Marriage and the Family in Canada*, edited by G. N. Ramu. Toronto: Macmillan, 1979.

――――――. *Marriage and Parenthood in Canada.* In process.

Rapoport, Rhona, and Rapoport, Robert N. *Dual-Career Families.* Middlesex: Penguin Books, 1971.

Rapoport, Robert, and Rapoport, Rhona. "Work and Family in Contemporary Society." *American Sociological Review* (June, 1965):381-94.

Raven, B.; Centers, R.; and Rodrigues, A. "The Bases of Conjugal Power." In *Power in Families*, edited by R. Cromwell, and D. Olson, pp. 217-32. New York: John Wiley, 1975.

Redekop, John H. "Continentalism: The Key to Canadian Politics." In *Approaches to Canadian Politics*, edited by John H. Redekop, pp. 28-57. Scarborough, Ont.: Prentice-Hall, 1978.

Redfield, Robert. "The Folk Society." *American Journal of Sociology* 52, 4 (1947):293-308.

Reed, Paul. "A Preliminary Analysis of Divorce Actions in Canada, 1969-1972." Paper presented at the Learned Society Meetings, Edmonton, 1975.

Reiss, A. J.; Duncan, O. D.; Hatt, P. K.; and North, C. C. *Occupations and Social Status.* New York: The Free Press of Glencoe, 1961.

Reiss, Ira L. "The Universality of the Family: A Conceptual Analysis." *Journal of Marriage and the Family* 2 (1965):443-53.

――――――. *The Social Context of Premarital Sexual Permissiveness.* New York: Holt, Rinehart and Winston, 1967.

――――――. *Family Systems in America.* 3d ed. New York: Holt, Rinehart and Winston, 1980.

Reiss, I. L.; Anderson, R. E.; and Sponaugle, G. C. "A Multivariate Model of the Determinants of Extramarital Sexual Permissiveness." *Journal of Marriage and the Family* 42 (1980):395-411.

Reiss, I. L., and Miller, B. D. *A Theoretical Analysis of Heterosexual Permissiveness.* Minneapolis: The Family Study Center, University of Minnesota, 1974.

――――――. "Heterosexual Permissiveness: A Theoretical Analysis." In *Contemporary Theories About the Family*, edited by W. Burr; R. Hill; F. I. Nye; and I. L. Reiss. New York: The Free Press, 1979.

Reiss, Paul J. "The Extended Kinship System: Correlates and Attitudes on Frequency of Interaction." *Marriage and Family Living* 24 (1962):334.

Reitz, Jeffrey G. "Language and Ethnic Community Survival." *Canadian Review of Sociology and Anthropology* special publication (1974):104-22.

――――――. "Immigrants, Their Descendants, and the Cohesion of Canada." In *Cultural Boundaries and the Cohesion of Canada*, edited by R. Breton et al. Montreal: Institute for Research on Public Policy, 1980.

Report on the CBC Task Force on the Status of Women. *Women in the CBC.* Toronto: Canadian Broadcasting Corporation, 1975.

Resnick, Phillip J. "Child Murder by Parents: A Psychiatric Review of Filicide." *American Journal of Psychiatry* 126 (1969):325-29.

—————————. "Murder of the New Born: A Psychiatric Review of Neonaticide." *American Journal of Psychiatry* 126 (1970):1414.

Reynolds, L. G. "A Break-even Analysis." *Personal Management* (February, 1977):22-31.

Richard, M. "Ethnic Intermarriage: As Reflected in the Characteristics of Husbands and Wives." Toronto CMA, 1971. Unpublished paper, Erindale College, University of Toronto.

Richer, Stephen. "Sex Role Socialization and Early Schooling." *Canadian Review of Sociology and Anthropology* 16, 2 (1979):195-205.

—————————. "Sex Role Socialization Outcomes as Manifested in Children's Drawings." 1980. Forthcoming.

Richert, Jeanne Pierre. "Political Socialization in Quebec: Young People's Attitudes toward Government." *Canadian Journal of Political Science* 6 (1973):303-13.

—————————. "Canadian National Identity: An Empirical Study." *American Review of Canadian Studies* 4 (1974a):89-98.

—————————. "The Impact of Ethnicity on the Perception of Heroes and Historical Symbols." *Canadian Review of Sociology and Anthropology* 11 (1974b):156-63.

Serbin, L. A. et al. "A Comparison of Teacher Response to the Preacademic and Problem Behaviour of Boys and Girls." *Child Development* 44 (1973).

Serbin, L. A., and O'Leary, K. D. "How Nursery Schools Teach Girls to Shut Up." *Psychology Today* 9 (1975):56-57, 102-03.

Shaheen, E.; Husain, S. A.; and Hays, J. "Child Abuse – A Medical Emergency." *Missouri Medicine* 72, 9 (1975):532-35.

Sharp, Henry S. *Chipewyn Marriage.* Ottawa: Canadian Ethnology Service. Paper no. 58, 1979.

Sherif, M. A. "A Study of Some Social Factors in Perception." *Arch. Psychology* 127, 187 (1935).

Sherriff, H. "The Abused Child." *J.S.C.M.A.* 60 (1964):191-93.

Shevky, E., and Bell, W. *Social Area Analysis: Theory Illustrative of Applicational Procedures.* Stanford, Calif.: Stanford University Press, 1955.

Simmel, Georg. *Sociologie.* Leipzig: Duncker and Humblot, 1908.

—————————. "On Superordination and Subordination." In *Theories of Societies* Vol. 1, edited by T. Parsons et al., pp. 540-44. Glencoe: The Free Press, 1961.

Simmons, J. L. *Deviants.* Berkeley: Glendessary, 1969.

Singh, B. K.; Walton, B. L.; and Williams, J. S. "Extramarital Sexual Permissiveness: Conditions and Contingencies". *Journal of Marriage and the Family* 38 (1976):701-12.

Skogstad, Grace D. "Adolescent Political Alienation." In *Socialization and Values in Canadian Society: Volume One – Political Socialization*, edited by Elia Zureik and Robert M. Pike. pp. 185-208. Toronto: McClelland and Stewart, 1975.

Skolnick, Arlene S., and Skolnick, Jerome H. "Rethinking the Family." In *Family in Transition*, edited by Arlene S. Skolnick, and Jerome H. Skolnick. Boston: Little, Brown, 1971.

Smelser, Neil J. *Economy and Society.* New York: The Free Press, 1956.

_____ . *Social Change in the Industrial Revolution*. Chicago: University of Chicago Press, 1959.

Smith, D. G. "Occupational Preferences of Northern Student." *Social Science Notes* 5. Ottawa: Department of Indian and Northern Affairs, 1974.

Smith, Michael R. "The Effects of Strikes on Workers: A Critical Analysis." *Canadian Journal of Sociology* 3, 4 (1978):457-72.

_____ . "The G. E. Strike: It's Starting to Hurt." *Business Week* (December 1969):20.

Snyder, E. E., and Spreitzer, E. "Attitudes of the Aged Toward Nontraditional Sexual Behaviour." *Archives of Sexual Behaviour* 5 (1976):249-54.

Soeur Ste-Madeleine-du-Sauveur. "Décision de la fille-mère au sujet de la garde de son enfant." Master's thesis, Département de Service Social, Université de Montréal, 1952.

Solomon, George F. "Psychodynamic Aspects of Aggression, Hostility, and Violence." In *Violence and the Struggle for Existence*, edited by David N. Daniels et al. Boston: Little, Brown, 1970.

Spanier, G. B. "Measuring Dyadic Adjustment: New Scales for Assessing the Quality of Marriage and Similar Dyads." *Journal of Marriage and the Family* 38 (1976):15-28.

Spicer, J. W., and Hampe, G. D. "Kinship Interaction After Divorce." *Journal of Marriage and the Family* 37 (1975):113-19.

Spindler, Louise S. *Menomini Women and Culture Change*. American Anthropological Association, Memoir no. 91, 1962.

Spinetta, John J., and Rigler, David. "The Child-Abusing Parent: A Psychological Review." *Psychological Bulletin* 77, 4 (1972):296-304.

Sponaugle, G. C. Gender Differences in Attitudes Toward Extramarital Sex. Paper presented at the Midwest Sociological Society Annual Meeting, Minneapolis, Minnesota, 1977.

Stanbury, W. T., and Siegel, Jay H. *Success and Failure: Indians in Urban Society*. Vancouver: University of British Columbia, 1975.

Statistics Canada. *Canada's Population*. Ottawa: Ministry of Supply and Services of Canada, 1979a.

_____ . *Canada's Families*. Ottawa: Ministry of Supply and Services of Canada, 1979b.

Steinmetz, Suzanne K., and Straus, Murray A. "The Family as Cradle of Violence." *Society* 10, 6 (1973):50-56.

_____ . eds. "Introduction." In *Violence in the Family*. New York: Dodd, Mead and Co., 1974.

Sternglanz, Sarah H., and Serbin, Lisa A. "Sex Role Stereotyping in Children's Television Programs." *Developmental Psychology* 10 (1974):710-15.

Stonequist, E. V. *The Marginal Man*. New York: Scribners, 1937.

Straus, Murray A. "Some Social Antecedents of Physical Punishment: A Linkage Theory Interpretation." *Journal of Marriage and the Family* 33 (1971):658-63.

_____ . "A General Systems Theory Approach to a Theory of Violence Between Family Members." *Social Science Information* 12, 3 (June 1973):105.

Sturino, Frank. "Family and Kin Cohesion Among Southern Italian Immigrants in Toronto." In *Canadian Families – Ethnic Variations*, edited by K. Ishwaran. Toronto: McGraw-Hill Ryerson, 1980.

Richmond, A. H. *Ethnic Residential Segregation in Metropolitan Toronto.* Ethnic Research Programme, I.B.R., York University, 1972.

——————. "Language, Ethnicity, and the Problem of Identity in a Canadian Metropolis." In *Ethnicity in the Americas,* edited by F. Henry, pp. 41-71. Chicago: Aldine Publishing Co., 1976.

——————. *Ethnic Variation in Family Income and Poverty.* Ethnic Research Programme, I.B.R., York University, 1979.

Richmond A. H., and Kalbach, W. E. *Factors in the Adjustment of Immigrants and their Descendants.* Ottawa: Statistics Canada, Minister of Supply and Services, 1980.

Rideman, Peter. *Account of our Religion, Doctrine and Faith, of the Brothers Whom Men Call Hutterites.* Suffolk, Great Britain: Hodder and Stoughton in conjunction with The Plough Publishing House, 1950.

Risman, Barbara J.; Hill, Charles T.; Rubin, Zick; and Peplau, Letitia Anne. "Living Together in College: Implications for Courtship." *Journal of Marriage and the Family* 43 (1981).

Roberts, J. "Characteristics of the Abused Child and His Family: An Agency Study." Unpublished thesis, Carleton University, 1968.

Robinson, Paul. *Where Our Survival Lies: Students and Textbooks in Atlantic Canada.* Halifax, Nova Scotia: Atlantic Institute of Education, 1979.

Robson, B. *My Parents Are Divorced, Too.* Toronto: Dorset Publishing, 1979.

Rodman, H. "Marital Power and the Theory of Resources in Cultural Context." *Journal of Comparative Family Studies* 3 (1972):51-69.

Romaniuk, A. "Modernization and Fertility: The Case of the James Bay Indians." *Canadian Review of Sociology and Anthropology* 11 (1974):344-59.

Rood-de-Boer, M. "Children's Suicide." Paper presented to the interdisciplinary Second World Conference of The International Society on Family Law dealing with Violence in the Family, 1977 06 13-17, in Montreal.

Rose, Albert, ed. *A People and Its Faith.* Toronto: University of Toronto Press, 1959.

Rosenberg, S. *Judaism.* Paramus, N.J.: Paulist/Newman Press, 1966.

Ross, H. L., and Sawhill, I. V. *Time of Transition, The Growth of Families Headed by Women.* Washington, D.C.: The Urban Institute, 1975.

Ross, Val. "How the Pattersons Survive on Strike Pay." *Chatelaine* (May 1979):44-45, 156-66.

——————. "The Arrogance of Inco." *Canadian Business* 52, 5 (May 1979):44-55, 116-42.

The Royal Commission Report on the Status of Women: Ten Years Later. An Assessment of the Federal Government's Implementation of the Recommendations. Ottawa: The Canadian Advisory Council on Women, 1979.

Rush, Gary B. "The Radicalization of Middle-class Youth." *International Social Science Journal* 24 (1972):312-25.

Safilios-Rothschild, C. "Family Sociology or Wives' Family Sociology: A Cross-cultural Examination of Decision-Making." *Journal of Marriage and the Family* 31 (1969):290-301.

——————. "The Study of Family Power Structure: A Review, 1960-1969." *Journal of Marriage and the Family* 32 (1970):539-52.

Sagarin, E. *Deviance and Social Change.* Beverley Hills, Calif.: Sage, 1977.

Samuel, Y., and Lewin-Epstin, N. "The Occupational Situs as a Predictor of Work Values." *American Journal of Sociology* 85 (1979):625-39.

Sanday, P. R. "Toward a Theory of the Status of Women." *American Anthropologist* 75: 1682-1700 (1973).

_____. *Farm Women.* Saskatchewan Women's Division, Department of Labour, 1977.

Sawer, B. J. "Predictors of the Farm Wife's Involvement in General Management and Adoption Decisions." *Rural Sociology* 38 (1973):412-26.

Scanzoni, John H. *Opportunity and the Family.* New York: The Free Press, 1970.

_____. *Sexual Bargaining: Power Politics in American Marriage.* Englewood Cliffs, N.J.: Prentice-Hall, 1970.

Scheff, Thomas J. *Being Mentally Ill.* Chicago: Aldine, 1966.

Schlesinger, Benjamin. *One in Ten. The Single Parent in Canada.* Toronto: Faculty of Education, University of Toronto, 1979.

_____. "Remarriage." In *Courtship, Marriage and the Family in Canada*, edited by R. N. Ramu, pp. 155-57. Toronto: Macmillan, 1979.

_____. "Children in One-Parent Families: A Review." *Conciliation Courts Review* (1981).

Schlossberg, N. K., and Goodman, J. A. "Woman's Place: Children's Sex Stereotyping of Occupations." *Vocational Guidance Quarterly* 20 (1972):266-70.

Schur, Edwin M. *Labeling Deviant Behavior.* New York: Harper & Row, 1971.

Schwartzman, Helen B. *Transformations, The Anthropology of Children's Play.* New York: Plenum Press, 1978.

Scott, Robert A. *The Making of Blind Men.* New York: Russell Sage, 1969.

Seeley, J. R.; Simm, R. A.; and Loosely, E. W. *Crestwood Heights.* Toronto: University of Toronto Press, 1956.

Selcer, B. "How Liberated are Liberated Children?." *The Radical Therapist* 2 (1972).

Sussman, Marvin B. "The Isolated Nuclear Family: Fact or Fiction?." *Social Problems* 6 (1959):333-40.

_____. *The Second Experience: Variant Family Forms and Life Styles.* Special Issue of *Family Co-ordinator* 24 (1975).

Sussman, Marvin B., and Burchinal, Lee. "Kin Family Network Unheralded Structure in Current Conceptualizations of Family Functioning." *Marriage and Family Living* 24 (1962):231-40.

Symons, Thomas H. B. *The Symons Report.* Toronto: The Book and Periodical Development Council, 1978.

Synge, J. "The Sociology of Canadian Education." In *Introduction to Canadian Society: Sociological Analysis*, edited by G. N. Ramu and S. D. Johnson. Toronto: Macmillan, 1976.

Tanner, Adrian. *Bringing Home Animals: Religious Ideology and Mode of Production of the Mistassini Cree Hunter.* St. John's: Memorial University of Newfoundland, 1979.

Tanner, J. M. "Physical Growth." In *Carmichael's Handbook of Child Psychology*, edited by P. Mussen. New York: John Wiley, 1970.

Tavuchis, Nicholas. "Ethnic Perspectives." In *Courtship, Marriage and the Family in Canada.* Toronto: Macmillan, 1979.

Teckenberg, W. "Prestige Ratings, Occupational Evaluation and Preference in the USSR in International Comparison." *Kölner Zeitschrift für Soziologie and Sozialpsychologie* 29 (1977):731-61.

Terr, Lenore C. "A Family Study of Child Abuse." *American Journal of Psychiatry* 127, 5 (1970):665-71.

Thibault, John W., and Kelley, Harold H. *The Social Psychology of Groups.* New York: John Wiley, 1959.

Thompson, Mary Lou, ed. *Voices of the New Feminism.* Boston: Beacon Press, 1970.

Time. "The Law as Male Chauvinist Pig." Canadian edition, 1974 03 25.

Tocqueville, Alexis de. *Democracy in America.* New York: Vintage Books, 1945.

Troyer, W. *Divorced Kids.* Toronto: Clarke, Irwin and Co., 1979.

Trudel, Marcel, and Jain, Genevieve. *Canadian History Textbooks.* Ottawa: Queen's Printer, 1970.

Turk, J. "Uses and Abuses of Family Power." In *Power in Families*, edited by R. Cromwell and D. Olson, pp. 81-94. New York: John Wiley, 1975.

Turk, J., and Bell, N. "Measuring Power in Families." *Journal of Marriage and the Family* 34 (1972):215-22.

Turner, Ralph. *Family Interaction.* New York: John Wiley, 1970.

Valle, F. "Kinship, the Family, and Marriage in Central Keewatin." In *The Canadian Family*, edited by K. Ishwaran. Toronto: Holt, Rinehart and Winston, 1971.

Veevers, J. 1971 Census of Canada. *The Family in Canada.* Catalogue 99-725. Ottawa: Statistics Canada, Minister of Supply and Services, 1977.

Veevers, Jean E. *Childless by Choice.* Toronto: Butterworths, 1980.

Vincent, Clark E. "Unwed Mothers and the Adoption Market: Psychological and Familial Factors." *Marriage and Family Living* 22, 2 (1960):112-18.

Vital Statistics, Vol. II, *Marriages and Divorces*, 1977. Ottawa: 1979.

_____, Vol. II, *Marriages and Divorces*, 1980. Ottawa: 1982.

Wakil, S. Parvez, and Wakil, F. A. "Campus Dating: An Exploratory Study of Cross National Relevance." In *Marriage, Family and Society*, edited by S. Parvez Wakil. Toronto: Butterworths, 1975.

Waller, Willard. "The Rating and Dating Couples." *American Sociological Review* 2 (1937).

Walster, Elain, et al. "Importance of Physical Attractiveness in Dating Behaviour." *Journal of Personality and Social Psychology* 4 (1966).

Ward, W. D. "Process of Sex-role Development." *Developmental Psychology* 1 (1969).

Wargon, Sylvia T. *Canadian Households and Families: Recent Demographic Trends.* Ottawa: Statistics Canada, Minister of Supply and Services, 1979.

_____ . *Children in Canadian Families.* Ottawa: Statistics Canada, 1979.

Wasserman, S. "The Abused Parent of the Abused Child." *Children* 14 (1967):175-79.

Watson, Roy E. L. "The Effects of Premarital Cohabitation on Subsequent Marital Adjustment." A paper presented at the 1981 Canadian Sociology and Anthropology Annual meetings in Halifax.

Weber, Max. *The Theory of Social and Economic Organization.* New York: Oxford University Press, 1947.

_____ . *The Protestant Ethic and the Spirit of Capitalism.* Totowa, N.J.: Charles Scribner's Sons, 1958.

Weekend Magazine, Winnipeg Free Press. 1978 02 11.

Weinstein, E. A. "Weights Assigned by Children to Criteria of Prestige." *Sociometry* 19 (1956):126-32.

Weitzman, Lenore J. "Love, Honour and Obey? Traditional Legal Marriage and Alternative Family Forms." *The Family Co-ordinator* 24 (1975).

Werblowsky, R. J. Z., and Wigoder, G., eds. *The Encyclopedia of the Jewish Religion.* Massada: P.E.C. Press, 1965.

Wertham, Frederic. "Battered Children and Baffled Adults." *Bulletin of the N.Y. Academy of Medicine* 48, 7 (1972):887-98.

Weston, J. T. "The Pathology of Child Abuse." In *The Battered Child.* 2d rev. ed., edited by R. E. Helfer, and C. H. Kempe, pp. 61-86. Chicago: University of Chicago Press, 1974.

White, W. L. et al. *Introduction to Canadian Politics and Government.* Toronto: Holt, Rinehart and Winston, 1972.

Whitehurst, Robert N. "Alternative Life Styles and Canadian Pluralism." In *Marriage, Family and Society*, edited by S. Parvez Wakil. Toronto: Butterworths, 1975.

_____ . "Non-traditional Family and Marriage." In *Courtship, Marriage and the Family in Canada*, edited by G. N. Ramu. Toronto: Macmillan, 1979.

Whitehurst, Robert N., and Frisch, R. "Sex Differences in Dating Orientations: Some Comparisons and Recent Observations." *International Journal of Sociology of the Family* 4 (1974).

Whitehurst, Robert N., and Plant, Barbara. "A Comparison of Canadian and American University Students' Reference Groups, Alienation, and Attitudes Toward Marriage." In *Canada: A Sociological Profile*, edited by W. E. Mann. Toronto: Copp-Clark, 1971.

Wilkening, Eugene A., and Bharadwaj, Lakshmi K. "Aspirations and Task Involvement as Related to Decision-Making Among Farm Husbands and Wives." *Rural Sociology* 33 (1967):30-44.

_____ . "Dimensions of Aspirations, Work Roles and Decision-Making of Farm Husbands and Wives in Wisconsin." *Journal of Marriage and the Family* 29 (1967):703-11.

Wilkening, Eugene A., and Guerrero, Sylvia. "Consensus in Aspirations for Farm Improvement and Adoptions of Farm Practice." *Rural Sociology* 34 (1969):182-96.

Wirth, Louis. "Urbanism as a Way of Life." *American Journal of Sociology* 44, 1 (1938):1-24.

Wolf, Margery. *Women and the Family in Rural Taiwan.* Stanford, Calif.: Stanford University Press, 1972.

Wolfe, D. "Power and Authority in the Family." In *Studies in Social Power*, edited by D. Cartwright, pp. 99-117. Ann Arbor, Mich.: University of Michigan Institute for Social Research, 1959.

Wright, Logan. "Psychological Aspects of the Battered Child Syndrome." *Southern Medical Bulletin* 58, 3 (1970):14-18.

Wurmbrand, M., and Roth, C. *The Jewish People: 4000 Years of Survival.* New York: Shengold, 1967.

Wuster, T. S. "Canadian Law and Divorce." In *Marriage, Family and Society*, edited by S. Parvez Wakil. Toronto: Butterworths, 1975.

Yelloly, Margaret A. "Factors Relating to an Adoption Decision by the Mothers of Illegitimate Infants." *Sociological Review* 13, 1 (1965):5-14.

Yinger, M. J. "A Research Note on Interfaith Marriage Statistics." *Journal for the Scientific Study of Religion* 7 (1968):98-99.

Young, Michael, and Willmott, Peter. *Family, Kinship in East London.* London: Routledge & Kegan Paul, 1957.

Zacharias, L.; Rand, W. M.; and Wurtman, R. J. "Growth in American Girls." *Obstetrical and Gynecological Survey* 31 (1976):325-36.

Zalba, S. "Battered Children." *Transaction* 8 (1971):68-71.

Zborowski, M., and Herzog, E. *Life Is With People.* New York: International University Press, 1962.

Ziegler, Suzanne. "Ethnic Diversity and Children." In *The Child in the City: Changes and Challenges,* edited by W. Michelson et al., pp. 345-409. Toronto: University of Toronto Press, 1977.

——————. *Demographic Influences on Adolescents' Cross-Ethnic Friendship Patterns.* Child in the City Report, No. 4. Toronto: Child in the City Program and the Centre for Urban and Community Studies, University of Toronto, 1979.

Zieglschmid, A.J.F. *Das-Klein - Geschichtsbuch der Hutterischen Brueder.* Philadelphia, Penn.: The Carl Schurz Memorial Foundation, Inc., 1947.

Zigler, Edward. "Controlling Child Abuse in America, An Effort Doomed to Failure." In *Child Abuse and Violence,* edited by David G. Gil, pp. 46, 47. New York: AMS Press Inc., 1979.

Zimmerman, Carl C. *Family and Civilization.* New York: Harper & Row, 1947.

Zuker, Marvin, and Callwood, June. *Canadian Women and the Law.* Toronto: Copp-Clark, 1971.

Zurick, Elia T. "Children and Political Socialization." In *The Canadian Family,* edited by K. Ishwaran, pp. 186-99. Toronto: Holt, Rinehart and Winston, 1971.